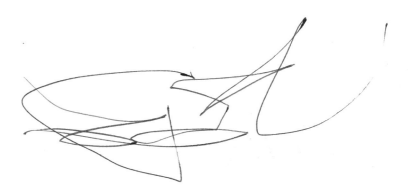

ALL·IN·ONE

CBAP®

Certified
Business Analysis
Professional

EXAM GUIDE

ALL·IN·ONE

CBAP®
Certified Business Analysis Professional

EXAM GUIDE

Joseph Phillips

New York • Chicago • San Francisco • Lisbon
London • Madrid • Mexico City • Milan • New Delhi
San Juan • Seoul • Singapore • Sydney • Toronto

The McGraw·Hill Companies

Cataloging-in-Publication Data is on file with the Library of Congress

McGraw-Hill books are available at special quantity discounts to use as premiums and sales promotions, or for use in corporate training programs. To contact a representative, please e-mail us at bulksales@mcgraw-hill.com.

CBAP® Certified Business Analysis Professional All-in-One Exam Guide

1234567890 FGR FGR 019

ISBN: Book p/n 978-0-07-162666-8 and CD p/n 978-0-07-162667-5
of set 978-0-07-162669-9

MHID: Book p/n 0-07-162666-2 and CD p/n 0-07-162667-0
of set 0-07-162669-7

Sponsoring Editor Tim Green	**Technical Editor** Julie Wiebell	**Production Supervisor** Jim Kussow
Editorial Supervisor Janet Walden	**Copy Editor** Jan Jue	**Composition** Apollo Publishing Service
Project Editor Emilia Thiuri	**Proofreader** Paul Tyler	**Illustration** Lyssa Wald
Acquisitions Coordinator Meghan Riley	**Indexer** Jack Lewis	**Art Director, Cover** Jeff Weeks

For my friends in Indiana and in Florida.

ABOUT THE AUTHOR

Joseph Phillips, PMP, Project+, CBAP, is the Director of Education for Project Seminars. He has managed and consulted on projects for industries, including technical, pharmaceutical, manufacturing, and architectural, among others. Phillips has served as a business analyst and project management consultant for organizations creating project offices, maturity models, and best-practice standardization.

As a leader in adult education, Phillips has taught organizations how to successfully implement business analysis techniques, project management methodologies, information technology project management, risk management, and other courses. He has taught for Columbia College, University of Chicago, Ball State University, and Indiana University, among others. He is a certified technical trainer and has taught over 10,000 professionals around the globe. Phillips has contributed as an author or editor to more than 30 books on technology, careers, business analysis, program management, and project management.

Phillips is a member of the International Institute of Business Analysis (IIBA), American Society for Training and Development (ASTD), and the Project Management Institute (PMI), and is active in local professional chapters. He has spoken on business analysis, project management, project management certifications, and project methodologies at numerous trade shows, PMI chapter meetings, and employee conferences. When not writing, teaching, or consulting, Phillips can be found behind a camera or on the working end of a fly rod. You can contact him through www.projectseminars.com.

About the Technical Editor

Julie Wiebell, MBA, PMP, CSM, is a project management consultant and educator working on her Ph.D. in Applied Management and Decision Sciences with a specialization in Information Systems Management. Her information technology and project management experience spans more than 15 years working with private, public, nonprofit, Fortune 100, and IT consulting firms. She is a past board member of the Project Management Institute Central Ohio Chapter (PMICOC) and a current board member of the East Tennessee Chapter (ETPMI), in addition to serving on the Honors Tutorial College Board of Visitors at Ohio University.

CONTENTS AT A GLANCE

CONTENTS

ACKNOWLEDGMENTS

More than once, I've said that I'm the luckiest guy in the room. I get to write and talk for a living—what could be better than that? I'm so grateful for the opportunity to write and must thank the wonderful group of people at McGraw-Hill for their belief in me to write yet another book. Thank you to Tim Green, my good friend and editor, for your guidance, patience, and confidence. Thank you to Meghan Riley—for keeping on top of this book and all its parts. Thank you, Jan Jue, for helping me to be a better writer. Emilia Thiuri, thanks for your hard work and attention to detail. Julie Wiebell, the technical editor for this book, has been a good friend and persistent editor. Thanks, Julie, for all of your hard work. Thank you to Janet Walden for keeping everyone organized. And thank you to Apollo Publishing for taking my scribbles and then creating all the artwork in this book. Finally, thank you to Jean Butterfield and Jan Benes for putting the parts of this book together and making it a reality.

I would also like to thank the hundreds of people who have attended my certification Boot Camps and management courses over the past years. Your questions and conversations have helped me create this book and will help thousands of others earn their certifications. Finally, thank you to my friends Martha Thieme, Don Kunhle, John and Cara Konzelmann, Lamont Hatcher, Phil Stuck, Laurie Lee Evans, Greg and Mary Huebner, Fred and Carin McBroom, Mike and Kelly Favory; my brothers, Steve, Mark, Sam, and Ben; my parents; and my son, KJ.

INTRODUCTION

This book has been written to help you pass your Certified Business Analysis Professional certification. It's also a handy reference for what business analysis is and the processes you'll utilize as a business analyst. I wrote this book with two purposes in mind: first, to help people like you pass their CBAP examination. Second, to help business analysts become better business analysts. Our profession is a tricky one; we're often the liaison between what stakeholders want and what reality can provide. My hope for you is that you pass your CBAP examination and that you become a better, happier business analyst.

The book is designed so that you can read the chapters in any order you like. However, if you examine the *Guide to the Business Analysis Body of Knowledge* (BABOK), you'll notice that the order of information presented is the same as the order of information in this book. In other words, you can read a chapter of the BABOK and then read a more detailed explanation in this book. This book is a guide to the guide. You'll also notice, if you haven't peeked ahead already, that all of the exam objectives are based on the BABOK, as are the chapter exams and the exams on the CD. You'll be well prepared to pass the CBAP by the time you reach the end of this book.

CBAP Exam Readiness Checklist

As of this writing, these knowledge areas and percentages of exam questions are correct. You should visit the IIBA web site at www.theiiba.org to confirm that the exam objectives have not changed.

Knowledge Area	Percentage of Questions	Chapter Number
Enterprise analysis	22%	Chapters 1, 5, 8
Requirements planning and management	22.7%	Chapters 1, 2, 8
Requirements elicitation	18.7%	Chapters 3, 8
Requirements analysis and documentation	20.7%	Chapters 2, 4, 6
Requirements communication	10.7%	Chapters 4, 8
Solution assessment and validation	5.2%	Chapters 6, 7, 8

Earning the Certified Business Analysis Professional Certification

In this chapter you will
- Meet the International Institute of Business Analysis
- Learn how to earn the Certified Business Analysis Professional Certification
- Qualify for the Certified Business Analysis Professional Certification examination
- Complete the exam application and audit
- Review the certification examination details

Welcome to the book that'll help you earn the Certified Business Analysis Professional (CBAP) certification. I know your time is precious and you don't want a book that drones on like a manual for a coffeemaker. This book is direct, to the point, and covers all of the exam objectives you must know to pass the CBAP examination. Here you'll find a concise explanation of the exam details, loads of practice questions and explanations, a detailed glossary, and a nifty CD with two practice exams and some training videos.

Let's get something straight from the start. I want you to pass your exam on the first attempt. You're studying to pass the exam, not just take it. The International Institute of Business Analysis (IIBA) is the governing body for the CBAP examination, so you'll have to play by their rules. This means that you'll have to use their nomenclature, terms, and processes when you study for and talk about the CBAP examination. Sure, sure, out there in your world you might have totally different terminology for how you do your business analysis work, but on the exam you'll have to use the terms IIBA provides. Sorry.

In this first chapter, I'm laying the groundwork for the examination. You'll learn all about the IIBA and how you can join (get out your checkbook). I'll cover the qualifiers for the examination, how you can verify your business analysis experience, and how to apply for the exam. In this first chapter, I'm also going to define how to pass an exam and how you'll abide by the IIBA rules. Ready to get to work? Good—let's go!

Introducing the International Institute of Business Analysis

The IIBA is a nonprofit entity headquartered in Toronto, Canada. IIBA aims to develop and propel the business analysis role and career. Its mission: "to develop and maintain standards for the practice of business analysis and for the certification of its practitioners." The IIBA is the governing body for the CBAP examination. They also approve and brand learning centers as Endorsed Education Providers, which are training companies that offer business analysis courses and seminars.

Relatively speaking, the IIBA is a young organization; they were created in October 2003 by 28 founding members. In 2006 they became an official not-for-profit entity. Each quarter since their inception their membership has grown, and their certification is growing in popularity and demand. As of this writing, the IIBA has over 100 chapters around the world; you can check their web site to find a chapter near you: www.theiiba .org.

The book that the CBAP examination is largely based on is *A Guide to the Business Analysis Body of Knowledge* (BABOK). The BABOK supports and defines the business analyst role, processes, and generally accepted practices of the community. In no way does this business analysis book capture every action, every nuance, of a business analysis, but rather it defines a framework that most business analysts would work within. The exam you're going to pass is based on the BABOK.

Exploring the IIBA

In earlier years the IIBA certification process didn't run as smoothly as it does now. In September 2008 the IIBA moved from a paper-based, proctored examination to a computer-based examination. Prior to this move, CBAP candidates would all convene in a central locale, usually at a related tradeshow, and take the examination on paper in unison. It was like taking the SATs in high school. You'd then have to wait a few weeks to get the results of your exam mailed to you. Oh the agony!

The computer-based examination is much more convenient. The exam allows CBAP candidates to register and pay for the examination online. The exam is offered through Castle Worldwide. I'll talk about the complete application process in a moment, but the computer-based exam is big news for the folks at the IIBA. It's a huge jump not only in convenience, but also in validity, to offer electronic testing and grading.

While the IIBA does not provide training as part of their services, they do endorse training providers who provide business analysis seminars. Their program, called the Endorsed Education Provider (EEP) program, requires the training provider to submit their course details for review by the IIBA. Each business analysis course that is to be certified by IIBA goes through a review process that determines the course's accuracy, how the course meshes with the BABOK, and that the course is taught by someone who's an expert in the course's topic.

The review process is completed by three business analysis professionals who are not affiliated in any way with the training center that's seeking approval by the IIBA. Of course the education providers have some other rules—you can see these online if you're really interested—but they mainly state that the EEPs will be good and will use quality instructors. EEPs do pay an annual fee and a per-course fee to the IIBA for the honor of being included in their EEP program.

Member chapters are another thing the IIBA organizes and approves. The IIBA chapters provide great avenues for networking, education, and chicken dinners on a regular basis. Typically chapter meetings meet monthly and have a guest speaker (often by guys who have written great books on business analysis—maybe I'll see you at your chapter event). In addition to monthly meetings, most IIBA chapters provide ongoing education, seminars, and group discounts for area workshops. You can find and join a local business analysis chapter through the IIBA web site.

As of right now, and according to IIBA, you first have to be a member of the IIBA to join a local chapter. Local chapters may also charge membership dues and a small fee for monthly meeting expenses. Check with your local chapter on what their costs and benefits are if you're curious. For point of reference, my chapter charges me $20 annually and $10 for every monthly chapter meeting I attend. Your chapter may be more or less costly, so plan accordingly.

Like any nonprofit, the IIBA is looking for volunteers to help support the organization. If you're looking to immerse yourself in the business analysis community, volunteering is a great way to meet new people, help establish direction for the IIBA, and get the inside scoop on how the IIBA works. Volunteer positions are posted, once again, through the IIBA web site and on many of the chapter web sites. You can expect to do work like field phone calls, review newsletters, help with chapter meetings and programs, and serve on different member committees.

Joining the IIBA

Now that you know the major details on the IIBA, I bet you'd like to join the organization, right? You can join the IIBA, as of this writing, for $95 per year. Once your payment has been received and processed, you're in the club. Your membership will expire one year from the last day of the month you joined. So I suppose if you want to stretch your dollars, join at the top of the month, and get a few extra days until you renew your membership. Yes, of course there's a renewal fee. Like the initial membership fee, this one is $95 for an additional year.

You can save a few dollars if your organization is a sponsor of the IIBA. IIBA Sponsors are organizations that provide services and products to the business analysis community, provide business analysis for other entities, or are just very generous with their checkbooks. As an IIBA Sponsor your company can use the IIBA logo, gain discounts on IIBA services, post your logo and company info on the IIBA web site, and post job openings on the IIBA career web site. As always, check with the IIBA, but here's a quick listing of the sponsor types your company may subscribe to:

- Premier Sponsor: $11,000 per year
- Industry Sponsor: $7,000 per year

- Corporate Sponsor: $5,000 per year
- Associate Sponsor: $3,000 per year

 NOTE To be an Associate Sponsor, the least expensive choice, your organization must employ 25 or fewer people.

If you'd like your company to become an IIBA Sponsor, you can complete an application on the IIBA web site. You can also check the IIBA Sponsors page to determine if your organization is currently a sponsor so you can take advantage of the membership fee discounts. You'll need to use your company sponsor identification number when you complete the membership form to receive the discount.

You can get some good benefits by joining the IIBA. Of course you'll receive networking opportunities at IIBA events, gain access to secure areas of the IIBA web site, and belong to a community of business analysts from around the world. You'll also get some additional benefits:

- Save $125 on your CBAP examination fee. (Remember, it only costs $95 to join the IIBA, so heck, join and actually save $30. That's a movie and four packs of licorice.)
- Surf all of the job postings on the IIBA career web site.
- Access the BABOK online.
- Access the IIBA forums, social and business networking groups, and other web-based services from our pals at the IIBA.

Once your application has been approved (read, your credit card is approved), you're in the club. IIBA will automatically e-mail you your receipt, your next renewal date, and most importantly, your membership identification number. You'll use this number to get your exam fee discount. You'll also periodically receive e-mails and newsletters from the IIBA—unless you opt out of their mailings.

Defining the Business Analyst Role

If you're prepping for this certification, you probably have a good idea of what a business analyst role is. You know what your responsibilities are in your organization and what's expected of you when you work with customers, project managers, subject matter experts, and other stakeholders. The IIBA, in their free Certified Business Analysis Professional Handbook, which you can download from their web site (www.theiiba. org), clearly defines the business analyst role. Their definition characterizes a business analyst role, the duties of a business analyst, and the confines in which business analysts are to operate. A business analyst role is responsible for several things within an organization:

- Identifies the business needs of the organization's clients and stakeholders
- Helps determine solutions to business problems
- Completes requirements development
- Completes requirements management
- Serves as a communications hub among business clients, project stakeholders, and the defined solutions team

As a business analyst your work is all about requirements. According to the IIBA, you work with customers, stakeholders, and clients to elicit, analyze, validate, and document business, organizational, and operational standards. The CBAP examination focuses on these activities, processes, and the outcomes of business analysis processes. In this book I'll cover all of the business analysis processes in detail, and you'll complete practice exams, create flashcards, and learn the IIBA approach to business analysis.

 NOTE It's important, I believe, to fully understand the IIBA definition of the role you serve, as this is what you'll be tested on through their exam. Knowing their interpretation of what you do will increase your odds of passing their exam.

Your goal is to pass the CBAP examination—my goal is to help get you there. To get there, and this should be evident by now, you need to learn the IIBA terms, definitions, and approaches. Your organization may have a slightly different approach than what's defined by the IIBA—and that's fine—just not for your CBAP exam. For example, some things you currently and typically do in your project as a business analyst may not synch with what's expected on the CBAP exam. On the exam, when you perform business analysis duties:

- You don't predetermine solutions; solutions are driven by the requirements of the business.
- You are not performing financial analysis.
- You are not managing projects.
- You are performing quality assurance.
- You are completing organizational development.
- You are testing software and solutions.
- You are training, coaching, and mentoring your colleagues.
- You are documenting the development of business solutions.

This is not to say that you don't perform these roles as part of your employment. It is to say, however, that the role of business analyst is distinctly different from these duties.

Qualifying for the CBAP Certification

Not everyone can take the CBAP examination—you have to qualify for the exam and certification. There's been some discontent over this approach to certification, but I think overall it's good for you and me, the qualified business analysts. If it were easy to become a CBAP, then everyone would do it. If everyone did it, then the value of the certification would decline as the market became saturated with certified business analysts. We've seen that happen already with certain information technology certifications, and the IIBA has learned from others' mistakes. Figure 1-1 is the complete chart to earning your CBAP. I'll walk through the entire process in detail now.

The process to become a CBAP isn't really that difficult. You'll need to evaluate if you think you qualify for the examination, complete an application, and cough up some bucks for the application and for the examination. I'll walk you through the whole process in one moment, but first know this: the IIBA can do whatever they want with their certification. While all of the information I'm about to share with you is accurate as of this writing, you should always cruise over to the IIBA web site and confirm the requirements, fees, and exam process. I'd hate for you to rely solely on my information here, as accurate as I am today, only to learn the fine people at the IIBA have changed some of their rules for the exam.

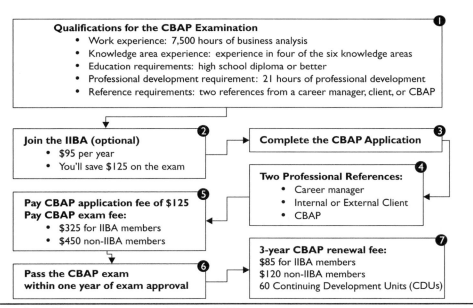

Figure 1-1 The many steps to earning your CBAP

Identifying the Typical CBAP Candidate

To qualify for the CBAP exam and certification, you'll need to have five years of business analysis experience within the last ten years. That's right—five years as a business analyst. The IIBA requires each CBAP candidate to prove and document their five years of experience as a business analyst in the context of the BABOK. When you complete your CBAP exam application, you're strongly encouraged to use the terminology and approaches discussed in the BABOK. You'll need to map your business analysis experience to the BABOK and to define how the work you've completed meshes with the expected duties of a business analyst from the IIBA point of view.

To give you an idea, here's a quick listing of what you'll find in the BABOK and where your five years of business analysis experience need to map to:

- Managing enterprise analysis and strategic planning
- Planning and managing requirements
- Eliciting requirements
- Completing requirements analysis and documentation
- Communicating requirements
- Performing solution assessment and validation

You'll also need to show how you've served as a business analyst within your organization. You can demonstrate this through your approaches to communication, leadership, and problem solving. In addition, you'll need to show how your organizational business knowledge allowed you to operate and improve as a business analyst within each entity you've served in.

If you believe that you do indeed qualify for the CBAP exam and are ready to move forward, you can begin your application at the International Institute of Business Analysis web site: www.theiiba.org. From here you can download the application form and begin documenting your experience, knowledge area skills, education, professional development, and professional references. The exam application, as of this writing, is paper based; you'll have to complete the application, print it, and then mail the application to:

Certification Manager
250 Consumers Road, #301
Toronto, Ontario
M2J 4V6
Canada

Again, I'll stress that this information is correct as of this writing, but you should always check with the IIBA web site. I have a hunch that the application process will move to a web-based form like other professional certification vendors use. I sure hope it does. I'll assume, for now, that you do have to mail your application to the IIBA, so you should send it registered mail or through an international delivery service so you have receipt of your application delivery. I'll now walk you through IIBA's current CBAP application process.

Starting the CBAP Application

Once you've downloaded the CBAP application from the IIBA, your first step is to enter all of your personal information. You'll need the following bits of information for the application:

- **Name** I encourage you to apply under your name as it appears on your driver's license or passport, so your ID and applicant names match. Testing centers are sticklers for this.

- **E-mail address** Use an e-mail address that you check frequently; this is how the IIBA will contact you.

- **Primary and secondary mailing address** This is where your certificate and other IIBA correspondence will be sent.

- **Phone numbers** So the IIBA can contact you if they need to.

- **Job title** While most CBAPs have the title of business analyst, the CBAP application also acknowledges that CBAPs may also be project managers, business systems analysts, or mysterious "others." If you choose "other," you'll have to elaborate on your business analyst activities and title.

- **IIBA membership number** If you've recently joined, you have an option on the application to indicate you've recently applied for membership.

- **Current employer** The IIBA assumes you're currently employed and doesn't provide an option if your situation is otherwise. You can, however, indicate that you're self-employed if that's the case.

- Number of employees in your current organization.

- Type of business your organization does.

The next section of the CBAP application is your education history. The requirement for the CBAP is that the applicant has a high school diploma, its equivalent, or higher education. CBAP does not reduce the required number of hours of work experience in exchange for higher education. All applicants, college grad or not, will need five years of business analysis experience to qualify for the exam. You will need to provide the highest level of education achieved and what you studied, as well as when and where you graduated.

Documenting Your Work Experience

This is the bread and butter of the CBAP application. The next section of the CBAP application is where you'll find a page titled "Work Experience." It's on this page that you'll need to document your 7,500 hours of work experience to equate to the minimum five years of business analysis experience. This can get tedious, as every project and organization you completed the work for needs to be identified and documented. This means if you've worked on 20 different projects to equate to 7,500 hours of business analysis experience, you'll have 20 different work experience sheets in your application. (And no, you can't use your resume instead of completing the forms.) The one caveat to that rule is that if you've worked on several small projects within one year, you should combine all of the smaller projects as one project toward your CBAP application.

When you begin completing each form, you should document your experience from the most recent projects first and the older projects last. While you don't need to document more than 7,500 hours of business analysis experience, I encourage you to document slightly more than that if possible. The reason is that IIBA can filter out business analysis experience or activities that they determine don't count toward the certification. If they remove projects from your application, you'll likely fall below the 7,500-hour requirement. Just remember, though, if you document more than the 7,500 hours of experience, the oldest project hours counted cannot be more than ten years from when you submit your CBAP application.

When I teach my CBAP boot camps, someone always asks immediately what does and what does not count toward experience as a business analyst. I bet you're wondering the same thing. The kind folks at the IIBA provide some examples of accepted and unaccepted types of activities. In addition, you can pretty much rely on the business analysis activities documented in the BABOK as a guideline for your application.

Here are some immediate examples of activities that do count toward your work experience. They're based on the examples in the CBAP Handbook, so don't use these verbatim. In fact, you should provide even more detailed examples of the work you did, because using this verbiage may raise eyebrows and red flags, and may cause your application to be scrutinized even more than usual. While these are provided as samples of things that do qualify, keep in mind this is in no way a comprehensive listing of all the different business analysis activities you could reference. Some approved business analysis activities:

- Requirements gathering
- Writing requirements documentation
- Determining project scope and objectives
- Identifying and documenting requirements risks
- Reporting on requirements progress
- Leading requirements gathering workshops
- Analyzing and documenting functional, nonfunctional, and user requirements
- Performing walkthrough activities and sign-offs of the requirements package
- Ensuring that requirements are met for the client, project stakeholder, or customer
- Reviewing testing strategy, plans, and cases

- Supporting QA and testing teams
- Determining corrective actions for defects, the priority of required fixes, and establishing workarounds for the defects

In contrast, here are some project activities that do not count toward your business analysis experience hours. Notice how many of these activities are similar to the business analysis activities that are approved. The determining factor is that the approved items focus on requirements, while these unapproved activities often focus on the project and project management duties. Basically any activity that is not clearly defined in the BABOK is not an approved business analysis activity. Use caution on your exam application; these activities do *not* count toward your business analysis experience:

- Selling requirements tools and software
- Managing projects
- Creating the project plan
- Creating the project charter
- Leading presentations on the progress of the project
- Creating and executing test scripts, reporting on testing status, and creating testing plans and strategies
- Programming
- Identifying project risks
- Providing status reports
- Tracking and managing defects
- Teaching business analysis training courses

Now that you know what you can and can't include on your exam application, you're ready to document the project details. Here's what you'll have to include for each project that you worked on as part of your 7,500 hours of business analysis experience:

- Start and end date of the project
- Project description or objective
- Your role(s) on the project
- Number of people, if any, that reported to you on the project
- Project name
- Project contact's name, e-mail, and your relationship to the project contact
- Organization name, contact information, and web site
- Total hours you worked on the project, minus the number of hours you completed non–business analysis activities, will equate to the number of hours you may count toward the 7,500 business analysis work experience

hours. The application makes you calculate the total number of hours you've completed on each project and the number of hours of business analysis work you've done on each project.

Don't let that last bullet point throw you for a loop. You could, for example, have worked for 2,500 hours as part of a project team but have spent 1,200 hours doing project work that didn't qualify as business analysis work. If that were the case, you'd only get to count 1,300 hours as business analysis experience.

NOTE The IIBA is a stickler when it comes to what does and does not count as work experience. Project management work is not the same as business analysis work.

Finally, for each project that you complete a work experience form for, you'll need to define the business analysis tasks you completed in each knowledge area and what deliverables those business analysis tasks created. Resist the urge to copy your activities and the deliverables you created as a business analyst. The IIBA warns that repetitive text will be rejected; they want you to clearly and accurately define what you did and what your activities created. Table 1-1 shows a mockup of the table that you'll have to complete for each referenced project on the CBAP application. The IIBA provides the experience area; you provide the business analysis tasks and deliverables.

Obviously, completing this CBAP application work experience section is going to be a tedious and time-consuming activity. Don't rush through the work. If you don't complete the work experience pages accurately, IIBA can reject your application, dock your experience hours, or both. If you accidentally include a business analysis task in the wrong knowledge area, the IIBA can even strike that experience from your application. Take your time and confirm the accuracy of your application before you send it off to Toronto.

For a more detailed explanation, watch the How to Earn the CBAP video now.

Experience Area	BA Tasks	BA Deliverables
Enterprise Analysis		
Requirements Planning and Management		
Requirements Elicitation		
Requirements Analysis and Documentation		
Requirements Communication		
Solution Assessment and Validation		

Table 1-1   Detailing Business Analysis Activities and Deliverables for Each Project

Documenting Your BA Knowledge Areas

CBAPs are smart people; you know this. To be a CBAP, however, you have to be a little bit more than just smart—you also have to prove your experience in the knowledge areas of a business analysis. You'll already do some of this when you document your thousands of hours of work experience, but you'll need to do just a bit more in this section of the CBAP exam application.

You'll be asked to rate your area of expertise in four of these six business analysis areas:

- Enterprise Analysis
- Requirements Planning and Management
- Requirements Elicitation
- Requirements Analysis and Documentation
- Requirements Communication
- Solution Assessment and Validation

You get to choose which four of the six business analysis areas you're experienced in—and the IIBA asks that you complete only four of the six. You'll use the following ranking for each of the four knowledge areas you want to demonstrate your strengths in:

- **Never**   You never do that task in your business analysis role.
- **Seldom**   You rarely perform the task.
- **Sometimes**   You have performed the task five to ten times in the last ten years.
- **Frequently**   You have completed the task 11 or more times in the last ten years.

For each of the knowledge areas, you'll be quizzed on the application on a given business analysis task, and you'll use the preceding scale to grade yourself on your experience in the given knowledge area activity. Next I'll walk you through the questions you'll have to answer in each knowledge area on your exam application.

Completing the Enterprise Analysis Knowledge Area Review

Enterprise analysis, according to the BABOK, comprises the activities that a business analyst uses to define and identify business opportunities for your organization. Think like an entrepreneur when you answer these questions. As a business analyst completing enterprise analysis, you'll also be helping an organization define its business architecture framework. The third part of enterprise analysis you do as a business analyst is to determine the best investment of an organization's funds when it comes to new business and technical systems. If one of the four knowledge areas you choose is enterprise analysis, you'll have to grade your strengths and weaknesses on the following questions:

- How often do you create or maintain the business architecture?
- How often do you conduct feasibility studies?

- How often do you determine project scope?
- How often do you prepare the business case?
- How often do you prepare the initial risk assessment?
- How often do you prepare the decision package?
- How often do you select and prioritize projects?
- How often do you launch a new project?
- How often do you manage projects for value?
- How often do you track project benefits?
- What other task(s) in this knowledge area do you perform that are not listed?

While you do have to answer every question, you don't have to have frequent experiences in all of these business analysis tasks to qualify for the exam. Just be honest in your personal assessment of how often you complete the work.

Completing the Requirements Planning and Management Application Area

When you complete requirements planning and management tasks, you are working with project and organizational stakeholders to determine what resources are needed for requirements gathering within your organization enterprise environmental factors, policies, and internal procedures. A business analyst completing these tasks is determining the key roles, managing the requirements scope, and serving as a communicator of the requirements gathering process. If you choose this knowledge area to be one of the four knowledge areas for your CBAP application, you'll have to answer the following questions:

- How often do you identify and document team roles and responsibilities?
- How often do you identify and consult stakeholders?
- How often do you define the BA work division strategy and allocate work?
- How often do you identify requirements risk and develop the risk management approach?
- How often do you identify key planning impact areas (for example, SDLC, life cycle methodology, risk, expectations, stakeholder needs and location, project type, and standards)?
- How often do you adjust the requirements management plan as required?
- How often do you select requirements activities (for example, elicitation, analysis and documentation, communication, and implementation)?
- How often do you estimate requirements activities (for example, identify milestones, work units, level of effort, duration, assumptions, and risks)?

- How often do you manage requirements scope (for example, baseline, structure, impacts, change management, and approval process)?
- How often do you measure and report on requirements activity (for example, determining, collecting, and reporting project and product metrics)?
- How often do you manage requirements change?
- What other task(s) in this knowledge area do you perform that are not listed?

Rely on your experience and interaction with project managers, business analysts, risk specialists, and subject matter experts as you define the requirements for the project deliverables. You are not required to have advanced experiences with every task, but you should show an accurate reflection of the work you've completed as a business analyst.

Completing the Requirements Elicitation Application Area

To define the requirements for an organization or project, you need to gather the requirements from the people who are doing the requiring. You need to talk with the clients, customers, and stakeholders to determine what opportunity, problem, or condition they want to act upon. You're eliciting, drawing out, their requirements through your communications, reviews, studies, and follow-up interviews with stakeholders. You'll also complete activities such as resolving conflicts, documenting the requirements, observing problems and studies, and facilitating workshops. If you consider requirements elicitation to be one of your four required knowledge areas to exhibit your business analysis expertise, you'll be faced with just two questions:

- How often do you elicit requirements?
- What other task(s) in this knowledge area do you perform that are not listed?

This is deceptively simple. Business analysts spend loads of time eliciting requirements, communicating with stakeholders and customers, and elaborating on the requirements to drill down to causal factors, true opportunities, constraints, and assumptions.

Completing the Requirements Analysis and Documentation Application Area

Once the requirements have been initially defined, the business analyst will analyze, frame, and document the requirements in order to find an appropriate solution to create the deliverables and benefits of the project or opportunity. The goal is not necessarily to define a project solution, but rather to frame the requirements so that the project team may complete the work to satisfy the identified requirements. If you consider requirements analysis and documentation to be one of your four required knowledge areas, you'll rank your experience according to the following questions:

- How often do you structure requirements packages?
- How often do you create business domain models?

- How often do you analyze user requirements?
- How often do you analyze functional requirements?
- How often do you analyze the quality of service requirements?
- How often do you determine assumptions and constraints?
- How often do you determine requirements attributes?
- How often do you document requirements?
- How often do you validate requirements?
- How often do you verify requirements?
- What other task(s) in this knowledge area do you perform that are not listed?

When you're answering these questions, reflect on your communications and elicitations with users, management, clients, lines of business within your organization, and any other stakeholders who were affected by the requirements you've gathered. You'll also need to think about the requirements verification processes and how you worked with the project managers, project team members, and clients to validate the requirements as they've been defined.

Completing the Requirements Communication Application Area

Communication is one of the most valuable skills a business analyst must have. Requirements communication happens through the business analysis activities, is done in tandem with requirements gathering and analysis, and is at the heart of requirements documentation. If you consider requirements communication to be one of your required four knowledge areas, you'll have to answer the following questions based on your experience:

- How often do you create a requirements communication plan?
- How often do you manage requirements conflicts?
- How often do you determine an appropriate requirements format?
- How often do you create a requirements package?
- How often do you conduct a requirements presentation?
- How often do you conduct a formal requirements review?
- How often do you obtain requirements sign-off?
- What other task(s) in this knowledge area do you perform that are not listed?

When you answer these questions on your CBAP exam application, you'll need to reflect on your experience with stakeholders to bring them to a common understanding of the project requirements. You'll also rely on your experience to get the stakeholders to approve the requirements of the project deliverable regardless of their technical, business, or cultural background.

Completing the Solution Assessment and Validation Application Area

The overall mission of requirements gathering is to define the requirements and then to find an appropriate solution. This knowledge area works with the project manager, technology team, project team, and stakeholders to analyze the detailed design documents. You'll define the logical phases of the project, the technical design, and the quality assurance activities. If you consider the requirements solution assessment and validation as one of your four required knowledge areas, you'll have to rank your experience by answering the following questions:

- How often do you develop alternative solutions?
- How often do you evaluate technology options?
- How often do you facilitate the selection of a solution?
- How often do you ensure the usability of the solution?
- How often do you support the quality assurance process?
- How often do you support the implementation of the solution?
- How often do you communicate the solution impacts?
- How often do you complete a post-implementation review and assessment?
- What other task(s) in this knowledge area do you perform that are not listed?

When you complete this section of the CBAP exam application, you'll want to think about the technical solutions you've identified requirements for, and how you and the technical team actually created the most appropriate solution. This knowledge area also includes change management activities, quality assurance, test plans, and mitigation of risk by implanting tests on the identified solution.

Confirming Your Professional Development

Part of the qualification for the CBAP is that you've completed professional development activities. Specifically, this means you've attended business analysis training courses. You must complete 21 hours of education that's directly related to business analysis within the last four years. The seminars you attend must be completed by the date you sign and submit your application. What this means is that you can't promise to complete a business analysis seminar later and submit your application anyway. All 21 hours of the training must be done before the application submission.

Some policies are attached to the type of training you may use to complete this CBAP requirement:

- All courses that you complete through an IIBA Endorsed Education Provider (EEP) are guaranteed to qualify. On your exam application, you'll have an opportunity to indicate that you completed the training through an EEP.

- You are not required only to complete the professional development through an EEP. You can complete the business analysis training through any training entity, but the IIBA will need to review the course outline.

- In-house business analysis seminars that you attend may qualify if the IIBA approves the seminar outline, which you'll submit at the time of your application. The IIBA asks that you provide a web address where the outline can be found.

- Underlying business analysis fundamentals courses may qualify. Chapter 8 in the BABOK lists all of the underlying CBAP skills. Here are some popular examples of underlying business analysis fundamentals training that could qualify:

  - Business analysis skills such as analysis techniques, issue management, communication, and usability.

  - Business knowledge on products, processes, markets, and internal systems.

  - Meeting management, presentation skills, and decision making skills.

  - Leadership seminars on coaching, goal setting, motivation, and interviewing may also qualify.

- Project management training does not qualify. The IIBA will openly (and it seems proudly) reject any project management training that you may reference as business analysis training. Save your ink and yourself a headache and don't try it.

- Programming and programming languages seminars do not count as business analysis training. These are really about project execution rather than requirements gathering.

- Testing courses do not qualify as business analysis courses unless they have been approved by the IIBA. Proceed with caution.

The required 21 hours of professional development can be achieved through one course or through multiple courses. The application is a bit vague on whether you're allowed to count a portion of a seminar toward business analysis professional development or if the whole course must focus on business analysis. My understanding, as of this writing, is that the IIBA wants the entire course to qualify for the business analysis professional development; you aren't allowed to cherry-pick outlines and build an aggregate of training solutions. It's all or nothing for each course you reference.

Providing Professional References for the CBAP Application

One requirement that has stumped a few CBAP candidates is the requirement to provide two professional references. This requirement has posed some problems for CBAP candidates who have moved from job to job, lost touch with older contacts, and may be in new positions as they apply for the CBAP. The IIBA stance is that you don't have to provide all of your professional references—only two references.

You must have known the references for at least six months. Your references cannot be project managers unless the project manager is your career manager. Your career manager is the person who completes your annual performance review. You may be tempted to add additional references to your application, but only two references will be reviewed by the IIBA. The references you select can be

- Career manager
- Client (internal or external)
- Certified Business Analysis Professional (IIBA-certified business analysis)

You get to choose which folks will be talking about you, so this really shouldn't be too difficult unless no one likes you much. In which case you should probably end your quest as a business analyst and become a lawyer. (I'm kidding, of course.) The people you choose as your professional references should have an idea of your role as a business analyst, the work you've completed in this role, and your strengths and weaknesses.

The two professional references must complete the official CBAP Candidate Reference Form, which you can download from the IIBA web site. Once your references have the document and have supplied their usual contact information, they'll have to answer the following questions about you:

- What is your relationship to the candidate? Career manager, client, or CBAP?
- For how long have you known the candidate?
- Candidate title?
- The candidate duties?
- What has been your professional relationship with the candidate?
- Please describe how effectively the candidate performs his/her business analysis duties.
- How would you describe the candidate's business analysis skills?
- How would you rate the candidate's skills from 1 to 5, where 1 is very low and 5 is very high?
  - Communications
  - Leadership
  - Problem solving
  - Business knowledge
  - IT knowledge
  - Enterprise analysis
  - Requirements planning and management
  - Requirements elicitation
  - Requirements documentation and analysis

- Requirements communication
- Solution assessment and validation
- What are the candidate's strengths?
- What are the candidate's weaknesses?
- Does the candidate display a high degree of personal integrity (that is, act honorably, honestly, justly, responsibly, and legally)? If no, please explain.
- Do you endorse this candidate as a business analysis professional?

Once your professional reference has answered all of these questions, she is to sign the document, seal the document in an envelope, and then sign her name across the seal of the envelope. No peeking! It's your responsibility to ensure that your professional reference completes the form and submits it to the IIBA.

Completing the CBAP Exam Application

The last chunk of the CBAP application is pretty easy and straightforward compared with the rest of the application. You must submit your $125 exam application fee with your exam. If you don't include your payment, your exam application won't be reviewed. You've got to pay the fee before IIBA will review your exam and report your status. Take note, the $125 application fee is nonrefundable. If your application for the CBAP exam is declined, you won't be receiving a refund.

Here's another quirky thing about the current exam application and the IIBA web site: where and how you'll take the exam. Traditionally, the CBAP exam was a paper-based exam; approved applicants would all rendezvous at a given time and locale and would complete the proctored exam in unison. You'd hear from the IIBA when your exam was graded a few weeks after you completed the test. Now, the exam is computer based and is hosted through Castle Worldwide.

The quirky thing I mentioned is that while the computer-based test is the preferred method, the CBAP exam application still asks where you'd like to complete the exam and on what date. The IIBA advises that applicants should reference their list of computer-based testing sites from their web site and should reference the city and computer-based test on the location section of the exam application. In other words, if you want to take the exam in Phoenix, you'd answer as Phoenix, Arizona—CBT. (Wow. What could possibly be easier?) You can also enter a time range of when you anticipate taking the exam, for example, June–July 2010. Once your exam application is approved, the IIBA will send you a confirmation letter with instructions on how to schedule your computer-based test through a web site.

The exam fee is $325 for IIBA memebers ($450 for nonmemebers)—this is in addition to the $125 application fee. You can, if you'd like to, submit your payment of $325 with your exam application. If you'd rather hang onto your dollars and stretch out the application process even longer, you can elect to pay for the exam once your application has been approved. Once your application is approved, you must pay the $325 exam fee at least 60 days prior to the exam date you indicated.

The final portion of the CBAP exam application is your signature and consent to the IIBA. You're consenting to allow the IIBA to collect and store your exam application information, your application reference forms, and your professional development information, and you're giving consent to the IIBA contacting your references. You're also allowed to choose if the IIBA can display your CBAP status on their web site once you've successfully completed the examination.

The final portion of the application also confirms your agreement to not divulge any information about the CBAP exam questions. You're not allowed to share any part of the exam with anyone orally, in writing, electronically, or by extrasensory perception. Everything that happens on the exam stays on the exam.

If you need to cancel and reschedule your examination once you've scheduled it, you must follow some rules. First, if you're still taking the paper-based test rather than the computer-based test, you need to notify the IIBA through their e-mail (certification@theiiba.org) as soon as possible. If your need to reschedule happens within 30 days of the exam's date, you'll be charged an administrative fee of $55. You'll have to pay the fee to the IIBA before you're allowed to reschedule your exam. So try to plan your emergencies well in advance of the exam date.

If you don't live in a cave, then you're probably taking the computer-based test. If you need to cancel and reschedule a computer-based test, you'll be charged $50 by Castle Worldwide regardless of when you cancel, reschedule, or move your exam date. It's Castle Worldwide's deal, not the IIBA's. If that steams you, then this will make your day: if you cancel within five business days of your scheduled exam start time, you lose all the examination fees that you paid. (That's right; it's like your favorite blackjack dealer pulling a 21 when you're sitting with a 19. If you don't play blackjack, just trust me that it's no fun when this happens.)

And just to be clear, if you cancel the computer-based test outside of five days of your test date but refuse to pay the $50 cancellation fee, Castle Worldwide considers your test cancelled. Their logic, I'm guessing, is that if you want to cancel the test but don't want to pay the $50 cancellation fee, then you've not really cancelled anything at all. Your test time will expire, and you'll forfeit your exam fee. Lesson to be learned? If you must cancel, do it outside of five days, and cough up the cancellation fee.

Reviewing the Exam Details

Once you've submitted your application, it's a waiting game as your pals at the IIBA review and approve your application. I'm a proponent of taking action and preparing to pass an exam rather than just taking it. If you believe that you qualify for the CBAP examination, I encourage you to take action by completing the CBAP exam application and beginning to prepare to pass the exam. By completing your application now, at the assumed onset of your studying, you'll let the IIBA review your application while you're studying to pass the exam. I think it's a mistake to study, then complete the application, and then take the exam at some distant, foggy point in the future. Work smart, not hard. Submit your application, and then begin studying for the exam.

The CBAP exam is a 150-question, multiple-choice exam. Each question will present four possible choices, and you'll have to choose the best answer for each question even if you don't like any of the choices presented. Do not leave a question unanswered; blank answers are wrong answers. You'll see a mixture of comprehension questions, where you'll need to recall the definition of terms, and situational analysis questions. The situational questions are scenario questions where you'll be placed in a scenario and have to choose the best course of action.

The CBAP exam is based on the business analysis knowledge areas where you have experience as a business analyst. Table 1-2 shows what you'll be tested on and the percentage of questions for each knowledge area.

NOTE   The IIBA doesn't report exactly how many questions you'll have in each category on each exam, so the number of questions reported here is still approximate.

Tailor your study sessions and efforts to the knowledge areas with the largest percentage of questions. Loads of resources besides this book can help you pass the CBAP examination. Of course I believe that this book is your best resource for the exam, but I'm biased. The IIBA recommends some other CBAP-related materials to help you study; I've sprinkled in a few of my own recommendations at the end of the list.

- **Business Analysis Body of Knowledge**   Download and review the BABOK. No offense to the IIBA, but the BABOK is like the printed version of sleeping pills. It's a good effort, but I've made good efforts to slam dunk a basketball, and that still hasn't happened. Still, your exam is based on the BABOK, and it won't hurt you to read it (well, not too much).

Knowledge Area	Percentage of Questions	Approximate Number of Questions
Enterprise Analysis	22%	33 questions
Requirements Planning and Management	22.7%	34–35 questions
Requirements Elicitation	18.7%	27–28 questions
Requirements Analysis and Documentation	20.7%	30–31 questions
Requirements Communication	10.7%	15–16 questions
Solution Assessment and Validation	5.2%	7–8 questions

Table 1-2   Estimated CBAP Exam Questions by Knowledge Area

- **IIBA web site**   I like the IIBA web site. It's organized, easy to navigate, and loaded with good information. In particular you should visit their frequently asked questions section for more information about the exam.

- **Training**   You must have 21 hours of professional development for your exam, so you might as well take a class or two to help you earn the CBAP. And now a blatant ad: I teach CBAP seminars to organizations around the world. If you'd like more information, come by my web site, www.projectseminars.com. Of course other wonderful training centers offer business analysis courses.

- **Business analysis mentor**   This is one of the best methods to learn business analysis skills. Emulating a business analysis professional that you admire can help you develop your own business analysis skills.

- **Join a study group**   This is a suggestion from the IIBA, not me. For some people it works, for others like me, it's a waste of time. All of the study groups I've ever joined were chitchat and commiseration times that didn't help me much to learn the material. If you're going to launch a study group, create some rules and boundaries, and establish a goal for the group—like passing the exam.

- **IIBA chapters**   Absolutely! You will meet some wonderful people in your local IIBA chapters who are happy to help you learn, advance your career, and be your friend. I can't praise the IIBA chapters and their leaders enough. I strongly encourage you to contact your local chapter and get involved. Many IIBA chapters offer training, mentoring, and guidance for the exam. Once you pass your exam, return the favor and help others do the same.

- **Flashcards**   Oh, boy. If you've ever taken one of my Boot Camp Seminars, you know how much I love flashcards. Repetition is the mother of learning, and flashcards are an instant way to learn the activities, processes, and business analysis tasks you'll have to know to understand the exam questions. Buy a big stack of index cards, and write the term on one side and the definition on the other. Don't buy preprinted flashcards; creating your own flashcards is part of the learning process.

- **Practice exams**   Every chapter of this book has 20 questions focusing on the content of the chapter. Answer these questions immediately after reading the chapter content, and continue to answer them until you can answer every question correctly. The CD in the back of this book has two 150-question simulation exams. I recommend you take the first exam once you've read this whole book. Continue taking the first exam until you can answer every question correctly. Then repeat the process with the second exam. Forget the movies for Friday night—you've practice exams to complete.

- **Create an incentive**   We all like rewards for a job well done. Create an incentive for you to pass the CBAP exam. Make it something that'll excite you and that's worth your time, attention, and energy. Promise yourself that you'll take a vacation day, buy some new music, or have a fancy dinner. Give yourself something to work toward that's special to you and that will keep you moving toward passing that exam.

Creating a Study Strategy

Here at the onset of your CBAP study efforts you should create a strategy of how and when you'll study. Use your business analysis skills to determine what the requirements are to pass the exam (I've done that in this chapter), but also use your skills to determine what the requirements are for *you* to pass the exam. You'll want to do some honest assessment of the knowledge areas, activities, and deliverables the IIBA expects you to know in order to pass the exam.

In each chapter I'll provide *key terms*. These key terms are excellent topics for your flashcards. As you move through the material and you see a term or concept that you're not familiar with, add it to your flashcards. Research the terms to fully understand their meaning and purpose. It's vital for you to understand the IIBA business analysis terms, as you'll need to apply them on the exam when you're answering situational questions.

As part of your study strategy, I also encourage you to study every day between now and when you're scheduled to pass your CBAP exam. You don't need hours and hours of daily time committed to the effort, but an hour a day would be ideal. In this hour create an approach that works best for you to retain the information. That approach might be reading this book, answering chapter exam questions, and then reviewing your flashcards. For others it might be answering the chapter exam questions first to pay attention to the information in each chapter. Mix up your approach, keep things fresh, and repeat until you've learned the material. Commitment to a daily—including weekends—study session will increase your exam success odds immensely.

Finally, complete your application as soon as possible and schedule your exam. Procrastination is one of your worst enemies when it comes to earning any certification. By scheduling your exam now, you're creating a deadline to pass the exam and get back to your life. Do it. I know you don't want to drag this process out any longer than necessary, and the only way to get through this studying and testing is to do the studying and testing.

All of your studying efforts lead to your goal: to pass the CBAP examination on your first attempt. You're studying to pass the CBAP exam, not just to take the test When your big day arrives, and it'll be here sooner than you think, get to the testing center at least 30 minutes before your exam is scheduled to start. Make certain you're well rested, that you know where the testing center is, and have a positive mind-set about passing your exam. In addition, you'll need the following for your exam:

- Your exam scheduling confirmation notice.

- Current identification with signature (valid driver's license, passport, or ID card).

- While the testing center should provide you with two pencils and some scrap paper, take some with you just in case.

Once you're seated in the testing center and your exam begins, you'll have 3.5 hours to complete the examination. No talking, noise, or tomfoolery is allowed in the testing center. You are allowed to take breaks, but you cannot pause the computer-based test once you've started it. Use your time wisely; you should be able to answer approximately 50 questions per hour, and you receive no extra credit for finishing the exam early.

Once you've completed the exam, your work will be graded immediately, and you'll know if you passed or not. Once you've passed the exam, you are a CBAP and can start bragging to everyone as such. You'll receive the CBAP logo via e-mail for your personal letterhead, and you'll receive some guidelines from the IIBA on how you're allowed to use the logo. The IIBA will also mail you a certificate suitable for framing, and a wallet card that is good for, um, keeping in your wallet.

Should a friend of yours—not you—fail the CBAP exam and want to retake it, they'll need to pay a $250 retake fee. Your friend will have to complete the official CBAP Exam Re-write Form available on the IIBA web site. The person taking the exam again can do so once within a year of when they originally submitted their CBAP exam application. The retake exam, however, must be at least three months after the failed attempt at the CBAP. If the individual, or anyone for that matter, doesn't pass the exam within the designated one-year period, he'll have to reapply and pay the full application and exam fees.

Maintaining the IIBA CBAP Certification

Once you've earned the CBAP certification, you'll have to complete some work to maintain the certification. This means you'll need to complete at least 60 Continuing Development Units (CDUs) within each three-year Continuing Certification Requirements (CCR) program. Each CBAP's three-year CCR cycle starts on the day they pass the CBAP exam and ends exactly three years later. You'll report your CDUs through the IIBA web site using the CBAP Certification Renewal Form.

In addition to completing the CDUs, you'll also have to pay a renewal fee; it's $85 for IIBA members and $120 for non-IIBA members. Your CBAP status is considered active as long as you've completed the CDUs and paid your renewal fees. If a CBAP fails to accrue the 60 CDUs, his CBAP status is changed to suspended, and his name is stripped from the online CBAP database. Once the suspended CBAP has earned the required 60 CDUs and paid the renewal fees, his status is changed back to active. If a suspended CBAP does not rectify the CDU problem and revert to active status within one year of being suspended, his CBAP designation is removed. If he wants to be a CBAP, the individual will have to start the entire certification process from scratch. No fun.

You can earn your 60 CDUs from six different categories. While no minimum amount is required from any category, there is a maximum number of CDUs you're allowed from any category. You can only count your participation in these activities if they are started after you've earned your CBAP. Here are details on the six CDU activities you can complete:

- **Formal academic education**   You can earn up to 40 CDUs per CCR cycle in formal academic education. The business analysis class must be offered for degree credit, and you must receive a passing grade in the class.

- **Professional development**   You can earn up to 30 CDUs per CCR cycle through professional development. You complete these seminars from EEPs or through training vendors who have their business analysis seminars approved by the IIBA. IIBA chapters can also grant CDUs for their meetings.

- **Professional activities**   You can earn up to 30 CDUs per CCR cycle through your professional activities. This category is reserved for activities that contribute to the business analysis knowledge area. Here are the breakdown and CDU values for this activity:

  - Author or coauthor a business analysis article that's published in a refereed journal to earn up to 30 CDUs per article.

  - Author or coauthor a business analysis article that's published in a non-refereed journal to earn up to 15 CDUs per article.

  - Serve as a speaker on business analysis at a conference, workshop, formal course, or through an IIBA chapter meeting to earn 10 CDUs per activity.

  - Moderate a discussion panel on business analysis, and you'll earn 5 CDUs.

  - Author or coauthor a business analysis textbook, and you'll earn 30 CDUs.

  - Develop content for a formal business analysis learning program, and you'll receive 15 CDUs.

- **Self-directed learning**   You can earn up to 15 CDUs per CCR cycle by spending at least 15 hours being coached, studying business analysis books, Internet resources, or other instructional sources. What a deal!

- **Volunteer**   You can earn up to 30 CDUs by volunteering through an IIBA chapter, in the community, or with charitable groups.

- **Professional experience**   You can earn up to 21 CDUs just by doing your job. It's based on the number of hours you spend completing business analysis duties over a three-year time frame. Here's the scoop:

  - Complete 1,000 to 1,999 hours of business analysis activities within a three-year time frame and you'll receive 7 CDUs.

  - Complete 2,000 to 2,999 hours of business analysis activities, and you'll receive 14 CDUs. If you've done 1,999 hours, find one more hour of work.

  - Complete 3,000 or more hours performing business analysis work within a three-year time frame, and you'll receive the maximum of 21 CDUs. You should also get a vacation.

If you complete more than 60 CDUs within your three-year certification cycle, you can apply up to 20 CDUs to your next certification cycle. The catch is that only CDUs earned in the last year of your certification cycle can be transferred to the next certification cycle.

Adhering to the CBAP Code of Ethical Conduct and Professional Standards

As part of your CBAP application and CBAP certification renewal process, you must sign and agree to abide by the CBAP Code of Ethical Conduct and Professional Standards. As with all IIBA documents, you can download your own free version from the IIBA web site. There's nothing shocking or unreasonable in this code of ethics, but if you're found guilty of violating the code, your CBAP status could be revoked.

The first section of the CBAP Code of Ethical Conduct and Professional Standards centers on your responsibility to the business analysis profession. You agree to comply with all of the IIBA rules and policies when it comes to applying to become a CBAP and maintaining your CBAP status. You'll report violations of the code to IIBA when there's clear and factual evidence of such violations, and you'll work with IIBA should there be an investigation into the breach of the code. You're also to communicate with clients and stakeholders whenever there's a circumstance that is a conflict of interest or a situation that could be construed as a conflict of interest or impropriety.

In your business analysis role, you agree that you will provide truthful advertisements and reflections of qualifications, experience, and skills. This also means that you won't accept assignments that you aren't fully competent and qualified to complete. The CBAP Code of Ethical Conduct and Professional Standards expects that you'll comply with laws, regulations, and standards that apply to your employment and services. That seems fair.

As a CBAP, you're also to advance the profession of business analysis. Specifically, according to the CBAP Code of Ethical Conduct and Professional Standards you are to

- Respect the intellectual work of others.
- Share the CBAP Code of Ethical Conduct and Professional Standards with other business analysts, clients, customers, and distant relatives.
- Advance the best qualified business analysis professionals. In particular, you are to advance certified business analysts who adhere to this code and to avoid those business analysts who don't adhere to this code or whose reputation might negatively impact the business analysis profession.
- Not tarnish other business analysts' reputations through malice or indifference.
- Maintain your education, competence, skills, and abilities through continuing education.
- Give generously of your time by training and mentoring others.

The CBAP Code of Ethical Conduct and Professional Standards also includes a section on your responsibilities to the public. As a CBAP, you're to be honest in your advertising, sales, cost and time estimates, and qualifications. You shouldn't take on assignments that you know you're unqualified to complete, but you should work to completely satisfy the scope of the services you've promised the customer to complete.

Don't deceive the customers for personal gain, but act honestly and in good faith that the public is doing the same.

Business analysts may become privy to information that is sensitive in nature. As a CBAP, and frankly as a good person, you are not to divulge that information. Keep private things private. Imagine a contract-based business analyst and how they may work for multiple entities. It'd be unethical for the business analyst to share information and insight into systems and operations of one client with other clients. This doesn't mean that the business analyst can't use what she's learned and apply it to different clients, but it does mean she shouldn't blab about specific operations, systems, and projects to all of her clients.

The CBAP is to use some common sense. No, the CBAP Code of Ethical Conduct and Professional Standards doesn't actually say that, but that's pretty much what you're expected to do as a CBAP. You can't take bribes, compromise projects, or make poor decisions for stakeholders that may just help your personal gain. Avoid conflicts of interest, impropriety, and even the appearance of both. Be honest, act in your customer's best interest, and do what's best for your client.

Chapter Summary

You've covered a lot of ground in this chapter. You've learned about the IIBA and their certification program, joining the IIBA, and finding a local business analysis chapter to join. The fee to join the IIBA is $95 per year of membership, and your local chapter may have a small annual fee to join. Your local chapter will likely also charge a small fee for each meeting—usually to offset room rental, dinner, and chapter events. I think it's a good idea to join the IIBA, not only for the networking and web resources, but you'll also save $125 on your exam fee—that alone is worth the membership.

The exam fee is $325, and the exam application fee is $125; these costs are in addition to the $95 to join the IIBA. Basically, to join the IIBA, apply for the exam, and to then take the test, you'll spend $420—which includes your $125 discount for joining the IIBA. So unless you're really opposed to joining organizations, you should join the IIBA and save some cash.

If you've decided that you're on your way to becoming a CBAP, you should complete your exam application as soon as possible. Completing the CBAP exam application is a time-consuming process, as you've got to document your education, professional development, and 7,500 hours of business analysis activity over the past ten years. You'll also need two professional references who can vouch for you as being a stellar business analyst.

As a CBAP applicant, you'll have to document how much time you've spent in at least four of the six business analysis knowledge areas, what experience you've had with a myriad of business analysis activities, and show what deliverables you've created from each activity. Once you've completed and signed the application, and submitted the form to the IIBA along with your payment and professional references, you'll be notified by the IIBA when they approve your application.

When your application is approved, you can schedule your computer-based test, the last hurdle to the CBAP. The test has 150 questions, and you'll have three and a half hours to complete the exam at a Castle Worldwide testing center. When you're done answering all of the questions or your time expires, whichever happens first, your exam is graded and your score is displayed on the computer screen. If you pass, you're certified. Congrats!

After your party, you'll then need to begin working toward maintaining your CBAP credential. You'll do this by earning the required 60 Continuing Development Units (CDUs) within your three-year certification cycle. You can earn these 60 units in a bunch of different ways including self-study and just working as a business analyst. In addition to your 60 CDUs, there's a CBAP renewal fee of $85 for IIBA members and $120 for CBAPs who aren't members of the IIBA.

While this chapter focused on the mechanics of the CBAP application and maintenance process, the remainder of this book focuses on passing the CBAP exam. I'll do that by detailing all of the content of the BABOK, activities, and outputs. You'll learn all of the details of the exam, complete practice tests, and learn the IIBA approach to business analysis. Your new goal, and my goal for you, is to earn your CBAP with as little pain and with as much joy as possible.

Key Terms

A Guide to the Business Analysis Body of Knowledge (BABOK)   The BABOK book is published by the IIBA and supports and defines the business analysis role, processes, and generally accepted practices of the community. The CBAP examination is based largely on the BABOK.

Business analyst   An individual who identifies the business needs of the organization's clients and stakeholders, helps determine solutions to business problems, completes requirements development, and performs requirements management. The business analyst also facilitates communications among clients, project stakeholders, and the defined solutions team.

CBAP Code of Ethical Conduct and Professional Standards   An IIBA document that defines the expected ethical and professional standards for all CBAPs.

Certified Business Analysis Professional (CBAP)   An individual who has the required education, professional development, and work experience, and has proven so by passing a business analysis exam governed by the International Institute of Business Analysis.

Completing the Solution Assessment and Validation   This business analysis knowledge area works with the project manager, technology team, project team, and stakeholders to analyze the detailed design documents. You'll define the logical phases of the project, the technical design, and the quality assurance activities.

Continuing Development Units (CDUs)   CBAPs must earn 60 CDUs per three-year cycle to maintain their CBAP status. CDUs can be earned through education, professional activities, and professional development.

Endorsed Education Provider (EEP)   Educational providers such as training centers or colleges have paid a fee to the IIBA to have their materials reviewed and endorsed by the IIBA as being accurate business analysis courses. EEPs may provide professional development courses and seminars that offer Continuing Development Units.

Enterprise analysis   These business analysis activities help define and identify business opportunities for an organization.

International Institute of Business Analysis (IIBA)   A nonprofit entity headquartered in Toronto, Canada. IIBA aims to develop and propel the business analysis role and career through its mission "to develop and maintain standards for the practice of business analysis and for the certification of its practitioners." The IIBA is the governing body for the CBAP examination and certification.

Requirements Analysis and Documentation   This business analysis knowledge area defines the analysis, framing, and documenting of the requirements in order to find an appropriate solution to create the deliverables and benefits of the project or opportunity.

Requirements Communication   This business analysis knowledge area happens throughout the business analysis activities and is done in tandem with requirements gathering and analysis. This activity documents and shares information about the requirements, status, and business analysis processes and their progress.

Requirements Elicitation   This business analysis knowledge area defines structured approaches to systematically and accurately draw out or confirm the project or opportunity requirements from the project stakeholders and clients.

Requirements Planning and Management   A business analysis knowledge area and activity that works with the project and organizational stakeholders to determine the required resources to complete the requirements gathering process. A business analyst completing these tasks is determining the key roles, managing the requirements scope, and serving as a communicator.

Questions

On your CBAP exam, you won't encounter questions from very much of the material in this chapter. This chapter, an overview of the CBAP process, didn't cover in much depth the CBAP exam objectives. You should, however, complete the following chapter exam anyway to get your brain reacquainted with answering situational- and definition-type test questions.

1. Where is the IIBA headquartered?

   A. Toronto

   B. New York City

   C. Newton Square

   D. San Francisco

2. When was the IIBA founded?

   A. October 2003

   B. October 2006

   C. January 1984

   D. March 1999

3. Marcy is a new business analyst, and Tom is mentoring her. Marcy would like some additional literature to read about the IIBA and the practices of a business analyst. Which book should Tom refer to Marcy?

   A. *PMBOK*

   B. *Business Analysis Body of Knowledge*

   C. *The All-in-One CBAP Exam Study Guide*

   D. *A Guide to the Business Analysis Body of Knowledge*

4. Mark is applying to become a CBAP. He is considering joining the IIBA to save $125 on his examination fee. Which one of the following is not a benefit of joining the IIBA?

   A. Mark can access the BABOK online.

   B. Mark can access the IIBA online forums.

   C. Mark can access the IIBA job posting forums.

   D. Mark can access the IIBA CBAP logos to use on his web site.

5. How many years of experience as a business analyst are required to become a CBAP?

   A. Three years within the last five years

   B. Five years within the last ten years

   C. Ten years within the last decade

   D. Three years within the last ten

6. Which one of the following is not a business analysis knowledge area?

   A. Managing Enterprise Analysis and Strategic Planning

   B. Planning and Managing Requirements

   C. Managing Requirements and Program Benefits

   D. Performing Solution Assessment and Validation

7. Fred is applying for the CBAP, but he is worried that his application will be rejected because of his lack of a college degree. What can Fred do to ensure his application will be approved even though he does not have a college degree?

   A. Fred does not need a college degree to apply for the CBAP; he must have graduated from high school.

B. Fred does not need a college degree to apply for the CBAP; he can document 1,500 additional business analysis experience hours in lieu of the college degree.

C. Fred does not need a college degree to apply for the CBAP; he must attend 32 contact hours of training in lieu of the college degree.

D. Fred cannot apply to become a CBAP; a college degree is required for all CBAP applicants.

8. Which one of the following activities may not be used toward your business analysis work experience on your CBAP exam application?

A. Writing requirements documentation

B. Project management

C. Determining project scope and objectives

D. Identifying and documenting requirements risks

9. How many knowledge areas must the CBAP applicant prove their business analysis experience in?

A. Six

B. Nine

C. Four

D. All of them

10. You are a business analyst in your organization and are mentoring Tracy on business analysis. Tracy is currently helping you identify new business opportunities for your organization. The process of identifying new business opportunities is known as what?

A. Research and development

B. Feasibility study

C. Enterprise analysis

D. Enterprise environmental factors

11. Jason is a CBAP for the Sunshine Organization, an IT development firm. He is currently identifying and documenting all of the requirement team roles and responsibilities for a newly identified project within the organization. Martin, the project manager, wants to know what business analysis process Jason is completing. What should Jason's answer be?

A. Jason is doing a project management activity and should stop.

B. Communications management

C. Roles and responsibilities identification

D. Requirements planning and management

12. In what business analysis knowledge area would a CBAP manage requirements conflicts?

   A. Requirements Communication

   B. Requirements Analysis and Documentation

   C. Requirements Elicitation

   D. Requirements Planning and Management

13. How many professional references will the CBAP applicant need in order to qualify for the CBAP examination?

   A. Four

   B. Two

   C. One

   D. Six

14. You are a business analyst for your organization and are working with Mary, the project manager of a new project. The project is a software development project that will connect your organization's manufacturing operations with existing customers. You are currently defining the logical phases of the project. Mary is uncertain of what phases should happen in which order, so you'll rely on historical information to help the process along. The definition of the phases is hosted by what knowledge area?

   A. Risk Management

   B. Solution Assessment and Validation

   C. Requirements Analysis and Documentation

   D. Requirements Elicitation

15. How many hours of professional development activities must you complete prior to submitting your CBAP application?

   A. 32

   B. 12

   C. 21

   D. 60

16. Hannah is completing her CBAP exam application, and she needs to list her professional references. She understands that she must have known the reference for at least six months prior to submitting the application, but she's confused as to what type of references she must identify. Which one of the following references does not qualify as a CBAP exam application professional reference?

   A. Career manager

   B. Client (internal or external)

   C. Certified Business Analysis Professional (IIBA-certified business analyst)

   D. Project manager

17. What must the professional references do with the CBAP Application Reference Form once they've completed it?

    A. Mail it immediately to the IIBA.

    B. Seal the envelope, sign the seal, and then mail it to the IIBA.

    C. Electronically sign the form and then submit it to the IIBA through their web site.

    D. Sign the form and fax it to the IIBA.

18. How much does it cost to apply for the CBAP examination?

    A. $125

    B. $325

    C. $450

    D. Nothing

19. How many questions are on the CBAP examination?

    A. 200

    B. 100

    C. 250

    D. 150

20. Your customer has requested that your organization create a new web site for his company. He'd like the web site to have blog, chat room, technical charting, and e-commerce abilities. You and your requirements gathering team are beginning to develop solutions for the customer. Your team creates four different alternative solutions. Alternative solution identification happens in which business analysis knowledge area?

    A. Risk Management

    B. Solution Assessment and Validation

    C. Requirements Analysis and Documentation

    D. Requirements Elicitation

Questions and Answers

1. Where is the IIBA headquartered?

    A. Toronto

    B. New York City

    C. Newton Square

    D. San Francisco

    A. The IIBA is headquartered in Toronto. All of the other choices are incorrect. While you certainly won't have a question on the CBAP examination on this particular content, this is an example of a comprehension-type question. You will have comprehension questions where you'll need to answer based on the definition of terms.

2. When was the IIBA founded?

   A. October 2003

   B. October 2006

   C. January 1984

   D. March 1999

   A. The IIBA was founded in October 2003 by 28 founding members. In 2006, they became an official not-for-profit entity. The other choices are incorrect.

3. Marcy is a new business analyst, and Tom is mentoring her. Marcy would like some additional literature to read about the IIBA and the practices of a business analyst. Which book should Tom refer to Marcy?

   A. *PMBOK*

   B. *Business Analysis Body of Knowledge*

   C. *The All-in-One CBAP Exam Study Guide*

   D. *A Guide to the Business Analysis Body of Knowledge*

   D. Marcy needs a copy of *A Guide to the Business Analysis Body of Knowledge*. A is incorrect, as "PMBOK" is an abbreviation for *A Guide to the Project Management Body of Knowledge,* not an IIBA favorite but it's a better guide for project managers than the BABOK. B is incorrect, as this is not as good a choice as D. This question is a good example of always choosing the best answer. Sure, you could argue that B and D are almost the same, but D is the correct name of the book, so it's the better choice. Always choose the best answer. If you chose C, I'm flattered but this is incorrect. You should choose your answers the way the IIBA expects you to answer the question.

4. Mark is applying to become a CBAP. He is considering joining the IIBA to save $125 on his examination fee. Which one of the following is not a benefit of joining the IIBA?

   A. Mark can access the BABOK online.

   B. Mark can access the IIBA online forums.

   C. Mark can access the IIBA job posting forums.

   D. Mark can access the IIBA CBAP logos to use on his web site.

   D. Mark won't be able to download the CBAP logos from the IIBA web site just because he's joined the IIBA. Mark will need to pass the CBAP exam and then follow the IIBA rules and policies for using the logos. A, B, and C are all valid benefits of joining the IIBA, so these choices are incorrect. This is a good example of how some of the questions want you to find the incorrect answer. Pay attention to what the question is asking, such as in "which one is not" or "all of the following except for which one" phrases.

5. How many years of experience as a business analyst are required to become a CBAP?

   A. Three years within the last five years

    B. Five years within the last ten years

    C. Ten years within the last decade

    D. Three years within the last ten

    B. You need five years of experience as a business analyst to qualify for the CBAP examination. Note that choice C is a bit of a trick, as ten years is a decade—that won't work.

6. Which one of the following is not a business analysis knowledge area?

    A. Managing Enterprise Analysis and Strategic Planning

    B. Planning and Managing Requirements

    C. Managing Requirements and Program Benefits

    D. Performing Solution Assessment and Validation

    C. Choice C is not a business analysis knowledge area. Choices A, B, and D are all valid choices, as there are six business analysis knowledge areas: Enterprise Analysis, Requirements Planning and Management, Requirements Elicitation, Requirements Analysis and Documentation, Requirements Communication, and Solution Assessment and Validation.

7. Fred is applying for the CBAP, but he is worried that his application will be rejected because of his lack of a college degree. What can Fred do to ensure his application will be approved even though he does not have a college degree?

    A. Fred does not need a college degree to apply for the CBAP; he must have graduated from high school.

    B. Fred does not need a college degree to apply for the CBAP; he can document 1,500 additional business analysis experience hours in lieu of the college degree.

    C. Fred does not need a college degree to apply for the CBAP; he must attend 32 contact hours of training in lieu of the college degree.

    D. Fred cannot apply to become a CBAP; a college degree is required for all CBAP applicants.

    A. Fred only needs to have earned a high school diploma to qualify for the CBAP certification. Choices B, C, and D are all incorrect choices.

8. Which one of the following activities may not be used toward your business analysis work experience on your CBAP exam application?

    A. Writing requirements documentation

    B. Project management

    C. Determining project scope and objectives

    D. Identifying and documenting requirements risks

    B. You'll need five years of business analysis experience to qualify for the CBAP examination. Your project management experience does not count toward the certification. The IIBA is very particular about project management activities and business analysis activities, so use caution in your CBAP application and documentation of professional experiences.

9. How many knowledge areas must the CBAP applicant prove their business analysis experience in?

   A. Six

   B. Nine

   C. Four

   D. All of them

   C. While there are six business analysis knowledge areas, you only have to document your experience in four of the six. Choices A, B, and D are all incorrect choices.

10. You are a business analyst in your organization and are mentoring Tracy on business analysis. Tracy is currently helping you identify new business opportunities for your organization. The process of identifying new business opportunities is known as what?

   A. Research and development

   B. Feasibility study

   C. Enterprise analysis

   D. Enterprise environmental factors

   C. Enterprise analysis, according to the BABOK, is composed of the activities that a business analyst uses to define and identify business opportunities for your organization. Think like an entrepreneur when you answer these questions. Choices A, B, and D are incorrect choices.

11. Jason is a CBAP for the Sunshine Organization, an IT development firm. He is currently identifying and documenting all of the requirement team roles and responsibilities for a newly identified project within the organization. Martin, the project manager, wants to know what business analysis process Jason is completing. What should Jason's answer be?

   A. Jason is doing a project management activity and should stop.

   B. Communications management

   C. Roles and responsibilities identification

   D. Requirements planning and management

   D. When Jason does requirements planning and management tasks, he is working with project and organizational stakeholders to determine what resources are needed for requirements gathering. A business analyst completing these tasks is determining the key roles, managing the requirements scope, and serving as a communicator of the requirements gathering process. A is incorrect, as Jason is defining the roles and responsibilities needed for requirements gathering, not the project team. B is incorrect, as Jason is not communicating requirements or status. C is incorrect, as this question is not as accurate as choice D.

12. In what business analysis knowledge area would a CBAP manage requirements conflicts?

   A. Requirements Communication

   B. Requirements Analysis and Documentation

   C. Requirements Elicitation

   D. Requirements Planning and Management

   A. Requirements Communication does include the management of requirements conflicts. Choices B, C, and D are incorrect choices because management of requirements conflicts does not happen in these knowledge areas.

13. How many professional references will the CBAP applicant need in order to qualify for the CBAP examination?

   A. Four

   B. Two

   C. One

   D. Six

   B. You'll only need two professional references to qualify for the CBAP exam. If you include more than two, only two can be used by the IIBA for their evaluation. Choices A, C, and D are incorrect.

14. You are a business analysis for your organization and are working with Mary, the project manager of a new project. The project is a software development project that will connect your organization's manufacturing operations with existing customers. You are currently defining the logical phases of the project. Mary is uncertain of what phases should happen in which order, so you'll rely on historical information to help the process along. The definition of the phases is hosted by what knowledge area?

   A. Risk Management

   B. Solution Assessment and Validation

   C. Requirements Analysis and Documentation

   D. Requirements Elicitation

   B. Phases are defined in the Solution Assessment and Validation knowledge area. Choices A, C, and D are all incorrect choices for Mary's problem.

15. How many hours of professional development activities must you complete prior to submitting your CBAP application?

    A. 32

    B. 12

    C. 21

    D. 60

    C. You'll need 21 hours of professional development prior to the date on your CBAP exam application. Choices A, B, and D are incorrect; note that choice D is the number of Continuing Development Units you'll need to maintain your certification once you've earned it.

16. Hannah is completing her CBAP exam application, and she needs to list her professional references. She understands that she must have known the reference for at least six months prior to submitting the application, but she's confused as to what type of references she must identify. Which one of the following references does not qualify as a CBAP exam application professional reference?

    A. Career manager

    B. Client (internal or external)

    C. Certified Business Analysis Professional (IIBA-certified business analyst)

    D. Project manager

    D. Hannah needs two references for her CBAP application. The references must be a career manager, client, or CBAP that she has known for more than six months. While Hannah could use a project manager who serves as her career manager, choice D does not clearly define this option. This is an example of choosing the best answer, as a project manager is not specifically defined by the IIBA as one of the three types of professional references the CBAP applicant may use.

17. What must the professional references do with the CBAP Application Reference Form once they've completed it?

    A. Mail it immediately to the IIBA.

    B. Seal the envelope, sign the seal, and then mail it to the IIBA.

    C. Electronically sign the form and then submit it to the IIBA through their web site.

    D. Sign the form and fax it to the IIBA.

    B. Once a professional reference has completed the CBAP Application Reference Form, he is to sign the form, seal it in an envelope, and sign his name across the seal. Choices A, C, and D are incorrect procedures for the form and CBAP application.

18. How much does it cost to apply for the CBAP examination?

    A. $125

    B. $325

    C. $450

    D. Nothing

    A. It will cost you $125 to apply for the CBAP examination. Choice B is the actual exam fee for members. Choice C is the total fee for the exam and the application fee, both of which you can pay at once when applying for the exam. Choice D is incorrect, as there is a fee for applying to take the CBAP examination.

19. How many questions are on the CBAP examination?

    A. 200

    B. 100

    C. 250

    D. 150

    D. There are 150 questions on the CBAP examination. You'll need to answer the 150 questions within three hours. Choices A, B, and C are all incorrect choices.

20. Your customer has requested that your organization create a new web site for his company. He'd like the web site to have blog, chat room, technical charting, and e-commerce abilities. You and your requirements gathering team are beginning to develop solutions for the customer. Your team creates four different alternative solutions. Alternative solution identification happens in which business analysis knowledge area?

    A. Risk Management

    B. Solution Assessment and Validation

    C. Requirements Analysis and Documentation

    D. Requirements Elicitation

    B. Alternative solutions are found during the Solution Assessment and Validation. This is a legitimate and encouraged business analysis activity. Choices A, C, and D are all incorrect choices.

Business Analysis Planning and Monitoring

In this chapter you will
- Determine a business analysis approach
- Identify the project stakeholders
- Manage risks within the requirements
- Plan the requirements elicitation activities
- Manage the requirements scope
- Manage changes to the requirements

This chapter focuses on one of the largest business analysis knowledge areas: Business Analysis Planning and Monitoring. This is the heart of your role as a business analyst, so many of the terms, activities, and approaches should already be familiar to you. As a reminder, be certain to answer the questions based on the IIBA's definitions of the terms and activities defined by them—not based on your day-to-day work.

The Business Analysis Planning and Monitoring knowledge area is all about you, the business analyst, defining the needed resources and tasks to complete the requirements gathering activities. You'll define the requirements activities based on the project, organizational structure, and existing standards, and then you and the business analysis team will elicit the requirements from the identified stakeholders.

This knowledge area is all about hands-on, time-intensive, critical work. It's considered critical because the project manager and the project team depend on you to provide the exact requirements for the project deliverables. Based on your analysis, the project manager and project team will create what you've asked for. This means you'll need to identify stakeholders and use the best business analysis activities for the requirements elicitation.

Part of this knowledge area is the human resources aspect of requirements gathering. You'll rely on your business analysis team to help gather requirements, so you'll need knowledgeable staff, and your staff will need to understand what is expected of them. As requirements are gathered, the team will need to react to schedule and scope slippage to capture, as efficiently as possible, the requirements for project objectives. This means the project manager will want to know enough information to be able to create time and cost estimates based on your requirements gathering results.

This knowledge area has six distinct tasks that you must know for your CBAP exam. I'll cover all six of these in detail:

- Plan the business analysis approach.
- Conduct stakeholder analysis.
- Plan the business analysis activities.
- Plan the business analysis communications.
- Plan the requirements management process.
- Manage the business analysis performance.

The outputs of these six tasks will help you determine what resources are needed for the project work. The outputs will also help the project manager determine what specific roles and responsibilities will need to be created and assigned to resources, or if the organization will need to procure or additional resources. These six tasks will also help you identify all of the project stakeholders and their stance on the project deliverables. There's much to cover in this chapter, so let's get to work!

Determining the Business Analysis Approach

Requirements planning is your job. The business analyst is responsible for determining what's needed by the customer and what the project must deliver in order to satisfy the problem or opportunity. Planning on how to gather requirements saves time, frustration, rework, and monies. Your effectiveness at properly gathering the requirements for a project will help the project manager better plan the project and the project team better execute the project.

Sometimes you don't get enough time to properly plan, gather, and document the requirements. When unrealistic expectations are placed on the business analyst to gather and document the requirements, troubles surface downstream in the project, in the execution, and in the morale surrounding the project. Part of the business analyst's responsibility is to communicate the time and expectations to complete requirements gathering. Lack of time and resources means a risk that all the requirements won't be gathered, created, or delivered.

Ideally, the business analyst will have sufficient time to work with the project manager on the best approach for requirements gathering. That's right; the business analyst should work with the project manager. The project manager and the project management team depend on the business analyst's effective requirements gathering. These two people should talk about what's the best approach for the business analyst to help the project manager to complete the project planning.

NOTE For your CBAP exam you won't have to know much about project management. In Chapter 9 of this book, however, I've included an in-depth look at the entire project management life cycle. Understanding the project management life cycle will help support your business analysis approach.

Planning for project requirements, managing scope, and reacting to scope change is an ongoing activity. Planning is not done once and then forgotten. Planning happens throughout the project until the project scope has been met. You can expect to interact with customers, project managers, the project team, and other stakeholders throughout the duration of the project as requirements shift in priority, or as the scope needs to be updated and changed.

When you plan the requirements, you'll need to consider many elements that will affect your approach to planning:

- Current standards and approaches your organization subscribes to
- Project-planning and requirements-gathering methodologies that the organization subscribes to
- Historical information from similar projects
- Inherent risks in the project work
- Expectations of the project stakeholders
- Stakeholder geographical locale
- Type of project

These things will help the business analyst consider the type of planning, type of requirements gathering, and what types of documents, conversations, and depth of planning will need to take place. You should always consider what organizational policies and standards already exist that may represent constraints or assumptions for the project; these may include policies, politics, and personalities.

 NOTE   *Organizational process assets* is a generic term to describe the existing templates, organizational business analysis procedures, historical information, and other standards that the business analyst can use to help the business analysis along. Governance standards, which are often requirements, are also considered to be an organizational process asset; consider Sarbanes-Oxley and COBIT as two examples.

Organizations often already have processes and procedures in place that direct the business analysis approach. When an organizational business analysis standard does not exist, then the business analyst works with the most appropriate stakeholders in the project to determine which approach and techniques are best for the project. Often it's the business need that drives the approach of the business analyst more than anything else.

Determining the Project Factors

Understanding why business analysis needs to take place can help the business analyst determine the best approach to the business analysis duties. The nature of the project work can help guide the business analysis work. All organizational endeavors usually fall into one of two categories that affect the business analyst:

- **Plan-driven endeavors** Most, if not all, elements and decisions of the project are explored, planned, and documented before the project execution begins. Plan-driven endeavors require the business analysis duties to be completed before the entire project plan is developed and approved. This approach requires a formal business analysis approach and documentation.

- **Change-driven endeavors** These endeavors describe projects that create deliverables in short bursts and are ideal for exploratory projects. Change-driven endeavors have a high-level project plan, but they only plan in detail for the most imminent activities. The business analyst usually provides an initial requirements list, sometimes called requirements envisioning, to allow the project work to begin. This approach allows the business analysis approach to be lighter, encourages more team interaction and conversational problem-solving, and provides documentation after the project has been completed.

Using the SDLC Methodology

For your CBAP exam you'll need to know a little bit about the System Development Life Cycle (SDLC). SDLC is a generic way of describing the life cycle of an information system and the phases the system goes through. SDLC has a lot of different flavors and theories about it, but you'll just need to know the broad, generic attributes.

Most SDLC approaches use phases to move the life cycle forward. A *phase* is a set of activities that creates a specific set of deliverables. The deliverables that are created in a phase allow the next phase to begin. When each phase ends, a new phase of the life cycle may begin based on the recently created deliverables. For example, you may have analysis, design, construction, implementation, operations, and maintenance of the information system. Some popular SDLC methodologies include

- **Waterfall** This methodology divides the project into phases, and the project manager focuses on control of time, cost, and scope. Figure 2-1 is an example of the waterfall. Loads of documentation occurs throughout the creation of the software or system. The waterfall approach is not the fastest or most flexible approach, but it does work. New project teams or teams that shift in resources often subscribe to this approach.

- **Incremental** This method uses a granular approach for quicker deliverables, easier risk management, and easier change control on the smaller segments of the project work. This approach can also use a series of waterfalls for phases and deliverables rather than one large waterfall model. This model is ideal for large projects but not so much for small projects.

- **Spiral** This approach, sometimes called the cinnamon roll, uses a series of planning, objective determination, alternative identification, and

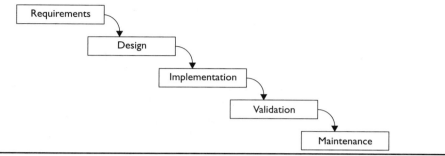

Figure 2-1 The waterfall model uses phases and documentation to control the work.

development for the life cycle. It's ideal for projects that have a low threshold for risks and choose to avoid or mitigate most project risks. The downside of this model is that it's unique for each project and can't usually be a template for future similar projects. The upside is that it's risk averse and provides accuracy.

- **Agile** Agile SDLC has a lot of different flavors, but they all have similar attributes: quick execution; daily meetings; isolated, protected developers; and adaptability to changes. The model uses small increments of planning and execution of the requirements. The benefits of this model are that the team can quickly create deliverables for the project stakeholders. The downside of this model is that an early mistake can cause huge ramifications and rework throughout the project.

These are just a few samples of the SDLC models. The business analyst should know which model the organization uses, which one the project manager wants to use, or which model is required based on the type of project that's under way. The model will help the business analysis team determine what requirements gathering approach is most appropriate and can guide the business analyst through requirements management and conversations with the project manager.

Consider the Project Life Cycle

The project life cycle is unique to each project. The phases that compose the project life cycle to build a piece of software will not be the same phases that you'd find in a construction project. Your industry, project, and organizational preferences will dictate the project life cycle you'll be gathering requirements for. The business analyst should be aware of the relevant life cycles the organization has used in the past and the industry standards that may affect the life cycle planning.

If you are familiar with the Project Management Institute (PMI) and their book *A Guide to the Project Management Body of Knowledge* (PMBOK Guide), you'll know that they make a clear distinction between the project life cycle and the project management life cycle. The project life cycle is unique to each project, while the project management life cycle is universal to all projects. The project management life cycle comprises initiating, planning, executing, monitoring and controlling, and closing processes.

The business analyst needs to be aware of the project's life cycle, phases, and generally accepted practices. One reason is that the business analyst and the project manager could participate in *rolling wave planning*. Figure 2-2 is an example of rolling wave planning, where the project is planned, then executed, then planned some more. Another reason for the business analyst's awareness of the life cycle is that on larger projects the requirements that are most immediate are planned in detail, while requirements that are off in the future are planned at a high level.

Consider Project Risks, Expectations, and Standards

Risks within the project, expectations of the project stakeholders, and relevant industry and organizational standards can all affect the business analysis planning. It's important to keep risk identification and management on the business analyst's agenda. Risk identification is an iterative process. Each time a new requirement is identified, a risk discussion should also be started. Remember that there's a difference between the requirements risk review and the project management risk review.

Expectations are sometimes just preconceived disappointments. It's not unusual for stakeholders to have an expectation of cost, duration, and deliverables that just doesn't jive with reality. Dealing with these expectations can be a challenge for the business analyst. Stakeholder expectations must be well documented, communicated, and explained to the project manager and project team so that the expectations can be addressed.

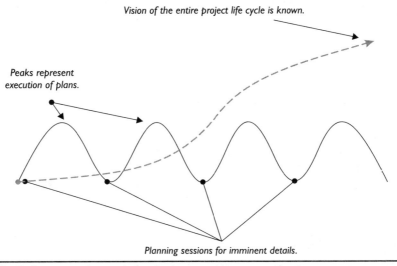

Figure 2-2   Rolling wave planning balances short- and long-term planning.

Also tied to expectations are the stakeholder priorities. When you're dealing with a large project, stakeholder priorities sometimes conflict with one another, shift, and offer competing objectives. Again, documentation of what's important to the stakeholders and periodic review of the priorities can help the project manager and the business analyst. A regular status review meeting with the project manager, project sponsor, and the key stakeholders can keep the business analysis activities on track.

A *standard* is a guideline or recommendation, while a *regulation* is a requirement. Standards are optional but are generally followed for best practices. It's up to the business analyst to identify all of the relevant standards for the industry, the type of project, and the identified requirements. Of course the business analyst should also document and communicate any regulations, which are not optional, to the stakeholders and project team.

Once the project is launched, planned, and the project work shifts into execution, change requests to the project scope will likely occur, and new requirements will be identified. When changes happen, the business analyst and the project manager need to be in sync on how the change management process will work. All changes, regardless of their size, must be considered and evaluated before they are folded into the project.

A change management system within the organization should be established that allows the project manager and the business analysts to determine the best course of action. All proposed changes should be evaluated on the following eight areas:

- **Scope**   What exactly is changing within the project and why the change is needed.

- **Time**   The amount of time the additional requirements will take in the project.

- **Cost**   The new requirements may demand additional materials, labor, or both, so additional costs may be added to the project.

- **Quality**   A review of how the addition will affect the project quality for better, for worse, or for no change at all.

- **Human resources**   The additional requirements may cause a need for additional staffing on the project, which is directly related to cost, time, and possibly procurement.

- **Communications**   The new requirements should be communicated to all affected parties, so they may voice their opinion on the proposed change.

- **Risk**   All new requirements must pass through risk identification and analysis, and determine if the new requirements introduce risk to the project.

- **Procurement**   The new requirement may necessitate procurement activities for the project.

These eight areas of the project are all linked together; a change in one of these elements may affect activities in the other elements. The linking of these areas is called *integration management*—it's a project management term, but it's applicable to the synergy between the project manager and business analyst.

Performing Stakeholder Analysis

Projects exist because of stakeholders and the promised return of the projects. *Stakeholders* are the people who are affected by the project purpose. It's important for the stakeholders to be identified as soon as possible—that's why it's one of the first business analysis activities. Stakeholders' attitude toward the project, their influence in the organization, and their authority levels over the project all must be considered by the business analyst and the project manager. Understanding a stakeholder's stance on the solution can help the business analyst gather requirements and manage the stakeholder more effectively.

While projects exist because of stakeholders, projects are managed by project managers—not business analysts. Business analysts are often the liaison between the end users and recipients of the project deliverables and the project manager. That shouldn't come as a surprise to you at all. However, what may come as a surprise is that the business analyst needs to identify all of the project team roles that will be needed to complete the requirements gathering process and the project work to create the project deliverables. While at first glance that seems a bit overwhelming, for a couple of reasons it's really not. First off, when you consider an organization and the types of projects it does, chances are it's doing the same type of projects over and over. A construction firm builds stuff. An IT shop is designing software. A manufacturer creates things. The types of projects are usually pretty similar from one to the next, so it shouldn't be a big mystery to the business analyst or to the project manager what types of resources are needed on the project.

When the business analyst goes about identifying the types of roles she'll need to complete the requirements gathering, they'll probably be the same people within the organization who specialize in the discipline the project centers around. She'll likely be utilizing some of the same people during the requirements gathering process who will be assigned to the actual project work. While in some huge companies this may vary slightly, it's not unusual to assume that the experts that offer advice during the business analysis activities will be the same experts completing the work during the project.

Finally, the business analyst and the project manager will work together to determine the roles needed for the project team. The business analyst is the person closest to the stakeholders during requirements gathering and will have an understanding of the work that needs to be done to create the requirements. This understanding will help the business analyst determine what roles are needed. In addition, the project manager can call upon past similar projects to help determine what types of roles are needed.

Identifying Project Stakeholders

If it weren't for stakeholders, business analysis, project management, and even operations would run much more smoothly. Then again, if it weren't for stakeholders, there just wouldn't be much to do. I'm being facetious, of course. Stakeholders are the most important element of business analysis and project management, because they are the driving force behind the requirements gatherings and project management business. Projects are done to satisfy some need or opportunity for the stakeholders.

It's an important part of business analysis to identify all of the stakeholders as early as possible during the project. If a business analyst overlooks a key stakeholder or groups of stakeholders, then the project is likely to suffer later. The overlooked stakeholder may have a large influence over the project that may cause rework, rescoping, and even business analysis duties. The rework will, no doubt, take additional time and monies to complete. Rework also negatively affects team morale, confidence in the business analyst, and causes frustration for all the other stakeholders. You can also expect the stakeholder who was overlooked in the stakeholder identification process to be less than happy and less than willing to help your project along.

If one of the stakeholders is a group of people, such as a department within your organization, then one person from that group should be designated to represent the interests of the group for the project. To start identifying stakeholders, the business analyst will need a list of the project team members, their roles and responsibilities within the project, contact information, and their functional managers. The business analyst should reference the organizational chart to determine which parts of the company are affected by the project and get contact information for these departments.

You can also identify stakeholders by considering the interfaces the project will deal with—vendors, subject matter experts, end users, and government agencies. A complete view of the origin of the project information, both incoming and outgoing, can help you identify the project stakeholders. All of the identified stakeholders should go into a stakeholder directory also known as the *stakeholder listing*. The project manager, project sponsor, and business analyst should review the stakeholder listing to identify gaps.

Another approach to stakeholder identification is to query your existing known stakeholders through a survey. The questionnaire can prompt other stakeholders who need to be included or can be a confirmation of all the identified stakeholders This questionnaire should have open-ended questions instead of "yes or no" answers. Let the participants ramble and point you to other stakeholders you may have overlooked. Some good questions to ask on the survey:

- Who is requesting the project deliverable?
- Who launched the request for the project?
- Who owns the problem or business opportunity the project will satisfy?
- Who is directly impacted by the result of the project?
- What roles in the organization will change because of this project's deliverable?
- Who is in control of the processes that this project may change?

You can add as many questions as you'd like, but generally fewer than ten prompts users to complete the form and return it. Make the survey too long, and it's likely to get ignored. Your survey should include a deadline and instructions for returning the form. Of course with all the technology that's available today, you have good reason to do a survey of this nature through a web form. It's faster, easier to collect the information, and easy to create. In either case, it'll take time to develop the survey, distribute it, and to give respondents an opportunity to answer the questions. When time's of the essence (and when isn't it?), a survey often isn't realistic to use.

A face-to-face interview with the known stakeholders is a great way to find stakeholders and to learn about your currently identified stakeholders. While it's a great approach, interviews can be time intensive. Again there's that pesky time issue, but it allows the interviewer to get immediate feedback, branch off into related questions, and can prompt the interviewee for additional information. You can ask dozens of questions in an interview to describe stakeholders. The goal is to capture stakeholders' project involvement, authority, and influence over the project, and to find how the project will impact them. Here are a few good interview questions for stakeholder identification:

- Who are their customers or suppliers?
- What are their key job functions or duties?
- What are their key business issues?
- How many computer systems do they use?
- How many end users do they represent or manage?
- What are their key business issues?
- Will one or more of their key issues be resolved by the project?
- What is the impact of excluding stakeholders' needs?
- What key issues or roadblocks do they face in this project (for example, geographic distance, cost, technology, and so on)?
- How many people in their organization are directly impacted by the project?
- Does the project's success create any negative impact for the stakeholder?
- What project goals can be eliminated or revised to remove the negative impact?
- Will one or more key business issues be resolved by this project?
- Will the project be successful if it does not remove all negative impact to the stakeholders? Can they live with the negative impact?
- What is the importance of each key project success criterion (consider schedule, delivery date, scope management, budget, and low risk)?
- Who is the key person who has authority to sign off for them? Does this key person have a backup?

The point of the questions is to generate as much information as possible about the project stakeholders. You want to document their position on the project, their influence over the project, and to acknowledge any political capital the individual stakeholders may sway toward the project. The problem with interviewing stakeholders is that the larger the project, the larger the number of stakeholders—and this means more and more time. Unfortunately, a large project can benefit most from a stakeholder information-gathering process like this one, so it's back to the time and cost issue and the challenge of conducting these interviews.

Once you've identified the project stakeholders, it's a good idea to begin categorizing them by needs, interests, contributions to the project, and the time frame of when you or the project manager will need to interact with the stakeholders. By grouping your stakeholders and their characteristics, you can identify trends, commonalities, and help with needs analysis, requirements gathering, and more stakeholder identification. While each project is likely to have different types of stakeholder groups, you should be familiar with these generic groupings for your CBAP exam:

- Key or secondary requirements source
- Project impact (high, medium, low, for example)
- Geographical location of the stakeholder
- Number of end users
- Business processes
- Existing systems in current business processes
- Interfacing business processes within the organization

The results of stakeholder grouping can help you create a matrix of stakeholders. You can identify each stakeholder's name or the group of stakeholders, business unit, location, their input on the project, and more. This information can help you and the project manager communicate with stakeholders about the project work, query information from them, and point you and your team to additional analysis.

Identifying Project Roles

Have you ever seen a one-person version of Shakespeare's play *Hamlet*? The actor has to shift between roles; one moment he's Hamlet, then it's Horatio, and then he's Claudius. It's fascinating to watch one person switch between roles and keep the play moving along. I bet you didn't think you'd read about Shakespeare here, did you? My point is that just as plays have different roles, projects have different roles. A role describes the function the person provides to keep the play, or in this case, the project, moving along.

The business analyst defines the roles that will be needed to keep the project creating the deliverables. Roles are generic terms that define the actions the person in the role completes. Roles are different from job titles, which is sometimes a gotcha for business analysts and project managers alike. *Roles* are generic descriptions of what the person (role player) actually does and not of the specific individual. For example, a trainer is an example of role, while Bob the Trainer is not. You do not want to attach individual people to the roles for a few reasons:

- **Flexibility** By keeping the roles generic in nature, you have flexibility in the project as to what roles are doing what activities.
- **Multiplicity** By keeping the roles generic, a number of people can satisfy different actions the role needs to complete. For example, you may need a role

to write and teach curriculum. Bob and Jane can both satisfy the role, as Bob can teach and Jane can write, or both Bob and Jane can teach and write in the role of trainer.

- **Future historical information** By keeping the roles generic, you can reuse the roles and their work assignments from project to project. If you use Fred the Developer instead of just the developer role, this will create complications when you adapt an older project plan to a new project plan.

- **Options** Chances are people may play more than one role in your project. You may have a person who can do the assignments of the quality assurance analyst, the business analyst, and the information architect all on one project team.

In addition to these reasons, your organization may have predefined roles and their expectations, definitions, and metrics for performance that you and the project manager have to manage and analyze by. It's important for the business analyst and project manager to work together to identify the required roles as early in the project as possible so functional management, other project managers, and the organization can plan accordingly. The availability of the roles and the people who play them will affect when the project can be completed.

Typical team roles you should know for your CBAP examination include

- **Application architect** This role defines the technical direction for the project's solution, creates the architectural approach, and serves as project expert for the project solution's structure.

- **Business analyst** This role elicits, documents, and reviews the requirements for projects. This role is the key facilitator for requirements gathering, planning, and communicating.

- **Database analyst** This role, sometimes called the DBA, designs, creates, and maintains databases for the project.

- **Developer** This role is the technical resource within the project and may serve as a designer, tester, coder, application developer, or other nomenclature. Developers help plan the operational transfer of the deliverable to the user.

- **End user** This role is the recipient and user of the project's deliverables.

- **Executive sponsor** This role is responsible for the project's funding, go/no-go decisions, and resource support, and approves schedules, budgets, and chief decisions. This role may also be known as the solution owner, project sponsor, or champion.

- **Information architect** This role, sometimes called the data modeler, helps assess the data requirements of a project, identifies data assets, and helps the project team complete data modeling requirements.

- **Infrastructure analyst** This role designs the hardware, software, and technical infrastructure required for the project application development, operations requirements, and ongoing solution.

- **Project manager**   This role manages the project management life cycle of a project to ensure that the project team is completing the project work with quality and according to the project objectives and requirements. This role works with the business analyst, executive sponsor, and key stakeholders to gain approval on project deliverables.

- **Quality assurance analyst**   This role maps the quality assurance requirements of the organization and the stakeholders to the project, ensures that the project deliverables meet the quality requirements, and works with the project manager and the project team on quality standards compliance.

- **Solution owner**   This role approves the project scope statement, phase gate reviews, solution validations, scope changes, and project success criteria. This role may often be the same as the executive sponsor, though sometimes the project customer may serve in this role.

- **Stakeholders**   This role is fulfilled by anyone who is affected by the outcome of the project deliverables. Stakeholders who make decisions on the project, influence the project requirements, or contribute to the project are sometimes called key stakeholders.

- **Subject matter expert**   This role is sometimes called the SME and consults the business analyst, project manager, and project team on decisions, directions, and other information needed to elicit requirements and build the project deliverables. This role can be someone on the project team, someone within the organization who provides expert judgment, or a hired consultant to contribute to the project work.

- **Trainer**   This role works with the project team to understand the deliverables and then teaches the users of the deliverables how to utilize the project's product. This person may teach, coach, write, and do instructional design to educate the users of the project's deliverable.

All of these team roles should be documented as part of the project management human resource plan. Depending on the organization, culture, and type of project being created, additional roles may need to be identified. The business analyst and the project manager will need to work together to ensure that all of the roles are identified and documented as early as possible in the project creation.

Defining the Role Responsibilities

While roles generally define who does what on the project, a responsibility specifies the amount of control over the decision, direction, quality, and accountability of the facets of the project. You could say that a role is what you do, while a responsibility is what you're accountable for. Roles and responsibilities go together, and the complete package of a role and responsibility must be decided before the project work gets too far along. You might know responsibilities as decisions, tasks, work packages, assignments, or some other terminology in your organization. For your CBAP exam a *responsibility* is the ownership of a specific activity to a specific project requirement—it is the action of completing the project work.

When a project manager, business analyst, and the project team define all of the tasks to be completed within a project, the roles, not the people's names, are assigned to the responsibilities. For example, you may have a project where the role of application developer has thousands of tasks to complete. This one role can be played by seven different people on your project team. The seven people playing the one role can collectively knock out the thousands of responsibilities that they are capable of and competent to do. It's the granular work of the project manager to determine which person is most suited to play the role based on any given responsibility.

While you should know the typical roles of a project team, you should also know some typical responsibilities linked to the roles:

- **Applications architect**   Is responsible for choosing and designing the architectural approach, high-level application design, and requirements review.

- **Business analyst**   Is responsible for the identification, documentation, and management of requirements. The business analyst will also manage requirements modifications and the change approval process.

- **Database analyst**   The DBA is responsible for the creation, management, configuration, design, and performance of any databases interacting with the project work, deliverables, or requirements.

- **Developer**   Participates in the requirements review, sign-off, and project deliverables approval and validation processes.

- **End user**   Participates during the requirements gathering process and may participate in user acceptability testing and pilot groups.

- **Executive sponsor**   Approves the requirements and the management processes.

- **Information architect**   Identifies data requirements and is involved in the requirements review, approval, and modification processes.

- **Infrastructure analyst**   Is responsible for designing the hardware, software, and technical structure to conform to the project requirements.

- **Project manager**   Is responsible for managing the project management life cycle, the project team's work, facilitating deliverable approval processes, and for the project success or failure.

- **Quality assurance analyst**   Participates in requirement review and validation, and ensures that project deliverables adhere to quality standards and scope fulfillment.

- **Solution owner**   Provides requirements and information, and approves functional requirements.

- **Subject matter experts**   Are responsible for contributing information, advice, and contributing to requirements gathering activities.

- **Trainer**   Develops training materials, facilitates knowledge transfer, and may participate in the development and approval of requirements.

The combination of a role and a responsibility ensures that all of the project tasks have been assigned and are accounted for. One of the most popular of several approaches to mapping roles and responsibilities is the RACI structure, as seen in Figure 2-3. The RACI structure is a form of a Responsibility Assignment Matrix (RAM). A RAM is simply a table that defines who does what. It uses a legend to show what type of participation a role has with a given activity. The RAM is great for mapping all levels of assignments as part of project planning.

Now back to the RACI, a form of RAM. The RACI chart use the following legend for each identified project task and for each identified role in the project:

- **Responsible** This role does the work and is responsible for its completion, quality, and adherence to defined requirements.
- **Accountable** This role is the decision maker regarding the responsibility.
- **Consult** This role must be consulted before the work begins and serves as a point of information for the activity's resources.
- **Inform** This role needs to be kept informed on the activity's completion.

It is possible for more than one role to serve in more than one category. For example, the application developer could have both the accountable and consult attributes on a particular activity. The accountable responsibility, however, should only be assigned to one role per activity. This is because you don't want multiple roles making decisions on each project assignment.

R - Responsible A - Accountable C - Consult I - Inform	Applications architect	Business analyst	Database analyst	Developer	End user	Executive sponsor	Information architect	Project manager
Requirement 1	R						A	
Requirement 2		I	A		R	I		I
Requirement 3	I	R		A			R	
Requirement 4	A			R	C			
Requirement 5		I	R		A	R		
Requirement 6		A		C			I	R
Requirement 7	C		C		R	A	C	

Figure 2-3   RACI charts map roles to responsibilities.

Another stakeholder chart is the Onion diagram. The closer a stakeholder is plotted to the project solution, the more involved the stakeholder is in the project solution, while the farther away the stakeholder is plotted, the less input and influence the stakeholder has over the project solution. A similar chart, though not as pretty, is a simple Stakeholder Matrix. This chart plots out the influence and impact of the stakeholders on the project solution.

Create a Requirements Communication Plan

When you consider the diverse backgrounds of people who are affected by any one project, it's easy to see why the business analyst must be comfortable talking and listening to stakeholders. Think of an IT project, for example, to change an organization's word-processing application. How the word-processing application is used throughout an organization is something you'd be interested in. You'd need to talk with all the different people who use that application and with the IT gurus to confirm that all parties understand how the application is used. A lack of understanding between the IT folks and the rest of the organization will result in frustration, loss of time, and possible loss of income for the organization. Your job, as the business analyst, is to be the hub of communications when it comes to project requirements.

Business analysts need a Requirements Communication Plan to document their intent and communication requirements for the business analysis activities. It's a plan to ensure that all of the proper communication channels are identified, documented, and communicated throughout the pre-project activities. It also serves somewhat as a schedule of communication so that the business analyst can work toward building the requirements, following-through with questions, and ensuring that the stakeholders receive all the information from the business analyst as well as contribute information to the business analyst.

Identifying the Communication Requirements

The Requirements Communication Plan also allows the business analyst to estimate what the communication needs are. Pausing and planning how much communication is needed for the analysis activities will help the business analyst to work smarter and more efficiently. In other words, if the business analyst knows what communications are required of her, she'll be able to provide more accurate communications among the stakeholders.

The business analyst will need to reference the identification of all stakeholders who need to participate in the communication. This means the business analyst will need to answer three questions as part of the Requirements Communication Plan creation:

- Who needs what information?
- When is the information needed?
- In what modality is the information required?

These three questions can help the business analyst identify the stakeholder demands and identify the information to be communicated, and it'll help the business analyst identify the most appropriate means of delivering the communication. The business analyst should also consider

- Each stakeholder's time availability to contribute to the project
- Each stakeholder's physical location and the communication challenges, time zone differences, language differences, and cultural differences such as holidays and customs
- What authority level the stakeholder has to contribute to the requirements
- The information that will be elicited during requirements gathering activities
- The best communication approach to elicit requirements
- The appropriate forms, templates, and other modalities to communicate identified requirements, conclusions, and requirements packages

While every project is different, a business analyst has little reason not to use a standardized template for the Requirements Communication Plan. The template could be standardized for all business analysts within an organization and then adapted to the current project. The danger, however, in using a standardized Requirements Communication Plan template is that the business analyst may assume the plan is complete rather than thinking and acting on the current project requirements. In other words, the business analyst might rush and not adapt the current plan to the current need.

Analyzing Communication Needs

Early in the business analysis duties, you'll need to identify all of the project stakeholders. This is part of the business analysis domain "Requirements Planning and Management." A fundamental part of communication is linked to the identification of all the stakeholders for a project. Should a stakeholder be missed in the initial stakeholder identification, additional work, additional time, and additional communications will be necessary.

The business analyst or, when working with other business analysts, the business analysis team must strive to ensure that all of the stakeholders have been identified so that the Requirements Communication Plan is accurate and inclusive. You can work with the project manager, the project sponsor, the solution owner, and other stakeholders to ensure that all of the stakeholders have been identified. Just ask these stakeholders who else should be included in the project communication.

The BABOK tells us directly that the business analyst is the chief communicator for everything about requirements. As the chief communicator, you've loads of responsibility riding on your shoulders to be certain that all stakeholders are identified and communicated with. At times the group of stakeholders may be massive. Consider an organizationwide switch from one software package to another. All of the end users are stakeholders, and all of their opinions are valid, but it doesn't mean that you'll need to speak with each individual in the group. When you're dealing with large groups of stakeholders, a representative should be appointed from the group, and you'll communicate directly with that individual.

You can use a Communications Requirements Matrix to help you identify the communication interaction of the stakeholders. This matrix can be adapted for whatever needs you have, but Figure 2-4 is a basic matrix you can use for your plan. The Xs in the figure represent which two corresponding stakeholders need to communicate with one another. Note that the Communications Requirements Matrix identifies who contributes to whom in this example—including the business analyst.

	Steve	Mark	Sally	Jane	Ben	Susan
Steve		X		X		X
Mark	X		X		X	
Sally		X		X		X
Jane	X	X				
Ben		X				X
Susan	X		X		X	

Figure 2-4   The Communications Requirements Matrix helps facilitate communication.

Defining the Requirements Risk Management

Risks are not a bad thing—but their impact can be painful. You probably take risks if you invest in the stock market, play poker, or drive a car. Some risks are worth accepting, and other risks you try to avoid. Your comfort level with accepting, avoiding, or mitigating risk events is called the *utility function*. Organizations have a utility function, too—and they may quantify their willingness to accept risks in a risk policy, risk analysis process, or even a risk department.

When it comes to business analysis, you'll need a broad understanding of risk events and an approach to capture, measure, and monitor risk. The business analyst focuses on risks in the requirements gathering process, while the project manager focuses on risks throughout the project. Some overlap occurs between the work you'll do as a business analyst and the project manager's activities. Much of this overlap will be based on your organization's policies and the scope of the project.

For your CBAP exam you'll also want to take note of the difference between a risk and an issue. A *risk* is an uncertain event that could have a positive or negative effect on the project. While most of your focus is on negative risk events, there are positive risk events: you might get a discount on some software, you may not have travel expenses, and a byproduct of the development could bring a profit to the organization. An *issue* is a negative risk that has come to fruition. Issues are conditions that you'll have to react to in order to offset the negative impact of the negative risk.

Identifying the Risks Within the Requirements

When it comes to risk management, you have to start with the requirements and all the possible risks that could be lurking within the requirements. You and your business analysis team will examine each project requirement to determine what risks may be lurking in the requirements, in the project, and among the stakeholders. This activity is not necessarily concerned with creating risk responses, though you may have some obvious responses to identified risks. The primary objective of this task is to list the requirements risks. Among multiple approaches to risk identification, the most common approaches are

- **Documentation reviews**   The business analysis team thoroughly review all the documentation of the requirements, desired future state, correspondence, and project objectives.
- **Brainstorming**   The business analysis team analyze each requirement and try to create a comprehensive list of all the possible risk events associated with the requirements.

- **Interviewing**   Just as the business analysis team used interviewing to gather the requirements, they may also use interviewing to identify risks within the requirements. The downside of this approach is the time-intensive nature of interviews with project stakeholders.

- **Root cause analysis**   Sometimes in risk identification the effect of a risk is more obvious than the actual causal factor of the risk event. Root cause analysis can uncover multiple risks that may contribute to the severity of a risk event.

- **SWOT analysis**   The business analysis team can identify the *strengths, weaknesses, opportunities,* and *threats* (SWOT) of each requirement to determine if there are risks to be documented.

- **Assumption analysis**   Testing the accuracy of assumptions made in the project. If an assumption proves to be false, it may generate one or more risks.

While these are the most common approaches to risk identification, some risk approaches may be unique to the type of project or work that's about to start. The goal of risk identification is not to judge any of the identified risks, but instead to capture as many of the potential risk events as possible. From the list of identified risks the business analyst can determine any categories of risks, trends, or risks that are linked together.

Some risks may also be universal to the requirements. These risks events should be documented even if the business analyst and the business analysis team know of their presence. Documenting the universal risks ensures that the risks are acknowledged, and the project manager and business sponsor can see the documentation. Examples of requirementswide risks include

- Inadequate stakeholder involvement with requirements gathering, identification, and analysis

- Vague requirements

- Conflicting requirements

- Lack of requirements management such as planning, change control, and governance

- Scope creep

All of the identified risks are documented in a risk register. The term *risk register* is traditionally used in project management, but it is acceptable for the business analyst to create the risk register and then to pass the identified risks on to the project manager. The project manager is responsible for end-to-end risk management, so it's typical for the business analyst to identify requirements risks and the project manager to manage the project risks.

Managing the Requirements Risk

Once the business analyst has identified the requirements risk, a structured approach to managing the risks is needed. The business analyst along with the key stakeholders, business analysis team, and the project management team will work together to manage the requirements risks prior to the project manager's risk management processes. A *structured* approach means regular reviews of the identified risks, requirements, and conditions within the organization. The business analyst should schedule weekly or biweekly risk reviews.

Each identified requirements risk should have some type of risk response. The status of the risk may affect what the risk response is, the escalation of the risk response, and conditions with the requirements gathering process. The risk responses can shift based on priorities, external events, and stakeholder concerns. A constant monitoring of the risk events is required so the business analyst and team can have an accurate assessment of the identified risks and their status.

The business analysis team should be involved with the requirements risk planning processes, and many of the business analysis team members may be assigned to monitor specific risk events. When a person is assigned to monitor a specific risk, they are sometimes referred to as the *risk owner*. The risk owner should be empowered to monitor the event and respond to the event if conditions change. Keep in mind, however, that risk management policies vary among organizations, so the risk owner in the requirements gathering activities may have little to no ability to respond to risk events.

NOTE   Let me stress the idea of a structured risk review: if the business analyst doesn't review the risk and requirements regularly, then risk management shifts from planning to firefighting. A methodical approach to requirements risk identification and control keeps risks in check and the business analyst in charge.

Once the risks have been identified, it's time for some simple qualitative analysis. Qualitative analysis is quick, shallow, and often based on experience. It's not a bad approach, but it can sometimes overlook the deeper testing that quantitative analysis provides. It's not a huge problem most of the time to do only qualitative analysis of requirements, because the project manager and team will do, and should do, a more in-depth analysis of each identified risk. For each risk the business analysis team should determine all of the following:

- **Likelihood**   The business analysis team should determine the probability of the risk event coming to fruition. The team should document the probability of the event by using a simple scale such as very low to very high, or a cardinal scale of 1 to 10. Your organization may use RAG Rating (Red, Amber, Green) for risk severity and likelihood.

- **Impact**   Just as the team measure the likelihood, they should also estimate the impact of the risk event with a similar scale. Things that should be estimated for each identified risk and its potential impact are

  - **Cost**   How much will the risk cost?

  - **Schedule**   What delays will the risk introduce?

  - **Scope**   What other parts of the project scope will be affected by the risk?

  - **Quality**   How will the risk affect the quality of the project, the scope, or other deliverables?

  - **Benefits**   What project benefits will be diminished if the risk event happens?

- **Intervention difficulty**   The business analysis team should determine how difficult it may be to act on the risk event to prevent the risk from occurring. This intervention measurement also determines how difficult it may be to respond to the risk event should it occur.

- **Precision of risk assessment**   This attribute rates the degree of confidence the business analyst has in the accuracy of the risk assessment. The more information that's known about the risk, the higher the degree of precision; if the requirement risk has never been identified or managed before, then there should be a corresponding low level of precision, because the confidence in the risk characteristics is unproven.

- **Mitigation strategy**   There are three initial approaches to dealing with identified risks:

  - **Avoid**   Avoid the risk by changing processes and activities to circumvent the risk event.

  - **Mitigate**   To *mitigate* a risk event is to spend more money, add time, or take extra steps in the processes to reduce the probability and/or impact of the risk event should it happen. Mitigation is a risk response.

  - **Assume**   To assume the risk is to accept the risk. This business analysis risk response is an acceptance of the risk event and is used when the identified risk event is particularly low in probability and impact. It could also be used when the identified risk is outside of anyone's control, such as the weather, the economy, or the pending laws and regulations.

- **Action plan**   This business analysis plan defines what the risk responses are and which members of the business analysis team will own which risks.

- **Contingency plan**   Should a risk event become an issue, there should be a contingency action, sometimes called a corrective action, to respond to the issue. The contingency plan also defines what the risk triggers are. A *risk trigger* is a warning sign or condition that the risk event is becoming an issue.

All of the results of risk identification and risk planning are documented and discussed with key stakeholders. It's not unusual to create a risk probability-impact matrix

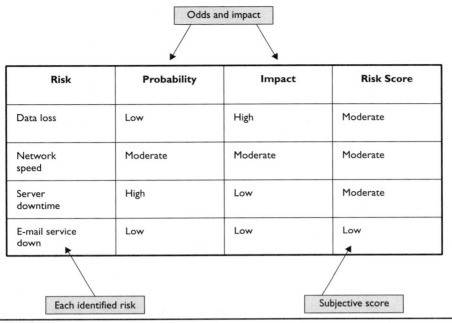

Risk	Probability	Impact	Risk Score
Data loss	Low	High	Moderate
Network speed	Moderate	Moderate	Moderate
Server downtime	High	Low	Moderate
E-mail service down	Low	Low	Low

Figure 2-5 A risk probability-impact matrix can help generate a risk score.

as seen in Figure 2-5 to visualize the risk events with the largest probability and impact on the project. Each risk event should be documented as to its characteristics and anticipated effect on the business analysis processes and overall benefits of the project.

Monitoring and Controlling the Risk Events

Monitoring risks is really confirming that the status of the risks has not changed. By monitoring risks on a regular schedule, the business analyst confirms that the status, impact, and probability of the risk events have not changed. In addition, regular monitoring allows the business analysis team to respond to the risk status if it does change. Regular monitoring means:

- Weekly confirmation of risk status
- Assessment of risk if it becomes an issue
- Comparison of initial and observed assessment of the risk on the requirements process
- Determination of risk response should the risk materialize

When the business analyst controls the risk event, he's taking action to maintain the risk event. Should the risk event come to fruition, he's to describe the impact of the risk event on the requirements, project, scope, and all other facets of the project and requirements that the risk event impacts.

Controlling the risk event also means the business analyst will execute the mitigation strategy according to plan. This is the avoidance, mitigation, and assumption of the risk event. The outcome of the mitigation plan should be documented. In the instances when the risk becomes an issue, then the contingency plan is enacted, and its results are documented.

Finally, the business analyst team should create lessons learned documentation. The lessons learned documentation is a record of what was experienced, what new knowledge came from the experience, and what the business analyst might have done differently. Lessons learned documentation becomes part of the organizational process assets and can help future business analysis teams avoid mistakes.

Seven Risk Responses

For your CBAP exam you'll need to know the three risk responses I've covered in this chapter: avoid, mitigate, and assume. That's nice, but technically you should know and use seven risk responses in your professional status as a business analyst. Here goes:

- **Avoidance** You know this one already. You're simply avoiding the risk. This can be accomplished many different ways and generally happens early in the project, when any change will result in fewer consequences than changes later in the project plan.

- **Transference** This is the transfer of the risk (and the ownership of the risk) to a third party. The risk doesn't go away; it just becomes someone else's problem. There's usually a fee for transference, and great examples include insurance, warranties, guarantees, and fixed-priced contracts with vendors.

- **Mitigation** You've seen this one already, too. Recall that this response is an effort to reduce the probability and/or impact of an identified risk in the project. Mitigation is done—based on the logic—before the risk happens. The cost and time to reduce or eliminate the risks is more cost-effective than repairing the damage caused by the risk. The risk event may still happen, but hopefully the cost and impact of the risk will both be very low.

- **Exploiting** Not all risks are bad; some risks you actually want to happen. When you want to take advantage of a positive risk, you exploit the risk. Some examples of positive risk exploitation: adding resources to finish faster than originally planned, increasing quality to recognize sales and customer satisfaction, and utilizing a better way of completing the project work.

- **Sharing**   Sharing is caring. The idea of sharing a positive risk really means sharing a mutually beneficial opportunity between two organizations or projects, or creating a risk-sharing partnership. When a project team can share the positive risk, ownership of the risk is given to the organization that can best capture the benefits from the identified risk.

- **Enhancing**   This risk response seeks to modify the size of the identified opportunity. The goal is to strengthen the cause of the opportunity to ensure that the risk event does happen. Enhancing a project risk looks for solutions, triggers, or other drivers to ensure that the risk does come to fruition so the rewards of the risk can be realized by the performing organization.

- **Acceptance**   You know this risk response. Acceptance is the process of simply accepting the risks because no other action is feasible, or because the risks are deemed to be of small probability, impact, or both, and a formal response is not warranted. You can accept both positive and negative risks.

There you go. Feel free to drop these risk management terms at parties, social mixers, and family reunions, but I'd save them for risk management meetings if I were you.

Choosing the Business Analysis Activities

As a business analyst, you know that you probably don't have the time or the need to do every possible business analysis activity for requirements. Management, customers, the project manager, and the project team are eager for you to complete the requirements gathering so that the project deliverables and benefits can be realized sooner rather than later. The longer you take to complete the requirements activities, the longer it'll be before the project team can deliver the benefits to the customers and the organization.

While it's true that the project scoping can't begin until you've gathered the requirements, it's also true that a rushed requirements process will likely result in project execution errors. It's important for the organization to give the business analyst the proper amount of time to do just the right amount of business analysis. A "proper amount of time" means that the business analyst can complete all of the appropriate business analysis activities so the project will go more smoothly, with less risk and less frustration than if the requirements processes were rushed by management, the project manager, and the customer.

"Select the requirements activities" means that the business analyst will need to determine what requirements activities are the most appropriate. The business analysis team will need time and resources to complete the five primary business analysis activities (the five beyond this chapter on business analysis planning and monitoring, of course):

- **Requirements elicitation**   This task determines which stakeholders should be identified as contributors to the requirements gathering process. Based on the stakeholder, type of project, and conditions within the organization, the business analyst will decide which elicitation activities are most appropriate. Once this activity is completed, then the business analyst should have the complete business and user requirements defined.

- **Requirements management and communication**   Communication is a key activity for business analysis. This activity defines what the types of communication, the best practices for communication, and the organizational requirements for communication may be. Based on the size of the project, organizational procedures, and requests from stakeholders, the business analyst will document and adapt the communication to what's best for the project.

- **Enterprise analysis**   The business analyst works with the organizational leaders, key stakeholders, and project managers to define opportunities, create the business analysis framework, and help management determine which projects are the best projects to invest funds into. Enterprise analysis follows the executive team's vision for the organization and supports the strategies and tactics of upper management.

- **Requirements analysis**   The business analysis activity defines the modeling and business analysis documentation technique the organization requires. Policies within the organization, business analyst preferences, or industry standards may influence the documentation and modeling approaches the business analyst uses.

- **Solution assessment and validation**   Once all parties agree on the requirements, then the solution for the requirements can be presented. This activity assesses the proposed solution(s) and validates that the solution can, or has, met the requirements of the stakeholders.

These five domains describe the complete arc of business analysis activities. The business analyst will need to determine, based on conditions and circumstances, which activities are the most appropriate and to what depth the activity should be executed. This process requires that the business analyst make a determination and documentation of the business analysis activities that need to be completed. Specifically, the business analyst documents what activities, resources, and documents she'll be creating, completing, and requiring to complete the business analysis work.

Estimate Requirements Activities

As a business analyst, you'll need to complete time, cost, and scope estimating activities. These are estimates for both the business analysis activities and the project activities. Here's one of those gray areas where the BABOK edges into project management. Your organization may have defined what estimates the business analyst is responsible for and what estimates the project manager is responsible for—that's fine. For your CBAP exam, however, you should be familiar with the approaches to estimating and assume that the business analyst will be involved in creating estimates for the project and the business analysis activities.

 For a more detailed explanation, watch the Funding the Project video now.

In all fairness, these estimates are to be high-level estimates, as the project manager and the project management team will most likely take the business analyst's estimates and refine them through their own estimating techniques. Just keep in mind for the exam that you'll estimate three things:

- **Scope**   The work that the business analysis team and the project team must do to complete the requirements of the customers and stakeholders
- **Schedule**   How long the estimated work will take to complete
- **Resources**   The funds the project and business analysis activities will require to complete the scope based on the schedule

If these three things remind you of the Triple Constraints of Project Management, you're right on track. As a refresher, the Triple Constraints of Project Management, sometimes called the Iron Triangle, shown in Figure 2-6, requires balance among time, cost, and scope. If any one area of the Iron Triangle is out of balance, then the other two areas are going to suffer as well. Your estimates will aim to keep these three things in balance with one another.

Figure 2-6
The Iron Triangle must be balanced for project success.

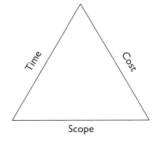

You will work with the project manager, the project management team, your fellow business analysts assigned to the requirements processes with you, subject matter experts, customers, and any key stakeholders to create a basis for your estimates. Your best input to the estimating processes is historical information. If your organization has done a similar project, there's no real need to create an estimate from scratch, as you have proven information to guide your estimating efforts.

Estimate Project Work for Milestones

Milestones are signs of progress within the project. You'll see milestones at the end of phases or when key deliverables are met. For example, the detailed design document is approved, the database is functional, or the foundation for a new construction is finished. Each of these deliverables allows the next phase of the project to begin. Milestones are timeless events that show significant advancement in the project.

Milestones are also signals that the project should be measured for quality, time, cost, and future expectations. Funding for the project is often tied to milestone delivery, as shown in Figure 2-7. As a milestone is reached, the project is funded for enough capital to reach the next milestone. This approach, called *step funding*, is excellent for cash flow forecasting, schedule scope validation, and project reviews, and keeps risk of lost capital segmented to each phase of the project.

Milestones can also be tied to calendar dates. This approach is good in planning to help determine what activities should be done by the determined date. The business analyst, the project manager, and management can make predetermined decisions about the project's future if certain things are not true by a deadline. For example, if the project fails to have certain activities completed by January 15, then certain deliverables in the scope will be cut, and the project's focus will be only on core deliverables moving forward.

Figure 2-7
Step funding
provides project
finances at milestone
completion.

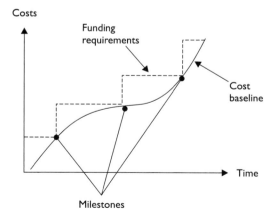

Whatever approach an organization takes to establishing milestones, they should document the milestone event, name it, and add it to the project plan. The ramifications of hitting or missing a milestone should be documented so everyone is aware of what's expected. The last thing a project manager wants is a delay in the project because someone's delaying a decision, financing, or approval for the next phase of a project at a milestone completion.

 NOTE It's not unusual for the project manager and the project team to receive bonuses and rewards based on milestone completion. The business analysts, management, and stakeholders should be ready to do their milestone-related activities so as not to delay the next phase of the project, which could hinder the project manager and team from reaching their rewards for completing the project on time.

You or the project manager should create a milestone chart as in Figure 2-8. This chart shows when the milestones were scheduled and when they were actually met. The difference between what was planned (the estimate) and what was actually accomplished shows the variance for the project. This variance can be measured in time and dollars. The project manager should explain any variances in a *variance report,* which is sometimes called an exceptions report.

Milestone	July	Aug	Sep	Oct	Nov	Dec
M1	△▼					
M2		△	▼			
M3			△			
M4					△ ▼	
M5						△

△ Planned
▼ Actual

Figure 2-8   Milestone charts show targeted and actual milestone completion.

Once the project scope has been clearly defined, the Work Breakdown Structure (WBS) should be created by the project manager. The WBS is a visual decomposition of the project scope. The project scope is subdivided over and over until the smallest unit of work, called a work package, is revealed. Work packages are project deliverables that correlate to the project activities.

The business analyst may create a high-level WBS, but a more detailed WBS is needed to see the smallest elements in the project deliverables. I know you're also recalling that the items in the WBS are things, not activities. The smallest things, the individual project deliverables, are called the *work packages,* and they map to *units of work.*

The units of work can then be mapped to the activities. Activities are broken down again into subactivities, and finally into individual tasks. According to the BABOK, tasks should be completed within a one- to two-week time frame. Each task will have one of three attributes:

- **Dependent task**   This task cannot start until other tasks are completed; this is sometimes called a successor task.

- **Predecessor task**   Other tasks cannot begin until this task is completed as it precedes them in the order of activities.

- **Independent task**   This task does not rely on other activities, and no other activities rely on this task completing.

The project manager and the project team members should contribute to this business analysis task, as they can offer advice and direction on the most likely order of events. The order of all of the tasks within the project will show the order of activities that will lead to the project milestones. When a milestone is reached, it's assumed, and validated, that all of the tasks to the milestone have been completed. In other words, you can't reach a milestone until all of the preceding tasks have been completed.

The next business analysis step is to estimate the effort per unit of work. This is where the roles and responsibilities matrix you created during business analysis planning can be handy. You can determine which role has what responsibility and how long the task will take to complete. You'll need several pieces of information to do duration estimating:

- Roles and responsibilities matrix
- Assessment of project team members and competencies
- Historical information from similar work within the organization
- Grouping of similar tasks to assign to individuals
- Geographical grouping of tasks

These items can help you determine the effort per activity to create a duration estimate. Once you've identified the relationship between activities and have created a time estimate for each activity, you'll schedule the activity on the calendar. Estimates initially assume that each activity will have at least one qualified resource per activity and that the resource will work on just the one activity until the task is completed. The reality, however, is that resources will likely have their time divided with demands in operations and other projects, and will be teaming with other resources to complete activities.

The initial estimate is loose, unreliable, and will require a more in-depth analysis to determine the number of actual days to complete a task. While a task may be scheduled for six days of effort, or 48 hours, it may take the resource eight calendar days to complete the 48 hours of effort. This is because of other obligations the resource may have within the project or within their day-to-day responsibilities.

Another fallacy business analysts sometimes believe is that the addition of labor decreases the amount of time to complete an activity. Not all activities are effort driven, where additional effort may reduce the amount of time for the task to complete. Consider the installation of software; regardless of how many people are scheduled for the task, the computer can only operate so fast. Activities whose durations cannot be reduced by the addition of labor are known as *fixed-duration* activities.

The final rule of duration estimating is to be aware of Parkinson's Law. Parkinson's Law states that work expands to fill the amount of time allotted to it. Say, for example, a team member reports to you that it'll likely take him 60 hours of effort to complete a task. If he's bloated his estimate to account for errors, any variance, or the fudge factor from a likely 40 hours of effort to the reported 60, it'll magically take 60 hours to complete the work. This is for several reasons:

- The team member may indeed make mistakes, have issues, or take his time to stretch the activity to the estimated 60 hours.

- If the team member completes the task at 40 hours, he's likely to not report the task as being done early because he's already committed to 60 hours to you.

- The team member may not start the activity until hour 20 and hope nothing goes wrong with the work for the next 40 hours knowing that he's committed to finishing the work by hour 60.

Parkinson's Law gives rise to constant battle in all projects. The best combatant to Parkinson's Law is an effort to record actual time to complete the project work. This is tricky, too, because the project manager or business analyst would need to closely monitor the project work and could impair the project team's ability to work and think. If the project manager can stress importance in estimating and in reporting completion of the work, and the project team buys into the rewards and recognition system, importance of the reporting, or demand for accurate timekeeping, you can build a database of actual durations.

The actual durations from your current project can serve as future historical information on other projects. Historical information is ideal for duration estimating, because it is proven information from past work. It's also ideal, because the business analyst and the project manager can review past projects to find variances in similar tasks and make adjustments in the current project to avoid repeating past mistakes.

The final approach the business analyst can take in activity duration estimates is to interview the project team members and subject matter experts. The interview process can help the business analyst understand the nature of the work, gauge estimates based on the interview, and create duration estimates from the team members who will be doing the assignments or who have completed similar assignments in the past. The persistent problem with interviewing, however, is that it is time intensive.

Identifying Project Assumptions and Risks

When you create time and cost estimates, you often have to rely on assumptions to predict how much the work will cost and how long the activities will take. If you want to be technical, and I'm sure you do, estimates are assumptions—you're assuming what the estimate is, what cost is, and how long it'll take to complete the work. Consider a project that's never worked with a particular software, type of material, or a new vendor. Almost all projects that have some untried element fall prey to the First-Time First-Use Penalty. The First-Time First-Use Penalty states that the first time you try something new, you can't know how long it'll take to complete and what the financial impact of the project may be.

It's like the first person to ever crack open an oyster and slurp it down—he may have suspected they'd taste great, but he didn't really know until he tried. It's the First-Time First-Use Penalty that makes lessons learned documentation and accurate recordkeeping so important for the project. By documenting the actual experiences with the new materials, software, vendors, or whatever it may be, the project manager and the business analyst can create historical information for future estimates.

The business analyst, project sponsor, project manager, and the key stakeholders should all review and sign off on the project assumptions early in the project. By gaining consensus on all the project assumptions, the business analyst communicates the assumptions and the impact should the assumptions prove false. Management may resist the acceptance of assumptions and want more assumption-validity testing before the project moves too far along.

Assumptions, should they prove false, will become risks for the project. Risks should be documented and measured for their probability and impact. The risks you, the business analyst, are most interested in are the risks directly related to the requirements gathering and management. The project manager will take your identified risks and fold them into his risk management plan. Risks on time and costs may be identified by you and your team, but these generally fall into project management risks.

As the project manager completes the sequencing of project activities in project planning, she may have an opportunity to examine the flow of work to determine where risks for scope, time, and costs can be mitigated. The flow of the project work is called a *project network diagram,* and Figure 2-9 is a small example of a project network diagram. Each activity must be completed before the project is complete, but the arrows show the order of activities.

If you were to add up the duration of all individual paths from the start of the project to its final activity, you'd discover the *critical path*—it's the path that has the longest duration. It's called the critical path, because if any of the activities on the path is delayed,

Figure 2-9
Project network
diagrams show
the sequence of
activities.

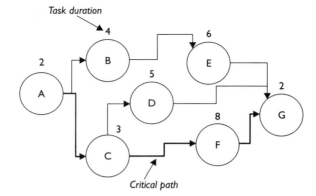

Task duration

Critical path

then the project will likely miss its end date. It's a project management process to calculate the critical path, so you won't have to worry about that for your CBAP exam. You will, however, need to consider risks surrounding the critical path for your exam. Your goal is to address the relationship of activities in the project network diagram and on the critical path, and to make adjustments to alleviate risks. Consider all of the following:

- Some tasks may happen in tandem with other tasks to reduce overall project duration.

- Lead time allows activities to overlap, while lag time adds "waiting time" between activities. Project usage of lead and lag can benefit the project schedule.

- Tasks that must start or finish on a particular date can create bottlenecks and risks within the project.

- Some activities are effort driven, and resources can be added to the task to decrease its duration; this approach is called *crashing*.

- High-risk activities may be better managed if they are removed from the critical path and positioned elsewhere in the project network diagram.

These recommendations are often the project manager's decisions, but the BABOK does reference these suggestions. The idea is that you'll make every effort possible to reduce the probability and impact of project risks to keep the project moving toward the completion with as few interruptions and delays as possible.

NOTE Many of the processes I'm discussing here can be managed and tracked through a project management information system such as Microsoft Project or Microsoft Excel. You could, I suppose, do this all with colored pencils and graph paper, but Microsoft Project can build the network diagram and show the critical path so quickly and easily that it's a worthy investment for any business analyst or project manager.

As the project moves into execution, the odds of scope change entering the project are quite high. Scope change should follow a predetermined, documented process to approve or decline each change. One aspect of the scope change process is the consideration of assumptions, risks, and the overall impact on the project. Should the change be approved, you'll likely need to update the requirements plan to reflect the added requirements, which will feed into project planning, scheduling, costing, and execution.

Communicating Requirements Activities Performance

Stakeholders want to know what's happening with their requirements, and they'll look to the business analyst, the project manager, the project sponsor, and anyone else they think can clue them into the requirements activities. One of the primary roles that you, the business analyst, and the project manager have is to communicate effectively, responsively, and persistently throughout the project. If stakeholders are asking questions about the project requirements, that's a good sign you'll need to communicate more—and it's a good sign the stakeholders are involved with the project.

Just as you don't want requirements that have subjective characteristics like "good," "fast," and "happy," your stakeholders won't want subjective reports on the project. They'll want quantifiable metrics that they can map to results. The metrics can be time, cost, performance, percentage of project completion, or any other agreed-upon and established project measurement. The goal of a metric is to show a quantifiable, relative measurement of performance.

The first set of metrics to be established is the project metrics. These are measurements of time, cost, scope, quality, and other project management attributes. Available systems can track and predict performance, though the leader is earned value management (EVM). EVM is a suite of formulas that can track project performance.

The second set of metrics is the product metrics. These measure how the product itself is performing, how it is measured, and any defects the product may have. The configuration management system is a tool that can help track the product characteristics as it focuses on quality, features, and functions.

No definite rule says which approach every project or organization should take on metrics and performance measurement. The arc of the rule is simply that metrics must be established, measured regularly, and communicated to the stakeholders. The project manager and the business analyst should work together on analyzing the project and product performance. The project manager needs the performance information to apply corrective actions, to communicate with project stakeholders, and to make decisions on the project. The business analyst needs the information for requirements tracking, stakeholder communication, and baseline measurement. A generally accepted approach to metrics measurement and communication is as follows:

- Establish a set of metrics before the project begins, and confirm that all stakeholders are in agreement with and understand all of the metrics.

- Define the collection, measurement, and communication process for the metrics before the project begins.

- As the project is in motion, the metrics should be collected on a regular schedule.

- The metrics are analyzed for project and product performance.

- The metrics are archived for future reference.

- The results of the measurement and analysis are communicated.

- Adjustments are made within the project to bring the conditions of the project, based on the results of metric measurement, back into alignment with project and product requirements.

This is an ongoing process throughout the project. As changes enter the project, the metrics should reflect the new additions, baselines, and activities so as not to skew the results of future measurements. The project manager and the business analyst must agree early in the project on the boundaries, responsibilities, and communications between one another so the project moves forward as planned.

Determining the Project and Product Metrics

The business analyst will need to establish project metrics as quickly as possible in the project so there's ample time for metric agreement among the project manager and the stakeholders. It's also important to establish metrics early so there's no delay in the project work and there's no gap between when the metrics are approved and project work that needs measurement.

Your organization may already have tools and techniques established for measuring project performance, such as EVM, Six Sigma, or industry standards specific to the project's field. Whatever the case, the approach must be documented and agreed upon early in the project. You can further customize the metrics to track cost or time per resource; for example, you could track how long a particular program worked on a certain project deliverable. This type of tracking could help for billing the project's requirements to several different stakeholders based on their requirements for the project.

It's not unusual for projects to use a chart of accounts to track costs by category, such as a resource, type of work, materials, or contractors. If this is the case, then the business analyst should include the chart of accounts to help track costs in applicable categories. When an organization is completing a similar project, the business analyst can use historical information from past projects to compare current performance to past performance.

Along with project metrics, the business analyst must also establish an agreeable set of product metrics. The product is the thing the project will create for the end users and customers. The business analyst must define and establish the product metrics along with the stakeholder. This means that each component of the project deliverable, the product, must have a measurable facet to it. This can, as you might guess, be darn tricky business.

The most common approach to creating product metrics is to determine why each component of the deliverable is being created. You can use the work breakdown structure, if it exists at this point of the project, to help you define the reason and benefit of each facet of the product. You must link project activities, particularly execution of the project plan, to the deliverable and justify the cost, time, and effort of the execution to the deliverable. You need to establish metrics that can link the project attributes to the product attributes.

When the business analyst determines the purpose for each project deliverable, she can then link it to the quality of the overall product. Quality, according to the PMBOK, is a conformance to requirements and a fitness for use. With this in mind, the metrics of each facet of the product must contribute to the overall quality of the project and be fit for use to satisfy the quality objectives. However, the "fit for use" must be defined as how fit, how fast, how many errors, and so on. The esoteric nature of quality demands that metrics be created to prove, or disprove, the presence of quality within the entities the project creates.

The product metrics should present themselves at a high level through the requirements elicitation process. The business analyst doesn't create these high-level metrics, but relies on the product team, product manager, and product customers to help define the requirements. The breakdown and analysis of the requirements will lead to metrics that can be used for measuring performance, trend analysis, and future historical information.

Chapter Summary

Requirements planning takes a big chunk of the business analyst's time, and it's a big chunk on your CBAP exam. You can expect many questions on requirements planning, so it's a wise choice to devote some time to the terms and principles in this chapter. You'll need to be familiar with requirements planning not only for your exam, but also in your day-to-day role as a business analyst.

One of the first steps of requirements planning is determining who will do what during the business analysis activities. You'll define your business analysis team roles and responsibilities so everyone is clear on who's doing what. A RACI chart is a quick and effective matrix to map out responsibilities among the team. Recall that a RACI chart uses the generic role rather than the specific team member names in most instances. In all instances, "RACI" stands for the legend of "responsible, accountable, consult, and inform" for the activities your roles will be doing.

On larger projects, you may be working with several business analysts, so you'll divide up the work to lighten the load. Your work division strategy can be based on skill sets, experience, geography, and even interest. Whatever approach you take, it's vital to document the responsibilities and for the business analysts to hold one another accountable for their duties.

One duty all business analysts on your team will need to be involved with is risk identification and planning. Recall that there are positive risks, which can help the organization and project, and negative risks, which aren't much fun. Your primary focus is on the negative risks that may cost the project in time or funds. Negative risks should be documented, and a risk response should be planned. When a risk comes to fruition, it becomes a risk issue, and a contingency plan is needed to address the realized risk event.

Another part of requirements planning is the estimation of time and cost for activities. Activities move the project toward its completion, and intermittent highlights throughout the project are known as milestones. Milestones are ideal times for requirements and quality reviews, and are sometimes called phase gates. Phase gates allow a project to move on to the next phase of execution based on what's been completed.

The collection of all the phases and milestones will eventually lead to the end of the project and, if all goes as planned, the requirements in physical form as deliverables. It's actually the summation of the project scope that will equate to the product scope. Before any execution starts, the business analyst and the project manager should be in agreement on what metrics will measure the project performance and the product performance. This lends itself to the quality of the project and, as far as requirements are concerned, the quality of the product.

Throughout the project, the project manager and the business analyst should make a constant effort to protect the project scope from unneeded change. All change requests should be documented and tracked. If a change is approved, then the requirements documents, project plan, and work activities are updated to reflect the change. Time and cost estimates may be adjusted as well, to reflect the new deliverables in the requirements scope.

I encourage you to spend a little extra time studying the BABOK and this chapter for your CBAP exam. Many of the processes and approaches in this chapter are broad and generic, as each company, even yours, may have a slightly different approach than what the IIBA deems generally accepted. Know the terms, theories, and approaches in this chapter, and you'll be well on your way to passing your CBAP exam.

Key Terms

Action plan   This business analysis plan defines what the risk responses are and which members of the business analysis team will own which risks.

Agile   An SDLC methodology that uses quick execution; daily meetings; isolated, protected developers; and adaptability to changes. The model uses small increments of planning and execution of the requirements. The benefits of this model are that the team can quickly create deliverables for the project stakeholders. The downside of this model is that an early mistake can cause huge ramifications and rework throughout the project.

Application architect   This role defines the technical direction for the project solution, creates the architectural approach, and serves as project expert for the project solution structure.

Assume   To assume the risk is to accept the risk. This business analysis risk response is an acceptance of the risk event and is used when the identified risk event is particularly low in probability and impact.

Avoid   Avoid the risk by changing processes and activities to circumvent the risk event.

Business analyst   This role is the key facilitator for requirements gathering, planning, and communicating.

Business Requirements Document   A snapshot of the requirements documentation that will serve as the requirements scope baseline (synonymous with Specification System Requirements Document).

Communications Requirements Matrix   This is a table to help the business analyst identify the communication interaction among the stakehoders.

Configuration management   Defines the features and functions of the approved change request and how it will be used as part of the deliverables.

Contingency plan   Should a risk event become an issue, a contingency action, sometimes called a corrective action, must be ready to respond to the issue. The contingency plan also defines what the risk triggers are.

Critical path   The longest path in a project network diagram to project completion. No delays are allowed on the critical path, or the project will be late for delivery.

Database analyst   This role designs, creates, and maintains databases for the project.

Dependent task   This task cannot start until other tasks are completed; this is sometimes called a successor task.

Developer   This role is the technical resource within the project and may serve as a designer, tester, coder, application developer, or other nomenclature. Developers help plan the operational transfer of the deliverable to the user.

End user   The recipient and user of the project's deliverables.

Enhancing   This risk response seeks to modify the size of the identified opportunity. The goal is to strengthen the cause of the opportunity to ensure that the positive risk event does happen. Enhancing a project risk looks for solutions, triggers, or other drivers to ensure that the positive risk will happen so the rewards of the risk can be realized by the performing organization.

Enterprise environmental factors   The policies, rules, and expectations of the organization that the business analysts are to follow; these are unique to each organization.

Executive sponsor   Responsible for the project's funding, go/no-go decisions, and resource support, and approves schedules, budgets, and chief decisions. This role may also be known as the solution owner, project sponsor, or champion.

Exploiting   Not all risks are bad; some risks you actually want to happen. When you want to take advantage of a positive risk, you exploit the risk. Some examples of positive risk exploitation are adding resources to finish faster than what was originally planned, increasing quality to recognize sales and customer satisfaction, and utilizing a better way of completing the project work.

First-Time First-Use Penalty   States that the first you try something new, you can't know how long it'll take to complete and what the financial impact on the project might be, because you've never attempted the activity before.

Functional requirements   Define the specific operations and characteristics of a system; definition of specific components and expectations for how those components are to operate.

Incremental   An SDLC method that uses a granular approach for quicker deliverables, easier risk management, and easier change control on the smaller segments of the project work. This approach can also use a series of waterfalls for phases and deliverables rather than one large waterfall model. This model is ideal for large projects.

Independent task   This task is not reliant on other activities, and no other activities rely on this task completing.

Information architect   This role, sometimes called the data modeler, helps assess the data requirements of a project, identifies data assets, and helps the project team complete data modeling requirements.

Infrastructure analyst   This role designs the hardware, software, and technical infrastructure required for the project application development, operation requirements, and ongoing solution.

Integrated change control   Project management process of examining all areas of the project and how a proposed change may affect time, cost, scope, quality, human resources, communication, risk, and any procurement issues.

Issue   A negative risk that has come to fruition. Issues are conditions that you'll have to react to in order to offset the negative impact of the negative risk.

Mitigate   To mitigate a risk event is to spend more money, add time, or take extra steps in the processes to reduce the probability and/or impact of the risk event should it happen. Mitigation is a risk response.

Nonfunctional requirements   Define how a system is supposed to operate. The qualities, characteristics, and constraints of any given system.

Organizational process assets   The collection of historical information, templates, processes, procedures, and other documents that support the business analysis duties.

Parkinson's Law   States that work expands to fill the amount of time allotted to it.

Predecessor task   Other tasks cannot begin until this task is completed, as it precedes them in the order of activities.

Project manager   Manages the project management life cycle of a project to ensure that the project team is completing the project work with quality and according to the project objectives and requirements. This role works with the business analyst, executive sponsor, and key stakeholders to gain approval on project deliverables.

Quality assurance analyst   This role maps the quality assurance requirements of the organization and the stakeholders to the project, ensures that the project deliverables meet the quality requirements, and works with the project manager and the project team on quality standards compliance.

RACI chart   A RAM that defines each participant role with the legend of *responsible, accountable, consult,* and *inform* for each activity.

Requirements analysis and documentation   The business analysis activity defines the modeling and business analysis documentation technique the organization requires. Policies within the organization, business analyst preferences, or industry standards may influence the documentation and modeling approaches the business analyst uses.

Requirements communication   Communication is a key activity for business analysis. This activity defines the types of communication, best practices for communication, and the organizational requirements for communication. Based on the size of the project, organizational procedures, and requests from stakeholders, the business analyst will document and adapt the communication to what's best for the project.

Requirements elicitation   This task determines which stakeholders should be identified as contributors to the requirements gathering process. Based on the stakeholder, type of project, and conditions within the organization, the business analyst will decide which elicitation activities are most appropriate.

Requirements traceability   A communication process that allows for each project requirement to be traced from its conception in the requirements documentation to its implementation in the project execution phase. Traceability ensures that each requirement is accounted for, and its implementation is tracked to execution, costs, and timing.

Requirements Traceability Matrix (RTM)   A table that tracks many actions to many requirements of the project. It maps the deliverables to the specific requirements and the verification that the deliverable does, or does not, satisfy the requirements.

Responsibility   Specifies the amount of control a role has over the decision, direction, quality, and accountability of the facets of the project; defines what the role is accountable for.

Responsibility Assignment Matrix (RAM)   A table that maps roles to responsibilities.

Risk   An uncertain event that could have a positive or negative effect on the project.

Risk trigger   A warning sign or condition that the risk event is becoming an issue.

Role   Defines the function the person performs on the business analysis team or the project team.

Sharing   Sharing a mutually beneficial opportunity between two organizations or projects, or creating a risk-sharing partnership. When a project team can share the positive risk, ownership of the risk is given to the organization that can best capture the benefits from the identified risk.

Solution assessment and validation   Once all parties agree on the requirements, then the solution for the requirements can be presented. This activity assesses the proposed solution(s) and validates that the solution can, or has, met the requirements of the stakeholders.

Solution owner   This role approves the project scope statement, phase gate reviews, solution validations, scope changes, and project success criteria. This role may often be the same as the executive sponsor, though sometimes the project customer may serve in this role.

Specification System Requirements Document   A snapshot of the requirements documentation that will serve as the requirements scope baseline (synonymous with Business Requirements Document).

Spiral   An SDLC approach, sometimes called the cinnamon roll, that uses a series of planning, objective determination, alternative identification, and development for the life cycle. It's ideal for projects that are sensitive to risk avoidance. The downside of this model is that it's unique for each project and usually can't be used as a template for future similar projects.

Stakeholders   This role is fulfilled by anyone who is affected by the outcome of the project deliverables. Stakeholders who make decisions on the project, influence the project requirements, or contribute to the project are sometimes called key stakeholders.

SWOT Analysis   The business analysis team can identify the *strengths, weaknesses, opportunities,* and *threats* (SWOT) of each requirement to determine the risks to be documented.

System Development Life Cycle (SDLC)   A generic way of describing the life cycle of an information system and the phases the system goes through.

Trainer   This role works with the project team to understand the deliverables and then teaches the users of the deliverables how to utilize the project product. This person may teach, coach, write, and do instructional design to educate the users of the project deliverable.

Transference   This is the transfer of the risk (and the ownership of the risk) to a third party. The risk doesn't go away; it just becomes someone else's problem. There's usually a fee for transference, and great examples include insurance, warranties, guarantees, and fixed-priced contracts with vendors.

Utility function   A person's or an organization's willingness to accept risk. The higher the utility function, the more willing the person or organization is to accept risk.

Waterfall   An SDLC methodology that divides the project into phases, with the project manager focusing on control of time, cost, and scope. Intense documentation happens throughout the creation of the software or system. The waterfall approach is not the fastest or most flexible approach, but it does work. New project teams or teams that shift in resources often subscribe to this approach.

Questions

1. You and the project manager are working on defining the roles and responsibilities for the requirements of a new project. Sarah, the project manager, wants to begin assigning individual project team members to the responsibilities, while you want to assign roles to the responsibilities. Sarah doesn't understand why you shouldn't just go ahead and assign the responsibilities to the people who'll be on the project team. Which one of the following is the best response to Sarah?

   A. Creation of the roles and responsibilities matrix is a business analyst task, not a project manager task.

   B. Roles allow multiple individuals to complete the project work.

   C. Roles should be generic in case a project team member leaves the organization.

   D. Roles make scheduling the project work easier, as you don't need to worry about availability of project resources.

2. Which role helps design the hardware, software, and technical infrastructure for a project?

   A. Infrastructure analyst

   B. Information architect

   C. Developer

   D. Infrastructure engineer

3. You're working on a new project for your organization. You've collected the project requirements and have identified the needed roles in your project. Management would like for you to create a standard chart that can show each role's involvement with the responsibilities you've created. What type of chart is management asking for?

   A. RAM chart

   B. RACI chart

   C. Pareto chart

   D. Roles and responsibility assignment matrix

4. You are mentoring Henry to become a business analyst. Henry wants to add more labor to some business analysis activities to reduce the amount of time it'll take to complete these tasks. You advise Henry that while that may initially work, he can't keep adding labor to the task to continue to reduce the task's duration. Which economic law prevents the business analyst from always adding more labor to a business analysis task to exponentially reduce the amount of time to complete the task?

   A. Pareto's Law

   B. Moore's Law

   C. Law of Diminishing Returns

   D. Law of supply and demand

5. You are creating a diagram to illustrate how involved each group of stakeholders is with the project solution. The diagram shows which stakeholders who are part of the organization participate in the creation of the project solution, and which stakeholders are outside of the organization, but still may contribute to or be affected by the solution. What type of diagram are you creating?

   A. Onion diagram

   B. Stakeholder matrix

   C. RACI chart

   D. Pareto chart

6. You are identifying risks that may be lurking in the project requirements. You and your business analysis team are to identify both positive and negative risks. Theresa, one of the members of your team, wants to know if they are also to identify issues at this point. What is the difference between an issue and risk?

   A. An issue is a negative risk that has happened in the project.

   B. An issue is a positive risk that has become a negative risk in the project.

   C. There is no difference between issues and risks.

   D. Issues have time and financial impacts, while risks may have only financial or only time impacts on the project.

7. What term describes an organization's willingness to accept risk?

   A. Positive risk

   B. Negative risk

   C. Utility function

   D. Opportunity costs

8. You want to create a matrix that shows the probability of a risk event happening and also link it to the overall effect on the project requirements should the risk event happen. This matrix could be completed with a cardinal or ordinal scale and will be based on qualitative analysis. What type of chart should you create?

   A. Pareto chart

   B. Probability-impact matrix

   C. Risk impact matrix

   D. Cause-and-effect chart

9. Your organization has hired an electrician to complete all of the electrical work in your project. The primary reason for hiring the electrician was because the electrical work was deemed too dangerous to be done by an employee. This type of risk response is known as what?

   A. Avoidance

   B. Mitigation

   C. Contingency

   D. Transference

10. A typical risk response to weather is known as what?

    A. Mitigation

    B. Acceptance

    C. Enhance

    D. Transference

11. Which Software Development Life Cycle is most sensitive to risk avoidance and uses a series of planning tasks as it moves through the software development?

    A. Waterfall

    B. Agile

    C. Spiral

    D. Incremental

12. You are working with the project manager to determine milestones within the project. Which one of the following is the most likely time a milestone will be evident?

    A. When the project charter has been signed.

    B. When the project passes a key risk event without the risk happening.

    C. When the project completes a quantitative analysis of the project deliverables.

    D. When the project completes a phase.

13. What must be true about change requests that affect the requirements scope?

    A. All change requests must be documented.

    B. All change requests must not affect the project's time or cost.

    C. All change requests must not introduce new risks.

    D. All change requests must add value to the requirements scope.

14. Your requirements scope has been approved, and it's time to start the time estimating activities. You gather your business analysis team, the project manager, the project team, and some other experts within your organization to begin estimating the project activities and the expected duration to complete the project work. What input is your best source of information for creating time estimates for activity durations?

    A. Historical information

    B. Subject matter experts

    C. Prototyping

    D. Project management information systems

15. You're working with the project team members to complete activity duration estimates. You warn the project team that they should provide a most-likely estimate to complete each task rather than bloating their estimated durations for the activities. What law are you trying to combat by stressing accurate time estimates?

    A. Moore's Law

    B. Parkinson's Law

    C. Law of Diminishing Returns

    D. Murphy's Law

16. What type of funding uses milestones as a sign to reinvest for the next phase of a project?

    A. Step funding

    B. Phased-gate estimating

    C. Milestone funding

    D. Opportunity cost

17. All of the following are baselines for projects except for which one?

    A. Requirements baseline

    B. Schedule baseline

    C. Cost baseline

    D. Quality baseline

18. You are working with the project manager to complete activity sequencing for a long project. Thousands of project activities are to be scheduled and sequenced, so you are using a project management information system to help with the calculation of the critical path. What is the critical path?

   A. It is the path in the project network diagram that has the activities with the most risks.

   B. It is the path in the project network diagram that is most important to the project stakeholders.

   C. It is the path in the project network diagram that takes the longest time to complete.

   D. It is the path in the project network diagram that can finish first in the project execution.

19. You have two activities that can overlap in the project network diagram. You take advantage of this and schedule the activities to overlap by one day to save time in the project schedule. When you allow activities to overlap to save time in the project schedule, you are doing what duration compression technique?

   A. Lag time

   B. Lead time

   C. Crashing

   D. Constraints

20. A project has an activity that can be greatly reduced by adding much labor to the activity. The activity is considered to be effort driven. When the project manager adds labor to the project, he is adding costs but saving on time for the project completion. What is this approach called?

   A. Fast tracking

   B. Crashing

   C. Resource leveling

   D. Labor compression

Questions and Answers

1. You and the project manager are working on defining the roles and responsibilities for the requirements of a new project. Sarah, the project manager, wants to begin assigning individual project team members to the responsibilities, while you want to assign roles to the responsibilities. Sarah doesn't understand why you shouldn't just go ahead and assign the responsibilities to the people who'll be on the project team. Which one of the following is the best response to Sarah?

   A. Creation of the roles and responsibilities matrix is a business analyst task, not a project manager task.

   B. Roles allow multiple individuals to complete the project work.

C. Roles should be generic in case a project team member leaves the organization.

D. Roles make scheduling the project work easier, as you don't need to worry about availability of project resources.

B. By using roles instead of specific resources, you can map multiple people to the roles. Individuals may serve in many different roles on a project. A is incorrect, as the project manager can certainly create a roles and responsibilities matrix. C is tempting, but not true. D is incorrect, as you'll eventually need to schedule individuals to serve as roles to complete the project work.

2. Which role helps design the hardware, software, and technical infrastructure for a project?

A. Infrastructure analyst

B. Information architect

C. Developer

D. Infrastructure engineer

A. The infrastructure analyst role designs the hardware, software, and technical infrastructure required for the project application development, operation requirements, and project ongoing solution. B is incorrect, as this role, sometimes called the data modeler, helps assess the data requirements of a project, identifies data assets, and helps the project team complete data modeling requirements. C is incorrect, as the developer is the technical resource within the project and may serve as a designer, tester, coder, application developer, or other nomenclature. D is also incorrect, as the infrastructure engineer is not a valid role for the CBAP exam.

3. You're working on a new project for your organization. You've collected the project requirements and have identified the needed roles in your project. Management would like for you to create a standard chart that can show each role's involvement with the responsibilities you've created. What type of chart is management asking for?

A. RAM chart

B. RACI chart

C. Pareto chart

D. Roles and responsibility assignment matrix

B. Management is asking for the standard RACI chart. A is not the best choice, because while a RAM is a type of roles and responsibilities chart, it is not a standardized chart; RAMs can use any legend you'd like, while RACI always uses the same legend. C, a Pareto chart, is a quality control tool to show categories of defects. D, the roles and responsibility assignment matrix, is not a standardized chart and is usually just called a RAM.

4. You are mentoring Henry to become a business analyst. Henry wants to add more labor to some business analysis activities to reduce the amount of time it'll take to complete these tasks. You advise Henry that while that may initially work, he can't keep adding labor to the task to continue to reduce the task's duration. Which economic law prevents the business analyst from always adding more labor to a business analysis task to exponentially reduce the amount of time to complete the task?

A. Pareto's Law

B. Moore's Law

C. Law of Diminishing Returns

D. Law of supply and demand

C. The Law of Diminishing Returns is what prevents Henry from continually adding labor to a task to diminish the task duration. A, Pareto's Law, is also called the 80–20 Principle; for example, 80 percent of your business comes from 20 percent of your customers. B, Moore's Law, is incorrect as this law, based on a statement by Intel's Gordon Moore, states that computer processing speed can double every 18 months. D is incorrect, as the law of supply and demand describes market conditions where a low supply and high demand equals higher prices and vice versa.

5. You are creating a diagram to illustrate how involved each group of stakeholders is with the project solution. The diagram shows which stakeholders who are part of the organization participate in the creation of the project solution and which stakeholders are outside of the organization, but still may contribute to or be affected by the solution. What type of diagram are you creating?

A. Onion diagram

B. Stakeholder matrix

C. RACI chart

D. Pareto chart

A. This is an example of an onion diagram. It's called an onion diagram because it looks similar to an onion; the closer the stakeholders are to the project solution, the more involved they are with the project solution. B is incorrect because a stakeholder matrix maps the level of influence a stakeholder may have over key project decisions. C is incorrect; a RACI chart is a roles and responsibility chart that uses the legend of responsible, accountable, consult, and inform. D is incorrect. A Pareto chart is a histogram that shows categories of failure; it's often used in quality control.

6. You are identifying risks that may be lurking in the project requirements. You and your business analysis team are to identify both positive and negative risks. Theresa, one of the members of your team, wants to know if they are also to identify issues at this point. What is the difference between an issue and risk?

    A. An issue is a negative risk that has happened in the project.

    B. An issue is a positive risk that has become a negative risk in the project.

    C. There is no difference between issues and risks.

    D. Issues have time and financial impacts, while risks may have only financial or only time impacts on the project.

    A. Risks that come into play are now issues. B, C, and D are all incorrect statements about project risks.

7. What term describes an organization's willingness to accept risk?

    A. Positive risk

    B. Negative risk

    C. Utility function

    D. Opportunity costs

    C. The utility function describes an organization's willingness to accept risks. Generally the higher the priority, the lower the utility function—which means the company is risk averse. Positive and negative risks describe the risk impact on the project should the risk event occur. D, opportunity costs, describes the total amount of an opportunity that must be surrendered to pursue a greater opportunity.

8. You want to create a matrix that shows the probability of a risk event happening and also link it to the overall effect on the project requirements should the risk event happen. This matrix could be completed with a cardinal or ordinal scale and will be based on qualitative analysis. What type of chart should you create?

    A. Pareto chart

    B. Probability-impact matrix

    C. Risk impact matrix

    D. Cause-and-effect chart

    B. You should create a probability-impact matrix that measures each risk event and assigns an overall score to the event. The Pareto chart shows categories of failure and is used in quality control. C, the risk impact matrix, is not a valid term. D, cause-and-effect charts, do not measure the probability and impacts of risk, but are useful for determining why quality defects, trends, or byproducts are happening.

9. Your organization has hired an electrician to complete all of the electrical work in your project. The primary reason for hiring the electrician was because the electrical work was deemed too dangerous to be done by an employee. This type of risk response is known as what?

   A. Avoidance

   B. Mitigation

   C. Contingency

   D. Transference

   D. This is an example of transference, as the risk doesn't go away but is transferred to a third party for a contracted fee. A, avoidance, avoids the risk altogether. B, mitigation, is steps that are taken to reduce or eliminate the probability and/or impact of a risk event. C, contingency, is incorrect, as this describes the reaction to a risk event should it become an issue.

10. A typical risk response to weather is known as what?

    A. Mitigation

    B. Acceptance

    C. Enhance

    D. Transference

    B. Acceptance is a common risk response to weather events—you can't control the weather other than schedule around it. Scheduling around the weather would be an example of the risk response avoidance and that would have been a correct choice—had it been offered. A, mitigation, is steps that are taken to reduce or eliminate the probability and/or impact of a risk event. C, enhancing the risk, is steps that are taken to ensure that the positive risk does happen. D, transference, is when the risk is transferred, usually for a fee, to a third party.

11. Which Software Development Life Cycle is most sensitive to risk avoidance and uses a series of planning tasks as it moves through the software development?

    A. Waterfall

    B. Agile

    C. Spiral

    D. Incremental

    C. Spiral uses a series of planning, objective determination, alternative identification, and development for the life cycle and is ideal for projects that are sensitive to risk avoidance. A, the waterfall life cycle, is a methodology that divides the project into phases, and the project manager focuses on control of time, cost, and scope. B, Agile SDLC methods, uses quick execution; daily meetings; isolated, protected developers; and adaptability to changes. The model uses small increments of planning and execution of the requirements. D, incremental, uses a granular approach for quicker deliverables, easier risk management, and easier change control on the smaller segments of the project work. This approach can also use a series of waterfalls for phases and deliverables rather than one large waterfall model.

12. You are working with the project manager to determine milestones within the project. Which one of the following is the most likely time a milestone will be evident?

A. When the project charter has been signed.

B. When the project passes a key risk event without the risk happening

C. When the project completes a quantitative analysis of the project deliverables.

D. When the project completes a phase.

D. Milestones are most evident when a project phase has been completed. A is incorrect, as the project charter launches the project and names the project manager. B is incorrect, as passing a risk does not usually constitute a milestone event in the project. C is not a valid choice for a milestone representation.

13. What must be true about change requests that affect the requirements scope?

A. All change requests must be documented.

B. All change requests must not affect the project's time or cost.

C. All change requests must not introduce new risks.

D. All change requests must add value to the requirements scope.

A. All change requests must be documented so they can be catalogued, tracked, and referenced. Verbal change requests are not valid. Choices B, C, and D are all incorrect statements about change requests.

14. Your requirements scope has been approved, and it's time to start the time estimating activities. You gather your business analysis team, the project manager, the project team, and some other experts within your organization to begin estimating the project activities and the expected duration to complete the project work. What input is your best source of information for creating time estimates for activity durations?

A. Historical information

B. Subject matter experts

C. Prototyping

D. Project management information systems

A. Historical information is your best input for estimating, as it is proven information. Choices B and C are both good inputs for time estimating, but A is the best choice because it is proven, while subject matter experts and prototyping are not. D is not an input for time estimating but can help record the outcome of time estimates.

15. You're working with the project team members to complete activity duration estimates. You warn the project team that they should provide a most-likely estimate to complete each task rather than bloating their estimated durations for the activities. What law are you trying to combat by stressing accurate time estimates?

    A. Moore's Law

    B. Parkinson's Law

    C. Law of Diminishing Returns

    D. Murphy's Law

    B. Parkinson's Law states that work expands to fill the time allotted to it. If the project team bloats their time estimates, then they'll likely use all of the estimated time to complete the work. A is incorrect, as Moore's Law describes the potential for computer processing speed to double. C is incorrect, as it defines the yield for the amount of labor added to a task to reduce the task's duration. D, Murphy's Law is not valid; it's an aphorism that whatever can go wrong probably will.

16. What type of funding uses milestones as a sign to reinvest for the next phase of a project?

    A. Step funding

    B. Phased-gate estimating

    C. Milestone funding

    D. Opportunity cost

    A. Step funding provides funds to the project as phases are completed. B, phased-gate estimating, may be linked to step funding but is really estimating for time and costs of each phase as the phase is set to begin. C is not a valid term, and D, opportunity cost, describes the total amount of an opportunity that is foregone to choose a more valuable opportunity.

17. All of the following are baselines for projects except for which one?

    A. Requirements baseline

    B. Schedule baseline

    C. Cost baseline

    D. Quality baseline

    D. The quality baseline is not a valid business analysis term; technically the quality baseline can be mapped to project and requirements scope. Choices A, B, and C are all valid business analysis baselines, so these choices are incorrect for this question.

18. You are working with the project manager to complete activity sequencing for a long project. Thousands of project activities are to be scheduled and sequenced, so you are using a project management information system to help with the calculation of the critical path. What is the critical path?

   A. It is the path in the project network diagram that has the activities with the most risks.

   B. It is the path in the project network diagram that is most important to the project stakeholders.

   C. It is the path in the project network diagram that takes the longest time to complete.

   D. It is the path in the project network diagram that can finish first in the project execution.

   C. The critical path is the path of activities in the project network diagram that takes the longest time to complete. It shows the earliest finish date for the project and allows for no delays of the activities on the critical path. There can be more than one critical path, as multiple paths can take the same amount of duration to complete. Choices A, B, and D are all incorrect descriptions of the critical path.

19. You have two activities that can overlap in the project network diagram. You take advantage of this and schedule the activities to overlap by one day to save time in the project schedule. When you allow activities to overlap to save time in the project schedule, you are doing what duration compression technique?

   A. Lag time

   B. Lead time

   C. Crashing

   D. Constraints

   B. Lead time allows sequential activities to overlap; for example, you could add lead time to an activity to paint a room with the priming the room activity. Lead time is a form of schedule compression. A, lag time, adds time between activities and is useful for waiting time—such as you must wait 24 hours for the primer to dry before you can begin painting. C, crashing, adds resources to a project so the project may finish faster. D, constraints, is not a valid option for this question.

20. A project has an activity that can be greatly reduced by adding much labor to the activity. The activity is considered to be effort driven. When the project manager adds labor to the project, he is adding costs but saving on time for the project completion. What is this approach called?

A. Fast tracking

B. Crashing

C. Resource leveling

D. Labor compression

B. Crashing adds labor to a project to finish the project work faster. Crashing generally drives costs up, because someone has to pay for the labor. A, fast tracking, is when the project manager allows complete phases of a project to overlap one another. C, resource leveling, is when the business analyst or the project manager determines a maximum amount of work hours allowed on a project by any one resource. For example, you may only work 45 hours per week on the project. Resource leveling often causes the project to extend in calendar days. D, labor compression, is not a valid term.

Eliciting Requirements

In this chapter you will
- Learn how to elicit requirements from stakeholders
- Lead focus groups
- Interview stakeholders
- Facilitate a requirements workshop
- Analyze business documentation
- Create a project prototype solution

I've some good news and more good news about this chapter: it's not very long, with just four business analysis processes to learn about. Maybe the better news is that this short topic accounts for nearly 20 percent of your CBAP exam (as of this writing). That equates to roughly 28 questions. Here's an exam tip: know these processes inside and out, as there's not as much information to know, but plenty of points to be had on the CBAP exam.

The four business analysis requirements elicitation processes are

- **Prepare for elicitation**   You'll need to know the business need, the business case, and the stakeholders you'll elicit information from, and you'll rely on your requirements management plan to guide you through the elicitation prep work.

- **Conduct elicitation activities**   This is the meat of the chapter and of your job. You'll be eliciting requirements through many different approaches, business analysis resources, organizational process assets, and the solution scope that your business analysis duties focus on.

- **Document elicitation results**   This is a process that you'll do in tandem with the elicitation activities. You'll create charts, models, and reports, record conversations, and produce supporting detail for future business analysis processes, project management, and decision making.

- **Confirm elicitation results**   As you collect and document requirements, you'll also need to confirm that requirements are accurate and are what the stakeholders are expecting from the project solution. This means you'll be working with the stakeholders to review what you've documented as the requirements.

You've probably already done many of the tasks in eliciting requirements in your role as a business analyst. You can rely on your experience leading brainstorming sessions, interviewing stakeholders, and hosting requirements workshops to help ease you past this exam objective. You'll need to recognize scenarios that call for a specific requirements elicitation activity, and you'll need to link requirements elicitation to other knowledge areas in business analysis.

You do requirements elicitation activities very early in the project, and then you ease off the elicitation. You can't do requirements gathering forever. You may have to, based on discovery, prototypes, identified gaps in the requirements, or competing objectives, revisit these tasks throughout the early stages of a project for clarifications, more information, or refinements to the requirements you've gathered.

Eliciting Stakeholder Requirements

When a business opportunity or problem is introduced to an organization, it's up to the business analyst to determine the exact requirements to solve the problem or to seize the opportunity. This is business analysis at its core. You'll need to work with, talk to, and study the stakeholders and their points of view, their understanding of the requirements, and their objectives. Basically, you've got to determine and document what the stakeholders want, why they want it, and when they want it delivered. Oh yeah, and don't forget how much (or how little) they'll want to spend for the solution.

To elicit stakeholder requirements, you've got to know some business analysis techniques and how to get people to talk about the requirements, and you'll need an understanding of how the organization operates. How the organization operates means more than the flow of processes, enterprise environmental factors, and who's in charge of what functions. Organizational operations include the undocumented but prevalent politics, agendas, and schemes that are in every company.

The business analyst will also need to be familiar with these skills to complete requirements elicitation:

- Information assessment
- Interviewing people
- Facilitating joint sessions among functional management, end users, customers, and other stakeholders
- Observing processes, workflow, and how tools, software, and other related resource are utilized within the organization
- Conflict resolution and consensus achievement among stakeholders
- Finding and leveraging patterns
- Writing
- Effective communications

You'll also use time management, planning, and resource management to effectively and quickly gather requirements. The goal of requirements elicitation is to determine what's needed by the stakeholders so a solution can be created in the least amount of time for the most accurate price.

Interviewing Project Stakeholders

A funny thing about eliciting and assessing information from stakeholders is that they have to be willing to participate. If stakeholders don't like the business opportunity, feel threatened by the identified problem, or think the solution isn't going to benefit them, they'll resist participating in your elicitation activities. Surprise, surprise. And then, even if the stakeholders do agree to participate, you may have some hostile opinions, negative attitudes, and competing objectives to deal with.

Let's hope that's the worst-case scenario for most business analysis activities. Usually, in my experience, the stakeholders want to participate in the business analysis work and are eager to share their requirements. Business analysts must identify all of the stakeholders, or they can miss requirements, risks, and a complete understanding of how the problem or opportunity affects all of the stakeholders. This can, of course, lead to lost time and monies, and to scope changes later in the project execution.

NOTE Business analysts who want to interview stakeholders need to be comfortable with the subject matter and comfortable talking with strangers. Don't underestimate the importance of being prepared for an interview

One of the most common approaches to eliciting information is interviewing. You'll need to identify the stakeholders who need to be interviewed, what their contribution to the project can be, and what their stake in the project outcome will be. Interviewing requires more than sitting down for a chat over a cup of coffee and firing off questions. Interviewing first requires preparation for the stakeholder. The business analyst needs to know several things about the stakeholder to be interviewed as part of the preparation:

- What resources, support, software, hardware, and processes does this person need to do their function in the organization?

- What things, resources, and/or services does the person create or provide for others within and without of the organization?

- What roles does the individual play in the organization, both in operations and projects?

- What are the enterprise environmental factors, procedures, regulations, or other policies that govern how the individual completes her work?

- What data flows through this individual? Consider who, what, where, when, and why.

Understanding this information prior to the interview can help a business analyst form other questions that are related specifically to the business problem or opportunity. The answer to these questions can also help the business analyst examine how the project will affect the stakeholder during its execution and once it moves into operations. This information can help you create a structured interview where you'll have a list of questions prepared for the interviewee.

The questions you'll create for a structured interview can be both open-ended and closed-ended questions. To be clear, open-ended questions invite the participant to ramble on about the problem, a situation, or process. Open-ended questions invite a dialogue between you and the participant, and may prompt follow-up questions. Closed-ended questions are for specific facts, like "how many servers do you support?" or "when are invoices processed?"

You can also use this information for an unstructured interview approach. An unstructured interview has some boundaries, but it's more open, to encourage ideas, thoughts, and concerns from the stakeholders. Unstructured interviews can be tricky to manage, because you want the interviewee to keep on topic, and it'll be the business analyst's job to bring the conversation back to the opportunity or problem.

With either approach the business analyst needs several things to conduct a successful interview:

- An understanding of the business, function, or processes the project will be centered in
- Interviewing experience and ability to react to stakeholders' queries and objections
- Ability to document the results of the interview
- Willing interviewees with an understanding of what the problem or opportunity is and how they need to contribute to the solution
- Empathy and rapport with the interviewee

For the most part, interviews are accomplished one-on-one, though it's possible to conduct group interviews. The problem with group interviews is that it may be difficult to facilitate the interview, document the response, and keep the group on task. It's a good idea, when possible, to hire someone to document the interviews, or to use a tape recorder and transcribe the conversation later. You'll also need to be certain that all of the people being interviewed contribute to the discussion. This can be tricky when managers and their employees are being interviewed together in a group setting.

When the interview is drawing to a close, be certain to give the interviewee the opportunity to address anything that may have been overlooked in the conversation. After the interview, you'll likely follow up with the participant about what was discussed, review your notes from the meeting, and offer the stakeholder a chance to clarify or add any information. You should communicate to the stakeholder that the follow-up isn't a guarantee of what will or won't be included in the actual project; it's just an understanding and confirmation of what was covered during the interview.

Managing Stakeholders

Chances are stakeholders will come from all over the organization when you begin requirements elicitation. You'll need to know who's from what department, who reports to whom, and what their role in the organization may be. Your organization will likely have charts or documentation on this information for you to refer to. This can help you interview, facilitate workshops, and know what's likely to be of interest to the stakeholders. Here are some common charts you should be familiar with:

- **Organization chart**   This traditional chart shows how the organization is broken down by department and disciplines. This chart is sometimes called the Organizational Breakdown Structure (OBS) and is arranged by departments, units, or teams.

- **Resource Breakdown Structure (RBS)**   This hierarchical chart, as seen in Figure 3-1, can break down the business problem or opportunity by the type of resources affected by the project. For example, your project might need several database administrators and programmers in several likely deliverables throughout the project. The RBS would organize all of the usage of the resources by their discipline rather than by where the discipline is being utilized. An RBS is an excellent tool for tracking resource utilization, resource costs, and helping formulate questions.

- **Responsibility Assignment Matrix (RAM)**   A RAM chart shows the correlation between project team members and the work they've been assigned to complete. A RAM chart doesn't necessarily have to be specific to individual team members; it can also be decomposed to project groups or units. When you first begin elicitation, you likely won't have a RAM to reference, but on larger projects with a series of elicitations this can be useful.

- **RACI charts**   A RACI chart is another matrix chart that uses only the activities of *responsible, accountable, consult,* and *inform.* Technically, a RACI chart is a form of the Responsibility Assignment Matrix, but I want to include it here as a separate entry. You'll definitely see this chart on your CBAP exam, and it can be useful during rounds of requirements elicitation.

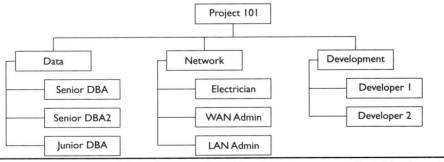

Figure 3-1   A Resource Breakdown Structure illustrates what resources are affected by the project.

For a more detailed explanation, watch the Charting the Stakeholders video now.

Understanding where a stakeholder fits into an organization and to whom the person reports can help you manage and prioritize objectives and conflicts. Every organization has a pecking order, but just because someone is at the bottom of the organizational chart does not mean they're automatically wrong and their opinions don't count. What it does mean, however, is that there is political capital to consider among the stakeholders, and understanding who wants (and demands) what can help your analysis.

Exploring Elicitation Techniques

You can use several different techniques besides interviewing to elicit requirements from stakeholders. While the interviewing technique may be the most direct and most common, you should know the details of some other business analysis approaches. Stakeholders won't always be available for interviews—or want to participate in your interviews. You might also be challenged with language differences, geographical challenges, and time constraints that can make interviewing difficult.

In this section, I'll explore five different face-to-face approaches to requirements gathering. You should know each of these for your CBAP examination. The approaches I'll cover in detail in this section are

- Leading a brainstorming session
- Hosting a focus group
- Observing the stakeholders
- Facilitating a requirements workshop
- Managing a stakeholder survey

These five approaches are where you'll likely have a generous number of questions for the requirements elicitation knowledge area on your exam. Spend a little time learning all about these approaches, and you'll be on your way to passing the CBAP examination.

Leading a Brainstorming Session

A brainstorming session is when a group of stakeholders comes together to attack a problem or opportunity with as many ideas as possible. The term "brainstorm" was created by advertising guru Alex Osborn in 1939. Little did he know that his term would become a key process in business analysis activities—and find its way onto your CBAP exam. You won't necessarily have to know about Alex Osborn, but you should know these specific things about brainstorming:

- Promotes diverse thinking for multiple options for a solution
- Reveals options that are available for the current issue
- Helps determine constraints on the project team, the project, or the organization and how they might be removed
- Explores solutions to problems within the project
- Explores solutions to business opportunities
- Encourages stakeholder participation
- Fosters team building

When leading a brainstorming session, the business analyst should encourage all of the participants to offer all ideas. Even if an idea is not practical, it may spur someone to think of a related or improved idea. What other people contribute can help the group formulate new ideas and solutions.

The brainstorming session should have a clearly defined topic that the suggestions, ideas, and thoughts center around. You do want to create boundaries for the session so participants don't ramble into areas that don't pertain to the topic at hand. You'll also want to create a time limit adequate for all members of the group to participate—though the ideal size for a brainstorming session is six to eight participants with a broad background of experience related to the topic.

When participants offer an idea, you should simply document it and not judge it. I like to use a whiteboard so everyone in the room can look over past ideas to help generate new ideas or link suggestions together. The facilitator shouldn't set a goal for a number of ideas, as this actually limits the maximum number of suggestions—you want as many as possible regardless of how radical the ideas may be. Brainstorming is a good practice to generate ideas if the participants are knowledgeable about the brainstorming topic.

Hosting a Focus Group

What if you could gather a sampling of your prospective customers into one setting and query them in a guided, structured meeting to determine their true feelings about your products and services? You'd have an example of a focus group. A focus group is a 1- to 2-hour meeting to gather ideas, determine opinions, and expose feelings about a product, service, problem, or opportunity. It's led by a moderator and feels conversational, though it's really quite structured.

The participants in the group should be qualified to voice their opinions and attitudes based on their experience or insight with the product or service. The ideal focus group has 6 to 12 people in it, though larger groups aren't unreasonable. When the moderator poses questions, the people in the group may reevaluate their stance based on what other people in the room say. The most common type of focus group has all of the participants in one room, though web-based focus groups are becoming easier to host.

When to host a focus group in a product life cycle depends on the goals of the focus group. Consider the varying goals for hosting a focus group based on how far along the product life cycle may be:

- **Development**   If the product is still in development, the focus group will evaluate the business opportunity, help determine requirements, and analyze existing requirements.

- **Prelaunch**   For products or services that are about to be launched, the focus group could help the organization determine how to best position the product or service in the marketplace.

- **Production**   If the product or service currently exists, the focus group could offer advice on improving the product or service, information on how they use the product or service, or what their perception of the existing product or service may be.

The type of participants in the focus group must also be evaluated based on the expected objectives of the activity. A homogeneous focus group, where all of the participants have similar characteristics, won't usually be as diverse in their attitudes about the product or service, but may offer specific insight into the development of the product or service. A heterogeneous group, where the participants represent a variety of users, backgrounds, and values, can offer differing points of view about the product or service. The heterogeneous group, however, may not state their opinions as easily in front of others who have differing opinions.

Obviously, the moderator should be someone who can generate conversation and camaraderie within the group. The moderator should be able to get all of the participants to contribute, guide the conversation, keep the group on track, and stay neutral on opinions that are offered in the group. The moderator should also have an assistant who can record conversations or videotape the group if necessary. The moderator is usually tasked with creating a qualitative report on the focus group. The qualitative report will help create themes for the product or service.

While focus groups are a great method to gather information from a group of people in one setting, this technique has several drawbacks. Depending on what the focus group's topic is, people may not want to share their opinion in front of others. What participants say in front of others may not be what people do in private or away from the group. It's up to the moderator to follow a crafted discussion to elicit genuine responses and trust, and to create a nonjudgmental space for an honest conversation among the group.

Observing the Stakeholders

If an organization would like to change or enhance an existing business process, then observing the stakeholders is an excellent approach to requirements elicitation. Stakeholder observation allows the business analyst to shadow a user to see exactly how the person completes his work, completes a process, or interacts with an existing system. If you've ever talked with someone about how they do their job and they've had difficulty explaining how and what they do, stakeholder observation is an excellent approach.

NOTE I had a client who loved for business analysts to do stakeholder observation. It got the business analysts out of their offices and into the field to really see the work. As he used to say, "Sometimes it's just easier to see someone peel a banana than describe how to peel a banana."

Passive stakeholder observation, sometimes called invisible observation, is when the business analyst observes the activity without interacting with the person doing the work. The business analyst observes the work many times, takes notes, and seeks to understand how the person completes the process by simply observing the task. Once the business analyst understands the process and the observation is over, then they'll interact with the person for clarifications about how they completed the work.

Active stakeholder observation is just the opposite of passive—you'll ask lots of questions as the person completes the process. The business analyst seeks to understand the reason behind every step in the business process to fully understand the process. Sometimes the business analyst will actually get involved in the work to fully understand the process and how the person completes the process.

NOTE Obviously business analysts can't get involved in processes where they aren't qualified, licensed, or might endanger themselves or others. No active stakeholder observations during open heart surgery, please. The business analyst might serve as an apprentice to the person completing the work to get close to the process, but not actually do the process.

It's important for both the business analyst and the person being observed to understand what the goal of the observation process is: to document how the process currently works, not to offer solutions, critiques, or judgment about the effectiveness of the current process. The observer should make the person completing the task feel comfortable, encourage them to "think aloud" as they complete each step of the process, and explain why each step is necessary as they work. The observer should document these thoughts and each step of the process.

Stakeholder observation is great for understanding work flow and business processes, and can help design and improve current processes. The key, however, is that the person doing the observation truly understand the process before tinkering with the process to make it better. That's why the notes of the analysis are distributed to the people who were observed to confirm or clarify the activity.

Where stakeholder observation is weak, however, is when the processes are more internal or thought-based rather than clearly defined steps in the process. For example, creative processes don't always follow the same step-by-step approach that a printing press does. Stakeholder observation can also be time-consuming, disruptive, and won't work for new processes—only processes that already exist.

Hosting a Requirements Workshop

A requirements workshop, sometimes called a Joint Application Design (JAD) workshop, is a fast method to bring the key stakeholders together to define the requirements for the project. Specifically, the requirements workshop can be used to clarify the project scope, refine existing requirements, and gain stakeholder consensus on the priorities of the project.

The requirements workshop should have all of the key stakeholders while not being too large to slow down the requirements gathering process and discussion. There should be a balance between the number of stakeholders in attendance at the workshop and the anticipated size of the project. In other words, you want to invite the most important stakeholders to the workshop without ignoring stakeholders who may have less to contribute. The workshop itself can last anywhere from less than a day to three days, though availability of the stakeholders may dictate when the workshop can happen and how long it'll last.

The facilitator has many responsibilities before, during, and after the workshop. For every workshop, the facilitator must prepare to lead the event to ensure it's productive and meaningful. Before the workshop the facilitator must

- Document what the business problem or opportunity is
- Communicate the purpose of the requirements workshop to the key stakeholders
- Create an agenda for the workshop
- Schedule a scribe or recorder to document the minutes and conversations of the workshop for future reference
- Complete interviews with the stakeholder to help facilitate the workshop

During the workshop, the facilitator will engage and interact with the participants to elicit information about the project. He'll need to work with the participants to help them reach consensus and agreement on conflicting views and competing objectives. Throughout the conversations, the facilitator will need to keep the session on track by following the agenda and the objectives of the workshop.

The facilitator should not be judgmental and should promote conversation among the participants while being friendly, conversational, and professional. He'll also need to establish and enforce the ground rules for the workshop so it's effective and the participants are kept on track. This means a clear introduction and statement about the rules, intent, and agenda for the meeting should happen at the start of the workshop. The facilitator should post the agenda and make certain all participants have a copy of the workshop agenda as well.

A good facilitator will keep all of the participants involved in the conversation without participating in decision making or the content of the discussion himself. This means the facilitator will need to ask questions, prompt participants, and follow up on conversations for more detail. Observing participants' nonverbal language, reactions to comments, and body posture can help the facilitator guide the conversation.

While a requirements workshop can be cost-effective and provide a fast approach to requirements gathering, it does have its weakness. The knowledge of the stakeholders in attendance can directly affect the effectiveness of the workshop. It's important that the right stakeholders attend the event to gather the correct and accurate requirements. Just as important is how effective the facilitator is at conducting and controlling the workshop.

Using a Requirements Survey

Surveys are a great method to quickly gain insight and feedback from a large group of stakeholders. Surveys can be anonymous, which is most common, or participants' identities could be known for follow-up questions from the survey. The trick with survey questionnaires, however, is to create the survey to present precise questions to the most appropriate group of stakeholders. Good survey results can help the business analyst develop additional studies, formulate requirements, and recommend solutions. A poor survey can be a waste of time and monies, and can cause confusion among the stakeholders.

NOTE   The Delphi Technique is a process that uses rounds of anonymous surveys to find consensus among the stakeholders. The results of each survey are compiled and then shared with the survey participants for feedback.

Surveys can use two types of questions, and each type has pros and cons:

- Closed-ended questions allow participants to choose one of many possible answers, but don't allow the participants to add comments, opinion, or insight. This survey type uses multiple-choice answers and is simple to tally and quantify results.

- Open-ended questions are essay questions where each participant can offer much insight, thought, and opinion to each question. While this approach can collect a wealth of varying information, it's time-consuming to quantify each result to form a consensus among the participants.

For a survey to be effective, with open- or closed-ended questions, consideration must be given to the intent of the survey. Whatever the meaning of the survey may be, from marketing efforts to requirements gathering, the survey creators should communicate why the survey is important so respondents are more likely to participate. Organizations might increase the number of participants in the survey by offering an incentive for completing the survey by a deadline, for example.

The business analyst must take many steps to create an effective survey:

- Document the survey purpose and which stakeholders should participate.

- Determine which types of questions, closed or open, are most appropriate for the survey type.

- Determine how respondents will receive, complete, and return the survey; consider paper-based, telephone-based, or web-based surveys.

- Determine the acceptable level of response rate and what incentives might be offered to help reach the response rate.

- Determine the need for pre- and postsurvey interviews to formulate the survey and to review its findings.

- Write the most appropriate survey questions in consideration of the participants' backgrounds, values, and interest in the survey purpose.

- Confirm the survey length (ten questions or fewer is ideal).

- Refine the survey questions so they're clear, easy to answer, and don't put the participant in a defensive stance.

- Test the survey and make any modifications to the survey if necessary.

Once the survey has been created and approved, you'll distribute the survey to your audience and wait for the results. You should have a deadline for survey results, and an offered incentive can help participants respond in a timely manner. Once the results have been received, you'll tabulate the response and communicate the survey results to the business sponsor. Based on the purpose of the survey, the next steps in the business analysis activities will happen.

I'm a big fan of surveys, as they're quick and easy to create, but they have some drawbacks you should be aware of for your CBAP exam. For starters, open-ended questions are tough to tabulate and they let stakeholders ramble—even to topics that aren't related to the survey's purpose. This isn't to say that closed-ended questions are better, as participants can just skip these questions if they don't want to answer them. You'll also find that closed-ended questions fall prey to participants checking "A" on all the answers, so the results can be skewed if the surveys aren't accurately completed.

Five Questions for Every Project Customer

In business analysis some things often are assumed, and with assumptions, things fall through the gaps. Every project customer should be asked these questions in some form. You can find these answers either in person or through a survey to ensure that all of the information is recorded.

Who are you?

No joke. You need to know who the project customers are and how to reach them. In large projects it's easy to overlook project customers who are affected by the project work, and then there's heck to pay when they're discovered later in the project. It's also important to create a directory of project customers (and other stakeholders) so you and the project manager can reach them when necessary. Don't overlook this first question.

What do you want?

I chuckled when a shopkeeper in Paris recognized that I couldn't speak French and in broken English she asked, "What do you want?" She was trying to help, but her question was pointed. As it turned out, it was an appropriate, though not-so-friendly, question, so she could help me make a purchase. It's no different in business analysis. Find out what the customer wants so you can help them.

Why do you want that?

Okay, the Paris shopkeeper didn't need to know why I wanted to buy a new pen, just that I wanted to buy one. Your job as a business analyst is to understand why the customer wants a certain something. They may be attached to a solution, and your job as the business analyst is to understand the reason behind their wants and to document the whole picture of what the customer is experiencing.

When do you want it?

As Benjamin Franklin said, "Time is money." Understanding the need of the project customer and when the need must be satisfied can help you formulate cost estimates for the solution. Generally the sooner it's needed, the more it's going to cost.

What's the most painful thing?

Sometimes the customer is trying to solve a pain. Understanding the pain is part of root cause analysis. The customer may be describing the effect of the pain and not the underlying problem at all. By identifying the customer's pain, so to speak, you can track down where the pain originates and present solutions to truly fix the problem.

Using Static Requirements Gathering

While face-to-face business analysis activities are often the most rewarding and productive, you can use other approaches to gather requirements. These static approaches are based on information that may already exist within the organization such as documentation, prototypes, or existing processes and procedures. Business analysis on an existing solution relies on problem solving; hands-on experience with the product, service, or processes; and time to fully develop requirements.

Note that these approaches require an existing amount of data and information to implement. In other words, you wouldn't be able to use these approaches for situations that are creating new solutions. I'll cover four static solutions in this section that you should be familiar with for your CBAP exam:

- Document analysis and documentation
- Interface analysis
- Project prototype solutions
- Reverse engineering approaches

These four requirements-elicitation techniques take time and resources to develop a complete set of requirements. These approaches could also be coupled with the face-to-face and live analysis techniques.

Performing Document Analysis

As a business analyst, you'll be dealing with loads of information. Much of the information you and other business analysts will be generating. Add to that pile all of the documentation that already exists within an organization, and that's a lot of information to sort through, analyze, and determine its worth. You'll need to be somewhat familiar with the document analysis techniques for your CBAP exam.

You'll most likely use document analysis when you're tasked with upgrading an existing system to a new system. This could be a technical system, work flow, or process engineering type of project. Document analysis is useful when there's a clear identification of how a system works based on experience, its process configuration, and what the system produces. You might also have to complete document analysis when the subject matter experts who created the system are no longer with the company. You'll have to figure out what the heck these experts did.

You'll also use document analysis as requirements elicitation activity for business opportunities and problem solving. Consider all the documents you'd research as part of this process:

- Business plans
- Market studies
- Contracts
- Requests for proposals and proposals
- Statements of work
- Memos
- Organizational processes, procedures, guidelines, and standards
- Information and literature from competing products
- Comparative product reviews, white papers, and published studies

All of this information should be reviewed by the business analyst team, the project team, and any subject matter experts for key information to aid the system upgrade, solve the business problem, or as part of requirements gathering. The goal is to sort out the relevant details from the information that won't contribute to the current project objectives. You'll also determine what relevant information needs clarification and additional analysis.

The advantage of document analysis is that you're starting with existing information to point you in the right direction for the project. You can use the existing information to determine and confirm project requirements. The disadvantage, however, is that you're limited to the documentation you can gather. This documentation may be wrong, incomplete, or outdated. In some organizations, hopefully not yours, the process of gathering all of the relevant information can be time-consuming, because the information is dispersed, guarded, or has been lost.

Completing Interface Analysis

An interface is just a link between two components. There are lots of links (interfaces) between you and the Internet. There's a link between you and your web browser—from your web browser to your computer's operating system down to the hardware. Your network cable physically links your computer and the network. There's even a link between your network and the Internet. There could be lots more interfaces along the route depending on what type of traffic you're generating on the network.

All of the interfaces in a system that's affected, or likely to be affected, by a proposed project, business problem, or opportunity need to be identified. All of the interfaces also have owners, real people who may or may not be thrilled about your business analysis duties. Business analysts need to identify three categories of interfaces:

- **User interfaces**   People who interact with one another, a system, or data moved between two users.

- **External systems**   Links between internal systems and external systems, such as vendors, regulatory agencies, and technical interfaces.

- **Hardware devices**   Links between any hardware device that may be affected by the proposed project. Consider servers, workstations, kiosks, and printers.

The goal of interface analysis is to document where the interfaces of a system are and where the system ends. It doesn't look for solutions or real insight into the problem or improvement of a system. Interface analysis most often ends with a diagram of the system, called a Context or Business Domain Diagram, as seen in Figure 3-2. Along with the Business Domain Diagram, the business analyst should create a data dictionary to define all or the part of the system that interacts with other parts of the system. The data dictionary serves as a glossary for the solution. It defines all of the terms and relevant business definitions for the project.

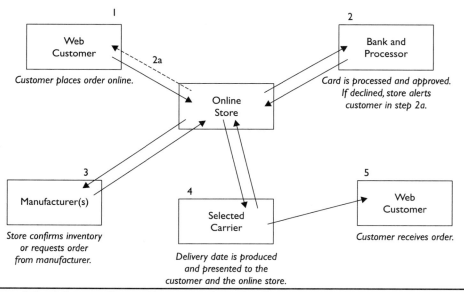

Figure 3-2   A Business Domain Diagram can help identify components and interfaces of a system.

You'll most often engage in interface analysis with user interface designers and data modelers when creating system-to-system requirements. This'll happen early in the business analysis duties so decisions, communication, and boundaries can be established among the system owners. The larger the system, the more owners will be affected and the more communication, collaboration, and risk management are needed for the project.

Creating a Prototype Solution

A prototype is a basic mockup of what the final project deliverable may look like. When it comes to application design, a prototype can be a quick and cheap approach for project customers to see and interact with a limited version of the proposed solution. The business analyst subject matter experts can create a a prototype so that the project customers can see, and confirm, what the final product should look like, how the product will operate, and offer input for clarifications and additional requirements gathering.

Prototypes are also good for the engineers, developers, and project team members to demonstrate their depth of understanding of what the customer is asking for. This is important, as it instills confidence in both the customer and the project team in the product design and requirements. Should the designers be off-base, however, the prototype they've created can serve as a baseline for adjustments, modification, and a deeper understanding of what the customer is requesting without spending tons of cash or hours of labor.

The functional scope of the prototype can be developed in two different approaches, depending on the project:

- **Horizontal method**   Quick, shallow, and wide view of the system without any real functionality behind the prototype. Easy to create, modify, and explain.

- **Vertical method**   Creates an in-depth analysis, deep prototype of just one portion of the system's functionality. Can be costly and time intensive, but proves the functionality of a system's key processes.

There are also two prototype approaches for system design and creation during the development life cycle:

- **Throw-away prototype**   As its name suggests, this prototype is simple and may often just be a sketch of the proposed system. It helps the customer and the developer see the system in recognizable components.

- **Evolutionary prototype**   This approach, sometimes called a working prototype, creates an operating prototype that will eventually evolve into the delivered solution. Each addition to the system evolves it another step until it reaches the complete scope of requirements and the project is closed.

Prototyping is a great tool for requirements elicitation, as it forces the developers, business analysts, project managers, and project customers all to visually inspect the prototype and confirm that the development is on track or that refinements are needed. It's an approach that requires early communication, feedback, and clarification of requirements on a relatively low-cost model that can serve as the foundation for the remainder of the project.

Prototypes do have their pitfalls, too. Seeing a visual mockup of the solution may cause the developers to spend more time in architectural design and technical theory rather than focusing on what the project requires. Granted, some in-depth analysis of the underlying system is needed, or too many assumptions may be made about the abilities, but prototyping should be quick and visual. Finally, prototypes may make promises to the customer that can't be kept in a reasonable amount of time or within the allotted budget.

Chapter Summary

Eliciting requirements is a crucial and key assignment for business analysts. What the business analyst discovers will serve as the foundation for project requirements, customer satisfaction, and the effectiveness of the project deliverables. This chapter covered several approaches to requirements elicitation, and the business analyst must recognize which technique is most appropriate for different scenarios.

In this chapter, you learned all about requirements elicitation and assessing the value of the information you gain from project stakeholders. Stakeholders may or may not be excited about the proposed project and may resist changes the solution may create. The business analyst will need to communicate with stakeholders about the requirements, the project, the stakeholder concerns, and competing objectives within the organization that can affect the current set of requirements.

You'll use both active and static requirements-gathering techniques. Recall activities such as brainstorming sessions, focus groups, and requirements workshops all require good facilitation abilities. You'll need to lead, control, and direct these group-based requirements elicitation activities. One-on-one activities, such as interviews and stakeholder observation, can also be valuable tasks for requirements elicitation, but can take longer to complete.

Static activities are usually about studying existing documentation, software, or processes. Consider documentation analysis and interface analysis. These require some existing set of products or documentation to determine new requirements for improving or replacing a product, service, or process. Prototyping creates a model of a proposed solution to help refine requirements and can evolve into a working solution for the organization.

Throughout the requirements elicitation process, you'll be creating many charts, documents, and reports about your requirements findings. This documentation will become supporting detail for future business analysis processes, additional requirements gathering, and input to the project solution. You'll work with the stakeholders to confirm that the findings you have are in synch with the requirements they have in mind. It's vital to confirm the elicitation results before the solution is proposed.

The CBAP examination will present approximately 28 questions on the activities in this chapter. You should be most familiar with this chapter, as the information-to-question ratio works in your favor. In other words, there's less information to know than for the other exam objectives for a heck of a lot of questions.

Key Terms

Active stakeholder   The business analyst seeks to understand the reason behind every step in the business process to fully understand the process. Sometimes the business analyst will actually get involved in the work as an active stakeholder to fully understand the process and how the person completes the process.

Brainstorming session   A facilitated meeting with a group of stakeholders to attack a problem or opportunity with as many ideas as possible. The term *brainstorm* was created by advertising guru Alex Osborn in 1939.

Closed-ended questions   Used in interviews and surveys, these questions can gain specific information, be multiple-choice answers, or provide yes or no answers.

Document analysis   A requirements elicitation technique that examines the current documentation of a project, product, organization, service, or process to help determine how these things may become better or may contribute to the existing business problem solution or opportunity.

Evolutionary prototype   Sometimes called a working prototype, this is an operating prototype that will eventually evolve into the delivered solution. Each addition to the system evolves it another step until it reaches the complete scope of requirements and the project is closed.

External systems interfaces   Links between internal systems and external systems such as vendors, regulatory agencies, and technical interfaces.

Focus group   A structured, facilitated meeting to gather ideas, opinions, and feelings about a product, service, problem, or opportunity.

Hardware devices interfaces   Identification of links between any hardware device that may be affected by the proposed project. Consider servers, workstations, kiosks, and printers.

Horizontal method prototyping   A quick, shallow, and wide view of the system without any real functionality behind the prototype. Easy to create, modify, and explain.

Interface analysis   Defines and documents all of the links between two or more components in a system.

Open-ended questions   Used in interviews and surveys, these questions can't be answered with a "yes" or "no" and allow the participant to elaborate on the question's topic.

Organization chart   This traditional chart shows how the organization is broken down by department and disciplines. This chart is sometimes called the Organizational Breakdown Structure (OBS) and is arranged by departments, units, or teams.

Passive stakeholder observation   Sometimes called invisible observation, this is when the business analyst observes the stakeholder's activity without any interaction with the person doing the work.

Prototype   A basic mockup of what the final project deliverable may look like.

RACI chart A matrix chart that uses only the activities of *responsible, accountable, consult,* and *inform* for assignment mapping.

Requirements workshop Sometimes called a Joint Application Design (JAD) workshop, this brings the key stakeholders together to define the requirements for the project. This meeting can be used to clarify the project scope, refine existing requirements, and gain stakeholder consensus on the priorities of the project.

Resource Breakdown Structure (RBS) This hierarchical chart can break down the business problem or opportunity by the type of resources affected by the project. An RBS is an excellent tool for tracking resource utilization and resource costs, and to help formulate questions.

Responsibility Assignment Matrix (RAM) A RAM chart shows the correlation between project team members and the work they've been assigned to complete. A RAM chart doesn't necessarily have to be specific to individual team members; it can also be decomposed to project groups or units.

Stakeholder observation A requirements elicitation approach where the business analyst observes the stakeholder working to determine how the work is actually completed.

Surveys A requirements elicitation technique to quickly gain insight and feedback from a large group of stakeholders. Surveys can be anonymous or participants' identities could be known for follow-up questions from the survey.

Throwaway prototype A simple prototype sample that may be just a sketch of the proposed system. It helps the customer and the developer see the system in recognizable components.

User interfaces User interfaces describe the actual users who interact with one another, a system, or data moved between two users.

Vertical method prototyping An approach that creates an in-depth analysis deep prototype of just one portion of the system's functionality. It can be costly and time intensive, but proves the functionality of a system's key processes.

Questions

1. You've been tasked with interviewing several stakeholders about a new software for their organization. Which one of the following pieces of information will help you the most as you prepare for the interview?

   A. Knowing what decisions, if any, this person makes about software purchases.

   B. Knowing who the person reports to within the organization.

   C. Understanding what data is currently available about this individual and his role in the organization.

   D. Understanding what type of data and information this individual sends and receives.

2. Which of the following statements is most accurate about closed-ended questions for an interview?

   A. You should never use closed-ended questions in an interview.

   B. You should use some closed-ended questions, as they allow the interviewee the opportunity to elaborate on the question's answer.

   C. You should use some closed-ended questions, as they prompt the interviewee for specific information.

   D. You should use all closed-ended questions in an interview to keep the interview duration to a minimum for all participants.

3. Which chart type can show how an organization is structured by department and disciplines?

   A. Organizational Breakdown Structure

   B. Work Breakdown Structure

   C. Responsibility Assignment Matrix

   D. Resource Breakdown Structure

4. What chart can help the business analyst identify the resources that will be needed throughout the solution implementation?

   A. Organization chart

   B. Resource breakdown chart

   C. Responsibility assignment matrix

   D. Work Breakdown Structure

5. You are the business analyst for your organization. Management has asked that you create a method to survey the respondents anonymously as part of your requirements gathering technique. They'd like for you to use rounds of anonymous surveys to build consensus among the stakeholders. What type of technique does management want you to use?

   A. Delphi technique

   B. Open-ended survey technique

   C. Close-ended survey technique

   D. Hybrid question survey technique

6. Which one of the following is not an output of a brainstorming session for requirements elicitation?

   A. Helps determine constraints on the project team, the project, or the organization and how they might be removed

   B. Identifies risks within the solution

C. Encourages stakeholder participation

D. Fosters team building

7. You want to perform a brainstorming session with your key project stakeholders. Your assistant Thomas wants to invite all of the stakeholders to the session. There are 37 stakeholders. What is the ideal number of stakeholders that should participate in a brainstorming session for a new product?

   A. 6–8 participants

   B. 10–15 participants

   C. 15–30 participants

   D. 30, but no more than 50 participants

8. Your organization has just created a new piece of software that will go on sale within a few weeks to the public. You are hosting a focus group for this new solution. What information should the focus group tell you about this newly created software?

   A. The focus group will evaluate the business opportunity, help determine requirements, and analyze existing requirements.

   B. The focus group could help determine the value of the new software.

   C. The focus group could help the organization determine how to best position the new software in the marketplace.

   D. The focus group could offer advice on improving the new software and offer insight as to what their perception of the software may be.

9. Mary Anne is observing a stakeholder completing a complex process as part of her requirements elicitation business analysis duties. She is stopping the stakeholder with every step of the work to ask questions about what the stakeholder is doing. How would you describe this scenario between Mary Anne and the stakeholder?

   A. Ineffective observation techniques

   B. Passive stakeholder observation

   C. Invisible observation

   D. Active stakeholder observation

10. A requirements workshop is sometimes referred to by what term when it comes to software development?

    A. Joint Application Design workshop

    B. Joint Committee Design workshop

    C. Joint Application and Software workshop

    D. Joint Application Development workshop

11. During interviews and focus groups what participant must keep the minutes and details of the conversation?

    A. Scribe

    B. Business analyst

    C. Project manager

    D. Business analyst assistant

12. You are the business analyst for your organization. You'd like to create a survey to quickly gather information about the business opportunity and gather requirements for the proposed project. You want to ensure that the respondents complete the survey within two weeks. What approach can you take to complete this survey with the given deadline?

    A. Offer an incentive for the stakeholders completing the survey within the two-week time frame.

    B. Offer the survey via the Internet.

    C. Deliver the survey with a coupon for a free coffee.

    D. Create a mandate that all of the stakeholders must complete the survey within two weeks, or they'll be reprimanded.

13. What type of interface exists between a stakeholder and an automated teller cash machine?

    A. External

    B. User

    C. Logistical

    D. Software

14. Mary Anne described how she'd like her software to operate and interact with web users. As she discussed the model, Marty sketched out the specifics on a cocktail napkin. Mary Anne reviewed the model and, with some clarifications, agreed that Marty had captured her basic requirements for the software. What term best describes this elicitation requirements activity?

    A. Interview

    B. Evolutionary prototype

    C. Throwaway prototype

    D. Focus group

15. You are the business analyst for your organization and are preparing to interview the stakeholders. You need to collect information from the stakeholders about how they currently fulfill orders that are taken over the Internet. You'd like the stakeholders to each discuss the order placement process and all the activities they do surrounding the process. What type of

elicitation would allow the stakeholders to freely discuss their role in the order taking process?

A. Structured interview

B. Unstructured interview

C. Focus group

D. Horizontal prototyping

16. You are documenting the roles of the stakeholders in your solution and need to create a chart to track the resources and how they're grouped by discipline. What type of chart should you create?

A. Resource Breakdown Structure

B. Organizational Breakdown Structure

C. Work breakdown Structure

D. RACI chart

17. Which one of the following is a negative aspect of interviewing stakeholders as part of requirements elicitation?

A. Limited number of people to interview

B. Time availability of the interview process

C. Determination of what the interviewee does for the organization

D. Documentation of the interview answers

18. At the end of an interview process what should the business analyst always ask the stakeholder?

A. How long they've worked within the organization.

B. What information they need to complete their functions within the organization.

C. How soon they expect a solution for the identified business problem.

D. If they have additional information to add to the interview.

19. You are hosting a brainstorming session. Why should you not set a goal of the number of ideas the participants should create for the proposed solution?

A. If the group doesn't reach the goal of the number of solutions, they may view the session as a failure.

B. If the group doesn't reach the goal of the number of solutions, the meeting will continue to run and the quality of ideas will suffer.

C. The group may rush to list as many ideas as possible to end the meeting as soon as possible.

D. Setting a goal on the number of proposed solutions sets a cap on the number of ideas and will limit good ideas beyond the identified goal.

20. You have proposed a two-day workshop to gather requirements from the key stakeholders in a potential business opportunity. It is uncertain if your organization should invest in a new project to seize the business opportunity, and you'd like focused input from the stakeholders. You and the business sponsor have discussed all of the elements the workshop should cover, and you agree with the proposed workshop. You need all of the following elements for the workshop to be successful except for which one?

A. Knowledgeable stakeholders in attendance

B. Structured agenda for each workshop participant

C. Clear identification of the project solution for the participants to discuss

D. Reservation of facilities, meals, and logistics

Questions and Answers

1. You've been tasked with interviewing several stakeholders about a new software for their organization. Which one of the following pieces of information will help you the most as you prepare for the interview?

A. Knowing what decisions, if any, this person makes about software purchases.

B. Knowing who the person reports to within the organization.

C. Understanding what data is currently available about this individual and his role in the organization.

D. Understanding what type of data and information this individual sends and receives.

D. Of all the items presented, D, understanding how an individual receives, processes, and sends data will help you the most during requirements elicitation in an interview process. You don't need to know what decisions this person makes about software purchases for an interview about a new software, so choice A is incorrect. Choice B is also incorrect, as the person's manager isn't necessarily being interviewed. The interview is to gather information about the proposed software, not organizational hierarchy. Choice C is also incorrect, as it describes a definition of a role and responsibility for the person being interviewed.

2. Which of the following statements is most accurate about closed-ended questions for an interview?

A. You should never use closed-ended questions in an interview.

B. You should use some closed-ended questions, as they allow the interviewee the opportunity to elaborate on the question's answer.

C. You should use some closed-ended questions, as they prompt the interviewee for specific information.

D. You should use all closed-ended questions in an interview to keep the interview duration to a minimum for all participants.

    C. You should use some closed-ended questions, as they do prompt exact answers. Choices A, B, and D are false statements about closed-ended questions and interviews, so these choices are incorrect.

3. Which chart type can show how an organization is structured by department and disciplines?

    A. Organizational Breakdown Structure

    B. Work Breakdown Structure

    C. Responsibility Assignment Matrix

    D. Resource Breakdown Structure

    A. The Organizational Breakdown Structure defines the hierarchy of an organization. B, the Work Breakdown Structure, is a visual decomposition of the project scope, so this choice is wrong. C, a Responsibility Assignment Matrix, maps roles to responsibilities within an organization, project, or business analysis activities. D, a Resource Breakdown Structure, is a chart that shows how organizational resources are utilized within a project.

4. What chart can help the business analyst identify the resources that will be needed throughout the solution implementation?

    A. Organization chart

    B. Resource breakdown chart

    C. Responsibility assignment matrix

    D. Work breakdown structure

    B. A resource breakdown chart shows a breakdown of the scope and what resources will be needed in each subdivision of the project. A, the organization chart, shows how an organization is structured by function or by management. C, The responsibility assignment matrix, is a table that maps resources to their tasks in the project. D, the Work Breakdown Structure (WBS), is incorrect. The WBS shows the deliverables for each component of the project, not the resources required to create the deliverables.

5. You are the business analyst for your organization. Management has asked that you create a method to survey the respondents anonymously as part of your requirements gathering technique. They'd like for you to use rounds of anonymous surveys to build consensus among the stakeholders. What type of technique does management want you to use?

    A. Delphi technique

    B. Open-ended survey technique

    C. Close-ended survey technique

    D. Hybrid question survey technique

    A. The Delphi Technique uses rounds of anonymous surveys to build consensus on project requirements. Choices B and C aren't really survey techniques, but descriptions of the type of questions a survey can have. Open-ended questions prompt the survey responder to answer questions in an essay format. Close-ended questions can be answer directly, like or yes or no. D, the hybrid question survey technique, is not a valid answer or survey type.

6. Which one of the following is not an output of a brainstorming session for requirements elicitation?

   A. Helps determine constraints on the project team, the project, or the organization and how they might be removed

   B. Identifies risks within the solution

   C. Encourages stakeholder participation

   D. Fosters team building

   B. Risk identification is not a typical output of a brainstorming session, but it is an output of the risk identification meeting. Choices A, C, and D are all acceptable outcomes of a brainstorming session.

7. You want to perform a brainstorming session with your key project stakeholders. Your assistant Thomas wants to invite all of the stakeholders to the session. There are 37 stakeholders. What is the ideal number of stakeholders that should participate in a brainstorming session for a new product?

   A. 6–8 participants

   B. 10–15 participants

   C. 15–30 participants

   D. 30, but no more than 50 participants

   A. Brainstorming sessions are highly interactive meetings, and results of participants need to be quickly documented, preferably in the meeting for all participants to see. The visual documentation of a brainstorming session can help other participants think of new ideas. If the number of participants is too large, such as answers B, C, and D, then the meeting may be ineffective and hard to manage. Having six to eight participants is ideal.

8. Your organization has just created a new piece of software that will go on sale within a few weeks to the public. You are hosting a focus group for this new solution. What information should the focus group tell you about this newly created software?

   A. The focus group will evaluate the business opportunity, help determine requirements, and analyze existing requirements.

   B. The focus group could help determine the value of the new software.

   C. The focus group could help the organization determine how to best position the new software in the marketplace.

   D. The focus group could offer advice on improving the new software and offer insight as to what their perception of the software may be.

   C. As this solution has already been created, the focus group will contribute information as to how the solution should be marketed. Choice A is ideal for a new, undeveloped opportunity. Choice B is ideal for a product that's currently in development. Choice D could be good for software that is being upgraded by the organization.

9. Mary Anne is observing a stakeholder completing a complex process as part of her requirements elicitation business analysis duties. She is stopping the stakeholder with every step of the work to ask questions about what the stakeholder is doing. How would you describe this scenario between Mary Anne and the stakeholder?

   A. Ineffective observation techniques

   B. Passive stakeholder observation

   C. Invisible observation

   D. Active stakeholder observation

   D. As Mary Anne stops the stakeholder at each step of the process, she's completing active stakeholder observation. As part of this activity, Mary Anne should have communicated to the stakeholder that she'd be stopping and asking lots of questions throughout the process. Choices A, B, and C are all incorrect answers. Note that choices B and C are the same, as passive stakeholder observation and invisible observation require the observer to be silent and just watch the process.

10. A requirements workshop is sometimes referred to by what term when it comes to software development?

    A. Joint Application Design workshop

    B. Joint Committee Design workshop

    C. Joint Application and Software workshop

    D. Joint Application Development workshop

    A. A requirements workshop during software development is also known as a Joint Application Design workshop. Choices B, C, and D are all incorrect choices and terms.

11. During interviews and focus groups what participant must keep the minutes and details of the conversation?

    A. Scribe

    B. Business analyst

    C. Project manager

    D. Business analyst assistant

    A. A scribe documents all of the conversations within the meeting. The BABOK mentions the term *scribe* several times when it comes to recording the details of a meeting. Choices B, C, and D are all incorrect.

12. You are the business analyst for your organization. You'd like to create a survey to quickly gather information about the business opportunity and gather requirements for the proposed project. You want to ensure that the respondents complete the survey within two weeks. What approach can you take to complete this survey with the given deadline?

   A. Offer an incentive for the stakeholders completing the survey within the two-week time frame.

   B. Offer the survey via the Internet.

   C. Deliver the survey with a coupon for a free coffee.

   D. Create a mandate that all of the stakeholders must complete the survey within two weeks, or they'll be reprimanded.

   A. By offering an incentive for the respondents, you'll likely receive more responses to the survey—assuming the incentive is something the stakeholders actually want. Choice B is incorrect, because the Internet delivery does not ensure that people will respond any sooner or at all. C is a good idea, but the free coffee coupon is received by the respondent regardless of completing the survey. D is wrong, because the mandate isn't applicable to all surveys, and the business analyst may not have any authority over the survey takers.

13. What type of interface exists between a stakeholder and an automated teller cash machine?

   A. External

   B. User

   C. Logistical

   D. Software

   B. This is an example of a user interface; recall that an interface is a link between any two components in a system. Choices A and D are legitimate interfaces, but these do not interact with people. Choice C is not a valid interface, so this answer is wrong.

14. Mary Anne described how she'd like her software to operate and interact with web users. As she discussed the model, Marty sketched out the specifics on a cocktail napkin. Mary Anne reviewed the model and, with some clarifications, agreed that Marty had captured her basic requirements for the software. What term best describes this elicitation requirements activity?

   A. Interview

   B. Evolutionary prototype

   C. Throwaway prototype

   D. Focus group

   C. A quick sketch of a system is an excellent example of a throwaway prototype. A is tempting, but the scenario doesn't really describe an interview. Recall that interviews just record information and don't offer suggestions. B is incorrect, as an evolutionary prototype is a working model that evolves over time. D is incorrect, as the scenario does not describe a focus group.

15. You are the business analyst for your organization and are preparing to interview the stakeholders. You need to collect information from the stakeholders about how they currently fulfill orders that are taken over the Internet. You'd like the stakeholders to each discuss the order placement process and all the activities they do surrounding the process. What type of elicitation would allow the stakeholders to freely discuss their role in the order taking process?

   A. Structured interview

   B. Unstructured interview

   C. Focus group

   D. Horizontal prototyping

   B. An unstructured interview allows each stakeholder to freely discuss their role in the order-taking process. It's more conversational than choice A, structured interview. Focus groups, choice C, bring a group of stakeholders together and a moderator guides the conversation. D, horizontal prototyping, is not the best choice, as this choice describes a wide, shallow view of a deliverable in a model format.

16. You are documenting the roles of the stakeholders in your solution and need to create a chart to track the resources and how they're grouped by discipline. What type of chart should you create?

   A. Resource Breakdown Structure

   B. Organizational Breakdown Structure

   C. Work Breakdown Structure

   D. RACI chart

   A. A Resource Breakdown Structure shows which resources are needed in the project and allows you to group the resources by discipline, project phase, or other attribute. B is incorrect as an Organizational Breakdown Structure shows the entire organization and who reports to whom. C is incorrect as a WBS is a decomposition of the project scope into work packages. D is also incorrect as RACI charts are a Responsibility Assignment Matrix.

17. Which one of the following is a negative aspect of interviewing stakeholders as part of requirements elicitation?

   A. Limited amount of people to interview

   B. Time availability of the interview process

   C. Determination of what the interviewee does for the organization

   D. Documentation of the interview answers

   B. Interviewing stakeholders can be a productive, but time-consuming process. Choices A, C, and D are all positive aspects of interviewing stakeholders, so these choices are incorrect.

18. At the end of an interview process what should the business analyst always ask the stakeholder?

    A. How long they've worked within the organization.

    B. What information they need to complete their functions within the organization.

    C. How soon they expect a solution for the identified business problem.

    D. If they have additional information to add to the interview.

    D. The interviewer should always give the interviewee the opportunity to add any relevant information to the conversation. Choices A, B, and C are all inappropriate questions to wrap an interview with, so these choices are wrong.

19. You are hosting a brainstorming session. Why should you not set a goal of the number of ideas the participants should create for the proposed solution?

    A. If the group doesn't reach the goal of the number of solutions, they may view the session as a failure.

    B. If the group doesn't reach the goal of the number of solutions, the meeting will continue to run and the quality of ideas will suffer.

    C. The group may rush to list as many ideas as possible to end the meeting as soon as possible.

    D. Setting a goal on the number of proposed solutions sets a cap on the number of ideas and will limit good ideas beyond the identified goal.

    D. Of all the choices presented, D is the most accurate. Setting a goal is actually setting a limit on the number of ideas the group may create. Choice A may be true, but it's not the primary reason for not setting a number goal for the group. Choice B could happen, but time constraints would likely force the meeting to end. Choice C may be true, but it's not as accurate as choice D according to the BABOK.

20. You have proposed a two-day workshop to gather requirements from the key stakeholders in a potential business opportunity. It is uncertain if your organization should invest in a new project to seize the business opportunity, and you'd like focused input from the stakeholders. You and the business sponsor have discussed all of the elements the workshop should cover, and you agree with the proposed workshop. You need all of the following elements for the workshop to be successful except for which one?

    A. Knowledgeable stakeholders in attendance

    B. Structured agenda for each workshop participant

C. Clear identification of the project solution for the participants to discuss

D. Reservation of facilities, meals, and logistics

C. You would not provide a clear identification of the project solution for the participants, as that's the point of the workshop. Choices A, B, and D are things that are required for the workshop, so these choices are incorrect answers.

Managing Requirements Communication

In this chapter you will
- Manage the scope of project requirements
- Manage requirements conflicts
- Create a requirements package
- Present requirements information
- Obtain stakeholder sign-off for requirements

If you ever think you're talking with people all day long as a business analyst, you're probably right. Communication is a constant business analysis activity, as you've got to talk with end users, experts, the project team, the project manager, management, vendors, and any other stakeholders who are affected by the proposed solution. Communication is a vital business analysis process and talent.

Half of communication, however, is listening. You've got to formulate your questions and thoughts to get the right responses from your stakeholders. It won't do you much good if you're constantly talking and stakeholders never contribute to the conversation. The point of communication is to elicit facts, opinions, and requirements from the project stakeholders.

This business analysis knowledge area will account for nearly 11 percent of your CBAP examination score. That equates to roughly 16 questions on communication. Five processes focus on communication:

- **Manage solutions scope and requirements** The business analyst works with stakeholders to form consensus on the solution scope that will be implemented.

- **Manage requirements traceability** The business analyst will create a system to trace requirements to solutions, business owners, stakeholders, other requirements, and documents created during business analysis processes.

- **Maintain requirements for reuse** The business analyst will take measures to archive and preserve requirements for the organization that can be utilized post-implementation for other similar projects and solutions.

- **Prepare requirements package**   The business analyst will create requirements documentation that is usable by and understandable to the stakeholders.

- **Communicate requirements**   The business analyst will accurately communicate with the stakeholders about the requirements, issues, risks, status, and other relevant information in a timely and concise manner.

Manage the Scope of Project Requirements

The scope of the project really represents everything that is required for the customer to accept the delivery of the project. While there are overlaps into time and cost concerns, the primary objective of managing the requirements scope is to ensure that all of the requirements are captured, documented, and planned for achievement in the project. Some of this business may fall into the realm of project management in your organization, but you should be familiar with this business analysis task for your CBAP exam.

The requirements scope serves as the baseline of project expectations for acceptance. The agreed scope of the requirements should be used by the project management team, project team members, and project customers as a point of reference for all future project decisions. Quality of the project deliverables is directly tied to achieving the requirements scope; should the deliverables not meet the stated requirements, then the project is faulty and quality has not been achieved to the documented level.

The project manager will need the requirements scope when change requests come from project customers. The requirements scope will serve as a point of reference for the original requests, and all future additions or subtractions from the requirements scope will need to be justified. The requirements scope should be protected from change once it has been agreed upon by all stakeholders—you don't want the change process to be easy, so the scope documentation must be rigid and exact.

Creating a Requirements Baseline

It's easy to see two baselines within project management: time and cost. The third baseline is not always so easy to see: the project requirements. A *baseline* is the standard agreement that all pending change requests are measured against. The requirements baseline is also the standard for changes that were not approved, such as scope creep, defects, or poor quality within the project. The results of unapproved changes must be corrected to be in alignment with the project scope.

When stakeholders sign off on the requirements scope, they're agreeing that these identified things will serve as the baseline for the project, and these things are demanded for the project to be accepted. The requirements baseline is the equivalent of the project solution scope. If the project does not create and utilize a scope baseline, then the project can wander, additions to the scope can sneak in, and it's next to impossible to have accountability for what's been created or forgotten during the project execution.

Requirements baselines that have been signed and agreed to by the customers are sometimes called the snapshot of the desired future state. This snapshot of requirements is what's referenced through project management in estimating, planning, resource management, and scope validation at the end of phases or when milestones are created. Your organization may have a more formal term for the requirements snapshot, such as the Business Requirements Document, Specification System Requirements Document, or simply the Detailed Design Document. Whatever name you apply to the requirements scope, the scope should be agreed to by all stakeholders and added to the project binder.

Creating Requirements Traceability Options

Requirements traceability allows for each project requirement to be traced from its conception in the requirements documentation to its implementation in the project execution phase. Traceability ensures that each requirement is accounted for, and its implementation is tracked to execution, costs, and timing. Traceability also ensures that all of the stakeholders are kept abreast of project progress, status of requirements, and a link between the requirements and the business benefit the deliverable creates. In longer, larger projects, it's vital to track each requirement from concept to implementation, as there are more details that can be overlooked, forgotten, or pushed to the edge of the project (by accident or on purpose).

You'll also find that requirements traceability will help the project manager and you manage and control the requirements scope. Traceability can assist with the scope management process by:

- Tracking functional requirements to business requirements or features of the deliverable to confirm the business analyst, project manager, and project team fully understand what the project customer is requesting.

- Tracking design functions to the functional requirements and features, which prevents scope creep. Recall that scope creep is the addition of small changes that bypass the scope change control process; the seemingly innocent changes steal time and cost from the project.

- Tracing all features of the project deliverables to work packages in the WBS to ensure that all deliverables are fully and accurately met.

- Tracing changes to the project scope to all elements of the requirements to determine what areas of the project deliverable may be affected by the proposed changes.

- Tracing changes to the requirements scope to time and cost impacts to measure their overall impact on the project.

- Tracing work packages and project activities to the requirements they are related to.

- Working with quality control to ensure that all work and deliverables are mapped to the requested requirements.

For each requirement that will be tracked, the business analyst should document and maintain all of the following information:

- **Requirement source** Identifies where the requirement originated and which stakeholders need to be communicated with about this requirement.

- **Requirements linking** Identifies which requirements are linked to other requirements in function, feature, or deliverable. This tracking helps determine the whole impact of changes to the requirements scope.

- **Requirements rationale** Defines why the requirement was included and what business goal(s) the requirement supports.

- **Requirements testing** Defines which requirements will need to be tested to validate delivery and acceptability.

- **Requirements interface** Defines what systems, processes, and functional organizations the requirement may interact with. This helps with requirements testing and scope change control.

To begin requirements traceability, the business analysis team and the project manager should agree on how the requirements will be traced, as there are several different approaches. All requirements should be assigned a globally unique identifier to specify the requirements throughout the project and traceability. Of course in order to create the unique identifier, the business analyst must have well-defined requirements that have been approved by the project stakeholders. All of the project deliverables must be met in order to satisfy the linked requirements.

One of the most common approaches for requirements traceability is a *Requirements Traceability Matrix* (RTM). The RTM tracks deliverables to the specific requirements and verifies that the deliverable does or does not satisfy the requirements. The RTM maps multiple elements of the project deliverable to satisfy the requirements. Wherever there's a gap between the defined requirement and the project deliverable, additional work needs to be done. If there is no relationship between the two identifiers in the table, then the business analyst will place a zero in the table's cell.

Maintaining the Requirements Scope

Changes to the project requirements aren't that unusual. External events, new technologies, shifts in priorities, and old-fashioned errors can all contribute to a desire to change the scope of requirements. Once the requirements have been created and signed by the stakeholders, the first reaction to change should be hesitant at best. Persistent changes to the requirements scope will only delay the project, frustrate the project manager and project team, and drive costs.

The change management process should be documented and explained to the project customer so there's no confusion on the process, fees, and reasons why change requests to the requirements may be delayed. Change requests must always be in writing with an explanation of why the change is needed. In addition, an identifier is attached to the change request so it can be tracked, reported, and archived. A typical change request process is shown in Figure 4-1, and I'll walk you through the process here.

- The change request is documented and entered into the information system. This can be Microsoft Project, Excel, a database, or even a word processor. The point is that you should document and electronically store the change request for easy reference, tracking, and for archiving its outcome.

- The attributes of the requirements scope change request are documented. When possible, determine and document the full impact of the requirements change request on work that's already been completed and the link between the change and other requirements.

- Integrated change control is the process of examining all areas of the project and seeing how the change might affect them. You and the project manager should consider time, cost, scope, quality, human resources, communication, risk, and any procurement issues.

- If a scope change is approved, it should be documented as part of configuration management. *Configuration management* defines the features and functions of the approved change request and how it will be used as part of the deliverables.

- An approved decision then gets documented into the requirements, and the project manager folds the decision into the project management plan execution, and control.

All change requests, approved or declined, are tracked and communicated to the appropriate stakeholders. There should be no question at the end of the project why a change request was or was not implemented. This helps as part of requirements traceability and scope validation by the project manager and the business analyst.

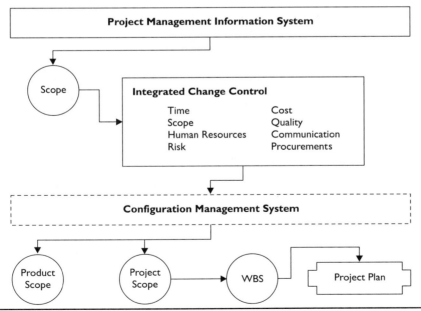

Figure 4-1   The control process must be well documented before the project begins.

Some changes happen without a proper change request: errors, scope creep, and misunderstandings by the project team executing the work. In these instances, the most prudent thing to do is to evaluate the unapproved change and see if it's worth the current time and costs to fix the error, or instead to leave the error in the project. In some instances it's more cost-effective to live with the mistake, while other times it's best to repair the problem to keep the project in alignment with the scope baseline.

NOTE If the choice is made to keep the error as part of the deliverable, there must be a change control process to gain approval to keep the error in the project. The customer may, and often does, object to the error, and the project team must fix the problem.

When changes to the requirements scope are approved, the requirements baseline must be updated to reflect the new changes. This is true for all changes that are made to the requirements scope—even when you take things out of the scope (called *de-scoping*). When items are removed from or added to the scope, you've changed the requirements scope, and a new version is needed. When you re-version the requirements baseline, you'll document the new version, what's been changed, and reference supporting detail for the change. You'll also update the Requirements Traceability Matrix for ongoing requirements tracking.

Using a Communications Formula

As a general rule, the larger the project requirements, the more communication the business analyst and the project manager can expect. Larger projects require more detail, and the project manager and the business analyst should expect to spend more time on communications when the project is a high-profile, large project. That shouldn't surprise anyone.

What may be a surprise, however, is how many opportunities there are for communications to break down. Consider all of the different people who can talk about your requirements—whether or not they have accurate information. Rumors, misconceptions, and misunderstandings can shake the confidence of project stakeholders.

There's a nifty formula to demonstrate project communication demands based on the number of project stakeholders. The formula is $N(N - 1)/2$, where N represents the number of project stakeholders, and the formula shows the number of communication channels in the project.

For example, consider a project with 81 stakeholders. The formula would be $81(81 - 1)/2$ or 3,240 communication channels within the project. That's 3,240 opportunities for communications to fail. Imagine a larger project, and you can see how easily communication can break down. Communication is key to stakeholder management.

Manage Conflicting Requirements

When it comes to project requirements, not everyone can have everything. Trade-offs, compromises, and flat-out denials aren't that unusual in business analysis, requirements gathering, and project management. Identifying, documenting, and facilitating the conflicting requirements are part of the business analyst's unpleasant duties. It's important to identify requirements without making promises initially to evaluate all wants, wishes, and demands of all the stakeholders represented. You don't want to paint yourself into a corner, so to speak, by making promises for project inclusion to any particular stakeholder without considering all of the other stakeholders and their needs as well.

Conflicts will happen among stakeholders but also within the requirements. Competing objectives, such as time and cost constraints, can often skew a project from feasibility. Urgent deadlines typically mean higher costs to achieve the deadlines, because of the added labor, additional quality control activities, and prioritized schedule. When organizations have a predetermined budget in mind for a given set of requirements, they may be setting up themselves, and the project, for failure, as reduction in costs may lower the quality of the deliverable. Expectations must be managed, and this is part of conflict management.

The goal of requirements gathering is to identify the business needs of the project. By understanding the symptoms of the problem and the problem itself, the business analyst can better serve the organization. Often the stakeholders want the symptoms treated without addressing the deeper issue that's causing their pain. Attached to the perceived stakeholder solutions may be pet projects, political aspirations, and personal agendas. It's the business analyst's role to cautiously pick through what's needed for the project success and the non-value-added requirements.

Identifying and Managing Conflicts

When you identify a requirements conflict, the first thing you'll need to do is record the conflict and its attributes in the *Requirements Issue Log*. The Requirements Issue Log can be as fancy as a database, though a spreadsheet will probably be just fine. You'll need to record the issue, the attributes of the conflict, the stakeholders involved, and the ramifications of the conflict on the other requirements within the project.

As the requirements gathering process moves forward, changes and updates to the recorded issue are probably likely. When you learn more information, the issue changes, or when the issue becomes resolved, you'll want to document that information as well in the Requirements Issue Log. It's important to keep accurate and timely information on requirements conflicts so they can be quickly and easily addressed.

Once the issue has been documented, then the business analyst should communicate with the stakeholders involved in the conflicting issue. The point isn't to heat up the situation, but rather to let all parties know that a requirements conflict exists, the conflict has been acknowledged and documented, and you're working toward a reasonable solution. For many issues the conflicts can be addressed through research, testing, and additional analysis.

Other conflicts, however, may require face-to-face negotiations among the stakeholders to reach a consensus on the conflict and resolution. In these instances it's important for the business analyst to create an agenda of the conflict resolution meeting, set the goal of the meeting, and to document the conversation. Meeting management techniques such as setting a time limit keep the stakeholders on target, and having minutes taken during the meeting can help keep the conversation civil and both parties working together for a solution.

All requirements conflicts should be documented, and an audit trail of their status and outcome is needed. This means that all communication, promises, and resolutions should be documented by the business analyst and communicated to the stakeholders. Once a resolution has been reached among the stakeholders, the business analyst should create a Conflict Resolution Document and obtain sign-off for the resolution. The resolution should also be referenced in the Requirements Issue Log.

Implementing Conflict Resolution

Let's face facts: the business analyst doesn't always have the power or position to sway stakeholders on some requirements conflicts. The stakeholders may be influential, powerful, and big decision makers in the organization. The lowly business analyst, or so it seems, is often the facilitator of the wants and demands of others. To some extent, that's the role of the business analyst, to determine the requirements of others. Unfortunately this often means that the business analyst does less analysis and more wish-granting.

When conflicts arise among stakeholders over requirements for the project, the goal should be to do what's best for the organization. You know that doesn't always happen, and you've probably seen management and others bully their way through conflicts. You've probably, I hope, also seen some cooperation among stakeholders to reach the best solution for the good of the project's deliverables. Here are some conflict resolution approaches that a business analyst can participate in:

- **Problem solving** This conflict resolution approach uses a spirit of cooperation among the stakeholders. Problem solving tackles the problem head-on and is the preferred method of conflict resolution. Sometimes this approach is defined as "confronting" rather than problem solving. Problem solving calls for additional research to find the best solution for the problem, and it's a win-win solution. It should be used if there is time to work through and resolve the issue. It also serves to build relationships and trust. The business analyst is the facilitator of the problem-solving technique.

- **Forcing** You've seen forcing used when the person in the conflict with the most power forces the decision. The decision made may not be the best decision for the project, but it's fast. As expected, this autocratic approach does little for relationship building and is a win-lose solution. You know a solution is being forced when someone with seniority or power makes a decision without considering the other parties' objectives.

- **Compromising** While compromising sounds nice, it really means that both parties must give up something. The decision made is a blend of both sides of the argument. Because neither party really wins, it is considered a lose-lose solution. The business analyst can use this approach when the relationships are equal and no one can truly "win."

- **Smoothing** This approach "smoothes" out the conflict by minimizing the perceived size of the problem. It is a temporary solution, but can calm stakeholder relations and boisterous discussions. Smoothing may be acceptable when time is of the essence or when any of the proposed solutions will not currently settle the problem. This can be considered a lose-lose situation as well, since no one really wins in the long run. The business analyst can use smoothing to emphasize areas of agreement between disagreeing stakeholders and, thus, to minimize areas of conflict. It's used to maintain relationships and when the issue is not critical.

- **Withdrawal** This conflict resolution has one side of the argument walking away from the problem, usually in disgust. You can recognize withdrawal when one party refuses to participate in the conflict resolution any longer and surrenders to the other stakeholders. The conflict is not really resolved, and it is considered a yield-lose solution. The approach can be used, however, as a cooling-off period or when the issue is not critical.

In all of these instances, the business analyst should document the conversation and the details of the conflict resolution meeting, and should update the Requirements Issue Log. Once the decision has been made about the conflict, the business analyst should obtain signatures from all parties involved in the conflict on a conflict resolution document. The signatures are part of the conflict audit and prevent stakeholders from raising the issue later in the project and claiming they weren't aware of the solution.

Determine the Requirements Format

One of the trickier parts of communicating project requirements to all of the stakeholders is to choose the most appropriate format for the communication. The business analyst does not want to speak above the stakeholders by being too technical about the requirements, nor does the business analyst want to speak below the expectations of the stakeholders.

The business analyst must choose the most appropriate method for communicating requirements to each type of stakeholder. This means that there may be several types of communication created for all of the different types of project stakeholders. The message of each communication about project requirements must be concise and contain the appropriate level of information for each stakeholder. It's a primary responsibility of the business analyst to communicate the requirements in the most appropriate format for the project stakeholders.

As a business analyst, you may find yourself creating multiple formats of the requirements to convey the information to multiple stakeholders in the communication method the stakeholders prefer. You may create diagrams, text descriptions, and even prototypes to help you convey the requirements details to the stakeholders.

In some instances the business analyst may need to create additional documentation to explain the project requirements such as user manuals, presentations, and even user stories. The reason the business analyst would take these extra communication steps is to ensure that the requirements are fully and completely understood by the stakeholders before the project work begins. A clear understanding between the business analyst and the stakeholders will ensure that the project execution and scope acceptance will go much more smoothly.

Identifying Communication Preferences

With multiple audiences of stakeholders such as executives, end users, and developers, the business analyst must identify the communication preferences for each audience. The goal is to set expectations for communication for all audiences about the requirements documentation and communication. This information should be included as part of the Requirements Communications Plan or included as an addendum to the requirements gathering. In either instance, the business analyst must understand the communication expectations of the stakeholders in order to satisfy those communication expectations.

 NOTE The best format to use for communicating requirements is the format that best satisfies the stakeholders' expectations for requirements. In other words, understanding what the stakeholders expect from the business analyst will make it easier to satisfy their needs.

Typical stakeholders and their communication expectations include

- **Executive sponsors and management** This group will likely want high-level requirements and summaries. They're not interested, usually, in the fine details and inner workings of the requirements. Management will want to see how the investment in the solution will help the organization grow, what the return on investment will be, and in some instances how operation costs can be cut by implementing the requirements.

- **Technical designers** These people will want the specifics of the requirements as they relate to the form, function, interface, and how the solution will be used once it's created. While business objectives are often included for technical designers, their primary focus will be on how the deliverables are to be utilized in the organization.

- **End users** The recipients of the deliverables, often the largest audience, need clear and easy-to-understand requirements. End users may be the group that is affected the most by the solution but with the least amount of influence over the solution.

- **Project team** The project team, if they're known at this point, will need information about the success criteria for the requirements so they can plan accordingly.

- **Quality assurance team** The QA group will want to know the business benefits so that they can create testing for the project deliverable. They'll also want to create plans based on the requirements to ensure that the proposed solution matches the expectations of the project customer.

- **Vendors** Depending on the type of project, the vendors will need information about the technical requirements, required materials, and other relevant requirements information.

Your organization may have templates already created for the business analyst to follow for requirements communication. If that's not the case, the business analyst should create communication documents to match what the stakeholders expect—which, in turn, means the business analyst must understand the expectations of the stakeholders when it comes to communication.

Formatting Requirements for Stakeholders

The type of stakeholder who will be reviewing the requirements information should help the business analyst determine what type of format to use for the requirements. The goal of communicating the requirements is always to clearly convey the requirements to confirm that the business analyst and the stakeholders both understand and agree on what the requirements are.

The audience also can dictate the formality and depth of the requirements package, but the organizational structure, type of project, and coordination with outside agencies or vendors may also influence the type of communication the business analyst creates. The business analyst should determine how formal the requirements package and associated documentation should be based on several factors:

- The size of the project may affect the formality of the requirements communication. This is especially true when the project is delivered in multiple coordinated phases and explicit, clear requirements need to be communicated for all participants across the entire project rather than just individual phases within the project.

- If the organization's departments and lines of business involved in the requirements are complex, integrated, and extend beyond the confines of the legal organization, then additional formalities for requirements may be needed. This means when vendors, government agencies, and partnerships are involved, the requirements documentation should be presented in a more formal manner.

- Mission-critical projects demand formal communications. When requirements are mission critical, the business analyst must take additional precautions to ensure that the exactness and clarity of the requirements communication is completely accurate.

- Executive sponsors demand formality. When dealing with upper management, you can typically expect the communication requirements to be formal.

- When government agencies will review the requirements, then a formal approach is needed to ensure compliance with the regulations. Consider any project that is subject to regulatory review to automatically require formal communication.

- Formal requirements communication is also needed when the requirements will be presented as part of a Request for Proposal (RFP) or Request for Quote (RFQ) for vendors.

NOTE A Request for Quote (RFQ) is a request from the buyer to the vendor to provide just a price for the stated work. RFQs are the same thing as an Invitation for Bid (IFB). A Request for Proposal is a document that asks the vendor to provide a much more detailed, solution-driven explanation of how the vendor would complete the work for the buyer. Proposals are time intensive and provide loads more information than a quote or bid. Business analysts might sometimes have a Request for Information (RFI) when they are gathering information to determine which type of solution would be best.

Not every instance, obviously, will require formal communications. What every instance will require, however, are requirements communicated in a way that stakeholders will actually read and understand. You want the stakeholders to actually read and understand the requirements, because you'll also need the stakeholders to approve what you've documented as the requirements.

NOTE The larger the project, the more detail you'll need to provide. Larger projects generally require formal communications rather than conversational requirements documentation. The more formal the documentation, the more time you'll need to create the documentation.

It's tempting to tailor each requirements communication to each group of stakeholders, and often that is the most appropriate approach for communicating requirements. However, multiple communications take time, redundancy, and thoroughness to ensure consistency through each depiction of the project requirements. A checklist can help the business analyst determine what needs to be communicated and to whom.

When the business analyst is considering multiple versions of requirements, she should consider several factors first:

- The level of detail the requirements must possess
- The information that must be communicated

- What each stakeholder audience needs to understand about the requirements
- Each stakeholder audience's preferred method of communication
- The characteristics of the requirement (technical constraint or business function)
- The extent that the requirement is traceable through phases, implementation, and project delivery

By considering the most appropriate communication for each audience, the business analyst can save time, frustration, and can always communicate effectively. Multiple version of requirements demand that the business analyst synchronize several documents when requirements are updated. Should the business analyst not update and communicate requirements changes across all versions of requirements, then stakeholders could be misled, confused, and angry.

If the business analyst fails to update the requirements documentation on several levels, an incorrect understanding of the requirements could cause a misunderstanding by the project manager or project team and lead to the wrong requirements being implemented. The business analyst must also consider that less formal documentation of project requirements may lead to additional risks of the stakeholder not completely understanding the project requirements.

Creating Work Products and Deliverables

The BABOK makes a clear distinction between work products and deliverables. Basically, a *work product* is a work-in-progress version of the requirements presentation. The *deliverable,* when it comes to requirements, is a document that clearly identifies the project deliverables the customer is expecting and that the project is to produce. The BABOK stresses that the business analyst must be careful when sharing work products with stakeholders.

You can probably imagine the danger in sharing work products with stakeholders rather than requirements deliverables. The work product may be taken as fact by the stakeholder when it's not fact, but rather just an intention, direction, or documentation of a conversation. At times it may be necessary to share work products with certain stakeholders, but the business analyst should take precautions and preface the documents as to their status in the requirements gathering process. Typical work products can include

- Meeting agendas and minutes
- Interview questions, notes, and conversations
- Business analyst facilitation notes from stakeholder meetings
- Issues logs
- Work plans and status reports
- Presentation slides
- Traceability matrixes

Deliverables are documents that the project manager will require to show evidence of the work that has been completed on the project and in business analysis duties. The supporting detail of a deliverable is not required as part of the deliverable, though it's a good idea to keep an archive of the supporting detail for future reference.

Create a Requirements Package

A requirements package is the collection of the business analyst's work results. It is the documentation, formulation, and organization of all the requirements the business analyst has gathered from the stakeholders, packaged in a comprehensive set of project requirements. It's the thing the business analyst creates to fully communicate the intent, demands, and requirements for the proposed solution. The requirements package is to be reviewed and approved by the project stakeholders prior to, generally speaking, the launch or continuation of the project.

There are instances, however, where the requirements package could consist of incremental creations for each proposed phase of a project. In these instances, the requirements package should reflect the supporting detail and exact expectations of the succeeding phase of the project. This approach allows the business analyst to append requirements subsets to the requirements package as the work progresses. The danger in this approach, however, is that errors and omissions in the increments package could cause an increase in project costs and delays in the project schedule, as work may be halted to fix defects and adjust the project scope.

In either instance, the requirements package must be complete and effectively written so that the stakeholders can comprehend the intent and demands put upon the project for the desired solution. An ambiguous requirements package will likely cause confusion, frustration, and misunderstandings in the project execution—which of course will mean additional costs and schedule delays in the project.

For your CBAP examination, pay special attention to the completeness and accuracy of the requirements package. The requirements package is the culmination of the work the business analyst has completed, and it's a reflection of the business analyst's performance in the organization. A sloppy, rushed requirements package will certainly result in either rework or defects within the project.

Preparing the Requirements Package

If you've ever taken a speech class, the professor probably told you that the key to giving a good speech was to first know your topic and then, secondly, to know your audience. That's pretty much the same advice you can follow for creating a requirements package. You need to know what the requirements are, and then know who you'll be presenting the requirements to.

Your first mission in the business analysis process is to identify what components should be included in the requirements package. You don't want to include too much information and bog down the requirements details with minutiae, but you also don't want to include too little information so that stakeholders miss the point of the requirements package. You want a balance of factual requirements, detail, and exactness to create a cohesive message of what the requirements are.

The requirements package isn't for you—it's for the stakeholders who will approve the requirements. So you must think, read, and ponder the points as if you were the stakeholders who will approve the requirements based on what you've created. The technical information may make perfect sense to you, but a stakeholder may not understand the technical jargon without adequate explanation.

In some instances, especially larger projects, the business analyst may need to create multiple versions of requirements packages for each audience that will need to approve the requirements. When the business analyst creates multiple versions of the requirements package to be reviewed and approved by different sets of stakeholders, she'll need to confirm consistency throughout all of the packages for the same deliverables.

Larger projects may also require the business analyst to present the same information to different sets of stakeholders in different formats. Some stakeholders may prefer a slideshow and formal presentation, while other groups want printed documentation they can review and study. The business analyst will need to assess the stakeholders and their preferred methods of receiving the requirements package.

The type of project will also affect how the requirements package is created and what's included in it. There's no standardized checklist for what should or should not be included in a requirements package, as each project may need different information based on its goals.

The size and scope of the project will affect the requirements package content. As a general rule, larger projects require more detail. Larger projects are generally higher-priority projects within the organization, so the business analyst can expect more information, multiple sets of requirements packages, and formal presentations to explain the requirements packages to different stakeholders who will approve the requirements. Smaller, lower-priority projects still demand attention to detail, but the amount of content may be less than for a high-profile project.

Internal projects are generally less detailed and less formal than a project your organization is completing for someone else. This isn't to say that internal projects aren't as important as external projects; it's just that when a business is completing projects for others, the level of professionalism, presence, and perceived image has a tendency to go up. Consider any firms that complete projects for other organizations: IT integrators, architectural firms, consultants, and even manufacturers.

Requirements that are created for clients are often based on statements of work documentation, Requests for Proposals, or Requests for Quotes. Customers have an expectation of professionalism and attention to detail, and will expect a complete and robust requirements package to show that the vendor understands their requirements to create the solution they're expecting as a result of their investment.

The type of project will also affect the content of the requirements package. A construction project is not going to have the same details as a software development requirements package. The application area will affect what the business analyst includes in the requirements package. There may be factors that the business analyst should reference simply based on the type of project that's being entertained. For example, laws, regulations, and standards will vary from industry to industry, and requirements will need to mesh with these constraints and should be referenced in the requirements package. Regulations are requirements and are mandatory. Standards are often seen as guidelines and are generally accepted, but are technically optional.

All requirements packages will need to be tailored to the stakeholders who will be reviewing the package for approval. The depth of information that should be included will vary from package to package, but often the project scope, if it's created at this point even in a preliminary format, should be included. The business analyst may also elect to include the identified business, functional, and technical requirements as part of the package. The audience that's reading the package can be assisted in understanding the proposed requirements with graphs, illustrations, and clear writing.

Building the Requirements Package

Every requirements package should have a table of contents. That's about the only thing you'll find consistent among all requirements packages, as every project type, every organization, and the corresponding groups of stakeholders will have varying expectations as to the exact content of the requirements package. The goal for all requirements packages remains the same: clearly and accurately define the project requirements for stakeholder approval.

You already know that the size and scope of the project may affect the requirements package content, but you must also consider the audience that will review the requirements package. The creation of the requirements package should be written to the audience that will approve the requirements. You'll want to create the requirements package from their perspective and according to what's most important to these stakeholders. How the information is presented is as important as the actual information that's presented.

Different stakeholders will have different needs and demands for the requirements package. You may have to create several requirements packages, and that's fine, but you should try to create them so they're easy to synchronize across all versions when changes or updates happen to the project scope. One approach that may be easier to manage than multiple requirements packages is to create a standard requirements package with an audience-specific preface. This approach would allow each audience to focus on their particular needs and still have access to the same underlying requirements for the entire project.

The categorization of stakeholders will help identify the expectations of each type of stakeholder and the contents of the deck of requirements. The most common stakeholder types and their requirements expectations are as follows.

Executive business sponsors   The executives will likely want a summation of the requirements, the project scope details, a return on investment assessment, business benefits, and the project costs and schedule. The executive stakeholders may be the only group that actually signs off on the requirements in some organizations.

Subject matter experts (SMEs)   The SMEs are the people who are closest to the project work, deliverable, or process affected by the implementation of the project. Their concern will likely be on assuring that the identified requirements actually achieve the requirements they've identified with the business analyst during the requirements gathering phase.

Quality assurance analysts The QA stakeholders will want to identify and focus on the critical success factors as identified by the business owners, subject matter experts, and the recipients of the project deliverables. This allows the QA analysts to test and measure the project deliverables to ensure that the execution of the project meets the actual requirements of the project scope and, in turn, achieves the expected quality.

 NOTE *Quality* is a conformance to requirements and a fitness for use. Quality is achieved by satisfying the project scope while balancing the project schedule and costs. The requirements must allow for quality to be achieved by setting realistic expectations of time, cost, and scope.

Outside customers and vendors These stakeholders will be concerned with the technical requirements, interfaces, security issues, and the documentation of any technical constraints they'll need to work with during the project execution. This group may also have contractual concerns where the project requirements will need to align with any obligations agreed to in the contractual relationship between the client and vendor.

Security, legal, and audit stakeholders This group of stakeholders will want to focus on the requirements of conformance to the corporate standards, laws, security, and potential audit requirements.

Technical solution providers These stakeholders will actually build the solution based on the gathered requirements. They will need the complete requirements package, a complete understanding of what the requirements will accomplish, and the functional and technical specifications of what the other stakeholders expect as a result of the project.

These are the most common stakeholders the business analyst will need to interact with. Your organization may have additional stakeholders who need to be addressed for requirements approval. Regardless of additional stakeholders, if they exist in your organization, the goal is still the same: communicate the project requirements to and obtain approval by the stakeholders.

Once the requirements package has been dispersed, the requirements might change. In these instances a change control system is needed. Changes to project requirements may have ramifications for the entire project—even for small, seemingly innocent changes. Changes should first be documented and then evaluated for their impact on the remainder of the requirements. For each change consider its effect on

- Overall project scope
- Time objectives
- Cost objectives
- Quality achievability
- Human resources
- Communication demands
- Risk
- Procurement

Changes may also affect the configuration management of the product the project will create. This will cause you to update the requirements package across all of the versions, and then to resubmit the changes to the stakeholders for approval. Whenever a change enters the requirements, the change should be documented in the revision log along with any supporting detail of why the change has occurred.

Conduct a Requirements Presentation

As a business analyst, you'll probably be doing loads of presentations in your career. Some of the presentations will be formal—PowerPoint slides and all—while the majority of your presentations will probably be less formal. In either case, you'll need to first determine why a presentation is needed and plan accordingly. Presentations often are needed to communicate with the stakeholders about the project status.

It's not unusual for presentations to happen throughout the life of the project, so you'll probably be working with the project manager on presentations about the requirements and the project execution. The business analyst may need to present with the project manager updates and clarifications about the project's ability to reach user expectations, refinements to project requirements, and how the project is achieving the stakeholder demands. This meeting is also to communicate how the project is reaching the objectives of each phase in the project.

Projects move through phases, as you can see in Figure 4-2, where each phase builds on the phase that came before. Usually the conclusion of a phase allows the next phase to begin. In project management, the closure of a phase often coincides with a milestone, and milestones call for the stakeholders to verify that the project deliverables to this point in the project are in sync with the project scope. This process is called *scope verification* and may be linked to payments if the project is being conducted under a client-vendor relationship.

Figure 4-2
Projects are dependent on the phases that precede the current phase.

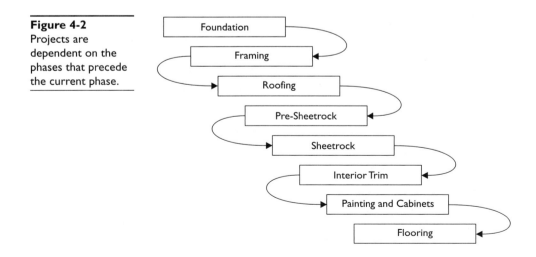

Business analysts are often the facilitators of the presentations, and you can follow some simple rules to ensure the meetings flow smoothly:

- Introduce all of the parties attending the meeting.
- Announce the meeting's objectives.
- When needed, provide some information about the project background.
- Discuss the project accomplishments to date, and present any appropriate deliverables the project has created.
- Meetings may end with a review of actions to be done by the customers, business analyst, and project manager.
- When deliverables are presented, the stakeholders should have an opportunity to review the deliverables and then sign a scope verification form.

When you conclude a meeting, formal or informal, you should document the outcome of the meeting. You'll probably have actions for the stakeholders, the business analyst (yourself), the project manager, and possibly the project team that's creating the solution. You should also document any of the requirements and deliverables that were not accepted by the customer and act with the project manager to achieve acceptability of the deliverables through corrective actions.

Hosting a Formal Presentation

Not every meeting needs to be a formal presentation. Sometimes a simple ad hoc meeting will suffice. It's the responsibility of the business analyst to determine the type of presentation that's most appropriate for the topics to be discussed. The purpose of the meeting should serve as a guide to determine if the meeting should be formal or if an informal approach is needed.

Formal presentations often require slides with key summation points to guide the conversation through the meeting. Slides are a great way of communicating the summation of the project while still providing enough detail to convey the project status. While you likely won't have questions about slide content on your CBAP exam, you should be aware, for practicality's sake, that presentations should be concise, direct, and well-organized. You don't want your message to be muddled in a barrage of animation, extraneous material, and graphics that don't contribute to the presentation.

You might host a formal presentation for many reasons, including

- To demonstrate how the project deliverables have met the quality standards
- To open a conversation about how the project will operate with other business processes within the project
- To gain scope acceptance and sign-off of the requirements
- To discuss requirements and/or deliverables testing processes
- To explore what solution may be the best approach to achieve the requirements before the project actually starts

- To review the project progress and discuss the next phases of the project work
- To discuss changes to the project scope

The business analyst may need to conduct a formal presentation for other reasons, such as when interacting with vendors and the general public. The business analyst should always be prepared, speak confidently, and use presentation slides, if any, to assist the message rather than to replace the message. Formal presentations generally include handouts for the audience as well, so there's an added layer of complexity for the handouts being easy to follow along with the presentation.

Hosting an Informal Presentation

Just because a presentation is informal doesn't mean that you shouldn't be prepared. The overwhelming majority of a business analyst's meetings are informal meetings for providing quick information, are conversational in tone, and seek open dialogue from the participants. Informal presentations are used for

- Quick check of the project requirements' completeness, status, and accuracy in implementation
- Confirmation that the project team understands the requirements
- Communication of the requirements to stakeholders who have no sign-off on requirements but are still affected by the changes the requirements provide
- Communication of the project requirements to project team members for training and clarification
- Facilitation between the key business users and the project team to ensure clarity

You may also use ad hoc meetings to discuss the project and its status with the project manager, project team, or stakeholders. Ad hoc meetings, sometimes called hallway meetings, are quick, informal conversations about the project and provide quick information exchange between you and the stakeholder. It's a good idea to follow up in writing any promises made in the ad hoc meeting, to ensure both parties are clear on what's been promised.

Communication Factors

To be an effective communicator in formal or informal presentations, you need to speak directly, clearly, and passionately about your topic. Think about some of your favorite speakers, professors, or performers, and you'll probably find that they have an ease and confidence in their ability to present. While some of this ease and confidence may come from years of experience as a presenter, I'd wager more of it comes from their knowledge and comfort with the material that's being presented.

When I first started teaching, a fellow professor told me that if I really wanted to know something, I should teach it. She was oh so right. I prepared my lessons intently, read beyond the classroom literature, and knew my topic beyond the classroom hours. The confidence I gained by being so prepared helped calm the jitters of public speaking, and I could focus more on my message than my speaking style. It's an approach I still use today whenever I present, and I encourage you to do the same.

Some communication terms may not help you directly to be a better speaker, but they'll help you understand the science and process of communication. When you consider that the bulk of your time as a business analyst is spent communicating, you should spend ample time preparing in order to communicate better. Here are some communication terms that it'll behoove you to know:

Sender-receiver models There is a flow and rhythm to conversation, formal or informal, and these are comprised of feedback loops. A feedback loop is a conversation. For example, I say the project is going well. And you then you ask for details about the cost and schedule. And then I respond to your question. Another example of a feedback loop is a meeting; all of your participants hear what the other team members say, offer feedback to the speaker, the speaker may respond, and so on. Basically, a feedback loop is a conversation between two or more speakers centering on one specific topic. You may occasionally, as part of your business analysis process, experience a barrier to communication. A barrier is anything that prevents communication from occurring at optimum levels. For example, if you and I are mad at each other, we're not going to communicate effectively—if at all.

Media The best modality to use when communicating is the one that is relevant to the information that's being communicated. Some communications demand a formal presentation, where others only warrant a phone call, an ad hoc meeting, or a quick e-mail. The right media is dictated by what needs to be communicated.

Writing style I like to write as though we're having a conversation, but this writing style, while easy to read (I hope for you), isn't always the best style for what's being communicated. You and I should adjust our writing style to the message and the audience that'll read the message.

Presentation techniques Some people can't stand being in front of an audience, but as business analysts, they often find themselves having to present. Presentation techniques such as confidence, body language, and visual aids promote or distract from the message the presenter is offering to the audience.

Meeting management techniques Ever attend a WOT meeting? That's a "waste of time" meeting. Meetings should have an agenda, and someone needs to keep the meeting minutes for the project. Informal meetings can drone on and on if you let them. I find it best in an informal meeting to stand rather than sit. Sitting is comfortable, while standing reminds me that the meeting's taking too long.

The good, old communication model demonstrates how communication moves from person to person. I like to think of each portion of the model as a fax machine to visualize all the components, as in Figure 4-3. Take a look:

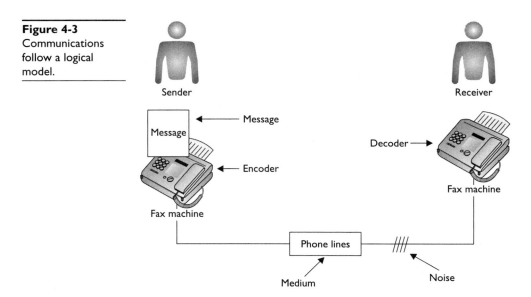

Figure 4-3
Communications follow a logical model.

Sender If I want to fax you a contract, I'm the sender. It's the same thing if I'm telling you a story. I'm sending the information.

Encoder This is the device that encodes the message to be sent. My fax machine is the encoder. If we're talking, my brain is the encoder.

Medium This is the device or technology that transports the message. The telephone line is the medium between our fax machines. In a conversation, the verbal and non-verbal languages are the medium.

Decoder This is the device that decodes the message as it is being received. Your fax machine is the decoder. When you listen to my story, your brain interprets the message—it's the decoder.

Receiver This is the person who receives the message. You receive my fax, jot a note to me, and then send it back through your fax machine to mine. When you send the message back to me, the communication model is reversed. When you laugh at the punch line, you're giving me some feedback that you got my joke.

Noise This is anything that interferes with or disrupts the message. It's possible that static on the phone line distorts the fax message between the two fax machines. Anything that distracts you or me from the message is noise. You don't always have noise in the communication model—if you did it'd be tough to transfer information. Noise is something that can happen, but thankfully, doesn't always happen.

 For a more detailed explanation, watch the Communication Novelties video now.

Being a good presenter takes preparation, knowledge of your topic, and practice, practice, practice. It's tempting to always host informal presentations, because they're practical and cause less stress. The truth is that the information to be presented should dictate what type of presentation is needed, not the comfort level surrounding the presenter.

Host a Formal Requirements Review

Despite your best efforts, in-depth conversations, and requirements elicitation, there's a chance you'll overlook, misunderstand, or goof on capturing a project requirement. That's okay, you're human. The point of the formal requirements review is to accommodate these rare mistakes by business analysts. Actually, and more precisely, the point of the formal requirements review is to have the project stakeholders confirm the accuracy of the requirements you've captured.

You need the project stakeholders, before and during the project, to participate in formal requirements review meetings. It's much more cost-effective to catch mistakes, errors, and omissions on paper than to fix problems that have already been implemented by the project team. Initially, formal reviews are completed with your fellow business analysts, certain key stakeholders, and subject matter experts. This gives you all a chance to confer on the requirements before the solution is implemented. As time progresses, you'll move through more formal reviews to maintain consistency between what is planned in the solution and what is implemented in the project.

Formal requirements review can include any or all of the following purposes:

- Review by all the stakeholders to ensure that all of the requirements have been captured
- Provide an opportunity to cut nonessential requirements (goodbye, pet requirements)
- Confirmation that the requirements are exact and easy to understand
- Review of the requirements for correctness
- Confirmation that the requirements will adhere to the organizational standards, policies, and quality expectations
- Review of requirements feasibility
- Opportunity for the stakeholders to prioritize the requirements

The formal requirements review usually includes all of the stakeholders or authorized representatives from large groups of stakeholders. When you've got a large group of stakeholders, such as end users, there may be a selection of stakeholders who represent the interests of the larger group of stakeholders. These representatives should be authorized to comment, give opinions, and approve the requirements on behalf of the stakeholders being represented. All participants in the meeting should review the requirements documentation before the meeting so they're prepared to discuss the requirements at length in the meeting.

Documentation of the conversations, questions, clarifications, and decisions that happen during this meeting is essential. Someone should take minutes and document the names, facts, and relevant meeting details. If a change, consensus, or issue is identified, this should also be documented by whoever is the minutes keeper. Sometimes proposed changes to the requirements may require additional analysis and then an additional requirements review.

Because requirements reviews happen throughout the project, usually at the end of project phases, your organization may call these meetings walkthroughs, inspections, or scope verification. Requirements review meetings should be scheduled with the project manager to ensure that approval of phase delivery, pending requirements decisions, and other input does not stall the project schedule.

Preparing for the Formal Requirements Review

As with many activities in business analysis, when it comes to a formal requirements review, success depends upon the preparation. This means that you, the business analyst, will need to prepare, along with the project manager and the key stakeholders. Key stakeholders for the formal requirements review meeting, at a minimum, are the people who will need to sign off on the requirements document. You may also have to select the people who can contribute to the accuracy of the requirements, such as your quality assurance leaders, stakeholder representative, and relevant vendors.

All participants should have a complete requirements document before the requirements review meeting. You'll want to schedule the requirements review to happen at an appropriate time after you've distributed the requirements document so that all of the participants can review the requirements document before your meeting. You don't want to distribute the requirements document at the meeting itself, as you need the participants to come to the meeting with a working knowledge of the requirements documentation.

In addition to scheduling the meeting with enough notice so that all of the key stakeholders can attend, don't forget to actually book a room and schedule Internet or teleconference facilities for the meetings. That might seem a little obvious, but it's been overlooked before. The business analyst should also follow up with the formal requirements review participants to remind them of the meeting, location, and information for connecting remotely if you're using web software or a teleconference as part of your review.

The business analyst manages the scheduling, organizing, and facilitating of the formal requirements review meeting. The project manager, however, also has a role to play in the review. You'll need to coordinate with the project manager as to what reviewers should receive the requirements documentation, who will attend the review meeting, and who will create the agenda for the meeting. There's a fine line between business analysis duties and project management duties, and both the business analyst and the project manager need to work together for the meeting to be successful. Typical roles for the formal requirements review include the following.

- **Requirements author**   This is the person who created the requirements document; typically this is the business analyst. The requirements review meeting can't happen without this person present.

- **Recorder**   This lucky person gets to record all the comments, suggestions, questions, and prompts for clarification about the requirements document.

- **Moderator**   This person actually facilitates the meeting. It's possible that this person is the business analyst, but generally this role is performed by a neutral person who can move the meeting along and stick to the meeting rules. The moderator has the responsibility of ensuring that all participants have reviewed the requirements documentation before the start of the meeting and of keeping stakeholders on track during the meeting.

- **Author peer reviewer**   This person completes a peer review of the requirements documentation to ensure that it meets the expected quality of the organization and inspects the requirements documentation for completeness. The author peer reviewer is often another business analyst.

- **Appropriate stakeholders**   The business analyst and the project manager may invite other key stakeholders who are not necessarily decision makers on the requirements but who can offer input and direction on technicalities and quality, and expert judgment about the content and accuracy of the requirements and deliverables.

Throughout all of the communication regarding the formal requirements review, you want to stress to the participants the purpose of the meeting as stated in the BABOK: to find and remove faults with the requirements. When faults are identified, they should be addressed, documented, and a set of actions should be agreed upon concerning the faults. If there are no faults and the parties agree with the requirements and the project deliverables, then there should be a formal sign-off of the requirements. I'll discuss that more later in this chapter.

Conducting the Formal Requirements Review Meeting

So the big day arrives; you've got the coffee, donuts, and yellow highlighters, and you're all ready for the requirements review. You don't have to have coffee and donuts, it's just amazing how food makes people attend meetings and participate. When you start the requirements review meeting, you should introduce yourself, give some background on the project (especially if there are participants such as vendors who aren't familiar with all of the project facets), and state the purpose of the meeting. If a moderator is leading the meeting, they'd do the same business and keep attendees on task.

The rules for a formal requirements review meeting are similar to hosting a formal presentation:

- Introduce the people in the room and their role in relation to the project.

- Remind the participants that the purpose is to find and remove any faults with the requirements, not the people who created the requirements.

- Define how the review process will happen.

- Lead the participants through a walkthrough of the requirements and, when appropriate, the deliverables.

- Document and assign activities for yourself, the project manager, and other stakeholders as needed.

The comments, questions, and inputs should also be documented. Suggestions for revisions to the requirements should be captured and confirmed for clarity among all the participating stakeholders. Close the meeting with a quick review and confirmation of the deliverables and requirements sign-off, or lack of sign-off if the requirements were not approved. You may also confirm any identified needs for quality improvements, the status of the requirements document, and whether additional reviewers need to comment on the requirements document before the project may move forward. Based on the outcome of the meeting, you may need to repeat the entire process to gain consensus before moving forward with the project.

All participants in the meeting must follow some simple rules. First, only the most appropriate stakeholders should attend. This means that supervisors, especially of the business analyst, should not attend the meeting unless they have direct input to the requirements or deliverables. While it's sometimes appropriate for supervisors to attend these meetings, they don't always have much to contribute. These folks can also change the dynamics of the meeting, shift control from the business analyst to themselves, and affect what the stakeholders may contribute. Second, the review is of the requirements, not of the author. And finally, participants must review and be familiar with the requirements documentation prior to the review meeting.

Obtain Requirements Sign-Off

In the David Mamet play and movie *Glengarry Glen Ross,* lead salesman Blake tells the lagging sales reps something that's stuck with me for years, "Get them to sign on the line which is dotted." It's a fantastic movie, though it's not one you'll want to watch with the kids. It's about sales, well, actually it's about closing sales. Sure, it's a long stretch from the typical day of a business analyst, but the movie addresses the lesson of getting your stakeholders to sign off on requirements.

You need the project stakeholders to sign off on the project requirements, as it's a signal that the requirements you've captured, documented, and presented are complete and accurate. Getting the stakeholders to sign off on the requirements is a risk reduction technique to avoid changes from popping into the project later. By having the stakeholders review the requirements documentation on their own and through the formal requirements review meeting prior to signing off on the documents, you're ensuring that all of the needs have been identified, agreed upon, and that the project is ready to move forward.

Obtaining Signatures for Requirements

I like the formality of stakeholders signing off on the requirements in ink, though for your CBAP exam this doesn't have to happen. Stakeholders can sign off on requirements in ink or electronically—either is acceptable as you're creating an audit trail of activity. By having the stakeholders sign off on the requirements, physically or electronically, you're holding them accountable for the inclusion of all requirements.

To get the signatures, you'll need to have a face-to-face meeting with your key stakeholders. Typically this is done in the requirements review meeting, and stakeholders can sign off on the requirements documentation at the conclusion of the meeting. Should there be errors, corrections, amendments, or other delays, follow-up reviews may be necessary. In either case, you'll need to present the requirements to the stakeholders first in printed form and then again at the presentation. You want to make certain the stakeholders do understand what they're signing and that they agree that the requirements are complete and accurate.

On most projects all stakeholders should sign all requirements. You might guess that this could get a little messy on larger projects where not all stakeholders would understand, or need to understand, all of the requirements in the project. In these instances, the stakeholders can sign off on a portion of the requirements that they have authority over, as long as they don't object to other requirements within the project. You'll need to take precautions in these instances, however, to ensure that all requirements are signed off on by at least one stakeholder and that no requirements are overlooked for approval.

In some instances a stakeholder refuses to sign off on a given requirement. In these cases the business analyst will discuss the issue with the project manager. Sometimes there is a legitimate reason for the refusal to sign off on requirements, and additional analysis and corrections are needed. It could be that the stakeholder doesn't understand the requirements, so you'll need a more in-depth explanation of what the requirements will accomplish. Finally, it could be a political objection to the requirements, and you and the project manager will need to discuss the refusal to sign and whether the project should continue, be delayed, or if the business owner needs to be brought into the scenario for resolution.

Requirements sign-off is the final step in the requirements communication process. The sign-off of requirements allows the project to continue. The sign-off documentation should become part of the project archives and may be needed during subsequent phases of the project for quality control and scope verification. All documentation relating to the project should be archived and will become part of organizational process assets. This is historical information for the organization to use on future projects, operational support, and updates and maintenance on the product the project creates.

Moving Through Project Milestones

In project management, milestones are timeless events that signal progress. For example, the successful creation of a home's foundation, the installation of a web server, or the working prototype for new software could all be milestones. Milestones usually come at the end of a phase and are the result of a significant deliverable within the project. Project management and business analysis often overlap, and both are linked, typically, to milestones to show progress within a project.

The sign-off of project requirements can be a milestone, as it shows progress has been reached within the project. Depending on how your organization is structured, your business analysis duties may come well before the project is initiated, though in my experience the project is initiated and planning starts all while business analysis activities are happening in the organization. My point being, your business analysis duties are outside the domain of project management, but the results of your work allow the project to move forward.

Requirements and project deliverables both need to be reviewed and approved by the stakeholders. Figure 4-4 shows some sample phases of a project where the result of each phase is a new milestone. Each phase is created, and the primary deliverable of the phase can be traced back to the project requirements. Every deliverable of the project must be verified and approved by the project stakeholder before the project can move forward. This verification, the requirements sign-off, ensures that all of the work to date is in sync with the requirements.

By involving the project stakeholders not only at the beginning of the project with the initial formal requirements review, but also throughout the project, you're ensuring accuracy with the project deliverables. You don't want the stakeholders to sign off on the requirements only at the beginning of the project and then not to see the results of progress until the project is declared completed. If there are mistakes in the execution of the project, then it becomes even more expensive, time intensive, and frustrating to fix the problems that could have been fixed during project execution.

The business analyst, the project manager, and the key stakeholders need to work together on the requirements gathering and verification of deliverables. Often, in my experience, there's an us-against-them mentality that creeps into the project. The customers may feel left out of the loop by the business analyst once the project moves into

Figure 4-4
Phases create milestones that show project progress.

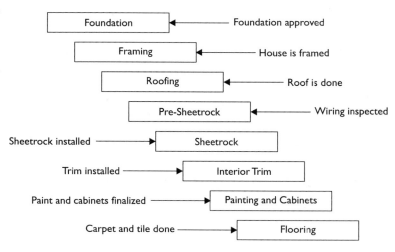

execution. The business analyst can feel isolated from the project manager once the requirements have been signed off. And the project manager can feel that the stakeholders and the business analyst are just pesky, because this is her project now, not theirs. Your experience and organization may be different, and I hope it is, but for your career and for your exam, communication among the stakeholders, the business analyst, and the project manager is paramount for project success.

Chapter Summary

Your first stop in official requirements communication is to create a Business Analysis Communication Plan. This plan will help guide you and your business analysis team through communications to ensure that everything that needs to be communicated, gathered, and documented is done accordingly. This plan can also help you ensure that you communicate to the right people, at the right time, with the right information. The business analyst is considered to be the chief communicator when it comes to project requirements. You're supposed to be the hub of communications, and the Business Analysis Communication Plan can help you stay organized.

As great as the Business Analysis Communication Plan is, it doesn't address specific conflicts in project requirements. For loads of reasons, conflicts could happen internal to the requirements or among stakeholders. When a requirements conflict is identified, the first thing that needs to happen is documentation of the requirements conflict in the Requirements Issue Log. You'll record the conflict, the status, and update the issue as progress is made. You'll communicate the conflict with the stakeholders and work with the stakeholders to find a resolution to the conflict. You can use conflict resolution meetings to bring the stakeholders together to discuss the conflict. Your goal is to find an acceptable resolution among the parties to allow the project to keep moving forward.

You'll be communicating with stakeholders often throughout the project, and knowing the most appropriate format for the message can help convey the message. In other words, you should allow the content of the message to dictate what format is best for delivery. Add to that idea the recipient of the message and his or her expectations for communication, and you'll be better prepared as a communicator. Not all groups of stakeholders need all the information regarding requirements; the business analyst should consider the message, the audience, and their expectations before communicating.

Formal presentations are venues to discuss the project deliverable and business processes affected by the requirements, and to gain sign-off of the project requirements. Informal presentations are quick meetings to discuss current status and issues with project deliverables, or to elicit and offer project information. Just because a meeting is less formal, however, doesn't mean that the business analyst shouldn't come prepared. An agenda, structured meeting techniques, and a time limit are good things to have for both formal and informal meetings.

One meeting that is always formal is the requirements review meeting. The goal of this meeting is to bring all the stakeholders together and to identify errors, gaps, or omissions in the documented requirements. The meeting participants should have received and read the requirements documentation before the meeting. The requirements review moderator should conduct the meeting to be civil, organized, and focused. Should errors be identified in the meeting, the requirements document should be updated, and subsequent review meetings may be necessary.

A subsidiary objective of the requirements review meeting is to obtain stakeholder sign-off. Once stakeholders agree that the requirements are accurate, they should sign off on the requirements either electronically or physically. Their sign-off acknowledges that the requirements are complete as documented and the project may move forward. In larger projects, stakeholders may sign off on portions of the requirements that are only relevant to them—as long as they don't have objections to other parts of the requirements. Should a stakeholder refuse to sign off on the document, the business analyst and the project manager should confer on whether the project should be halted or whether the lack of sign-off affects current project activities.

As you can imagine, you'll be creating loads of paperwork, e-mails, faxes, reports, and other requirements-related information. All of this information should be archived as part of your business analysis duties. This information can become part of organizational process assets and reused for future, similar projects. Always archive the requirements information—this saves time and monies for future projects within the organization.

For your CBAP examination, you should be familiar with the demands of the business analyst when it comes to communication. You always need to communicate the most accurate information at the most appropriate time to the correct stakeholders.

Key Terms

Author peer reviewer   This person completes peer review of the requirements documentation to ensure that it meets the expected quality of the organization and inspects the requirements documentation for completeness. The author peer reviewer is often another business analyst.

Barrier   Anything that prevents communication from occurring at optimum levels.

Communications formula $N(N - 1)/2$ where N represents the number of project stakeholders, and it shows the number of communication channels in the project.

Compromising   Requires that all parties in the conflict must give up something. The decision made blends both sides of the argument. Because neither party really wins, it is considered a lose-lose solution. The business analyst can use this approach when the relationships are equal and no one can truly "win."

Conflicting requirements   When two or more requirements conflict in scope, time, cost, or objective. Conflicting requirements should be documented in the Requirements Issue Log, and a conflict resolution process should begin. Updates to the resolution should be documented in the issues log as well.

Decoder   The device that decodes the message as it is being received.

Deliverable   A document that clearly identifies the project deliverables the customer is expecting and that the project is to produce for the stakeholders.

Encoder   The device that encodes the message to be sent.

Feedback loop   A conversation between one or more speakers centering on one specific topic.

Forcing   Forcing is used when the person in the conflict with the most power forces the decision. The decision made may not be the best decision for the project, but it's fast. As expected, this autocratic approach does little for relationship building and is a win-lose solution. You know a solution is being forced when someone with seniority or power makes a decision without considering the other parties' objectives.

Formal requirements presentation   A structured meeting to review requirements status, changes, and progress. Formal presentations are often hosted by the business analyst for all of the stakeholders to attend.

Formal requirements review   A meeting that brings together all of the stakeholders to identify any errors or omissions in the identified requirements. Should no errors exist, requirements sign-off is needed.

Informal requirements presentations   Somewhat structured, but less formal, and conversational in nature.

Media   The best modality to use when communicating is the one that is relevant to the information that's being communicated. Some communications demand a formal presentation; others only warrant a phone call, an ad hoc meeting, or a quick e-mail. The right media is dictated by what needs to be communicated.

Medium   This is the device or technology that transports the message.

Meeting management techniques   Meetings should have an agenda and order, and someone needs to keep the meeting minutes for the project.

Milestone   The significant deliverable of a project phase; it is a timeless project event that shows progress toward completing the project requirements.

Moderator   This is the person who actually facilitates the requirements review meeting. It's possible that this person is the business analyst, but generally this role is performed by a neutral person who can move the meeting along and stick to the meeting rules. The moderator has the responsibility of ensuring that all participants have reviewed the requirements documentation before the start of the meeting and of keeping stakeholders on track during the meeting.

Noise   Anything that interferes with or disrupts the message. Anything that distracts you or me from the message is noise.

Problem solving A conflict resolution approach that uses a spirit of cooperation among the stakeholders. Problem solving tackles the problem head-on and is the preferred method of conflict resolution. Sometimes this approach is defined as "confronting" rather than problem solving. Problem solving calls for additional research to find the best solution for the problem, and it's a win-win solution. It should be used if there is time to work through and resolve the issue. It also serves to build relationships and trust. The business analyst is the facilitator of the problem-solving technique.

Project phases The incremental progression of the project through logical, work producing sections of a project. The end of a project phase results in a project deliverable and often coincides with a milestone.

Receiver The person who receives the message.

Recorder The person who records all the comments, suggestions, questions, and prompts for clarification about the requirements document during the formal requirements review meeting.

Regulations These are enforced requirements and are mandatory.

Requirements author The person who created the requirements document; typically the business analyst. The requirements review meeting can't happen without this person present.

Requirements format The format and designated information of the requirements document; there may be multiple versions of the requirements document depending on the stakeholders in the project.

Requirements Issue Log Central log to document conflict issues, the attributes of the conflict, the stakeholders involved, and the ramifications of the conflict for the other requirements within the project.

Requirements package The collection of the business analyst's work results. It is the documentation, formulation, and organization of all the requirements the business analyst has gathered from the stakeholders, packaged in a comprehensive set of project requirements.

Requirements sign-off The stakeholders signing off on the requirements—demonstrates the stakeholder approval of the identified requirements. Stakeholders can sign off on requirements in ink or electronically—either is acceptable, as you're creating an audit trail of activity.

Sender The party sending the message is the sender.

Sender-receiver models The flow and rhythm to conversation, formal or informal, are comprised of feedback loops.

Smoothing This approach "smoothes" out the conflict by minimizing the perceived size of the problem. It is a temporary solution, but can calm stakeholder relations and boisterous discussions. Smoothing may be acceptable when time is of the essence or when any of the proposed solutions will not currently settle the problem. This can be considered a lose-lose situation as well, since no one really wins in the long run.

Standards   Often seen as guidelines and are generally accepted, but are technically optional.

Withdrawal   This conflict resolution technique has one side of the argument walking away from the problem, usually in disgust. You can recognize withdrawal when one party refuses to participate in the conflict resolution any longer and surrenders to the other stakeholders. The conflict is not really resolved, and it is considered a yield-lose solution. The approach can be used, however, as a cooling-off period or when the issue is not critical.

Work product   A work-in-progress version of the requirements presentation.

Writing style   The tone, language, and formality of a written topic.

Questions

1. You are the business analyst for a large project that has nearly 50 stakeholders. You need a document that can guide you and your business analysis team as to who needs what information at different points during the analysis process. What document can best serve your needs?

   A. Communications Requirements Matrix

   B. Business Analysis Communication Plan

   C. RACI chart

   D. Project scope statement

2. There are 76 stakeholders in the current project. How many communication channels exist in this project?

   A. 76

   B. 152

   C. 77

   D. 2,850

3. There are 56 stakeholders currently in the project, and next week there will be an additional four stakeholders. How many more communication channels will exist next week on this project?

   A. 4

   B. 6

   C. 230

   D. 1,770

4. Nick is the project manager of the JGH Project, and Susan is the business analyst. Robert Templetone is the business owner. There are 29 stakeholders in this project. Who is the chief communicator?

A. Nick

B. Susan

C. Robert

D. Each stakeholder representative

5. You are the business analyst for the NHG Project, which has 72 stakeholders. You need to create a document to track the communication requirements among the project stakeholders as far as who contributes information to other stakeholders. What type of document would satisfy this requirement?

A. Communications Requirements Matrix

B. RACI chart

C. Pareto chart

D. Responsibility Assignment Matrix

6. When conflicting requirements have been identified, what is the first action the business analyst should take?

A. Contact the stakeholders who are affected by the conflicting requirement.

B. Contact the project manager to discuss the conflicting requirements.

C. Document the conflicting requirements in the Requirements Communications Plan.

D. Document the conflicting requirements in the Requirements Issue Log.

7. Which conflict resolution approach requires both parties in conflict to give up something?

A. Problem solving

B. Confronting

C. Withdrawal

D. Compromising

8. Marty tells Tom that he's been the lead designer for six years at Company ABX and because of this, the decision on the conflicting requirement will be decided by him. This is an example of what type of conflict resolution?

A. Withdrawal

B. Forcing

C. Ineffective

D. Compromising

9. What is the danger in creating multiple versions of the requirements documentation so that all stakeholders can understand the requirements?

A. Overlaps in the documentation

B. Synchronizing the documentation

C. Time wasted in redundancy

D. Confusion as to which requirements are accurate

10. Why would a business analyst create multiple versions of the requirements for the different groups of stakeholders?

A. Each stakeholder needs a clear understanding of the requirements.

B. Each stakeholder may demand their own set of requirements.

C. Each stakeholder has different levels of competency.

D. Each stakeholder doesn't need to see all of the requirements.

11. What type of requirements information would the executive sponsors of a software design project most likely want to review?

A. Technical design documentation

B. All of the requirements specifications

C. Return on investment information

D. Project scope statement

12. All of the following are true statements about the formality of requirements communication except for which one?

A. The size of the project may affect the formality of the requirements communication.

B. If the organization's department and lines of business involved in the requirements are complex, integrated, and extend beyond the confines of the legal organization, then additional formalities for requirements may be needed.

C. Mission-critical projects demand formal communications.

D. Projects that require an investment of more than $10,000 require formal communications.

13. What is the risk of sharing a work product with a project stakeholder?

A. The work product may be taken as factual and be misinterpreted by the stakeholder as promised information.

B. The work product may conflict with other requirements the stakeholders want in the project.

C. The work product may cause the stakeholder to include more requirements.

D. The work product may cause the stakeholder to withdraw funding for the project if they're not in agreement.

14. What is created as a result of the business analyst's work?

    A. Deliverables

    B. Requirements

    C. Milestones

    D. Requirements package

15. What is created at the end of a project phase?

    A. Milestone

    B. Scope verification processes

    C. Requirements review process

    D. Funding requests

16. Which of the following best describes quality in a project?

    A. Quality is the totality of all the project requirements.

    B. Quality is a conformance to the stakeholders.

    C. Quality is using the highest grade materials for the project deliverables.

    D. Quality is a conformance to requirements.

17. When a change is considered for the project requirements, which one of the following is not reviewed in consideration of the requirements change request?

    A. Time to implement the change

    B. Cost to implement the change

    C. The person who submits the change request

    D. The human resources that may be affected by the proposed change

18. You are the business analyst for a project to create a software package. A change to the identified requirements has been approved by your organization's Change Control Board. What should you do with the change information?

    A. Communicate the change to the project manager.

    B. Document the change in the revision log.

    C. Document the change in the Requirements Issue Log.

    D. Communicate the change to the business owner.

19. What component of the communication model is responsible for transferring the message between parties?

    A. Medium.

    B. Transfer agent.

C. Language.

D. It depends on the format of the message.

20. Tom and Sally are business analysts for your organization and are currently in a disagreement about a project requirement. Tom and Sally are refusing to communicate with one another, so you bring the two together for conflict resolution. The refusal of Tom and Sally to communicate is known as what?

   A. Noise

   B. Barrier

   C. Nonverbal communication

   D. Paralingual communications

Questions and Answers

1. You are the business analyst for a large project that has nearly 50 stakeholders. You need a document that can guide you and your business analysis team as to who needs what information at different points during the analysis process. What document can best serve your needs?

   A. Communications Requirements Matrix

   B. Business Analysis Communication Plan

   C. RACI chart

   D. Project scope statement

   B. The Business Analysis Communication Plan identifies who needs what information, when they need it, and in what modality. A, the Communications Requirements Matrix, demonstrates the interaction among stakeholders. C, a RACI chart, is a Responsibility Assignment Matrix using the legend of responsible, accountable, consult, and inform. D, the project scope statement, does not include contribution of information during business analysis duties.

2. There are 76 stakeholders in the current project. How many communication channels exist in this project?

   A. 76

   B. 152

   C. 77

   D. 2,850

   D. The formula to calculate the number of communication channels is $N(N - 1)/2$. In this instance it means that $76 \times 75 = 5,700$. This number is then divided by 2 for 2,850 communication channels.

3. There are 56 stakeholders currently in the project, and next week there will be an additional four stakeholders. How many more communication channels will exist next week on this project?

   A. 4

   B. 6

   C. 230

   D. 1,770

   C. Using the communications channel formula of $N(N - 1)/2$, you'd first calculate the current number of communication channels, which is 1,540. Then you'd calculate the second amount, which is 1,770, and find the difference, as the question is asking how many more channels will exist next week. The result is C, 230 channels.

4. Nick is the project manager of the JGH Project, and Susan is the business analyst. Robert Templetone is the business owner. There are 29 stakeholders in this project. Who is the chief communicator?

   A. Nick

   B. Susan

   C. Robert

   D. Each stakeholder representative

   B. The BABOK clearly states that the business analyst is the chief communicator on the project. A, Nick, the project manager, may play a role in communication as will Robert, choice C, but Susan is the chief communicator for the CBAP examination.

5. You are the business analyst for the NHG Project, which has 72 stakeholders. You need to create a document to track the communication requirements among the project stakeholders as far as who contributes information to other stakeholders. What type of document would satisfy this requirement?

   A. Communications Requirements Matrix

   B. RACI chart

   C. Pareto chart

   D. Responsibility Assignment Matrix

   A. The Communications Requirements Matrix is a table of all stakeholders showing the mapping of which stakeholders will contribute information to other stakeholders. B, a RACI chart, is a Responsibility Assignment Matrix using the legend of responsible, accountable, consult, and inform. C, a Pareto chart, is a quality control chart that shows categories of defects. D, a Responsibility Assignment Matrix, is a chart that can assign roles to responsibilities.

6. When conflicting requirements have been identified, what is the first action the business analyst should take?

    A. Contact the stakeholders who are affected by the conflicting requirement.

    B. Contact the project manager to discuss the conflicting requirements

    C. Document the conflicting requirements in the Requirements Communications Plan.

    D. Document the conflicting requirements in the Requirements Issue Log.

    D. The business analyst should always first add the information to the Requirements Issue Log. Choices A, B, and C are all invalid actions to take when a conflicting requirement has been identified.

7. Which conflict resolution approach requires both parties in conflict to give up something?

    A. Problem solving

    B. Confronting

    C. Withdrawal

    D. Compromising

    D. Compromising requires that both parties surrender something in exchange during the resolution. A, problem solving, is when both parties work together for the best solution. B, confronting, is another name for problem solving. C is incorrect, as withdrawal is when one party leaves the argument and surrenders to the other party.

8. Marty tells Tom that he's been the lead designer for six years at Company ABX and because of this, the decision on the conflicting requirement will be decided by him. This is an example of what type of conflict resolution?

    A. Withdrawal

    B. Forcing

    C. Ineffective

    D. Compromising

    B. This is an example of forcing the decision. A is incorrect, as withdrawal is when one party leaves the argument and surrenders to the other party. Choice C is not a valid conflict resolution term. D, compromising, is when both parties surrender something in exchange in the resolution.

9. What is the danger in creating multiple versions of the requirements documentation so that all stakeholders can understand the requirements?

    A. Overlaps in the documentation

    B. Synchronizing the documentation

    C. Time wasted in redundancy

    D. Confusion as to which requirements are accurate

    B. It is often necessary to create multiple versions of the requirements documentation so that the stakeholders can best understand the requirements, but the danger is that when something changes in the requirements, the business analyst overlooks synchronizing all of the versions. Choices A, C, and D may be valid choices in some instances, but B is the best answer according to the BABOK.

10. Why would a business analyst create multiple versions of the requirements for the different groups of stakeholders?

A. Each stakeholder needs a clear understanding of the requirements.

B. Each stakeholder may demand their own set of requirements.

C. Each stakeholder has different levels of competency.

D. Each stakeholder doesn't need to see all of the requirements.

A. The goal of creating versions of the requirements is to educate each set of stakeholders on the most appropriate information. Choices B and C are not valid choices. Choice D may be valid as a general statement, but it does not fully answer the question.

11. What type of requirements information would the executive sponsors of a software design project most likely want to review?

A. Technical design documentation

B. All of the requirements specifications

C. Return on investment information

D. Project scope statement

C. Executive sponsors will most likely want to see how the return on investment will happen for the project. The technical team would like to see A, the technical design document. Choice B is more likely for the project team. And choice D is not valid, as the project scope statement may not even be created at this point in the project.

12. All of the following are true statements about the formality of requirements communication except for which one?

A. The size of the project may affect the formality of the requirements communication.

B. If the organization's department and lines of business involved in the requirements are complex, integrated, and extend beyond the confines of the legal organization, then additional formalities for requirements may be needed.

C. Mission-critical projects demand formal communications.

D. Projects that require an investment of more than $10,000 require formal communications.

D. Of all the choices, only D is a false statement about the formality of the requirements communication. The budget of a project should have little influence over the formality of the communications.

13. What is the risk of sharing a work product with a project stakeholder?

A. The work product may be taken as factual and be misinterpreted by the stakeholder as promised information.

B. The work product may conflict with other requirements the stakeholders want in the project.

C. The work product may cause the stakeholder to include more requirements.

D. The work product may cause the stakeholder to withdraw funding for the project if they're not in agreement.

A. A work product has not been approved yet, so it generally should not be shared with a stakeholder. In some instances when the work product is shared, the business analyst should express the status of the requirement in the work product. Choices B, C, and D are not valid statements about sharing the work product with a stakeholder.

14. What is created as a result of the business analyst's work?

A. Deliverables

B. Requirements

C. Milestones

D. Requirements package

D. A requirements package is the culmination of the business analyst's work. A, deliverables, are the results of project work. B, requirements, are the demands, wants, and needs of the project stakeholders. C, milestones, are reached by completing project phases.

15. What is created at the end of a project phase?

A. Milestone

B. Scope verification processes

C. Requirements review process

D. Funding requests

A. Milestones are reached by completing a project phase. B, scope verification processes, may happen at the end of a phase, but they are not created by the phase completing. C, requirements review process, may be associated with milestone completion, but the process is not created by the phase completion. D, funding requests, may be linked to milestones but not always, so this choice is incorrect.

16. Which of the following best describes quality in a project?

A. Quality is the totality of all the project requirements.

B. Quality is a conformance to the stakeholders.

C. Quality is using the highest grade materials for the project deliverables.

D. Quality is a conformance to requirements.

D. Quality is a conformance to requirements and a fitness for use. Choices A, B, and C do not define quality in a project.

17. When a change is considered for the project requirements, which one of the following is not reviewed in consideration of the requirements change request?

A. Time to implement the change

B. Cost to implement the change

C. The person who submits the change request

D. The human resources that may be affected by the proposed change

C. The person that submits the change is not considered as part of the change approval. All change requests should review time, cost, scope, quality, human resources, communication, risk, and procurement as part of the change approval process.

18. You are the business analyst for a project to create a software package. A change to the identified requirements has been approved by your organization's Change Control Board. What should you do with the change information?

A. Communicate the change to the project manager.

B. Document the change in the revision log.

C. Document the change in the Requirements Issue Log.

D. Communicate the change to the business owner.

B. Whenever a change has been approved, the business analyst needs to document the change in the revision log. As part of the change process, the communication of the change would happen between the business owner, relevant stakeholders, and the project manager, so choices A and D are incorrect. Choice C is not valid, as conflicting requirements are recorded in the Requirements Issue Log, not changes.

19. What component of the communication model is responsible for transferring the message between parties?

A. Medium.

B. Transfer agent.

C. Language.

D. It depends on the format of the message.

A. Medium describes the agent that transfers the message between two or more entities. Choices B, C, and D are not valid terms used in the communication model.

20. Tom and Sally are business analysts for your organization and are currently in a disagreement about a project requirement. Tom and Sally are refusing to communicate with one another, so you bring the two together for conflict resolution. The refusal of Tom and Sally to communicate is known as what?

A. Noise

B. Barrier

C. Nonverbal communication

D. Paralingual communications

B. Tom and Sally are experiencing a barrier to communication. A, noise, is something that distracts from the message, like static on a telephone call. C, nonverbal communication, usually supports the communication model and does not describe the scenario. D, paralingual, is a term to describe the pitch, tone, and inflection that may affect the communication meaning.

Working as an Enterprise Business Analyst

In this chapter you will

- Examine the duties of a business analyst
- Conduct feasibility studies
- Prepare the business case
- Conduct risk assessments
- Prepare a decision package
- Select and prioritize projects

In your work as a business analyst, you've probably completed many of the activities in this chapter already. You've worked with your management team, stakeholders, and clients to select projects and to shift projects based on needs, priorities, and opportunities. Of course the projects you shift around are based on the business cases and feasibility studies you've completed. Every project and opportunity that an organization selects to invest time and funds in must fit within the organization's architecture, mission, strategy, and goals.

Business analysts work with executives, functional managers, project managers and both internal and external clients to determine the optimum investments for new projects and opportunities. A project is a short-term endeavor that will create something unique and individual for the organization. Projects have a definite ending; organizations, hopefully, do not. Organizational opportunities are usually centered on profitability or reducing costs. Business analysts work at the enterprise level to help determine which projects and which opportunities should be funded.

The immediate goal of a business analyst is to capture the current state of an organization and then to frame the desired future state of an organization. Often the business analyst will draw out the requirements of a project or opportunity to determine the feasibility of reaching the desired future state of the organization. Sometimes this process is a stand-alone project for the organization rather than a pre-project activity. In either instance the goal of the activity is the same: to determine the requirements to reach the desired future state and whether those requirements are worth the risk, effort, time, and cost to achieve.

You'll need to be familiar with five enterprise analysis processes for your CBAP examination:

- Define the business need.
- Access capability gaps.
- Determine the solution approach.
- Define the solution scope.
- Define the business case.

While you may or may not have in-depth experience determining value, worth, and cost justification at the enterprise level, you'll need to know the activities and processes in the Enterprise Analysis knowledge area for your CBAP examination. Obviously this is a knowledge area that demands your attention and that will challenge your knowledge of the IIBA approach to enterprise analysis.

Defining the Enterprise Business Analyst Role

To be most effective as an enterprise business analyst, you have to know what it is you're to analyze. You can't do your duties as a business analyst at the enterprise level unless the executive of the organization has completed her mission and vision for the entity. Without some direction and vision, the business analyst can't find projects and opportunities that align with the strategic plans and goals of the executives. Once the executive team has established clear goals, which is typically early on in an organization's life, then the business analyst can recommend new programs, projects, opportunities, and prioritization of these new ventures.

In the BABOK most of the business analyst activities are pre-project driven, but it's important to realize that not all of business analysis is centered on projects. Some business operations, lines of business, and ventures are part of operations rather than projects. Business analysis is a vital pre-project activity, however, that helps an organization determine which projects should be funded, given a go/no-go decision, or even stopped. You won't have to know much about project management for your CBAP examination, but know this: business analysis activities may appear to overlap project management, but distinct differences exist between the two.

Business analysts create the scope and requirements for the project, and project managers control and execute the activities to create the scope. Business analysis activities and project management activities often happen in tandem, especially in large, long-term projects. For your CBAP examination, you'll need to recognize the owners of certain business analysis and project management responsibilities. Here's a quick listing of the roles you'll see throughout the remainder of this book and on your CBAP exam:

- **Executive team** These people make up the organization's upper management, who create the vision, leadership, direction, strategy, and tactics for the organization.

- **Business sponsor**   This is an individual within an organization who has the positional power and decision-making ability to launch new projects, to start new organizational initiatives, and to grant resources to business analysts and project managers. Business sponsors are sometimes called the project sponsors, as they may charter new projects.

- **Enterprise governance group**   This is a committee of organizational leaders who ensure that groups, functional departments, projects, and other members of the organization are following the established organizational rules, procedures, and business directives of the organization.

- **Project manager**   This individual oversees the project processes, deliverables, and project team. The project manager has a predefined amount of autonomy over the project and works within the established boundaries to deliver the project scope as planned. The business analyst and the project manager often work closely together, but have distinct responsibilities.

- **Business analyst**   This is you. The business analyst is responsible for preparing feasibility studies, business cases, decision packages, project scope, and requirements, and for validating the business case, project scope, and project deliverables.

The project manager, business analyst, and the management team of the organization must be in sync with who does what, who makes what decision, and what boundaries are established between the project manager and the business analyst, while still allowing teamwork between the business analyst duties and project management. Table 5-1 links the organizational roles and deliverables to the expected activities from the business analyst.

As more businesses shift to a management-by-projects approach, where every deliverable is treated as a project with definite expected deliverables, processes, and procedures, the role of the business analyst becomes more important. For your CBAP examination, you'll need to recognize the demand for a business analyst to be involved with business stakeholders, project managers, and the IT staff when new projects and solutions are proposed. For the CBAP, center the proposed project, investment, and desired future state around what's best for the organization's health, longevity, and return on investment (ROI).

Participating in Strategic Planning and Goal Setting

Organizations are traditionally chunked into three divisions, as seen in Figure 5-1. The top layer, the *executive* layer, has the fewest people but the most influence over the organization's direction. This top layer of an organization creates the vision, provides the leadership and mission, and establishes the strategic goals. The executives of an organization, regardless of the organization's size, must provide a clear description of where the organization is and where the organization wants to go.

Activity	Owner	Deliverables	Business Analyst Duties
Develop the strategic plan	Executive team	Strategic plan	Competitive analysis. Create benchmark studies. Plan and lead strategic planning sessions.
Develop strategic goals	Executive team	Strategic goals Organizational themes and benefit measurements	Plan and lead strategic planning sessions.
Perform feasibility studies	Business analyst	Feasibility studies	Identify alternative solutions. Examine feasibility of options. Determine most feasible solution.
Develop business cases	Business analyst	Business cases	Create project scope. Create time and cost estimates. Quantify benefits. Create business case document.
Project proposal	Business sponsor	Executive presentation Decision package	Create executive presentation documentation. Create decision package.
Select and prioritize opportunities	Enterprise governance group	Project selection Project priority Project charter	Facilitate portfolio management meeting. Present new project proposals.
Launch new projects	Project manager	Project plans	Assist with project initiating and planning. Collaborate with system architect on project solution.
Manage projects for value	Business analyst	Updated business case at control gates	Work with project manager to update the business case. Help executives make decision to continue to invest in project based on project performance, discovery, risk, and findings.
Track project benefits	Business sponsor	Balanced scorecard reports	Ensure metrics are present, analyzed, and reported to business sponsor. Track actual and planned performance.

Table 5-1   Business Analyst Organizational and Project Management Activities

The middle layer is the *functional* layer. This layer, sometimes called middle management, operates by function such as sales, information technology, marketing, and other functional activities. The purpose of the functional layer is to lead and accomplish the strategies, tactics, and operational architecture of the organization. The functional layer

Figure 5-1
Organizations are divided into three layers.

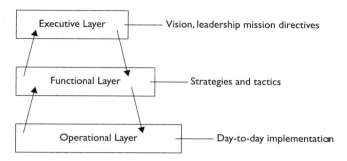

Each layer must support the layer above it.

of an organization manages departments, project management offices, and lines of business.

The bottom layer of an organization is the *operational* layer. This is a somewhat vanilla way of describing the employees who are functional managers or executives. These individuals actually do the labor and create deliverables that allow the organization to exist. The operational layer is the implementation of the business objectives. The operational layer has the most people and the least amount of directional decision-making abilities.

In this pyramid model, each layer must support the objectives of the layer above it. Each layer has specific purposes, but the purposes must be clearly defined or chaos ensues. Strategic planning is an important business analysis activity, as its outcome may affect the direction of the organization and have an impact on different levels of the company. When a new project is proposed, the business analyst completes strategic planning to determine

- How the proposed project meshes with the executive layer's vision and goals
- How the project may affect the functions of the organization and the internal and external clients of these functions
- How the project may be accomplished with operational resources the company has
- The impact on the environment and market
- The current technical culture and structure of the organization
- The identification of ongoing business issues, risks, and concerns
- How the organization will remain profitable and competitive

The business analyst is a key role in an organization's strategic planning and goal setting activities. The business analyst must understand the vision and direction of the organization and help others acquire that same understanding. The business analyst is at the center of strategic planning and works with internal and external clients to examine the long-term effect a project or investment may have on an organization's ability to reach and maintain its mission, purpose, and strategic goals. Business goals, projects, and identified problems can be generated from several locales in and out of an organization:

- **Top down**   Upper management identifies a need for a strategic goal.
- **Bottom up**   The organization experiences problems with processes, functions, or operations that must be resolved.
- **Middle-based**   Management needs more information in order to maintain or improve current operations.
- **External drivers**   Customers, competition, or regulation force new projects, problems, and demand for solutions.

The origin of a business goal holds sway over the priority an organization places on achieving that goal. For example, a government regulation may take precedence over a middle-based goal to improve an internal process.

Developing Strategic Goals

The business analyst works with the executive team to help create the strategic goals of the enterprise. Developing the enterprise strategic goals usually happens concurrently with the strategic plan development, though some organizations may revisit strategic goal setting quarterly or yearly. Strategic goals are specific, obtainable, measurable things that can be achieved through opportunities and projects. Vague, subjective goals, such as "improve customer service," must be elaborated into quantifiable specifics that can be measured, planned for, and achieved.

An approach organizations often take with the business analysis activity is to create strategic themes. Themes compartmentalize strategic goals and allow the goals to be broken down into smaller projects and opportunities. For example, the broad strategic theme of "increase corporate revenue by adding new services" could be chunked into specific revenue-generating goals for an organization. Strategic themes and strategic goals are usually centered on adding revenue, reducing costs, and adding value to internal and external clients; they increase corporate competence, learning assets, and knowledge management.

 EXAM NOTE   Are your goals SMART? SMART is an acronym for a way to measure a goal to determine if it's *specific, measurable, achievable, relevant,* and *time-bounded.* (The first letter of each attribute spells the word "smart.")

As strategic themes require a way to measure progress, many organizations use a corporate scorecard to track progress, adherence to a theme, and as a barometer for potential project success. In for-profit entities, financial goals are typically highest in scorecard weight, while not-for-project groups have mission, financial responsibility, and impact as measurable factors. The idea of the Balanced Scorecard uses four predetermined metrics to measure the components of an organization:

- **Financial**   This metric states the specific financial goals of the organization, such as reduce costs by 10 percent and increase revenue by 8 percent.

- **Customer**   This metric states the goal for customer satisfaction, which could be to earn a 98 percent approval rating on a customer service survey. It could also measure customer retention and new customer additions to be measured.

- **Internal**   Internal processes are measured between periods, and goals are set to improve process performance. Industry benchmarks, such as IT and construction, could also be used as internal metrics for measurement.

- **Learning and innovation**   This goal measures new product development, measurable competencies achieved, skill development, and proper application of knowledge learned to projects, operations, and issues.

A similar scorecard can be applied to government agencies where accountability, rather than financial goals, is a concern. These scorecard factors stem from the Global Balanced Scorecard for U.S. Government:

- **Customer**   How do our customers perceive us?

- **Financial**   What's the best utilization of our funds to reach the best results?

- **Internal**   What must we excel at?

- **Innovation**   How do we improve and create value?

For the CBAP examination, you should be familiar with the idea of scorecards for profit, not-for-profit, and government agencies. The purpose of a scorecard is to iden-tify measurable goals, strategic themes, and purpose, and then to aim projects and operations to achieve the goals. Strategic goals, like strategic planning, may change based on environmental, cultural, and economic conditions. When strategic goals change, the scorecards must reflect the updated strategic plans.

Serving as an Enterprise Business Analyst

A business analyst serving at the enterprise level helps make decisions that can affect the entire organization. A business analyst in this role works with executives, func-tional management, internal and external clients, and project managers to gather, doc-ument, and analyze projects, opportunities, and organizational changes. Changes to IT, for example, are classic examples of enterprise-level changes that require a business analyst to evaluate each change, measure the risk, and help to document proposed solutions. All changes to business processes at the enterprise level, IT-driven or not, require a clear understanding of why the change is needed or proposed.

As a general rule, the larger the project, the more information is needed to make decisions about the project. A primary objective of business analysis is to gather and provide just the right amount of supporting detail for the organization to make the investment decision. Too little information and it's time wasted and frustration; too much information and the decision is bogged down in minutiae. For the CBAP exam, you should be familiar with how much effort is needed for project decisions based on the size of the proposed change. Table 5-2 shows the project type, risk exposure, and project impact on the enterprise.

Project size	Small	Medium	Large
Anticipated risk	Low risk	Low-to-moderate risk	High risk
Estimated duration	Less than six months.	Six to 12 months.	More than 12 months.
Schedule constraints	Schedule is flexible.	Minor schedule variations, firm deadline.	Deadline is fixed. Schedule delays are unacceptable.
Complexity	Defined scope, achievable solution.	Problem is difficult to understand. Solution is unclear. Solution may be difficult to achieve.	Problem and solution are difficult to define. Solution is difficult to achieve.
Strategic goals	Internal.	Some lines of business impacted. Impact is low-priority risk.	Affects enterprise core service. Tied to key organizational incentives.
Level of change	Single business unit.	Number of business units.	Enterprisewide.
Dependencies	No major dependencies.	Some major dependencies. Interrelated projects.	Major dependencies. Interrelated projects affected at high risk.

Table 5-2 Project Attributes Help Business Analyst Determine Effort

Based on this table the business analyst will determine how many of the statements are true for each proposed project or organizational change. The more elements that are true, the larger the amount of effort is required. Risk is an uncertain event or condition that may have a positive or negative effect on the organization. Accepted risk, as in all ventures, may result in a loss of the invested dollars. The amount of risk an organization is willing to assume must be in proportion to the amount of reward the organization will receive.

High-risk projects require strenuous, in-depth business analysis and are characterized by their enterprisewide impacts and two or more categories in the "Large" column of the table. Low-to-moderate-risk projects typically have four or more attributes in the "Medium" column. Some projects may be categorized as low-to-moderate risks if they have but one entry in the "Large" column and three or fewer entries in the "Medium" column. Finally, low-risk projects don't generally require much enterprise-level business analysis, but do require some benefit-costs analysis to ensure the investment is worth the risk exposure.

Examining the Outputs of Enterprise Business Analysis

For your CBAP examination, you should always examine the question, especially situational questions, in the context of how large the project or opportunity is. The size of the project may help you determine what business analysis activities you are to complete or what documents you should be creating for the project team. The output of business analysis creates the supporting detail that the project manager and the project team will use to frame and guide the project.

For the large, high-risk projects, you'll create several documents that will help the project management team in their efforts. I'll discuss each of these documents in more detail throughout the book, but for now just know which document is needed for which size project.

Large, high-risk projects require several documents:

- Enterprise architecture
- Feasibility study
- Business case
- Risk rating
- Decision package

Medium, low-to-moderate risk projects require some documents to serve as supporting detail for the project manager:

- Business case
- Enterprise architecture

Depending on the size and conditions of the project, the business analyst may need to create any of the documents she'd normally create with the large, high-risk projects.

Small, low-risk projects require but two things:

- Simplified business case
- Simplified business architecture to provide context for the project manager

As the phases of the business analysis progress, more information will come available for the business analyst to examine. As more information becomes available, the business analyst is able to elaborate more on the required documents for the defined size of the project. If the project or opportunities grow or the level of risk exposure changes, the business analyst is expected to react with more analysis and supporting detail that will lead to the decision package.

Creating and Maintaining the Business Architecture

Business architecture doesn't mean that you're building skyscrapers, technology, or bridges. Business architecture is an esoteric, intangible structure that constitutes a business entity. It is the culture, enterprise environmental factors, business structure, and policies that guide and direct the selection, funding, and management of programs and projects. Business architecture is often based on the purpose, mission statement, and intent of the organization. It defines what the organization does, its business strategy, objectives, long-term goals, and vision for the organization. The business architecture defines its stakeholders in the form of internal and external clients, regulatory agencies, employees, vendors, and partners.

Business analysts are becoming more involved in the creation and maintenance of the business architecture. Specifically, the business analyst may help create the unified documentation, models, diagrams, and the current and desired future structure of the organization. The business analyst may create these documents to help define the business architecture:

- **Vision and mission** While existing organizations likely already have a mission statement or vision, it may evolve and change based on culture, climate, and competition. The business analyst can help elicit the requirements and define the desired future state and purpose of the organization.

- **Enterprise environmental factors** These are part of the business architecture that defines the policies, procedures, and rules that project managers and employees must follow. Enterprise environmental factors are unique to each organization.

- **Organizational structure** The structure of the company is documented and often diagrammed through organizational charts. Matrix structures may show overlaps between departments or reporting project offices. Business analysts may also identify geographical locations, managers, and utilizations.

Every organization has a business architecture, whether it's documented or not. For your CBAP exam, you'll need to know that the role of the business analyst is becoming more ingrained into the documentation of the business architecture; specifically, senior business analysts may be involved with creating and maintaining the business architecture at the enterprise level.

In today's world, when the business architecture changes, so technology must change to be in alignment with the business processes. Part of business architecture is the identification and documentation of the supporting information technology systems, platforms, and topology. Should the business architecture be modified, the IT must also be modified, as it's part of the business framework.

Developing the Business Architecture

All projects are about change. When a project is proposed, what's really being entertained is changing the business, cultural, or communal environment by creating a new product or service, or by removing something from the environment. When a project aims to change something, the business architecture is evaluated to determine if the project is warranted, if the project fits within the current business architecture, and how the change may affect the business process and supporting IT systems.

To facilitate the creation of new projects and to continue to develop the existing business architecture, the business analyst completes several activities:

- Documents the current business architecture by identifying the organizational structure, organizational product, services, and strategy

- Documents the organizational functions, services, internal processes, and geographical locations

- Develops the business architecture in consideration of the organization s strategic vision

- Completes analysis on the difference between the current business architecture and the desired business architecture

- Determines effort, time, cost, and feasibility of moving from current business architecture to the desired business architecture objectives

- Documents the process for new project assessment, which is part of organizational portfolio management, and helps identify how new opportunities can be recognized and achieved by the organization within the defined constraints of the business architecture

Obviously, larger, mature organizations will likely have more control, in-depth business planning, models, and established processes than smaller, newer organizations. This is not to say that newer organizations or mature companies are better or worse than one another, but rather that the maturity of the organization typically indicates the depth of business analysis required for structured business architecture development. In either entity the goal of business architecture development is the same: to provide a consistent, yet flexible, framework for allowing new projects and opportunities to enter the organization, and to provide structure and restraint for organizational decisions.

According to the BABOK, it's the senior business analysts along with the executive team who serve as the business architects. Just keep in mind that business architects are creating systems, documentation, and components so business decisions can be made as efficiently as possible. Business architects need these skills and knowledge:

- Understanding and application of generally accepted business practices

- Relevant knowledge of industry domains

- IT-enabled business solutions

- Emerging business concepts, strategies, and practices

- Internal lines of business and how they interact

- Organization of the enterprise knowledge

- How the organization's business issues drive the organization demand for technology

- Business process engineering

- Business analysis abilities

- Business modeling, concepts, rules, policies, and terminology

Each organization will have its own enterprise environmental factors that will affect how much control, input, and creating of the business architecture is required. Mature organizations will likely have much of the business architecture already defined, either by design or by the evolution of its practices. Smaller, more nimble organizations may be able to shift their business architecture faster than larger organizations and react to market conditions, competition, and changing organizational priorities. In either instance, the business analyst is needed to help the organization document and create the business architecture.

Creating the Business Architecture

An organization may create or update their business architecture for many different reasons, so there's no defined step-by-step process. All business architecture creation, however, will need to determine the scope of the business architecture effort required to complete the work. Changes to the business architecture will affect the entire organization, so it's typically a time-intensive and resource-consuming process. There must be a clear understanding of the current architecture and how the intended architecture is to be used within the organization. Executives, functional management, project managers, and the IT groups will need to buy-into the process and participate in the creation as facilitated by senior business analysts. The business architecture must address all stakeholders who are being affected by the change or creation of the architecture:

- Executives and middle management
- Individual contributors
- Project management teams
- Operational teams
- Shareholders
- Customers and end users
- Government and regulatory agencies

The business analyst and key stakeholders will need to determine the best approach and structure for creating or modifying the architecture. This includes making decisions on which organizational diagrams, flowcharts, and process mappings need to be updated to reflect the finished architecture. This will require an evaluation of how the organization completes its operations, its strategic goals, and the viewpoint from the varying lines of business.

Throughout the creation or modification of the business architecture, the business analyst will need to consider

- What tools and techniques are most appropriate for creating, modeling, forecasting, and archiving the business architecture structure, historical data, and the outputs of the business analysis processes and activities

- How the business architecture will be used throughout the organization and the involvement of all the correct stakeholders, decision makers, government compliance, vendors, and clients

- The architecture creation strategy, whether it's an architecture modification or an entire new architecture using a top-down approach

- The creation of a desired new architecture, the documentation of the organization's current architecture, or both (both may be done if the organization has an informal, loosely documented architecture and a desire to create a more sophisticated document architecture)

Part of creating or updating the architecture also involves the creation of new architecture drawings and documents. The architecture documents specifically define the structure of the organization, its hierarchy, dependencies, systems, policies and procedures, and the persistent connection with the IT groups. A tool that can be helpful in ensuring that all components of the business architecture have been addressed is a Requirements Traceability Matrix (RTM).

As a business analyst, you've probably used RTMs before. An RTM is a way of identifying and documenting categories of needs, specific requirements within the categories of needs, functional or operational identification for each identified requirement, and any additional characteristics that need to be addressed such as budget, status, delivery of work, and whether the work delivered satisfies the identified requirement. RTMs may also have columns for comments, owners of the deliverable, and other relevant information. See Figure 5-2.

	Op1	Op2	Op3	Op4	Op5	Data	Status	Owner	Comments
REQ1	X		X	X	X	487	Fun	PM1	Currently functional
REQ2	X	X	X		X	7,321	Open	PM1	Open for review
REQ3	X	X		X		.99	Test	Pr2	Currently testing
REQ4		X	X			12.32	Prog	Pr2	Development
REQ5	X			X			Prog	BA3	Development
REQ6			X	X			Init	FM1	Initiating
REQ7	X			X		7.55	Test	IT1	Testing
REQ8			X		X		Fun	ITCIN	Currently functional
REQ9						475	Open	PS	Open for review

Figure 5-2 A Requirements Traceability Matrix (RTM) can track requirements and satisfaction of the identified requirements.

One business architecture framework approach that you'll find in the BABOK, and likely on your CBAP examination, is the Zachman Framework. It's a matrix, created by John Zachman, that provides structure and helps stakeholders describe complex enterprises. The Zachman Framework uses predefined questions that must be answered for each component of any organization. The results are captured in the matrix as in Figure 5-3. While you won't have to create a Zachman Framework for your CBAP, you should be able to recognize it based on the standard questions and components it defines.

You might also see a more direct business architecture creation technique called the POLDAT Technique. This data collection framework uses six categories whose first letter spells POLDAT:

- **Process** Each defined business process that provides value from the organization to the client

- **Organization** The lines of business, functional departments, management teams, staffing, roles, skills and knowledge, and other identifiable operational duties that make up a portion of the enterprise

- **Location** The physical location of the business units, offices, and any other entity that has a physical address as part of the enterprise

- **Data** The information that serves as what the BABOK calls "the currency" of the enterprise; this is the information that the enterprise needs to function

Answer these questions.

	What Data and entities	How Processes	Where Location	Who Stakeholders	When Schedule	Why Motivation
Scope						
Business Model						
System Model						
Technology Model						
Detailed Representations						

Use these objects.

Figure 5-3 A Zachman Framework can help create the business architecture.

- **Applications**   The software that allows employees to act quickly and efficiently

- **Technology**   The information systems beyond the application that support the operations of the enterprise

Know these approaches for the CBAP examination—you'll likely see them there. The advantage of these approaches is that a framework can guide the business analyst through the enterprise architecture creation and help capture all of the requirements for the organization. With these predefined compartments, it's easier and more precise to focus on one element of the business at a time. As always, document your outcomes and supporting detail, and archive the information in case it's needed for reference later.

Modeling the Business Architecture

You can also use business models to help create or modify the business architecture. The outcome of using models is still the same, to capture all of the organizational strategic requirements, but the approach is different. Based on the organization, the amount of effort estimated to create the architecture, experience, urgency, and comfort, the business analyst may choose any one of these models for the business architecture:

- **Component business model**   This is the most common business model and was formulated by IBM. It provides a direct and traditional view of an enterprise, providing nomenclature to lines of business, functional units, departments groups, and other organizational resources. Each service, deliverable, or information that provides value to the customer should be documented.

- **Business process model**   A *process* is an activity that brings about a specific, desired result. A business process model, sometimes called an activity model, captures all of the activities within a business, the inputs and outputs of each activity, and the required resources to complete each activity. Business process models traditionally show the hierarchy of an entire organization rather than a department-by-department viewpoint.

- **Use case model**   Captures the business processes by showing how customers, vendors, management, departments, and other enterprisewide stakeholders interact with the business. By capturing how resources interact with one another through the business processes, it should become more apparent how the organization is to be structured.

- **Class model**   A class model captures the relationship of information within an organization, how information is exchanged, and the flow of information.

- **Business scenario**   A business scenario is a hypothetical situation that portrays how the organization's processes are to operate. Business scenarios can depict typical operations, planned processes, and responses to situations when things don't go as planned. The outcomes of business scenarios can help the business analyst define the business architecture by defining the relationship of organizations in (and out of) the organization, process interaction, and expected outcomes of operations.

- **Knowledge management** According to the BABOK, knowledge management is becoming a more and more important tool for business analysts to use during business architecture creation. Knowledge management is the collection, storage, accessibility, and accuracy of the wealth of information an organization creates.

In addition to these modeling tools and techniques, the business analyst can use more sophisticated software tools to help create the business architecture. You won't need to know any specific software tools for the CBAP examination, but you should know that software can help document the business processes, create diagrams and charts, and archive the business architecture creation for future refinements. Most software-driven tools are either modeling tools or archival tools—though some newer applications boast the ability to do both.

Once the business architecture has been finalized and there's a consensus that the architecture meets all of the identified requirements, then the business architecture report needs to be created. This report finalizes the documentation for the business architecture, explains why the architecture has been created, and provides supporting detail for decisions made during the creation of the business architecture. This final report will need to address operations, project management, functional management, and the connection and required support of IT.

Once the business architecture report has been written and newly defined or updated, business architecture must undergo a quality review. The purpose of the quality review is to find consensus on the accuracy and completeness of the defined business architecture. That is, can a new opportunity or project successfully be launched, managed, and benefits realized based on the business architecture? The Requirements Traceability Matrix may be called upon again to ensure that all of the identified requirements were met and the supporting detail was examined.

The key stakeholders, executives, and even hired subject matter experts may be needed to review the business architecture to ensure its completeness. The strategic goals and purpose of creating or updating the architecture is what must be measured against the results of the business architecture creation. All stakeholders should ask if the architecture can support current and future objectives, operational strategies, and if the structure of the architecture is fully documented.

Should errors or omissions be discovered during this quality review, then the business analyst and the organization will need to refine the structure and repeat the process. The quality review should also provide an opportunity to confirm, test, and benchmark the performance metrics for projects and operations. The performance metrics, such as sales, profitability, and customer satisfaction, should be linked to the organization's strategic goals.

Determining Capability Gaps

For-profit businesses exist for one reason: to make a profit. While they may have lofty goals, help the community, and provide services for people around the world, their fundamental purpose is to make a profit. Even though not-for-profit organizations also have a financial reasoning to their existence, their mission and objectives are not necessarily centered on revenue, and they often have an obligation to the monies they've raised and the people they represent. In either instance, for your CBAP examination, you must understand the fundamental reason why a business exists. In scenario-driven questions, determine the goal of an organization and how the question supports the organization's strategy to reach its goals.

As businesses create or modify their business architecture, they'll constantly refer to their organizational goals, strategic goals, and mission. Once the architecture has been approved, the next step is action in alignment with the business architecture and strategic goals. The actions, as far as the business analyst is concerned, will come through opportunities, programs, and projects. In all of these actions, the first step is evaluation and consideration of the best approach to realize the benefits that the opportunities, programs, and projects may have to offer. Alternative identification is an approach to consider all of the available and possible solutions and then to pare down the solutions to the most likely and feasible options.

Capability gaps describe the void between what the organization can currently do and what the organization must do to achieve their business goals. Capability gaps are detailed through gap assessments, feasibility studies, expert judgment, and projects to establish the depth of the gap and the means to overcome it.

A feasibility study researches the possible solutions to determine each solution's likelihood of meshing with the business architecture, with the organizational mission, and of reaching financial, operational, and technical achievability. Obviously not every solution is possible, so the feasibility studies can help determine which solution will give the biggest reward for the cost and effort generated toward the solution. Choosing only the least costly in terms of finances isn't always the best choice; the business analyst should determine more than cost, but should also consider

- Risk of choosing one alternative solution over another
- Commitment of resources
- Risk of the project
- Estimated cost
- Estimated schedule
- Time lapse before any benefits, return on investment, or deliverables are realized
- Quality concerns of the proposed solution
- Resource, competencies, facilities, and other gaps that the solution may present
- Cost-to-benefit ratio of each solution

Every project and opportunity is different, so the preceding list is by no means all-inclusive. When creating a feasibility structure, you'll consider whatever other facets may affect the operations, lines of business, customers, or the ongoing health of the organization. Understanding the purpose of the project will help you determine which solution can offer the best for the enterprise as a whole. Massive proposals for programs and large projects may often treat the feasibility study as its own project. Business analysts create feasibility studies

- When the executive layer is creating new strategic goals and strategies
- When the portfolio management team is evaluating programs, projects, and opportunities to resolve problems, such as cutting costs, and to seize opportunities, such as new profit-generating projects
- During the requirements gathering activities of a proposed project, program, or opportunity, to determine the most viable solution to satisfy the stakeholder strategic goals

You, as a business analyst, will likely determine capability gaps whenever your organization has major changes in its organizational climate. When your company proposes new products and services, new lines of business, mergers and acquisitions, or changes to the enterprise environmental factors within the organization, a feasibility study should be created. The end result, a capability gap assessment, leads to the recommended solution option. The recommended solution, based on your findings, will be elaborated upon in a business case.

Preparing for the Feasibility Study

For your CBAP exam, you'll need to know the skills and knowledge areas a business analyst will need to create a feasibility study. Keep in mind, my focus here is on you passing the CBAP examination; while all of the information I present is accurate and applicable to all organizations, your company may already have a methodology created for business analysis and feasibility studies. That's great. For your exam, however, you'll need to use and recall the terminology the IIBA has established. Don't worry, the underlying processes for most of the terms and activities are probably the same as what you use in the real world, but the names may be slightly different for the CBAP exam.

The IIBA assumes that you, the business analyst, have relevant knowledge of software development, IT infrastructure, and information systems. You won't necessarily have to know any particular software packages, but conceptually you should understand technology, infrastructure, and general themes of IT for your exam. In light of this, one of the first stops in creating a feasibility study is an assessment of the business analyst's skills and competencies. You should have a deep understanding of the business objectives, strategic goals, and IT. For each project, you'll need to know why the project is being proposed, what will be changed, and have a general idea of how the organization will function once the project has been completed.

It's unreasonable to expect one person, the business analyst, to have all of the skills required to perform a complete analysis of most proposed projects, programs, and opportunities. No one knows everything (as I've been told more than once), so the business analyst needs to recruit some help to complete the business analysis to create the feasibility study. To complete the feasibility study, the following skills are needed:

- Research and information analysis
- Research planning and leadership of the analysis processes
- Technical writing
- Organizational skills
- Communication skills to perform interviews, create documentation, and conduct ad hoc meetings
- Flexibility to work independently and in team efforts

Participants who contribute to the feasibility study will need a clear understanding of what they are to do, when they are to do it, and to whom they'll communicate the results of their work. A work authorization system can help you keep the feasibility study progressing and hold people accountable for their assignments. If the feasibility study is for a significant change or large project, the study may be treated as its own project. In this case, you'll also need project management skills to complete the study. Chapter 9 in this book offers a view of project management, but for now I'll touch lightly on the process. You can follow along using Figure 5-4, which shows the project management life cycle and how it may map to a feasibility study. This is a brief overview of the project management processes, just to give you an idea of how a project moves from concept to final deliverable.

- **Initiating**   The project is charted with a broad vision of what the project is to create. A preliminary project scope statement may be created that calls for the creation of a feasibility study to determine the recommended solution option. The project manager is named and given autonomy over the feasibility study project.
- **Planning**   The project is planned based on the determined requirements for scope, time, cost, quality, human resources, communications, risk, and procurement. The constraints and assumptions of the project are documented, and the execution of the project is planned.

Figure 5-4
The project management life cycle is universal to all projects.

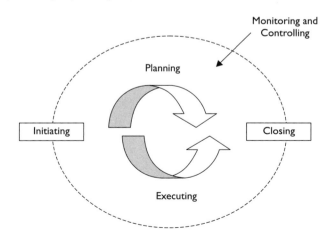

- **Executing** The project plans that have been created are now executed. The project manager ensures that the work is done with quality, that the project team is completing their assignments, and that the outcomes of the work are documented. Communication of the feasibility study, among the project team and other stakeholders, follows the rules of the project communications management plan.

- **Monitoring and controlling** In tandem with project execution, the project is monitored and controlled. The creation of the feasibility study—its schedule, costs, scope, and quality—are all controlled, evaluated, and the results documented. When issues, risks, or unacceptable work arise, the project shifts back into planning to address the situation.

- **Closing** The project phase or entire scope has been completed, and the project manager performs administrative closure. This includes sign-off from the customer on the scope validation, final findings, and archiving the project documentation. An operational transfer plan may address the feasibility study resources and how they're released from the project.

Not all feasibility studies will need a project, but it's not unusual for a feasibility study to be treated as a project or to follow the logical project management life cycle. For your CBAP exam, you should be topically familiar with the project management life cycle, but the IIBA draws a distinction between project management and business analysis.

 NOTE If you're certified as a Project Management Professional (PMP), you may notice some subtle differences between the Project Management Institute's definition of terms and the IIBA's definition. The CBAP is based on IIBA's approach, so adjust your studying and terminology accordingly for the IIBA CBAP exam.

Determining the Purpose for the Feasibility Study

You know that an organization can create a feasibility study for a bunch of different things: new software, buying a competitor, a new line of business, reducing costs, eliminating waste, and thousands of more reasons. Each business analyst tasked with creating a feasibility study must understand the underlying purpose of why the study has been launched:

- Assessing current capabilities
- Assessing desired capabilities
- Addressing a business problem
- Seizing a business opportunity

All feasibility studies will fall into one of these categories. Which type of study the business analyst is to do will determine the approach and requirements that will need to be addressed. This means the business analyst will need to have some initial assessments, meetings about the feasibility study, and a clear understanding of what the organization, enterprise, client, or other stakeholder wants the study to address. These preliminary activities will lead to the findings that will serve as the foundation for the study and research activities.

When a business analyst and his resources are creating a feasibility study to address a business problem, they'll need to determine and document the problems the organization wants to solve. This can be massive, as stakeholders may often see the end result of the problem without clearly understanding the root cause of what they're experiencing. In this type of feasibility study, the business analyst and team will need to address:

- The problem to be solved in its entirety
- The effects the problem is generating
- The causal factors that are contributing to the problem
- A decomposition of the problem to granular areas to be analyzed
- The impact of the problem on the organization, including lost time, cost, effort, morale, and marketplace perspective
- Anticipated timing and cost to the problem resolution

The most likely approach to solving a business problem is root cause analysis, which determines the causal factors, contributing factors, and the effect of the problem. Root cause analysis does not solve the problem, but can uncover the factors that are contributing to the problem the organization is experiencing. Findings are often graphed in a cause-and-effect diagram as seen in Figure 5-5.

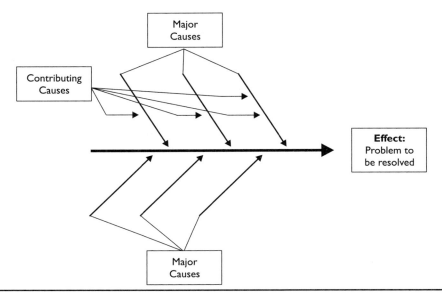

Figure 5-5   Cause-and-effect diagrams are also known as Ishikawa diagrams.

A cause-and-effect diagram is also known as a fishbone diagram or an Ishikawa diagram. The diagram can be massive, as each contributing factor must be reviewed to determine what things, events, and processes may be contributing to it. In most cases, a combination of contributing factors creates the problem the organization is experiencing. The feasibility study will create the recommended solution option based on all the options the business analyst uncovers through the study.

A feasibility study of new opportunities requires the business analyst to study the opportunity in its entirety. The business analyst and her team will evaluate the opportunity, define the opportunity in detail, and document the scope that represents the opportunity as it is understood. There's a partnership between the business analyst and the organization. Lines of communication must exist for the business analyst and the organization to provide financial prospectuses, legalities, and marketplace analysis to lead to the recommended solution for the organization. In other words, management shouldn't push an agenda and look for the business analyst to support their beliefs. The business analyst's job is to uncover and evaluate the most appropriate solution for the business opportunity. For your CBAP exam, remember the business analyst is not to create evidence for preselected, recommended solutions through the feasibility study, but rather to uncover many options and then create a recommended solution option.

Planning the Assessment Efforts

As with anything in business analysis, you need planning to address the approach, effort, and scope, and to determine the objectives of the capabilities assessment. You can't rush in and start tinkering with processes, interviewing stakeholders, and drawing loopy diagrams, and still expect to achieve much of anything. Business analysts must have a logical and structured approach to creating the capabilities assessment. That is, first understand why the assessment is needed: for a business problem or opportunity. When the assessment foundation is created, you can then assemble a team of the most appropriate resources to help you generate the study.

NOTE The BABOK recommends over and over that business analysts use a team of skilled resources. You don't have to know everything about IT, business, and project management. You just have to know where you can find the most skilled resources for your business analysis duties.

You'll lead and assign your business analysis team to the following tasks:

- Determine and document the specific objectives that your recommended solution must meet. The objectives must be measurable, achievable, and proven in order to qualify as a possible solution.

- Develop benefit criteria that all proposed solutions may be measured against. Proposed solutions will be quantitatively measured against the established criteria to determine which solutions are most feasible and which are not.

- Define, document, and communicate with the business analysis team the activities that will be conducted to generate the assessment.

- Define, document, and communicate what the study is to create based on the requirements and expectations of the stakeholders.

The requirements must be documented, reviewed, and approved by the business sponsor. The sponsor should approve the defined requirements of the assessment so there's a clear understanding of the expectations of you and your team. You'll also need the sponsor to approve the plans, timings, and budget you've created to generate the capabilities assessment, including your approaches to the work, communication strategies, and the quality control expectations.

Finally, it's also important that you and the business sponsor agree at the launch of the study on the measurable criteria your assessment efforts will generate. If objections or modifications occur, they should be added to the documentation and reviewed again for approval. You want to communicate the understood requirements and goals as early in the process as possible to reduce waste and frustration, as well as to increase productivity.

Conducting a Current State Assessment

A current state assessment can be part of a feasibility study performed by the business analysis team to determine the current status and capabilities of the organization. An understanding of the current organizational status can be compared with the desired future status of the company. This is helpful in studying both opportunity and problem-solving undertakings. By having a clear picture of where the organization is—its priorities, objectives, and strategic goals—the study team can focus its efforts more in sync with what's expected and prioritized by the organization.

The study team will review documentation, graphs, and stakeholders to determine and document the following information as part of the current state assessment:

- **Strategy**   The strategic goals of the organization should be readily available from the business architecture documentation. A review of the goals helps the study team focus on what's important for the organization.

- **Business area**   The opportunity or problem may affect many areas of the organization's business. Each line of business or department that is affected by the opportunity or problem should be documented as part of the current state assessment. This documentation should include a directory of affected stakeholders and organizational charts of each business area affected.

- **Locations**   The geographical locations should be examined and documented. This information should also be readily available for the business architecture.

- **Data and information**   Based on the topic the assessment will examine, the location, type, quantity, and flow of data and information should be studied and referenced.

- **Infrastructure** The recommended solution will often affect the technical infrastructure of the organization. The problem or opportunity that is being studied may affect the technical infrastructure, so this current status should be documented as a baseline for future reference.

- **Processes** The business processes that interact with the problem or opportunity should be documented.

- **Marketplace** The current competitive arena should be documented, including the market analysis, competition, emerging markets, and any relevant regulatory, compliance, or government changes that may affect the business.

The current state analysis may serve as point of reference throughout the study or project implementation, or even as a marker in case of a contingency rollback plan. The study team should collect an accurate picture of the current status, but a time limit should be imposed so that the study may shift forward to analyze the opportunities, solutions, and predicted future status of the organization based on its findings.

Creating a Feasibility Study

You can use many approaches to creating a feasibility study for your organization. You'll need to know and recognize these approaches for your CBAP examination. I suspect many of these tools you already use as a business analyst. You'll also see these tools pop up throughout the remainder of the book, so I'll define each one in detail here and won't in the future. If you're unfamiliar with these tools, add them to your flashcards, since you'll probably see these tools on your exam.

The first batch of tools is used when conducting the current state assessment:

- **Organization charts** These will show the hierarchical structure of the company and which units of the company are affected by the feasibility study.

- **Geographical maps** As you might guess, these show the physical location of the business units that can help address logistical concerns such as shipping, travel, communication, and IT issues.

- **Data flow diagrams** These capture and display the type and traffic of information within the organization.

- **Technology architecture diagrams** These map the topology and relationship of the IT infrastructure.

- **Process flow diagram** These diagrams capture the inputs and outputs of current, and sometimes future, process instances within the organization.

- **Domain modeling** This term gets thrown around way too much in IT and in business development. The concept of domain modeling is simply to chart out the area that's under construction, analysis, or creation, so that all stakeholders can visualize the areas that are affected. In IT, you may use domain modeling in a software creation initiative to show the functions of the software and its physical connections. In business, you might use domain modeling to visualize interfaces for process engineering, procurement systems, change management, and configuration management.

- **Six sigma programs**   These quality improvement approaches rely on data and statistical analysis to measure accuracy, efficiency, and trend analysis.

- **Root cause analysis**   This process investigates root causes, contributing causes, and causal factors that are creating the effect to be solved (which may turn out to be a business problem).

The next chunk of tools and techniques is recommended to be used during the planning of the feasibility study:

- **Standard project management activities**   Business analysts can rely on their project management expertise to plan, execute, control, and then close the feasibility study process.

- **Brainstorming**   This approach attempts to find as many solutions as possible, regardless of the proposed solutions' feasibility, practicality, or merit. This is a fast, subjective approach.

- **Work Breakdown Structure**   The WBS is a visual decomposition of the scope; it is deliverables based and typically does not include activities.

As the feasibility study evolves, the business analyst can use these additional tools to lead the study team to as many potential solutions as possible:

- **Cause-and-effect diagrams**   These diagrams visualize the result of the root cause analysis study. These are sometimes called fishbone diagrams or Ishikawa diagrams.

- **Business process reengineering**   This approach studies the current flow of business processes; looks for strengths, weaknesses, opportunities, and threats (SWOT); and considers minor adjustments to entire new designs to investigate improvements.

Once potential, viable solutions have been identified by the study team, these tools and techniques can be used to determine the feasibility of each option:

- **Market surveys**   To test customer acceptance of the solution and to measure marketplace demand.

- **Technology feasibility assessment**   Tests and documents the option to determine if it is within the organization's technical abilities, cost acceptance, and current limitations of the IT systems.

- **Interviews**   The business analyst and study team will interview business staff, IT staff, financial staff, project managers, and other stakeholders to gauge willingness, acceptance, and achievability.

- **Prototyping**   This approach creates just the component of the solution that has the highest risk of failure. If the team is able to move past the component's risk, then the remainder of the project can move forward. If the team cannot move past the risk, the solution is scrapped and a new solution is pursued.

- **Risk analysis**   The probability and impact of each solution's risk is quantitatively measured and analyzed for time, cost, and effort considerations.

- **Benchmarking**   Benchmarking compares two or more systems, states, services, products, or things to determine the best viable choice.

- **Competitive analysis**   This is a marketplace study to determine the feasibility of a proposed solution as compared against the competition.

- **Environment impact analysis**   Each option is measured for its impact on the environment in consideration of culture, compliance, regulation, and laws.

- **Technology advancement analysis**   Examines the most recent technical solutions that may be applied to the business problem or opportunity.

- **Cost-benefit analysis**   Measures the early known cost and benefits to create a cost-benefit ratio of each potential solution. The cost-benefit analysis will be elaborated on during the business case creation.

- **COTS**   Examines in-house creation versus a commercial off-the-shelf (COTS) solution.

- **Issue identification**   Identifies and documents the issues of each possible solution that may affect the business.

- **Pareto chart**   This diagram, as seen in Figure 5-6, shows the categories of defects, range of solution costs, income potential, and other categorization of components from largest to smallest.

Figure 5-6
A Pareto chart shows categories of defects from largest to smallest.

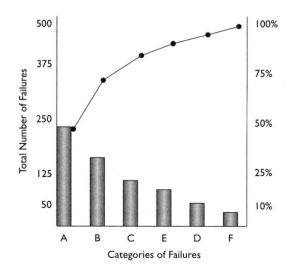

- **Analytic Hierarchy Process**   This approach uses both qualitative (subjective) and quantitative (in-depth) analysis for each solution to compare and contrast each solution based on a series of comparisons.

- **Decision Analysis**   This statistical reasoning approach allows the study team to measure and compare the probabilities of the outcome of each identified solution.

- **Decision tables**   A decision table is a matrix that illustrates the logic of decisions and leads the study team to a recommended option based on the qualifiers the table identifies and on the initial feasibility study requirements for the proposed solution.

- **Structured problem-solving techniques**   These approaches are really systems to receive and retrieve information within an organization. They keep communication happening, involve stakeholders, and plot out expected responses based on a survey, form, or structured interview.

A business analyst will use these most common approaches to create a feasibility study. Certainly there are more approaches, but these are the usual suspects when it comes to business analysis and feasibility study. You'll likely see these terms on your CBAP examination and throughout the remainder of this book. You don't need to have years of experience in any of these approaches, but you will need a topical understanding of these tools as I've given here.

Completing the Feasibility Study

The feasibility study team can now begin formulating possible solutions to recommend as an output of the feasibility study process. One of the most practical approaches is external research to determine how other organizations conquered similar problems or took advantage of similar opportunities. While every project is different, you will rarely find a project that is so unique there's no available information internal or external to the organization.

By leveraging external research, the study team can assess a wealth of information to address each of the requirements the feasibility study demands. External research allows the study team to quickly and efficiently document as many options as needed to satisfy the various components of the to-be-determined solution requirements. It's not likely that any one article or case study on the Web will answer all of an organization's problems, but many articles or case studies can address many different pieces of a proposed solution.

While many different solutions may be uncovered, one option always is to do nothing. I'm not saying doing nothing is always the best option, but it is an option. An organization may elect to do nothing because of risk, cost, schedule, changing market conditions, low return on investment, or changing priorities. Just because an organization can do a project doesn't always mean that they should do the project. Keep this in mind for your CBAP exam: when it comes to feasibility studies and possible solutions, doing nothing should be included in the list of possible options.

With each possible solution, the business analyst and team should document the possible solution in as much detail as possible. One approach, as shown in Figure 5-7, is to create a Work Breakdown Structure (WBS). A WBS is a visual breakdown (sometimes called a decomposition) of the solution to illustrate all of the components of the possible solution. Most WBS diagrams are deliverable based and don't show activities. A WBS in business analysis helps the stakeholders visualize the scope of the effort the possible solution entails. Based on the size and complexity of what's being studied, the WBS can be as granular as needed by the stakeholders.

Every possible solution that is entertained as part of the feasibility study should be documented and assessed to include the economical, technical, and operational feasibility of the solution. This can include creating prototypes for risk assessment and technical achievability. Business analysts might also create market surveys to determine the demand for the solution in relation to the cost to create the solution.

As many solutions are IT driven, interviews with the technical units of the organization are needed to determine the stability of each proposed solution. The business ana-

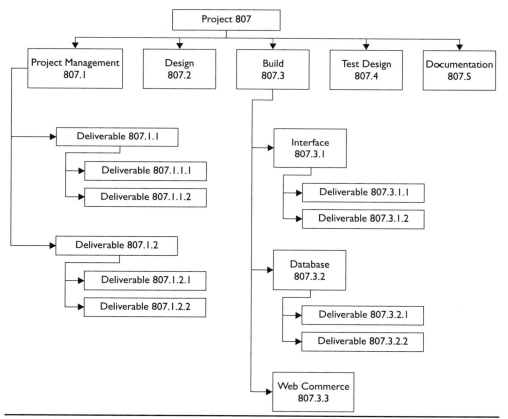

Figure 5-7   Work Breakdown Structures are visual breakdowns of the project scope.

lyst will need to confirm that the solution is based on proven technology that doesn't isolate the organization and that provides growth, stability, and scalability for future endeavors. This means that the business analyst and the IT groups will need testing, interviews with experts, time, and a budget to complete these assessments.

As the feasibility study process winds down, the business analyst will need to continue to communicate the study's status to executive management, business process owners, unit managers, the study team, and any subject matter experts throughout the enterprise. The business sponsor of the study should be kept abreast of the work throughout the study—no surprise there. The final output and communication of the feasibility study is, as expected, a feasibility study report.

The feasibility study report identifies each of the available solutions for the opportunity or business problem to be solved. For each opportunity that has been identified, the business analyst will include the overall feasibility and likelihood of the option. Feasibility study reports should include

- Executive summary
- Business problem or opportunity statement that the study aims to examine based on the current state assessment and external research
- Identified feasibility study requirements
- Description of each possible solution
- Description of the assessment methods used during the feasibility study
- Narrative on the results of the assessments, expected results, actual results, quantitative score methods, and any other relevant information on the study activities
- Identified risks and their probability, impact, methods used for risk analysis, and any potential risk responses
- Issues that may harm or hinder the proposed solutions from being implemented
- Assumptions and constraints used in the feasibility study and their impact if they prove to be false
- Ranking of the proposed solution, the ranking score, and criteria
- The recommended solution and supporting detail for the proposed solution
- Appendixes with all supporting details, research findings, or information about where the feasibility study information is archived

NOTE   An assumption is anything that you believe to be true but have not proven to be true. For example, you might assume that the proposed software will work with the current operating systems, hardware, and other systems. Until you actually test the software, however, you really don't know the accuracy of the assumption. Assumptions that prove false can become a risk.

The organization may require that the final feasibility report also include a description of how the proposed solution may or may not mesh with the current enterprise strategic goals, business architecture, direction, and desired future state of the organization. Some solutions may conflict with the current state of the organization, but align with the desired future state of the organization.

You might also need to include in your final feasibility study report the technical alignment with the current technical enterprise environment and the desired future. Issues such as dual support, scalability, and backward compatibility of software and systems may need to be addressed. In this same vein, you may need to address commercial off-the-shelf (COTS) software as opposed to creating the solution in-house. Don't be surprised to see these technical issues pop up on the CBAP exam.

Determining the Solution Scope

Project managers don't typically get assigned to a project until it's been chartered. Recall that the project charter is the document signed by someone in the performing organization with enough authority to grant the project manager the power to manage the project and its resources. The business analyst, however, needs to create a solution project scope document to present to the portfolio management governance group so they can determine if the project is worthy of being chartered in the first place. It's a gotcha! You'll need a project manager to help you scope the project, but the project hasn't been approved yet.

The document that you'll create is the solution scope document that establishes the boundaries, initial requirements, broad cost and time estimates, and sets the expectations for what the project should do and create for the organization. In your organization you may be both the business analyst and the project manager, and that's great. For your CBAP exam, the business analyst and the project manager are two different people. To create the project scope, you'll need, for your exam, the assistance of a senior project manager.

You and the project manager will work together to create the solution scope document so that you can then create the business case for the proposed project. This high-level scope document is based on the solution options you've already created and will serve as the foundation for the business case you'll present for the project. To create the scope, you'll also likely need a business lead, a technical lead, and any other subject matter experts who can contribute to the framing of the scope. You and these leads are dubbed the *proposal team,* and you'll create a decision package for the executive sponsor of the project.

Scoping the Solution Requirements

You and your proposal team will need to quickly determine what will and will not be in the solution scope. Based on your initial research, you should already have a good idea of what will satisfy the business problem or opportunity, and your goal is to present the quickest, most cost-effective, and robust solution for the organization. A scope creation mind-set is to balance the amount of time, cost, and effort in return for the project deliverables and benefits. You and the proposal team will need to examine the benefits and trade-offs of the project constraints and deliverables, and to make your project solution scalable. This means, ideally, that the portfolio management governance board can trim scope to fit the funds and time available without compressing the schedule or expectations.

 NOTE In the real world, where you and I live, we know that management often leaves the scope in place but trims the estimate time and cost. Politics, culture, and personal objectives cloud the issue even more. For your exam, everything is perfect, balanced, and works out just fine—unless the question tells you otherwise. You can't read into the question beyond what's presented. Answer the questions IIBA's way, and then go back to work in the real world with your CBAP credentials.

To define the solution scope, you'll need to establish and create four things:

- Business objectives of the proposed solution based on the identified problem or business

- Description of the deliverables; this may be products, services, environment, profits, problems solved, and other outcomes

- Assumptions and constraints for the solution

- Definition of the expected effort to create the expected deliverables

 NOTE A constraint is anything that limits your option. Time and cost limits are examples of constraints.

The solution scope can use standardized approaches like process reengineering approaches, architectural frameworks, and International Organization for Standardization (ISO) models, depending on the project's focus and the organizational requirements for creating the scope. The Capability Maturity Model, industry standards, culture, political capital, and general business knowledge are all viable inputs to creating the project scope document. You'll basically need to know what's expected in your industry and in your organization, based on the current solution you'll be presenting. For your CBAP examination, the IIBA can't be too specific on scope creation practices because of all the different background industries represented by the CBAP candidates. In other words, it'd be unreasonable for a construction business analyst to answer questions about software development models on the CBAP exam.

 NOTE The International Organization for Standardization is abbreviated ISO instead of IOS because of the translation of the name into all the different languages that use their models, such as the ISO 9000 or 10000 series. ISO is used because *iso* means "uniform" in Greek and translates well to an international community. You won't see that on your exam, but it's a fun fact to know and tell.

Writing the Solution Scope Statement

Once the proposal team has been created and an approach to creating the solution scope has been agreed upon, it's time to dig in and create the document. Your proposal team will each bring different talents to the activity, but for your exam, you should be familiar with the fundamentals of project management.

The proposal team will need to interview, document, and collaborate with experts throughout the organization and, likely, experts from outside the organization. Discussions will focus on capturing the most effective requirements time, cost, and project deliverables to be represented in the scope. Supporting detail for all claims should also be referenced. The proposal team will likely include the scope diagrams, schematics, process configuration identification drawings, and any other artwork to ensure that the scope is fully understood.

The creation of the project scope statement should create, include, or reference all of the following project deliverables:

- Product description and scope
- Supporting detail of how the scope was formulated and created
- How the scope aligns with the business objectives and strategic goals of the organization
- Expected milestones, funding requirements, and limitations
- Expected policies, standards, regulations, and other external project constraints
- Project constraints and assumptions
- High-level business requirements and objectives
- Dependencies, organizational systems the project will interact with, and support data for the project work
- Context diagram to illustrate a visual model of solution scope
- Product breakdown structure—a visual decomposition of the product (or service) the solution will create

The creation of the solution scope will be presented to the business sponsor for approval. You'll also interact with and need to communicate with the business projects and the IT management affected by the solution scope. Ultimately it's the portfolio management governance board that will need to approve the solution scope, cost and time estimates, and the approach of the project work.

The solution scope will serve as the foundation for the project's business case. You can expect that solution scope will undergo significant changes as more information becomes available. The refinements of a project scope pass through *progressive elaboration,* a term to describe the evolution of exactness as more detail is discovered.

Creating the Business Case

For large projects or programs, your organization may ask that you take the feasibility study one step farther and develop a business case. A business case is not something you store your files and folders in (har-har, I know). A business case is a document that reports on the value that the business will gain by investing in the initiative. It s basically your fact-based opinion on what the project or program will bring to the organization in terms of dollars, experiences gained, benefits, and overall value in relation to the amount of funds the organization will have to invest.

Business cases justify the investment into the project you've been studying. You'll need to research the financial aspect of the proposed project more than any other area when dealing with the business case—especially for risk-laden projects, projects with many variables, and assumptions. The business case documents how the deliverable will be able to compete in the marketplace, the expected competition, and insight into market trends for your organization's product or service that's being proposed.

The business case will need to examine the cash-flow forecast for the project or program and determine when monies will be invested, the duration of the investment, and the expected return on the investment. You'll use some financial prediction, studies, and any historical information to predict the cost and time to break even. Generally speaking, the longer the organization's funds are invested, the higher the risk because of unknown variables that may enter into the project, program, marketplace, or organization.

Quantifying the Project Costs

The business analyst will need to quantify the net cost of the project. This includes determining the initial funding, intermittent funding, and the total cost of ownership for the deliverable. The net cost will also need to examine the life cycle costing of the deliverable; *life cycle costing* is the price tag for supporting the deliverable once the project has been completed and the solution becomes part of the organization's operation. In some instances, the life cycle cost may be passed on to the client; for example, an organization creates a piece of software for a client. The client, not the organization that created the initial software, pays for the ongoing support, training, and maintenance of the software.

Another cost is the opportunity cost. An organization experiences opportunity cost when it must forego other opportunities to seize the current opportunity. The opportunity cost is the total amount of the opportunity it had to let go of. For example, a company has two projects it could choose from. Project A is worth $750,000 and Project B is worth $987,000; the company can only choose one project due to effort, time, and available resources. The company is going to choose Project B because it is worth more than Project A. The opportunity cost is $750,000—the total amount of the project that was passed over to do Project B.

When it comes to quality, two types of costs should be examined by the business analyst completing the business case:

- **Cost of conformance to quality** These are expenses that must be spent to achieve the expected level of quality by the organization. Consider training, correct materials, additional resources, and in some instances safety, inspections, and compliance issues.

- **Costs of nonconformance to quality** These are the costs of not conforming to the expected level of quality. For example, if the project team doesn't have the correct training, then the project may take longer to complete, cost more due to errors and omissions, and customers may reject the deliverables.

IT costs are often difficult to capture because of the ever changing nature of IT. The costs of IT can fluctuate greatly based on seemingly small changes to or requirements for the project scope. The business analyst must communicate the range of variance for any cost estimate he attaches to the business case in IT projects. Traditionally IT projects suffer from the First-Time, First-Use Penalty. This penalty states that if the project has never been done before, there's no real way of knowing how much the project will cost or how long it will take to complete. No executive wants to hear that.

When you consider that business cases are usually done for large projects or programs that may last several years, you have other financial concerns. Primarily you'll want to consider the time value of money. Here are some formulas and concepts you should know for your CBAP examination that will help you and the executives quantify the project costs.

Benefit/Cost Ratios

Just like they sound, benefit/cost ratio (BCR) models examine the cost-to-benefit ratio. For example, a typical measure is the cost to complete the project and the cost of ongoing operations of the project product, compared against the expected benefits of the project. For example, consider a project that will cost $575,000 to create a new product, market the product, and provide ongoing support for the product for one year. The expected gross return on the product, however, is $980,000 in year one. The benefit of completing the project is greater than the cost to create the product.

Payback Period

How long does it take the project to "pay back" the costs of the project? For example, the DRE Project will cost the organization $500,000 to create over five years. The expected cash income on the project is $40,000 per quarter. From here it's simple math: $500,000 divided by $40,000 is 12.5 quarters, or a little over three years to recoup the expenses.

This selection method, while one of the simplest, is also the weakest. The cash inflows are not discounted against the time to begin creating the cash. This is the *time value* of money. The $40,000 per quarter five years from now is worth less than $40,000 in your pocket today.

For a more detailed explanation, watch the Time Value of Money video now.

Considering the Future Value of Money

Discounted cash flow accounts for the time value of money. If you were to borrow $100,000 for five years to pay for a project, you'd be paying interest on the money. If the $100,000 were invested for five years and managed to earn a whopping 6 percent interest per year, compounded annually it'd be worth $133,822.60 at the end of five years. This is the future value of the money in today's terms.

The formula for future value is $FV = PV (1 + I)^n$, where:

- FV is future value
- PV is present value
- I is the interest rate
- N is the number of periods (years, quarters, and so on)

Here's the formula with the $100,000 in action:

1. $FV = 100,000(1 + .06)^5$
2. $FV = 100,000(1.338226)$
3. $FV = 133,822.60$

The future value of the $100,000 five years from now is worth $133,822.60 today. This means that the proposed project had better be worth more than $133,822.60 in five years, or the organization is better off to invest the monies some other way.

Considering the Present Value of Money

In other words, if a project says it'll be earning the organization $160,000 per year in five years, that's great, but what's $160,000 five years from now really worth today? This puts the amount of the cash flow in perspective with what the projections are in today's money. We're looking for the present value of future cash flows: $PV = FV \div (1 + I)^n$.

Let's plug it into the formula and find out (assuming that the interest rate is still 6 percent):

1. $PV = FV \div (1 + I)^n$
2. $PV = 160,000 \div (1.338226)$
3. $PV = \$119,561$

$160,000 in five years is really only worth $119,561 today. If we had four different projects of varying time to completion, cost, and project cash inflows at completion, we'd calculate the present value, and choose the project with the best present value, as it'll likely be the best investment for the organization.

NOTE You should be able to look at the present value of two proposed projects and make a decision as to which one should be green-lighted. The project with the highest PV is the best choice if that's the only factor you're presented with.

Calculating the Net Present Value

The net present value (NPV) is a somewhat complicated process, but it allows you to predict a project's value more precisely than the lump sum approach of the present value formula does. NPV evaluates the monies returned on a project for each period that the project is in existence. In other words, a project may last five years, but there may be a ROI (return on investment) in each of the five years the project is in existence, not just at the end of the project.

For example, your company may be upgrading its warehouse facilities throughout the United States. The company has 1,000 warehouses; as each site makes the conversion to the new facility design, the project deliverables will begin, hopefully, generating cash flow as a result of the project deliverables. The project can begin earning money when the first site is completed with the conversion to the new facilities. The faster the project can be completed, the sooner the organization will see a complete ROI.

Here's how the NPV formula works:

1. Calculate the project's cash flow for time unit (typically quarters or years).
2. Calculate each time unit total into present value.
3. Sum the present value of each time unit.
4. Subtract the investment for the project.
5. Take two aspirins.
6. Examine the NPV value. An NPV greater than 1 is good, and the project should be approved. An NPV less than 1 is bad, and the project should be rejected.

When comparing two projects, the project with the greater NPV is typically better, though projects with high returns (PVs) early in the project are better than those with low returns early in the project. Here's an example of an NPV calculation:

Period	Cash Flow	Present Value
1	$15,000.00	$14,150.94
2	25,000.00	22,249.91
3	17,000.00	14,273.53
4	25,000.00	19,802.34
5	18,000.00	13,450.65
Totals	$100,000.00	83,927.37
Investment		78,000.00
NPV		$5,927.37

NOTE You likely will not have to calculate NPV for your exam. I've included the whole scenario here to provide an understanding of the formula. Basically, better than 1 is good; less than 1 means your project is losing money.

Considering the Internal Rate of Return

The last benefit measurement method is the internal rate of return (IRR). The IRR is a complex formula to calculate when the present value of the cash inflow equals the original investment. Don't get too lost in this formula—it's a tricky business and you won't need to know how to calculate the IRR for the exam. You will need to know, however, that when comparing IRRs of multiple projects, the projects with high IRRs are better choices than projects with low IRRs. This makes sense. Would you like an investment with a higher rate of return or a lower rate of return? As a general rule, an IRR greater than 1 is good.

Finalizing the Business Case

Once the finances have been quantified, any major risks addressed, and the return on investment fleshed out for management, you can begin formalizing the final business case for management. The business case, along with the feasibility study, will go to management as the foundation for the decision package so that the project may receive a go or no-go decision. There are some techniques you might use to finalize the business case in addition to the financial tools I've already discussed. The first is the *SWOT analysis*. SWOT is the documentation of the project's *strengths, weaknesses, opportunities,* and *threats.*

You might also use *Activity Based Costing* (ABC), which examines the true cost of any business process the project may invoke. It examines the performance of resources, activities resources will complete, and includes the cost-effectiveness of nonhuman resources, such as equipment and facilities. ABC focuses its attention on the total cost of ownership the project creates and includes life cycle costing.

Once the analysis is complete, the business analyst can begin assembling the business case. A typical business case includes

- Executive summary
- Business case summary
  - Project rationale for preferred option
  - Current business process
  - Description of the problem or opportunity
  - Objectives of the project or program
  - Project scope
  - Business benefits
  - Project costs
  - Assumptions and identified constraints
  - Business and staff impact analysis

- Technology impact analysis
- Open issues and concerns
- Cursory implementation plan
- Project execution approach
  - Financial metrics
  - Privacy impact assessment
  - Alternative identification
- Key selection criteria
  - Project and objective weighting
  - Constraints and limitations
- Preferred alternative solution
  - Business benefits
  - Cost of solution
  - Assumption the solution makes
  - Business and staffing impact analysis
- Risk management plan
  - Risk assessment
  - Qualitative risk analysis
  - Risk responses
  - Benefit realization
- Conclusion and recommendations

The business case is presented to the executive sponsor, who will likely present the findings to the portfolio management governance board. This set of documents will serve as their decision package to determine if the risk is in balance with the anticipated reward of investing in the project. Since you, the business analyst, will be the person who knows the most about the potential project, you'll often accompany the sponsor in the discussion of the business case.

The portfolio management governance board will review the business case and will come to a decision on the investment of the project. If the board decides to invest in the project, program, or opportunity, then shuffling of priorities may result. Projects can be paused, scope and budgets trimmed, and entire efforts stopped all because of new opportunities within the enterprise. Once a project is chartered, however, management will review the project at milestones to test the project's validity, review cost and schedule control, and to confirm that the project should move forward. Milestones usually happen at the end of a phase, so it's appropriate that these milestone-linked reviews are often called phase gate reviews.

Chapter Summary

Working as an enterprise business analyst takes patience, tenacity, and critical thinking skills. You have to listen to stakeholder requirements, understand the business vision and strategy, and correlate proposed projects, programs, and solutions to the mission of the vision. Your job requires laser focus, communication, leadership, and the ability to quickly absorb details, process questions, and then research with your business analysis team the problem or opportunity.

In this chapter you learned all about creating or modifying the business architecture. The business architecture establishes the bones and structure of the entity you're working in and can have significant effects on the enterprise. Business architects create systems, documentation, and components so business decisions can be made as efficiently as possible. To create the business architecture, you'll need an understanding of how the architecture will be used throughout the organization and which stakeholders will be most affected by the creation or modification of the structure.

Feasibility studies are another important activity business analysts often are tasked with completing. For larger undertakings the feasibility may be its own project, while smaller initiatives don't require the formal project charter, budget, and schedule. In either case, the goal of the feasibility study is to determine the feasibility of all the available viable options. The business analyst will work with management, project managers, IT units, and all the relevant stakeholders to collect, process, and document information about the proposed project, program, or initiative.

For your CBAP exam, know that the business analyst may also be responsible for creating the preliminary project scope document. The project scope is all of the work that's required to satisfy the project objectives. The project scope creation requires that the business analyst work with a project manager, though a project manager may not yet be assigned to the project. The project manager and the business analyst will work with subject matter experts to create a high-level Work Breakdown Structure. Recall that a WBS is a visual decomposition of the project's scope and is made up of deliverables the project creates.

Depending on the size of the proposed project, program, or opportunity an organization may have, the business analyst also creates a business case. This document details the value the business will gain by investing in the initiative. The focus is on what the organization will gain in terms of return on investment, new skills learned, market position, savings, and any other values the opportunity presents. The project risks are examined to determine if it's worth accepting the risk in relation to the potential rewards.

For your CBAP exam, you should be familiar with the processes in this chapter. Enterprise analysis is a big topic, and I've tried to pare it down to the most essential, core activities the BABOK addresses. You'll likely have 33 questions on the information in this chapter, so don't skimp on your study efforts, as this chapter represents 22 percent on your CBAP exam. I encourage you to create your flashcards based on the key terms from this chapter. Be familiar with the activities, processes, and deliverables the business analyst creates.

Key Terms

Activity Based Costing   Examines the true cost of any business process the project may invoke. It examines the performance of resources, activities resources will complete, and includes the cost-effectiveness of nonhuman resources such as equipment and facilities.

Alternative identification   An approach to consider all of the available and possible solutions and then to pare down the solutions to the most likely and feasible options.

Analytic Hierarchy Process   This approach uses both qualitative (subjective) and quantitative (in-depth) analysis for each solution to compare and contrast each solution based on a series of comparisons.

Assumption   Anything that you believe to be true but have not proven to be true.

Balanced Scorecard   A management approach that tracks and grades financial performance, customer satisfaction, internal processes, and enterprisewide learning and innovation.

Benchmarking   Benchmarking compares two or more systems, states, services, products, or things to determine the best viable choice.

Benefit/cost ratio (BCR) models   Examine the cost-to-benefit ratio.

Business analyst   A person responsible for preparing the business architecture, feasibility studies, business cases, decision packages, project scope, and requirements, and validating the business case, project scope, and project deliverables.

Business architecture   The intangible structure that constitutes a business entity. It is the culture, enterprise environmental factors, business structure, and policies that guide and direct the selection, funding, and management of programs and projects.

Business case   A document that reports on the value that the business will gain by investing in the initiative.

Business process model   Sometimes called an activity model, it captures all of the activities within a business, the inputs and outputs of each activity, and the required resources to complete each activity.

Business process reengineering   This approach studies the current flow of business processes, looks for strengths, weaknesses, opportunities, and threats (SWOT), and considers everything from minor adjustments to entire new designs to investigate improvements.

Business scenario   A hypothetical situation that portrays how the organization processes are to operate. Business scenarios can depict typical operations, planned processes, and responses to situations when things don't go as planned.

Business sponsor An individual who has the positional power and decision-making ability to launch new projects and organizational initiatives, and to grant resources to business analysts and project managers.

Cause-and-effect diagram Also known as a fishbone diagram or an Ishikawa diagram. The diagram can be massive, as each contributing factor must be reviewed to determine what things, events, and processes may be contributing to it. In most cases, a combination of contributing factors creates the problem that the organization is experiencing.

Closing The final project management process group, where the project's phase or entire scope has been completed and where the project manager performs administrative closure. This includes sign-off from the customer on the scope validation, final findings, and archiving the project documentation.

Competitive analysis This is a marketplace study to determine the feasibility of a proposed solution as compared against the competition.

Component business model This is the most common business model and was formulated by IBM. It provides a direct and traditional view of an enterprise providing nomenclature to lines of business, functional units, departments, groups, and other organizational resources.

Constraint Anything that limits your options. Time and cost limits are examples of constraints.

Cost of conformance to quality These are expenses that must be spent to achieve the expected level of quality by the organization. Consider training, correct materials, additional resources, and in some instances safety, inspections, and compliance issues.

Cost-benefit analysis Measures the early known cost and benefits to create a cost-benefits ratio of each potential solution. The cost-benefit analysis will be elaborated on during the business case creation.

Costs of nonconformance to quality These are the costs of not conforming to the expected level of quality. For example, if the project team doesn't have the correct training, then the project may take longer to complete, cost more due to errors and omissions, and customers may reject the deliverables.

COTS Examines in-house creation versus a commercial off-the-shelf (COTS) solution.

Current state assessment Part of the feasibility study to determine the current status of the organization. An understanding of the current organizational status can be compared with the desired future status of the company.

Data flow diagrams Capture and display the type and traffic of information within the organization.

Decision Analysis   This statistical reasoning approach allows the study team to measure and compare the probabilities of each identified solution outcome.

Decision tables   A decision table is a matrix that illustrates the logic of decisions and leads the study team to a recommended option based on the qualifiers the table identifies and the initial feasibility study requirements for the proposed solution.

Domain modeling   Domain modeling charts the area of organization that's under construction, analysis, or creation so that all stakeholders can visualize the areas that are affected.

Enterprise environmental factors   Part of the business architecture that is the definition of the policies, procedures, and rules that project managers and employees must follow. Enterprise environmental factors are unique to each organization.

Enterprise governance group   A committee of organizational leaders that ensure groups, functional departments, projects, and other members of the organization are following the established organizational rules, procedures, and business directives of the organization.

Environment impact analysis   Each option is measured for its impact on the environment in consideration of culture, compliance, regulation, and laws.

Execution   The third project management process group, where the project plans are executed. The project manager ensures that the work is done with quality, the project team is completing their assignments, and the outcomes of the work are documented.

Executive team   These people make up the organization's upper management who create the vision, leadership, direction, strategy, and tactics for the organization.

Feasibility study   The research of the possible solutions to determine each solution's likelihood of meshing with the business architecture, the organizational mission, and of reaching financial, operational, and technical achievability.

Future value   Determines the future value of an amount of funds based on the present value of the funds. The formula for future value is $FV = PV (1 + I)^n$, where FV is future value; PV is present value; I is the interest rate; and N is the number of periods.

Geographical maps   Show the physical location of the business units and can help address logistical concerns such as shipping, travel, communication, and IT issues.

Global Balanced Scorecard for U.S. Government   A scorecard that measures government agency performance, customer perception, financial and internal responsibilities, and innovation.

Initiating   The first project management process group, where the project is charted with a broad vision of what the project is to create. The project manager is named and given autonomy over the feasibility study project.

Internal rate of return   A complex formula to calculate when the present value of the cash inflow equals the original investment.

Knowledge management   The collection, storage, accessibility, and accuracy of the wealth of information an organization creates.

Monitoring and controlling   The fourth project management process group, where processes are completed in tandem with project execution. The project work is monitored and controlled.

Net present value   Evaluates the monies returned on a project for each period that the project is in existence; based on the present value formula for each period.

Organization charts   Show the hierarchical structure of the company and which units of the company are affected by the feasibility study.

Pareto chart   Shows the categories of defects, range of solution costs, income potential, and other categorization of components from largest to smallest.

Payback period   The amount of time it takes the project to "pay back" the costs of the project.

Planning   The second project management process group, where the project is planned based on the determined requirements for scope, time, cost, quality, human resources, communications, risk, and procurement.

POLDAT Technique   A requirements gathering and business architecture technique that captures information about processes, organization structure, location, data, applications, and technology.

Portfolios   The organizational management of projects, programs, and undertakings that support the vision, strategy, and tactics of the enterprise. Portfolio management is the measurement, selection, and management of the funds, time, and effort to support the enterprise ventures beyond day-to-day operations.

Preliminary scope   A document that establishes the boundaries, initial requirements, broad cost and time estimates, and sets the expectations for what the project should do and create for the organization.

Present value   A formula that determines the present value of a future amount of money. The present value formula is $PV = FV \div (1 + I)^n$, where FV is future value; PV is present value; I is the interest rate; and N is the number of periods.

Process flow diagram   These diagrams capture the inputs and outputs of current, and in some instances future, processes within the organization.

Programs   A program is a collection of projects working together with a common vision to take advantage of benefits that would not be realized if the projects worked independently of each other.

Project   A short-term endeavor that will create something unique and individual for the organization. Projects have a definite ending.

Project life cycles   A project life is the unique life and phases of a project. A project life is unique to each project; for example, the project life cycle of a software development project does not have the same project life cycle as a bridge construction project.

Project management process groups Five project management process groups are universal to all projects: initiating, planning, executing, monitoring and controlling, and closing.

Project manager This individual oversees the project processes, deliverables, and project team. The project manager has a predefined amount of autonomy over the project and works within the established boundaries to deliver the project scope as planned.

Prototyping This approach creates the highest-risk component of a proposed solution to determine if the solution is feasible in light of the known risk. In other words, the team must create the solution to determine if the actual solution may be created considering the largest known risk.

Requirements Traceability Matrix (RTM) Table that facilitates the identification and documentation of the categories of needs, specific requirements within the categories of needs, functional or operational identification for each identified requirement, and any additional characteristics.

Root cause analysis This process investigates root causes, contributing causes, and causal factors that are creating the effect to be solved (which may turn out to be a business problem).

Six sigma programs These quality improvement approaches rely on data and statistical analysis to measure accuracy, efficiency, and trend analysis.

Structured problem-solving techniques Receive and retrieve information within an organization. They keep communication happening, involve stakeholders, and plot out expected responses based on a survey, form, or structured interview.

Subprojects A smaller project within a larger project. Subprojects are managed as their own project, reporting to the project manager of the parent project.

Technology advancement analysis Examines most recent technical solutions that may be applied to the business problem or opportunity.

Technology architecture diagrams Map the topology and relationship of the IT infrastructure.

Theme Premise of a strategic goal; allows the large organizational goals to be broken down into smaller projects and opportunities.

Use case models Captures the business processes by showing how customers, vendors, management, departments, and other enterprisewide stakeholders interact with the business.

Work Breakdown Structure The WBS is a visual decomposition of the scope; it is deliverables based and typically does not include activities.

Zachman Framework A matrix, created by John Zachman, which provides structure and helps stakeholders describe complex enterprises. The Zachman Framework uses predefined questions that must be answered for each component of any organization.

Questions

1. Your organization uses the Balanced Scorecard approach to measure performance. Which one of the following is not a metric used in the Balanced Scorecard?

   A. Financial

   B. Customer

   C. Quality

   D. Learning and Innovation

2. You are the business analyst for your organization and are reviewing a proposed project. The project will likely last 18 months, and there are some high-probability and high-impact risks within the project. What must the organization do in light of project risks?

   A. No risks can be accepted within the project, so the project should be scrapped.

   B. The risks within the project must be removed before the project may begin.

   C. Risks within the project are acceptable as long as there is a proven way to recover from the risks should they happen.

   D. Risks within the project are expected, but the risks the project offers must be in relation to the reward the project will bring.

3. Which document will you not need to create on a large, high-risk project during the business analysis activities?

   A. Project charter

   B. Business architecture documentation

   C. Feasibility study

   D. Business case

4. You are a business analyst for the McTeely Company. You are creating a table to capture the needs of the organization, its categories of needs, and characteristics of the project such as budget, work delivery, and expectations of quality. What type of a table are you creating for your organization?

   A. Risk Probability-Impact Matrix

   B. Requirements Traceability Matrix

   C. Pareto chart

   D. Requirements Identification Matrix

5. What matrix structure uses predefined questions and helps the business analyst create the business architecture framework?

   A. Zachman Framework

   B. Feasibility studies

   C. Requirements Traceability Matrix

   D. Decision table

6. Management has asked that you create and document the business architecture framework for the organization based on the existing strategic goals, vision, and direction. They've asked that you use a data collection framework that will capture processes, locations, and technical information about the company. What approach should you use for this activity?

   A. Zachman Framework

   B. Feasibility studies

   C. POLDAT

   D. Root cause analysis

7. Which modeling approach was made popular by IBM and provides a traditional view of an enterprise?

   A. Component business model

   B. Business process model

   C. Use case model

   D. Business scenario model

8. John is a business analyst for his organization and has created a model for the Business Architecture Creation Project. His model shows users interacting with the organizational lines of business, customers purchasing their products, and describes the processes vendors, departments, and employees' experience when they interact with the organization. What type of a model has John created?

   A. Business process model

   B. Class model

   C. Component business model

   D. Use case model

9. A cause-and-effect diagram is also known as what?

   A. Root cause

   B. Decision tree

   C. Ishikawa diagram

   D. Fishhook diagram

10. You've been assigned to create a feasibility study for a large project in your organization. This new project will likely change much of the business architecture, the services your organization offers, and may affect several lines of business. What step of the feasibility study should you complete first?

   A. Create the project charter.

   B. Initialize the project.

    C. Create a business case.

    D. Create a current state assessment.

11. What document creates a visual description of the project scope with a focus on deliverables and not project activities?

    A. Work Breakdown Structure

    B. Pareto diagram

    C. Process Configuration

    D. Project Scope Statement

12. You are the business analyst conducting a feasibility study for your company. The opportunity you are studying is for a new, lightweight radio-controlled airplane that can carry a digital recording camera. The airplane can be used in land surveys, topographical research, and some military uses. Management has asked that you physically test the model airplane to determine if the cost is worth the investment to mass-produce the product. What feasibility approach is management asking for?

    A. Prototype

    B. Functional analysis

    C. Product breakdown

    D. Risk probability analysis

13. What feasibility analysis approach compares two or more products to create a baseline?

    A. Technology advancement analysis

    B. Environment impact analysis

    C. Benchmarking analysis

    D. Cost-benefit analysis

14. What chart shows categories of failure from largest to smallest?

    A. Fishbone

    B. Ishikawa

    C. Pareto

    D. Flowcharting

15. Which one of the following is an option that should always be included in the list of possible solutions for a proposed project?

    A. Do the project in small phases.

    B. Do the project with many subprojects.

    C. Do not do the project.

    D. Outsource the project.

16. You are the business analyst for your organization and are completing a feasibility study on a newly proposed product. You have identified several assumptions that you had to make in order to create the feasibility study. Management is concerned that the assumptions you have made may prove to be false. If management is correct, what will the assumptions become in the proposed project?

    A. Constraints

    B. Risks

    C. Bottlenecks

    D. Points of project failure

17. What is the difference between the project life cycle and the project management life cycle?

    A. There is no difference; they are the same.

    B. The project life cycle is universal to all projects, while the project management life cycle is unique to each project.

    C. The project life cycle is unique to each project, while the project management life cycle is universal to all projects.

    D. The project life cycle describes how long the project's product or service will exist, while the project management life cycle describes the duration of the project work from initiating to closing.

18. A project has been proposed to management that promises to be worth $987,500 to the organization once it's been completed. The project is likely to take three years to complete and will cost $545,000 to complete. What formula will help management decide if they should invest in the project based on the current value of promised project deliverable?

    A. Payback period

    B. $FV = PV (1 + I)^n$

    C. $PV = FV \div (1 + I)^n$

    D. $PV = NPV \div (1 + N)^i$

19. Which costing approach considers the true cost of all the business processes the project may invoke?

    A. Total Cost of Quality

    B. Indirect Costing

    C. Direct Costing

    D. Activity Based Costing

20. You are the business analyst for your organization. You have completed the feasibility study and the business case for a newly proposed project that you

believe should be given a go decision. The business sponsor asks you to come with her to the meeting where the proposed project will be reviewed. You're needed in case there are any specific questions about the project. Who will you and the business sponsor be presenting the project proposal to?

A. Project manager

B. Organizational program manager

C. Customers of the project

D. Portfolio management governance board

Questions and Answers

1. Your organization uses the Balanced Scorecard approach to measure performance. Which one of the following is not a metric used in the Balanced Scorecard?

A. Financial

B. Customer

C. Quality

D. Learning and Innovation

C. Quality is not one of the four metrics used in the balanced scorecard. A, B, and D are incorrect choices, as these are three of the four metrics used in the scorecard; the fourth metric is internal.

2. You are the business analyst for your organization and are reviewing a proposed project. The project will likely last 18 months, and there are some high-probability and high-impact risks within the project. What must the organization do in light of project risks?

A. No risks can be accepted within the project, so the project should be scrapped.

B. The risks within the project must be removed before the project may begin.

C. Risks within the project are acceptable as long as there is a proven way to recover from the risks should they happen.

D. Risks within the project are expected, but the risks the project offers must be in relation to the reward the project will bring.

D. Risk is not a bad thing; it is the impact the risk may bring that is considered negative. All projects have some amount of risk, but the accepted risk must be managed and in proportion to the reward it brings. Choices A and B are incorrect, because projects do carry risk. Investment in a project is an example of risk acceptance, because the project could fail and the investment be lost. Choice C is incorrect, because risks must be anticipated but it does not answer the question as completely as choice D.

3. Which document will you not need to create on a large, high-risk project during the business analysis activities?

A. Project charter

B. Business architecture documentation

C. Feasibility study

D. Business case

A. The project charter is a document that is created once the project is launched. Since the project has not been launched yet, there's no need for a project charter. You will, however, need to create the business architecture, the feasibility study, and the business case as part of your business analysis activities, so choices B, C, and D are incorrect answers.

4. You are a business analyst for the McTeely Company. You are creating a table to capture the needs of the organization, its categories of needs, and characteristics of the project such as budget, work delivery, and expectations of quality. What type of a table are you creating for your organization?

A. Risk Probability-Impact Matrix

B. Requirements Traceability Matrix

C. Pareto chart

D. Requirements Identification Matrix

B. You are being asked to create a Requirements Traceability Matrix. Choice A, a Risk Probability-Impact Matrix is a table to help quantify risk exposure. Choice C, a Pareto chart, shows categories of failure from largest to smallest. Choice D is not a valid term.

5. What matrix structure uses predefined questions and helps the business analyst create the business architecture framework?

A. Zachman Framework

B. Feasibility studies

C. Requirements Traceability Matrix

D. Decision table

A. The Zachman Framework uses predefined questions and framework components to help guide the business architecture framework creation. Choice B, feasibility studies, determine the feasibility of any of the possible solutions. Choice C, a Requirements Traceability Matrix, is a table to capture the needs of the organization, its categories of needs, and characteristics of the project. Choice D, a decision table, is a tool to model complicated logic. It uses if-then scenarios to help the business analyst create a decision or solution in the feasibility study.

6. Management has asked that you create and document the business architecture framework for the organization based on the existing strategic goals, vision, and direction. They've asked that you use a data collection

framework that will capture processes, locations, and technical information about the company. What approach should you use for this activity?

A. Zachman Framework

B. Feasibility studies

C. POLDAT

D. Root cause analysis

C. Management is asking that you use the POLDAT model to capture data on the process, organization, location, data, applications, and technology. Choice A is incorrect, as the Zachman Framework is a table to help build the business architecture. B is incorrect, as feasibility studies are where the POLDAT model is used. Choice D is also incorrect, as the question does not describe the root cause analysis process.

7. Which modeling approach was made popular by IBM and provides a traditional view of an enterprise?

A. Component business model

B. Business process model

C. Use case model

D. Business scenario model

A. The component business model was created by IBM and provides the traditional view of an enterprise. Choice B is incorrect, as a business process model captures all of the activities within a business, and the inputs and outputs of each activity. Choice C is incorrect, because a use case model demonstrates how users interact with the business, its processes, and resources. Choice D is also wrong, because a business scenario model is a hypothetical, ideal description of how the business should operate in different scenarios.

8. John is a business analyst for his organization and has created a model for the Business Architecture Creation Project. His model shows users interacting with the organizational lines of business, customers purchasing their products, and describes the processes vendors, departments, and employees' experience when they interact with the organization. What type of a model has John created?

A. Business process model

B. Class model

C. Component business model

D. Use case model

D. This model demonstrates how users interact with the business, its processes, and resources. Choice A is incorrect, as a business process model captures all of the activities within a business, and the inputs and outputs of each activity. Choice B is incorrect, because a class model captures the relationship of information within an organization, how information is exchanged, and the flow of information. C is incorrect, as a component business model provides a direct and traditional view of an enterprise, providing nomenclature to lines of business, functional units, departments, groups, and other organizational resources.

9. A cause-and-effect diagram is also known as what?

   A. Root cause

   B. Decision tree

   C. Ishikawa diagram

   D. Fishhook diagram

   C. A cause-and-effect diagram is also known as an Ishikawa diagram. A, B, and D are all incorrect names for the cause-and-effect diagram. Note that choice D is close, but incorrect. The cause-and-effect diagram may also be known as a fishbone diagram, not a fishhook diagram.

10. You've been assigned to create a feasibility study for a large project in your organization. This new project will likely change much of the business architecture, the services your organization offers, and may affect several lines of business. What step of the feasibility study should you complete first?

   A. Create the project charter.

   B. Initialize the project.

   C. Create a business case.

   D. Create a current state assessment.

   D. The creation of the current state assessment can capture where the business currently is and serve as a baseline for where the business wants to go—the desired future state. Choices A, B, and C are incorrect, as these documents are created after the current state assessment.

11. What document creates a visual description of the project scope with a focus on deliverables and not project activities?

   A. Work Breakdown Structure

   B. Pareto diagram

   C. Process Configuration

   D. Project Scope Statement

   A. The Work Breakdown Structure is a visual breakdown of the project scope with its focus on project deliverables and not project activities. Choice B, the Pareto diagram, is a chart that shows categories of failure from largest to smallest. Choice C, process configuration, is usually a flowchart that shows the order and interaction of processes. Choice D, the scope statement, is also incorrect, as the scope statement is what the WBS is based on; this document is not a visual representation.

12. You are the business analyst conducting a feasibility study for your company. The opportunity you are studying is for a new, lightweight radio-controlled airplane that can carry a digital recording camera. The airplane can be used in land surveys, topographical research, and some military uses. Management has asked that you physically test the model airplane to determine if the cost is worth the investment to mass-produce the product. What feasibility approach is management asking for?

    A. Prototype

    B. Functional analysis

    C. Product breakdown

    D. Risk probability analysis

    A. Management is asking for a prototype of the airplane. Choice B, functional analysis, is an analysis of all the functions of the plane. Choice C, product breakdown, is a decomposition of the entire project—usually in a schematic drawing. Choice D, risk probability analysis, is a study of the likelihood of an identified risk event happening.

13. What feasibility analysis approach compares two or more products to create a baseline?

    A. Technology advancement analysis

    B. Environment impact analysis

    C. Benchmarking analysis

    D. Cost-benefit analysis

    C. Benchmarking creates a baseline by comparing two or more things such as systems, products, or resources. A, B, and D are all incorrect, as these things do not compare one thing to another.

14. What chart shows categories of failure from largest to smallest?

    A. Fishbone

    B. Ishikawa

    C. Pareto

    D. Flowcharting

    C. Pareto charts can show categories of failure from largest to smallest. Choice A, fishbone, is a diagram that can be used in root cause analysis. Choice B, Ishikawa, is the same thing as a fishbone. D, flowcharting, shows the flow of a process, information, or activity.

15. Which one of the following is an option that should always be included in the list of possible solutions for a proposed project?

    A. Do the project in small phases.

    B. Do the project with many subprojects.

    C. Do not do the project.

    D. Outsource the project.

    C. Of all the options presented, only C is a viable choice, as not doing the project is always a viable option to be presented by the business analyst. Choices A, B, and D would not be a viable solution for all projects.

16. You are the business analyst for your organization and are completing a feasibility study on a newly proposed product. You have identified several assumptions that you had to make in order to create the feasibility study. Management is concerned that the assumptions you have made may prove to be false. If management is correct, what will the assumptions become in the proposed project?

    A. Constraints

    B. Risks

    C. Bottlenecks

    D. Points of project failure

    B. If the assumptions that have been made prove false, then the assumptions may become risks within the project. Choices A, C, and D are incorrect, as false assumptions don't necessarily become constraints, bottlenecks, or points of failure.

17. What is the difference between the project life cycle and the project management life cycle?

    A. There is no difference; they are the same.

    B. The project life cycle is universal to all projects, while the project management life cycle is unique to each project.

    C. The project life cycle is unique to each project, while the project management life cycle is universal to all projects.

    D. The project life cycle describes how long the project's product or service will exist, while the project management life cycle describes the duration of the project work from initiating to closing.

    C. The project life cycle is unique to each project regardless of the scope, industry, or expected deliverable. The project management life cycle is universal and consists of project initiation, planning, executing, monitoring and controlling, and closing.

18. A project has been proposed to management that promises to be worth $987,500 to the organization once it's been completed. The project is likely to take three years to complete and will cost $545,000 to complete. What formula will help management decide if they should invest in the project based on the current value of promised project deliverable?

    A. Payback period

    B. $FV = PV (1 + I)^n$

    C. $PV = FV \div (1 + I)^n$

    D. $PV = NPV \div (1 + N)^i$

    C. You should use the present value formula to determine if the project is worth investing the funds. The project needs to beat the rate of return to be a feasible investment.

19. Which costing approach considers the true cost of all the business processes the project may invoke?

    A. Total Cost of Quality

    B. Indirect Costing

    C. Direct Costing

    D. Activity Based Costing

    D. Activity Based Costing examines the true costs of all business processes that the project interacts with. Choice A, the total cost of quality, describes the funds the project will have to pay to achieve the expected level of quality. Choice B, indirect costing, describes a project expense that can be shared with others, such as splitting the cost of a backhoe, consultant, or other resource. Choice C, direct costing, describes a project cost that cannot be shared with any other entity and is used solely by one project.

20. You are the business analyst for your organization. You have completed the feasibility study and the business case for a newly proposed project that you believe should be given a go decision. The business sponsor asks you to come with her to the meeting where the proposed project will be reviewed. You're needed in case there are any specific questions about the project. Who will you and the business sponsor be presenting the project proposal to?

    A. Project manager

    B. Organizational program manager

    C. Customers of the project

    D. Portfolio management governance board

    D. The portfolio management governance board will make the go/no-go decision.

Analyzing and Documenting Project Requirements

In this chapter you will
- Create the requirements documentation
- Structure the requirements packages
- Create a business domain model
- Analyze functional requirements documentation
- Determine the project assumptions and constraints
- Validate and verify the project requirements
- Create data and behavior models
- Rely on usage models

As a business analyst, you know that lots of people depend on you: project customers, the business owner, the project manager, the project team, end users, and more, depending on the project you're working toward. This knowledge area, Requirements Analysis and Documentation, is one of the most important areas of business analysis. All of these stakeholders depend on you to accurately analyze and document an acceptable solution—failure to do so will have tremendous ramifications for the whole project.

Your documentation of an acceptable solution for the business problem or opportunity will affect how the project team goes about creating and implementing the solution. Obviously, if you don't have clear documentation and a solid understanding of the solution, no one else in the project will either—it all starts with you. This means you'll be creating analysis models, case studies, and detailed documentation on what the project team is to create.

In this knowledge area you'll also work with key stakeholders, the project manager, the project team, and even subject matter experts to ensure accuracy in the proposed solution. The documentation and models you create will serve as inputs for time, cost, and resource estimates for the project. You get more than one crack at creating your documentation; however, you'll be doing iterations of analysis to ensure the accuracy of your models so the downstream project activities are accurate as well. You'll need to know about six processes from this chapter:

- Prioritizing requirements
- Organizing requirements
- Specify and model requirements
- Defining assumptions and constraints
- Verifying requirements
- Validating requirements

This portion of your CBAP exam is chunky. This chapter has loads of terms and lots of business analysis processes, too. I'm sure many of the activities I'll describe here you're already doing, while others may be new to you. Don't worry—just soak it all up, take notes on new approaches, and keep a positive attitude toward passing your exam. I'm certain you can do this!

Prioritize Requirements

During your business analysis duties, you'll hear stakeholders demand requirements, tell you the solution must have a particular feature, or suggest a requirement that'd be nice to have. These imperatives are really clues to you as to what's important to the stakeholder. On larger initiatives, you'll likely find competing objectives, loads of requirements from a smattering of stakeholders, and requirements ranking from demands to wishes. You'll need an approach to prioritize what requirements are most important to the organization.

Once you've prioritized the requirements, you can then go about determining which needs should be implemented right away and which need additional analysis. You'll also be able to plan for time and cost objectives based on what's most sensitive to the organization. For example, deliverables that have penalties for being late may demand a higher priority when it comes to execution. The prioritization of requirements is more than just what the customer wants first; it's what the organization needs first.

Setting Priorities for Requirements

Perhaps the most effective method for prioritizing requirements is to determine the business value for the identified requirements. Each requirement can be assessed for its costs, benefits, and overall value to the organization. The business value of a requirement might also be measured with the risk elements of implementing or not implementing the identified requirement. This includes the consideration of the cost element and the risk distribution of the execution.

For example, a requirement that has a prominent risk may be executed first to see if the risk comes to fruition. If the risk does happen and it's a project killer, then there's been a minimal amount of funds and time spent on the solution. The exploration and implementation of a risky requirement can actually save the organization time and effort in the long run. This doesn't mean that high-risk requirements always take a higher priority; it's just a useful approach to prioritization.

Sometimes it's best to start with the easiest requirements first. This allows the project team to continue to work on riskier, more difficult-to-achieve requirements while the project is in motion. The implementation difficulty and the likelihood of success are requirement attributes that may demand expert judgment, but applying those criteria enables the project to progress while you're planning the remainder of the solution implementation.

The law is the law. Regulations and compliance-based requirements demand implementation and are usually bumped up the requirements priority ladder. Regulations are requirements that must be included in the solution and project execution. Risk analysis of these requirements should be completed through quantitative analysis to measure the time, cost, and overall quality impacts of the solution.

Some requirements are needed now in order to allow other higher-priority requirements to be implemented later. These requirements are called *mandatory dependencies* because it's mandatory to complete these requirements before future requirements You can't start the framing on the house until the foundation has been created. You might also know this as hard logic—it's just the way the work has to be done to satisfy the project requirements.

Finally, stakeholders may dictate which requirements are most important. A consensus among the stakeholders could shift the prioritization of the requirements. Their consensus could be based on any of the requirements attributes, a sense of urgency, or time and cost factors for the stakeholders. Whatever their reason, requirements priorities should always be documented and should reference supporting detail as to why the decisions were made.

Analyzing Requirements for Priority

You won't always have control over which requirements take precedence over others. You'll have to document why the requirements have been prioritized even if you don't agree with the organizational or stakeholder reasoning. This process overlaps stakeholder management to some extent, as stakeholders may not be willing to negotiate, compromise, or budge on the priorities. Typical challenges you'll face when it comes to prioritizing requirements:

- **Nonnegotiable requirements** Sometimes stakeholders know exactly what they want even if their demands are mutually exclusive, conflicting, and contradicting. You'll experience this when a stakeholder tells you that all of the requirements are of equal importance—they all are high priority.

- **Unrealistic estimates** The implementation team can affect the prioritization of the project work by grossly overestimating the time or cost of certain requirements. They'll expect additional time, monies, or both—or they'll want you to remove some other requirement to offset the work they're overestimating.

One approach you can use with stakeholders to prioritize the requirements is the *MoSCoW Analysis*. This approach breaks out each requirement into one of four imperatives:

- **Must** These requirements must be implemented for the solution to be deemed a success.

- **Should** These requirements should be implemented in the solution, but are not vital to the solution's success.

- **Could** These requirements would be nice to include in the solution if possible, but they're not the most important of the requirements.

- **Won't** These requirements have been identified but are now not going to be implemented into the project solution due to cost, complexity, timing, or any number of other reasons. These requirements may be implemented into the solution later.

All requirements should be prioritized and their level of prioritization documented for the solution. Not all requirements need prioritization when the execution of the solution begins, but it's ideal. You can expect stakeholders to negotiate on requirements when time and cost estimates are created, which may mean a shift in the overall requirements prioritization for the project.

Organize Project Requirements

Here's a word you should know for your CBAP exam: *iterative*. Iterative means you'll be completing the tasks, activities, and other business analysis duties over and over throughout the project. You, the business analyst, will be performing the processes of business analysis iteratively throughout the requirements-gathering processes. It's a word that you'll find over and over in the BABOK, and it's a concept that rings true with most business analysts. After you define the project requirements, you'll often refine the project requirements—it's not a one-shot deal.

Part of the job of a business analyst is to continue to define and refine the scope of the problem or opportunity the project will focus on. This means ongoing testing, interviewing, and investigation to gather the most accurate requirements, information, and supporting detail. Because the definition of requirements is an iterative activity, it helps the project customer, project manager, and the project team to have the best information to estimate, work accurately, and create reliable work packages.

Iterations of interviews and project documentation will require loads of communication with the project key stakeholders. All of this communication, documentation, and supporting detail needs to be organized. Consider all of the people you and members of the business analysis team will consult with:

- Users
- Senior management
- Customers
- Public (considered an external stakeholder)
- System and process owners who are affected by the project proposed solution

Your interviews with these stakeholders will help you create the project documentation, supporting detail for project decisions, and work records. You'll also be creating, of course, the actual requirements documentation. The project stakeholders will need to validate the requirements documentation. This isn't always easy, as there will likely be competing objectives and priorities, so at a minimum you want some consensus prioritization based on cost, needs, and even political capital.

Creating the Business Requirements Documentation

Through analysis, investigation, and requirements review, the business analyst aims to gain an understanding of the problem or opportunity presented. This business analysis moves through iterations of testing, interviews, and reviews. Key stakeholders, that is, the stakeholders who have decision-making powers, will review the requirements. The key stakeholders have the most influence over what will and won't go into the project scope.

Based on each review of the identified requirements, the business analyst will need to compile the comments, revisions, and additions and present the requirements to the stakeholders again. Once again the key stakeholders will review the requirements, and then the business analyst will compile any new information until the requirements have been agreed upon and there's a consensus among the stakeholders for the requirements documentation.

These iterations of requirements review are completed through many different activities, though not all of these are necessary for every project:

- **Structure requirements**   The requirements are logically organized and documented.
- **Create a business domain model**   This is a visual representation of how the business does or should work in regard to the project requirements. In particular, it defines each process that is affected by the project, how the process should work, and how the process interacts with other processes, functions, and project-affected users in the organization.
- **Analyze user requirements**   Documents what the user expects the solution to do; in a software project, this is the creation of the User Requirements Document (URD). Users must agree that the business analyst understands and has captured what they want accomplished in the solution.

- **Analyze functional requirements** Functional requirements describe how the solution will function, what it will do, and what its expected outcomes are. This is usually a more technical document than the URD, but it should mesh with the users' requirements.

- **Analyze supplementary quality of service requirements** The business analyst and key stakeholders must agree on what the expected level of *quality of service* for the project deliverable will be. This term lends itself most to IT solutions where a benchmark has been created for an acceptable level of quality, and the solution is measured above or below the defined benchmark. In other words, based on the solution and previous history, what are the expected level of quality and the acceptable level of errors in relation to the expected quality? Generally, the higher the quality of the demand, the more mission-critical the solution is, and the higher the costs to achieve the solution.

- **Determine assumptions and constraints** This is an ongoing activity to define, test, and document the assumptions and constraints of the requirements. Recall that an assumption is something that you believe to be true but haven't yet proven to be true. A constraint is anything that limits the project options, such as a deadline or predetermined budget. Assumptions and constraints can both become project risks.

- **Determine requirement attributes** All of the identified requirements have attributes, which should be documented; attributes can include status, associated risks, cost and time estimates, dependencies, resources needed, and more.

- **Verify requirements** The verification of the known requirements is an opportunity for the business analyst to confirm with the stakeholders that all of the requirements have been captured, documented, and are accurately represented. In other words, the business analyst gets to ask the key stakeholders, "Do we have the requirements correct?"

- **Validate requirements** Validation of the requirements is a test of the actual deliverables, a prototype of the deliverables, or a small batch run.

 NOTE An argument has always centered on the difference between "validate" and "verify." *Verify* means "approve what we've captured before we do the work." *Validate*, like scope validation, means "prove that we've accomplished what's been asked of us."

These requirements analysis and documentation activities continue to happen until the key stakeholders agree that the requirements are accurate, achievable, and will accomplish the user requirements and the functional requirements. The remainder of this chapter delves into each of these business analysis activities in detail.

Exploring Solution Development Approaches

Let's face facts: business analysts need to do requirements gathering so they understand the problems, in order to develop solutions for the identified problems. Business analysts, along with the project manager and the stakeholders, are problem solvers—but the business analysts are at the core of finding solutions, so everything starts with them. That's why it's so important to have accurate and complete requirements gathering and to invest time in exploring solutions.

With several different approaches to solution development available, you should be able to work in more than one approach, even if you have a favorite. For your CBAP exam, you'll be presented with scenarios about solution development, and you'll need to choose the most appropriate solution development methodology for the given scenario. In the real world, the culture and environment of the organization will usually dictate what approach you'll need to take.

The first solution-development methodology focuses on process improvement, and it's simply called *business process analysis*. This approach examines and documents how the work is currently done and usually diagrams the work, as in Figure 6-1. As you might suspect, because so much of business is driven by technology, this approach may include an analysis and documentation of the organization's IT systems.

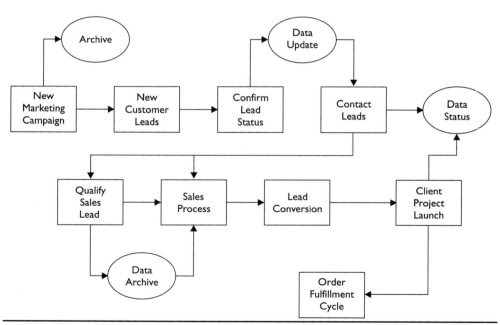

Figure 6-1 Business process analysis maps the known process of the business.

Business process analysis is known by many different names: business process mapping, business process reengineering, business process transformation, and business process modeling. Granting slight differences between the implementation of business process analysis and these pseudonyms, the intent is always the same: examine the business process for improvement.

What that improvement may be, however, depends on the problem the organization is experiencing. Business process analysis may be looking to reduce costs, decrease delivery time, increase productivity, become more efficient, or a hundred other goals. The path to process improvement is first to examine the current process work flow and then to develop an improved model based on what's currently known.

Another approach is the *object-oriented analysis* of an information system. This approach dissects a system, specifically an IT system, and shows how information, called *messages,* is passed from one entity in the system to another. The entities in the system are called *classes,* and the messages consist of data and information on how the data was created.

If you're a programmer, you probably know that object-oriented analysis is at the heart of the *Unified Modeling Language* (UML). UML was defined by the Object Management Group and allows the project team and business analysts to quickly visualize and document the components of a software program and the systems the software and users interact with.

NOTE If you're unfamiliar with UML, don't worry—you won't have to know much about it for your CBAP exam.

The final solution development approach you'll need to be familiar with is *structured analysis.* This approach, also a software development analysis tool, considers an IT system as a series of processes, and each process contributes to other processes within the system. All processes stem from some user interaction. Data is also tracked in structured analysis and is seen as the result of processes and user input.

One of the most common structured analysis charts is the flowchart. *Flowcharts* show the flow of information from one process to another. You'll use flowcharts to show the logical progression of work, data, activities, or any other complex system and how the entities within the flowchart are to work with each other. To create a flowchart, as in Figure 6-2, you need to know the boundaries of the chart; in other words, where will the flowchart start and end.

Flowcharts don't always just flow forward. You can create conditional branching, loopbacks, and even performance responsibilities for each defined entity in the chart. It's also a good idea to create a legend or accompanying text to explain how the flowchart's to work, so the user has a clear understanding of the intent of the chart. Common components of a flowchart include

- **Activities** These are the processes, work, or functions represented by rectangles.

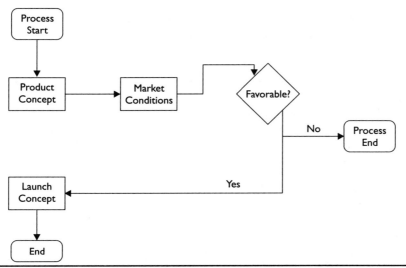

Figure 6-2 Flowcharts show the flow of decisions, data, and actions.

- **Flow** The flow is the direction of the data, represented by arrows.
- **Branches** When conditions allow the flow of activities to branch into multiple streams, a diamond is used to represent the split in the flowchart.
- **Forks** Sometimes the path will need to choose one of two paths to continue; this is called a fork. Forks in the flowchart are represented by a double line above the two paths in the flowchart.
- **Joins** Just as the flow can split into two paths, two paths can merge together through a join. Joins are also represented by a double line, but joins come after multiple paths.
- **Other items** Depending on your industry, you can have other items in your flowchart, like documents, databases, storage, and other media.
- **Starting point** This is the first item in the flowchart, and it's represented by a rounded rectangle.
- **End point** This is the final item in the flowchart, and it too is represented by a rounded rectangle.

Dataflow diagrams represent how data is entered into a system and what happens to that data once the system receives it. This diagram is great to visually represent how data moves through users, databases, retrieval, and storage for developers, management, project managers, and other stakeholders. The hierarchy of a system is broken down over and over until the individual processes that manage the data are revealed within the system.

NOTE   The first step of breaking down a system is to create a dataflow diagram called the *Context Diagram*.

Typical dataflow diagrams begin with an external entity, usually a person, but it could be another system, and this external entity is always represented by a rectangle in the chart. When data is entered into the system, a data *store* is also represented—these are represented by two parallel lines. When data is acted upon, it's called a data *process*, and the dataflow diagram represents this action with a circle. The last component is the data *flow* piece of the chart, and it's represented by an arc that shows the direction of the data flow. Check out Figure 6-3 for a small dataflow chart.

On a larger scale of structured analysis is an *entity relationship diagram*. This diagram considers the whole picture of an organization rather than just the IT systems the business interacts with. An entity relationship diagram visualizes all of the components of an organization and the relationships among the organization: customers, suppliers, vendors, employees, management, and resources like data, facilities, and equipment. This is an ideal model to capture communication requirements and channels within an organization.

Components of an entity relationship diagram are

- **Entities**   It's good for an entity relationship diagram to have entities; these are the people, resources, vendors, and data sources that contribute to the communication and processes within the organization.

- **Attributes**   The characteristic of the entity identified in the chart; consider the details of a piece of equipment, contact information for a vendor, or employee information.

- **Unique identifiers**   Each entity in the chart needs to be uniquely identified. Consider all of the system engineers who could be included in the chart; the unique identifiers distinguish between Marcy the system engineer and Steve the system engineer. This is used for each entity in the chart: vendors, equipment, and so on.

- **Relationships**   These show how communication flows from one entity to another. The rules of the organization, established flow of communication, and demands for communication are considered.

Figure 6-3
Dataflow charts capture the path of data input, storage, and output.

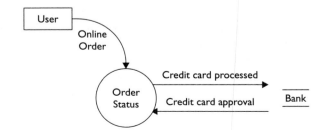

In the chart, the relationship line between entities includes a minimum and maximum count of the number of occurrences between one entity and another. Each occurrence represents an exchange of information that contributes to the relationship. The count is called the *cardinality* of the relationship—the higher the cardinality, the more communication is required between the two entities.

Structure Requirements Packages

A requirements package is a single item in the project scope based on the customer requirements. The potential scope solution is broken down into smaller and smaller requirements until the business analyst, the project manager, and other key stakeholders have a clear understanding and a significant amount of detail on each individual requirement of the project.

The more detail that's available on the requirements, the more accurate the solution for the business problem or opportunity will be. Structuring the requirements package is similar to creating the Work Breakdown Structure, and both provide an accurate reflection of customer and organizational expectations for the project deliverable.

The idea is that by "decomposing"—and yes, that's the preferred word to "breaking down"—requirements, all of the participants in the process will have a clear understanding of the project requirements. A clear understanding of the customer requirements will contribute to a more precise solution, better communications, and a more cost-effective project management approach. It's considered to be a cost benefit, because this process helps to eliminate waste, non-value-added activities, and miscommunication in the project team.

I'm often asked how far the requirements should be decomposed. I don't think it's very practical to decompose the requirements down to every keystroke in the application or every nail in the house—that'd take forever and would just be silly. There are a couple of schools of thought here. The first is that the decomposition should map to the 8/80 Rule. This is a common rule with project management, and it states that the smallest item in the decomposition should take no more than 80 hours and no less than 8 hours of labor to create. In other words, don't get too granular or leave chunky requirements in the model.

The other school of thought, and this is what I subscribe to, is that the requirements should be decomposed in enough detail that requirements are clearly understood. If the business analyst (or project manager) doesn't understand what the requirement does, what it demands, then it needs to be broken down more. If you're doing a smaller project, it's unlikely you'll need to break down the requirements into great detail. A large, hulking set of requirements, however, demands a fine decomposition to understand all that's needed for the project to be successful.

The decomposition of problems leads to solutions. By breaking down identified problems into smaller components, you can create rough time-and-cost estimates to help determine project feasibility for the identified solution. Breaking down large problems into smaller components also allows multiple projects to tackle individual components rather than creating large, complex projects within the entity. This is part of your organization's portfolio management processes to determine the initiation of projects or programs.

To create the requirements package, you first have to know where the solution will start and end—these are the solution boundaries. You don't want your solution to overstep or overextend the defined boundaries. You'll need to define what resources will interact with the solution and when that interaction will occur. Along with the resources, the solution requires you to define any other system that will contribute to or take from the solution.

Creating a Goal Decomposition

Goals are the results the stakeholders want for the project. Goals can be to increase revenue, reduce costs, brand distributed software, or just about anything else the stakeholders think is important and should be included in the project deliverable. Stakeholders, along with the business analyst, define the project goals during the enterprise assessment. Once the goals have been identified, they shift into the business analysis planning and management activities.

Including goals in the project solution is all about one thing: achieving customer satisfaction. It's imperative to have clearly identified goals as part of business analysis, the project requirements, and the proposed solution. In larger projects, where many stakeholders are involved, you'll probably encounter competing goals among the stakeholders. This is when a business owner, or even upper management, needs to get involved to provide leadership on trade-offs, competing objectives, and conflict resolution before the project execution gets under way.

The goals that have been identified must also be documented and agreed upon by the key stakeholders. These goals become part of the project requirements and should be broken down just as the project requirements are—they aren't treated separately from the project; they are part of the project. It's useful to track goal achievement for specific stakeholders to promote goodwill, synergy, and to show progress.

While most goals are objective, such as a specific feature in a software package, other goals may not be. Subjective goals are dangerous, as they can't easily be measured. Part of the business analyst's job is to establish metrics for measuring subjective goals, such as improving customer satisfaction, creating a good network, or making order processing faster. These are subjective goals that need metrics tied to them to show what's an "improvement," what "good" really means, and how "fast" may be interpreted differently among the stakeholders.

Dividing Solution Features and Functions

Features are how the stakeholder visualizes the project deliverable acting as part of the solution. Features can be visualized in a feature scheme to ensure that both the business analyst and the stakeholder understand one another. Features are generally identified in the high-level requirements of the project and then incorporated into the detailed requirements. Features, like all high-level requirements, are broken down into functional and supplemental requirements. The project team will use the identified features as part of their project planning and execution to ensure the stakeholders receive what they were promised.

When it comes time to close the project, the project manager, the business analyst, and the stakeholders will complete validation. Recall that validation is a confirmation of what the project has created to be in sync with the solution scope. Features are what the stakeholders will be looking for, and their evidence is a signal that the project was done according to plan. This is why it's important to identify and document the features of the project deliverable as part of the project requirements.

Functions define how something behaves. *Functional* decomposition identifies the high-level functions of a system, organization, or service, and breaks them down into subfunctions and activities. Functional decomposition ensures that all of the active characteristics of the proposed solution are identified, documented, and can be tracked. Functional decomposition aims to capture all of the processes within the system, software, or service the project is to create.

As with all decomposition activities, the goal is to decompose the identified functions to a level of detail that's useful—neither too large nor too small. With functional decomposition, there's a general rule that you continue to decompose the function until it cannot be split into two or more subfunctions.

Unfortunately, some solutions are presented with little or no business analysis to support the chosen solutions. Consider an executive decision to use new software, add a service to the organization, or purchase an off-the-shelf solution. While these decisions may have repercussions for lack of business analysis or feasibility studies, the solution may still need to be decomposed to identify the requirements the solution demands.

Solution-driven decomposition takes the identified solution and decomposes it to identify the components of the solution. The components then can be evaluated to determine how they'll interact with existing systems and processes, staffing demands, the learning curve to work with the solution, and any number of other considerations based on what the identified solution may be.

Working with Stakeholders

If it weren't for stakeholders, your projects and business analysis duties would be so much easier. I'm kidding, of course. If it weren't for stakeholders, there wouldn't be any business analysis duties or projects. Stakeholders are all of the people who have an interest in the execution and outcome of the project based on their needs, wants, and demands. "Stakeholders" is often a generic term to describe the people who create the expectations for the project.

Stakeholders, especially the end users and project customers, need to be involved as much as possible in the decomposition process, as it helps everyone visualize what the project, the project solution, and the requirements truly compose. Large, dreamy requirements can be interpreted so many different ways, while a detailed decomposition of the project requirements is exact and nails down project expectations.

The project manager, business analyst, and the business analysis team members are also stakeholders, as they're affected by the project execution and outcome. Decomposition of the solution helps identify responsibilities, project roles, and resource expectations of the solution. Decomposition of the requirements does, to some extent, overlap with project management activities, but it increases an understanding of what the project scope boundaries are.

A key part of stakeholder management is communication. You need a defined set of stakeholders and a defined policy, schedule, and plan to manage communication. Project management requires a communication management plan, but the business analyst should contribute to this plan. Communication is what keeps the business analysis and the project execution moving along.

Analyze Solution Requirements

Part of business analysis is to understand and document how users will interact with and use the deliverable of the project. The anticipation of how the solution will be utilized in the organization is discussed, analyzed, and documented as *user* requirements. The documentation of user requirements is important, because both the solution provider and the recipients of the solution agree that the expectations are the same.

Larger, complex projects, however, make the documentation of user requirements more difficult. Consider all of the competing objectives, the learning curve of the solution, and even interest in what the project is to create for the users. Management will often have to intercede on conflicting user requirements, while the business analyst and the project manager will need to work to gain consensus among the stakeholders on what the deliverable is to create for the organization.

Functional requirements are the identification of how the solution will operate once it's been created and released into the organization. Functional requirements, like user requirements, are documented and agreed upon before the solution's implementation. The expected behavior of the solution is documented and communicated to the key stakeholders. Behaviors are responses to conditions and they include

- The effect the behavior has upon the problem
- How people and systems will interact with the proposed solution
- Compliance with all appropriate standards and regulations

The functional requirements do not have to be tied to a specific functional solution. The functional requirements are written in such a way as not to constrain the possible solutions, but to define the requirements that the selected solution must have. In other words, the functional requirements should define how the solution operates, not what the solution is.

Writing the Requirements Documentation

User and functional requirements may overlap each other. You need to pay attention to the documentation of the requirements to ensure no duplication in requirements, no conflicts within the requirements documentation, and to ensure a clear understanding among the stakeholders. Requirements should be written clearly, precisely, and exactly, so there's no confusion or misinterpretation of what the requirements are. Follow these rules when writing requirements:

- State the requirements as simply as possible.

- Avoid complex conditional clauses.

- Confirm that terminology is accurately defined and used consistently throughout the requirements documentation.

- Don't make assumptions; spell out acronyms and define new terms.

- Don't group requirements; define them one at a time.

Your goal as a business analyst is to create well-formed requirements for your stakeholders. Anyone related to the project should be able to read the requirements documentation and understand what the project is to do. The reader should be able to understand what the solution is, the conditions that will define when the solution has been reached, and what people are responsible for what elements of the solution.

Good writing uses the active voice and defines what the subject must do. For example, "the database administrator creates the database." Passive voice can leave things open for interpretation, is not as commanding as active, and makes me sleepy. Avoid the passive voice; here's an example: "The database was created by the database administrator." Your requirements want strong, imperative roles and responsibility definitions. Leave nothing to interpretation.

Requirements documentation should also define any rules, policies, or regulations that may affect the outcome of the requirements. You should reference relevant organizational policies, rules, regulations, and laws that may affect how the solution is allowed to be implemented. An assumption that your stakeholders understand all of the relevant rules and regulations can lead to misunderstanding, trust issues, and frustrations later in the project.

Visualizing the Requirements Document

Sometimes it's easier to examine a chart, matrix, or model to evaluate what the requirements of the solution are. As a business analyst, you want the project stakeholders to clearly understand what the requirements are to eliminate confusion and wasted time and funds. Charts, matrixes, and models can also help the requirements-gathering process to ensure that all of the requirements have been identified and documented. You can use these items later in the project implementation as part of the solution validation process to ensure that all of the requirements have been met.

A matrix is simply a table that maps a set of components against another set of items. For example, you might create a matrix that lists all of the functional requirements and maps them according to the project objectives. When any two components in a matrix intersect, some action, input, or output is demanded from the requirement components. You can use a legend to define what action and expectation is needed between the two components.

If a picture is worth a thousand words, then it's a great idea to use pictures in your requirements documentation. Specifically, you'll use diagrams to illustrate the requirements and how they'll interact with one another, users, the organization, and systems within the organization. Diagrams help everyone clearly see the problem, the proposed solution, and how the solution may come into being. Diagrams are great for

- Illustrating how an organization will interact with the solution
- Diagramming the flow of activities within the project
- Documenting the chain of power, flow of communication, and other organizational attributes for the stakeholders
- Mapping the physical location of the solution

Diagrams can become very complex, so you should try to keep them as neat and simple as possible. A legend can help the reader identify the parts of the diagram and understand the intent of the business analyst. Always keep components approximately the same size and color in the diagram, unless the difference in color and size is significant to the understanding of the diagram. Finally, create diagrams for the widest audience; consider the culture and language of the participants viewing the diagram.

Models can also help stakeholders understand and relate to the requirements more easily than a textual documentation can. Models are a mesh of textual elements, matrixes, and diagrams, and they present all or a portion of the proposed solution. You'll typically find yourself using a model in complex solutions and long-term project schedules. You'll find several benefits to using models:

- Core requirements are focused on, and the business analyst can filter out descriptions, opinions, and other noise.
- Complex systems and solutions can be understood more easily through models.
- Models can shift the viewers' perspectives on the system.
- Models can help ensure that all of the business requirements are captured.
- Models can help the business analysis team define a solution design.

Models can be formal or informal, depending on the organization, but both should be created with clearly defined boundaries, terminology, and designs. The complexity of the model often depends on how complex the problem is, the timeline for the implementation, and the number of requirements already identified.

Within the model, the business analyst can create views; *views* represent only a portion of the model that is most appropriate to specific stakeholders. For example, the manufacturing stakeholder may only want to see requirements that affect her operations, rather than the entire model. Views allow the business analyst to narrow the focus of the model to a select set of stakeholders to increase communication and understanding.

Two common views for information technology projects are physical and logical views. The business analyst will typically create the *logical* view, as it defines all of the business requirements for the organization. The application developers will then create the *physical* view, as this information is most specific to what they'll be creating.

Analyzing the Solution Quality

Whatever solution the organization chooses, to be acceptable, it must meet the expectations surrounding the solution. The conformance-to-requirements business is pretty easy to see; the solution must create deliverables that satisfy the requirements that the business analyst has collected. The *fitness* part of a solution, however, can be a little tricky.

If you were to create a piece of software for me that allowed me to post information to several web pages from my word processor, we'd have a set of requirements that would map out all of the requirements. The requirements elicitation process, led by a business analyst, would capture everything I wanted the software to do. If your software met all of the requirements but had bright, flashy colors, error messages, and only worked when I typed the entries in all capital letters, there'd be a fitness for use problem. While technically you may have met all the requirements, the software wouldn't be fit for use.

The fitness for use goes above and beyond the conformance to requirements that maps to the quality of service. The solution has to meet both the stated requirements and the implied requirements of the customer. The environmental conditions that the solution has to interact with, the network, the data, access to remote servers, reliability, and even the competency of the users all affect the quality of service and must be considered when designing a solution.

These environmental issues are considered nonfunctional requirements according to the BABOK. They're considered nonfunctional because these are stakeholder demands and needs that may affect how the functions of the solution are allowed to work. Quality requirements, design constraints, and external systems that the solution must operate with are all common examples of nonfunctional requirements. Nonfunctional requirements are considered constraints and should be documented during the requirements elicitation process.

 NOTE I like business analysts, the IIBA, and the effort put forth in the BABOK; however…"quality of service" is a really loose term in my humble opinion. Quality of service has for years been linked to networking and the reliability of the network. In recent years, quality of service ("QOS" in the network side of the house) maps to the ability to throttle bandwidth for different network services, types of data, and overall communication. "Quality of service" in the BABOK, however, hints at that traditional point of view, but they really open it up to include more than that. And now I step down from my soapbox. Carry on.

Identifying Supplemental Requirements

Supplemental requirements are part of the quality of service requirements. These are elements that most projects must consider as part of their requirements, constraints, and quality to meet the expectations of the project customers. The business analyst should always consider these requirements in any type of project, though I think you'll find the CBAP exam leans more toward application development, for example, than construction.

The first supplemental requirement is the environmental requirement. This is not a nod toward the environment such as the rainforest, per se, but more toward the environment the project work and deliverable will exist in. You'll have to consider the environmental requirements that affect the project's ability to directly reach its goal. Consider all of the following environmental requirements:

- **Political environment** Every organization has politics that may influence project decisions. While you may elect to not document these politics directly, you need to consider which individuals may have power over the solution.

- **Regulations** Regulations are never optional. Your project and proposed solution may have industry regulations that you must adhere to. Always consider the regulations, even pending regulations, as these may hinder or constrain the project's ability to quickly and cost-effectively meet the identified requirements.

- **Standards**   Industry standards are sometimes optional. Standards are guidelines that are usually followed, but you won't be breaking any laws if you don't follow them. Your organization may also have standards such as forms, documentation, and processes that must be followed on most projects.

- **Market**   The condition of the market is an excellent example of an environmental requirement that you have little control over. Market conditions can affect how you buy and sell, price your services and goods, and have an impact on whether the project is even launched or allowed to proceed at all.

- **Enterprise environmental factors**   This term describes the conditions within your organization that may constrain options on the project. Consider culture, policies, rules, the chain of command, the power of the business analysts, the project manager, and the project team.

- **Audit requirements**   Projects may require data about the data they produce in case they're audited by an outside agency. This "data about data" is called *metadata,* and while it's a pain in the neck to create and consider, it's required for consistency and often by law, depending on the industry the project is taking place in.

- **Globalization and localization**   It's not unusual for projects to span countries. Projects that span multiple countries must consider all of the laws, languages, and cultural issues of each country the project interacts with. You'll also have to consider time zone issues, languages, and monetary concerns such as the exchange rate.

- **Legal requirements**   Projects and solutions must adhere to the relevant laws. There may be some industry-specific laws the business analyst should consider or seek legal advice on when there's a question of legality.

 NOTE   I like to say that *regulations* are requirements and are never optional. *Standards* are guidelines and can sometimes be optional. This helps me keep these terms straight in my head.

In today's business world, technology drives and supports business like never before. This fact introduces the second environmental requirement: interface requirements. *Interface requirements* is a term to describe how technical systems interact with one another and with the users of the technology.

Consider the hardware, software, data collection and storage, and how users, engineers, and database administrators all interact with the technical infrastructure within an organization. You'll also need to consider how, and if, the customers outside of the enterprise interact with any of the technical infrastructure and how the solution may affect them.

A hardware interface is any physical connection between technical devices. Consider servers, workstations, and other systems and the physical link between them—the network and the Internet. A *network topology* is a map of the network and every link on that network, as in Figure 6-4. Each identified component should be documented as to its contribution, how it interfaces with other technology, and what effect it may have on the project or the project may have upon it.

Software interfaces is a term to describe every technological interface that is not a physical thing such as a server or printer. Software interfaces are applications, processes, operating systems, databases, and data that are transmitted across and through hardware interfaces. The consideration of these interfaces is mandated by the business analyst, because these interfaces could be immensely affected by any technical solutions—or the interfaces could adversely affect the proposed technical solution.

Above all of this technology are the *operational* requirements. The solution that the business analyst presents must define how it'll interact and possibly affect operations for the better. The business analyst will need to examine the *stress* (sometimes called the load) on the hardware and software interfaces when users start using the new solution. The maximum amount of users, data throughput, and even acceptable downtime will all need to be examined and documented as part of any technical solution. Mission-critical applications, network solutions, and security of the data are part of operational requirements.

Environmental regulations, hardware interfaces, and software interfaces will introduce loads of terms to the project and to the stakeholders. Most organizations probably also have their own acronyms for internal processes and procedures. All of these terms can get muddled in the business analysis documentation, and misunderstood terms can diminish the effectiveness of the requirements. This is why a glossary of terms should be included with the requirements, so all stakeholders have clear definitions of what's being communicated.

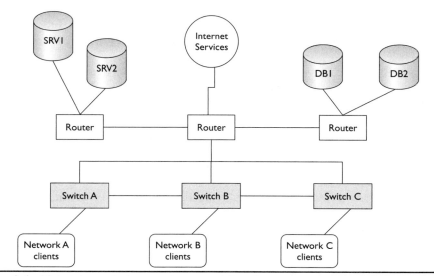

Figure 6-4   Network topologies map the network interfaces.

Your organization may have privacy requirements for its users, both public and internal, that you have to abide by. Privacy requirements are part of environmental requirements, because it's often a legal requirement or corporate policy that dictates how your solution, your business, will protect user data and information. All privacy requirements should be documented and clearly expressed to the relevant stakeholders. Failure to abide by the defined privacy requirements can have costly legal and professional ramifications.

Meeting Expected Quality

If quality is conforming to requirements and creating something that's fit for use, then it's reasonable to expect quality to be designed into the solution. Quality expectations from the project customer, project manager, and the business analyst should be in sync when it comes to the end result of the project. Quality designed into a new solution should always consider and quantify

- Design of the project solution
- Reliability of the solution
- Usability from the end user's perspective
- Maintenance of the solution when it moves post-project and into operations
- Testing of the solution components
- Scalability of the solution across the enterprise, future growth, current processes, and existing technology

You should also consider the learning curve of the solution. The *learning curve* describes how long it'll take to learn the new solution and how much the learning will cost the organization. Many solutions expect an initial drop in efficiency as the users learn how to use the new solution, as in Figure 6-5. Over time, however, efficiency should increase to a new plateau. The learning curve, also called *regression analysis,* identifies how far backwards in efficiency an organization will have to go in order to go forward in efficiency and productivity.

Figure 6-5
The learning curve describes a dip in performance before new efficiencies.

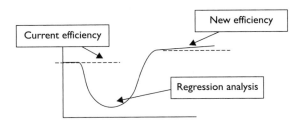

NOTE Just because a worker can be more efficient, doesn't mean they'll be more productive. Parkinson's Law states that work expands to fill the amount of time allotted to it. If a new solution can reduce the amount of time it takes to complete an operational task by 8 hours, it doesn't automatically convert to 8 hours of realized productivity. The worker may stretch the work by filling the time with web surfing or other activities. Efficiency and productivity are not the same thing.

Another quality requirement that you must consider is the failure and disaster recovery piece of the proposed solution. Disaster recovery has become a new theme for most IT projects, as its focus is on maintaining operations should there be a disaster. Business analysts should consider solutions for ongoing operations, data recovery, redundancy, partial and complete system failure, and testing procedures. This portion of the requirements process should also include instructions for implementing a disaster recovery plan, a mitigation plan, and steps for operating in the worst-case scenarios.

Many solutions may have safety issues that need to be addressed. You should document any safety procedures that should be followed when working with the solution, and document the risks users may face if they do not follow the outlined safety procedures. There may also be laws and regulations that dictate user and employee safety for the solution.

Safety issues are part of two known costs associated with quality:

- **Cost of conformance to requirements** These are the monies that an organization must spend to ascertain the expected level of quality: the correct tools, software, safety equipment, and training.

- **Cost of nonconformance to requirements** These are monies that an organization will pay in fines, lawsuits, loss of sales, and loss of customers should they not achieve the expected quality in the project. Consider a project that does not provide the project team with the proper safety tools or training. If someone gets injured, then there'll be repercussions. These costs also include time delays, waste of materials, loss of team morale, and poor deliverables.

 EXAM NOTE When it comes to quality, you can count on the phrase "what get measured is what gets done." You need quality metrics in your requirements so everyone knows when you've achieved quality in the deliverables. Business analysts should identify metrics to measure the reliability, validity, and timeliness of each requirement.

Training is also a quality requirement that should be documented. This is training for the project team to complete the work and for the recipients of the project deliverables. An assessment of the available resources will help determine competency gaps related to the skills needed to complete the project work. You'll also need to examine the solution and determine through your research what type of education, manuals, and support will be needed for the project deliverables.

Identifying Constraints and Assumptions

Throughout requirements gathering, you'll be on the lookout for constraints and assumptions. As a reminder, and to beat you over the head with this business, a *constraint* is anything that can limit the options of the project. An *assumption* is anything that you believe to be true but haven't proven to be true. Both constraints and assumptions can become risks in the project, and then it's all doomed! Well, maybe not doomed, but you'll wish you'd dealt with the constraints and assumptions earlier rather than later.

Constraints are usually pretty easy to identify: just look for anything that you have to do, are required to do, or that places demands on the project. Typical constraints are schedules, cost limits, and must-haves for the project deliverables. You might also face constraints such as when you have to deal with a particular vendor, even if you don't like them, or when you have to use the boss's daughter on the project, even if she's only home from college for the summer, isn't really qualified, and spends her days surfing the Web for fun. (Now, that's purely anecdotal; I've no such work experience with a team member like that.)

Some tricky constraints are tied to human resources. The project may have demands for resources that don't exist within the organization, or you may not have enough resources for the project to finish by a given deadline. Considering resources is tricky in business analysis, because all of the project may not be mapped to dates, but it's a good idea to at least consider if resources are available for the project.

Assumptions, on the other hand, can be tougher to identify. Sometimes the nature of the work relies on assumptions for planning. Consider construction in the northern United States: it's usually better to construct things in the summer months than the winter months, but you don't really know what the weather is going to be. You might also have to plan based on assumptions in technology, competencies, and available resources in the organization. All projects go into motion with one major assumption: that the project won't get cancelled once the work is under way.

Documenting Identified Constraints

Once you've identified the constraints, you'll need to write them down. Surprised? When it comes to your CBAP exam, be certain to look for answers that have you document stuff. The CBAP exam, and your business analysis practices, should love documentation and love to document constraints. The documentation of constraints isn't so you can tell stakeholders "I told you so" when the constraints wreck the project. You document the constraints so you and the project manager can plan for addressing and managing the constraints in the project.

 NOTE Documenting the constraints is also a great way to communicate the risks associated with the constraints. It's funny how some people seem to take things more seriously once you've written constraints down.

Business constraints are constraints that are imposed on the project. Business constraints generally include

- Predetermined deadlines and schedules
- Assigned budgets
- Requirements for specific resources to complete the project work
- Competency and training of the project team
- Considerations for project execution and the affected lines of business
- The scope of the project, as it's what the project is to create

All of the business constraints should be documented and reviewed with the project manager, the business owner, and the key stakeholders. Everyone should agree that the identified constraints are valid. The validation of the constraints makes it easier to negotiate for concessions in the project to alleviate the pressure and demands constraints add to the project.

Technical constraints are tied to the architecture decisions in a technical, IT-based project. You'll encounter and document technical constraints for the project, which means you may need to rely on a subject matter expert to help identify the constraints. Typical technical constraints include

- Software development languages
- Hardware platforms
- Software the project deliverable will interact with
- Resource utilization
- Restriction on the data usage, size, and other data elements

When it comes to technology, every organization, site, and project has different characteristics, so you'll need to carefully examine each solution for constraints. There's no blanket list of technical constraints to consider across every technical project. Your organization may also have its own guidelines that the project is expected to adhere to—these technical guidelines are constraints. Finally, as the project progresses, new constraints may be identified, and these too should be documented and presented to the key stakeholders.

Documenting Assumptions

Along with documenting the project constraints, you're also going to document the project assumptions. Based on all of the project details, research, business analysis, and input from subject matter experts, the project manager, the project team, and any other relevant stakeholders, you'll need to clearly and fully document assumptions that have been made in the project.

While I've stated (more than once, I know) that assumptions are things that you believe to be true but haven't proven to be true, they're technically more than just that.

My definition is the broadest definition of an assumption, but you'll also need to document the things that you know to be true and that you believe won't change in the project execution. Assumptions also include the known factors that would affect the project, for better or worse, if the conditions changed.

NOTE Assumptions are tied to project risks. Negative risks are things that hurt the project, while positive risks actually help the project. You can have both positive and negative assumptions in every project.

Here are samples of things that may be currently known and that are usually assumed not to change:

- Availability of project resources
- Availability of project budget
- Reliance on identified vendors
- Accuracy of project requirements
- Abilities of the project team
- Law, standards, and regulations

A project can have countless other assumptions that you have to consider. Should any of these assumptions change, the project could be affected. Sometimes a change in assumption could be seen as a boon to a project, such as an assumption in the cost of a certain material. Consider the cost of fuel, shipping, and travel; these are variable costs that can change based on market conditions. The shift up or down on costs could help or hinder the project as a whole.

Determine the Requirements and Attributes

You'll elicit requirements through a series of interviews with stakeholders, prototypes, and other elicitation approaches—and then you'll document the requirements. It won't do anyone much good if the documents are not documented in clear, concise language that fully captures what the stakeholders are requesting from the project. The requirements document is evidence of what the stakeholders have asked for, and it communicates the business analyst's understanding of their needs and wants for the project solution.

The requirements document does not estimate time and costs, as these are project management activities. Rather, the requirements documentation leads to the project scope statement, since it portrays what the customer needs and what the project should create. The requirements documentation may also serve as more than just the project scope. It could be an input to the procurement process if the project work is being completed by a vendor.

Part of your business analyst job is to do more than elicit and document requirements. You also need to document the attributes of the requirements, that is, what the requirements are really asking for, the characteristics of the requirements, and who asked for what. These attributes will help the project manager communicate during the project, manage the execution of the project to achieve the requirements, and will help you and the project manager prioritize requirements.

The documentation of the requirements will also help when it comes to change management. When changes are proposed to the project scope, the project manager, change control board, and you need to know what the change may impact within the scope and how the change, if it's approved, will affect the rest of the project. Change management requires communication among the stakeholders, and knowing who asked for what can help the project manager communicate the change and how it may impact other project requirements.

 NOTE Changes can be sneaky attempts by stakeholders to promote their own interests over other competing project objectives. By identifying project requirements, you can trace change requests back to the original stakeholders and any issues or conditions surrounding their requirements.

Each identified requirement should be isolated as part of documenting the requirements. As each requirement is isolated from other requirements, you can add the details about the requirements, resources used, expected completion dates, risks, and other information. Recall that each requirement should have a unique identifier and that this identifier can then be cross-referenced with supporting, related, or succeeding requirements. You can also then track resources, risks, and issues across all of the requirements based on the identified project attributes.

Creating a Requirements Document

The performing organization may already have a form or template for capturing and documenting project requirements. That's fine if one exists—use it! You may have to, in some instances, create your requirements documentation, as the project is unique or your organization does not have predefined requirements documentation. For your CBAP examination, you should be familiar with some of the common requirements documents:

Vision Document

A vision document is a high-level view of the project solution. It defines a "vision" of what the project is to create for the organization. Vision documents are ideal for projects that will go through rounds of planning and where the project scope is defined through iterations. If you're familiar with the PMBOK, then you may recognize this approach as progressive elaboration. Progressive elaboration is where you start with a broad vision of the project and then, through planning, you provide more and more detail until the exactness of the project is determined.

Business Process Description

Like the vision document, the Business Process Description defines the project at a high level of what the project should create. Where this document differs, however, is that the Business Process Description also includes a summary of the current business model, all of the known user requirements, and any of the functional requirements that have been defined. This document may also move through iterations of planning.

Business Requirements Document

This document clearly defines the behavior of a project solution for the customers and end users. It's most common for software development projects, and it's based on the business requirements defined early in the business analysis activities. This document is great for confirming that the business analyst, the project manager, and the stakeholders all agree on what the project should create.

Request for Proposal (RFP)

This document, often just called an RFP, is part of the procurement process in an organization. It is a request for a vendor to create a fully defined approach for the requirements of the project. For example, an RFP to create a web site might include the number of pages, the content management system, the shopping cart software, the electronic fulfillment requirements, and more. It's a document that asks the vendor to provide a solution for the project—it's more than just a price request.

Request for Quote (RFQ)

This document, sometimes called an RFQ, asks the vendor to create a price for the exact requirements that have already been defined. For example, you could ask a vendor for a quote for 80 copies of a particular off-the-shelf software. You don't need any fancy ideas or suggestions as you'd expect with a request for proposal. An RFQ just wants a price for the already defined requirements.

Software Requirements Specification

Depending on the situation, this document may also be called a System Requirements Specification. This requirements documentation defines the expected behavior and implementation of the software or system the developers will be creating for the project customers. This documentation starts with a definition of the problem domain and the functional requirements that will help create the solution. The document will also include the expected quality of service and will communicate any relevant assumptions or constraints the developers will need to manage as part of the solution.

It's not unusual to create more than one of these documents depending on the size of the problem domain and the audience of the requirements document. For example, you may start the fun with a vision document, and then create a Business Requirements Document as more information becomes available. You could also create an RFP to see what the vendor's cost and approach for the project may be. The goal of these documents, especially those that interact with vendors, is not to create time and cost estimates, but to document and capture the requirements that will feed into the project.

Assigning Requirement Attributes

All requirements also have attributes that elaborate on the requirements and provide more communications to the users, customers, project manager, and even vendors when they're involved. The requirement attributes are more than just the functional and business requirements; they'll help the project team plan on how to achieve the requirements, analyze risk, and judge quality of service.

The wording of the requirements can help the business analyst, the customers, and the project manager all agree on the urgency of the requirements. Consider these imperatives and how they'll affect the project requirements:

- **Shall and must** The requirement is mandatory for the project. For example, the application must be compatible with Microsoft SQL Server.

- **Should** The requirement is desirable. The application should allow the user to interact with reporting software.

- **May** The requirement is optional. The application may allow users to post results as a web page or a printed page.

- **Will** The requirement will be provided by a solution outside of the current project. ABC Consultants will provide the physical security of the project solution.

These imperatives for each requirement can help everyone understand the responsibility of the project team and what the project deliverables will be expected to provide as part of the solution. Project planning processes will research and expound on these requirement attributes. These imperatives and requirement attributes will be revisited during the project scope validation process to confirm that the project team has indeed created what the project customer expected.

In addition to the imperative to describe what's expected of the solution, you should also know these common requirement attributes for your CBAP exam:

- **Absolute reference** Each identified requirement will have its own unique identifier that will not be assigned to any other requirement within the project. If a requirement is removed from the project, so is the absolute reference of the requirement.

- **Acceptance criteria** This requirement attribute defines the condition that proves the requirement has been delivered.

- **Author of the requirement** This attribute simply defines the individual who demanded or is the authority of the requirements. It's useful to document this person in case there are follow-up questions or additional communication is needed.

- **Complexity**   A scale, definition, or essay on how complex the requirement will be to implement.

- **Ownership**   This attribute defines the business entity or group within the organization that will be the business owner of the requirements once they're released into production. Note that this attribute is different from the author of requirement attribute, as the ownership can describe a business unit, while the author of requirements defines a single person.

- **Priority**   Defines the order in which the requirements should be implemented. This is particularly useful when creating deliverables in stages for the project customers.

- **Source**   The source is the authorized entity that has the authority to approve requirements and may need to be involved in the change control process of a project. The source is usually higher than the owner and author of the requirements within the organization.

- **Stability**   Most requirements pass through rounds of planning and definition. The more fully defined the requirements are, the more stable they are deemed to be. At some point the requirements are considered stable enough to start work. It's important to accurately judge the stability of the requirements, as unstable requirements that result in wasted efforts and monies will probably increase frustration among you, the project manager, and the project customers (not too good for you).

- **Status**   This attribute is linked to the stability of the requirements, as it keeps track of each requirement and what its current status in the project may be: proposed, accepted, verified, or implemented.

- **Urgency**   Stop the presses! This requirement is superimportant! Well, maybe not. This requirement attribute defines how urgent the requirement is and when the customer needs it to be delivered as part of the solution.

You might also find yourself including other requirement attributes like maximum cost, geographical locations, resources, versioning of the requirements, and other attributes that are unique to your organization. That's fine, as long as you explain the attributes and everyone understands why you're documenting the additional requirements information.

Verifying Project Requirements

Once you've elicited requirements, documented requirements and their attributes, and found an acceptable level of stability with the clients for the project manager to begin project work, there's one last step to complete. This step is your safety net between you, the project manager, the project team, and the project customers: verify the project requirements.

The verification of the project requirements is an immensely important step, because it's the last activity, between the requirements elicitation and the commitment of resources, before the project requirements become a reality. You'll work with the customers, users, project manager, and business owners to review each requirement and confirm the understanding of the requirements for execution in the project.

One of the primary reasons it's important to verify requirements is to prevent waste. If you skip this step, then there's a good chance the requirements won't be as accurate as you believe, and the project manager and the project team will need to scrap time and work they've invested and start on clearer requirements. This is, as you might guess, a huge pain in the neck and frustration ensues. It'll also cause the project to get off on a bad foot, and the project may never recoup its costs and time for the lost work based on poor requirements.

When requirements are poorly defined and are unverified, then it's really an error or omission that will affect the project scope. The project scope is based on the requirements documentation, and changes to the project scope, regardless of the reason, create a series of steps that also take time and sometimes monies to incorporate. All changes must be evaluated for understanding, their purpose for entering the project, and their effect on all the other project requirements. You can imagine, I'm sure, the wasted time and monies from poor requirements and not completing the requirements validation.

Confirming Stakeholder Requirements

The goal of verifying requirements is to work with the stakeholders to confirm that you, the business analyst, have captured everything they've asked for. You want to review the requirements and first confirm that your requirements documentation is accurate, thorough, and written in an easy-to-understand format. You'll want to look for some key attributes of the requirements before moving ahead with the project manager and the key stakeholders. In particular you want to confirm all of the following:

- No duplicate requirements or overlaps exist between identified requirements.
- The requirements are feasible, achievable, and the available technology and resources are capable of implementing the identified technology.
- The requirements are fully defined, and expectations of deliverables are clearly stated.
- The requirements don't include assumptions about how the solution will be implemented, only what the end result of the project will provide.

Well-defined requirements use measurable metrics and avoid ambiguous terms like "good," "fast," and "high." You want to capture sufficient detail about each requirement that there's no confusion or misunderstanding of what the project manager and the project team are to accomplish. Poor requirements will lead to wasted project resources. You'll work with the project stakeholders to confirm each of the requirements, the requirement attributes, and the completeness of each requirement.

Assessing the Quality of Requirements

The quality of the requirements is directly linked to the quality of the project. If the requirements are loose, ambiguous, and ill-defined, then the project manager and project team will have to revisit the requirements for additional information, clarification, and analysis. The elicitation and analysis of the requirements are the primary functions of the business analyst—not the project manager. Just as you wouldn't complete project planning, quality control on project deliverables, or procurement processes, you can't expect the project manager to complete business analysis duties.

There are eight conditions for each requirement that you should confirm prior to the project execution. These eight criteria help you and the project stakeholders review the completeness and accuracy of the requirements before project execution. You should be familiar with these criteria for your CBAP exam:

- **Necessary**   Each requirement should have cohesive value and contribute to meeting defined business goals and objectives as stated in the project charter, vision document, and the business case.

- **Complete**   The requirements are fully defined, which means that all constraints, assumptions, potential risks, attributes, and conditions of the project are documented. The complete attribute also means there is enough accurate information that the project team may begin creating the requirements based on the documentation provided.

- **Consistent**   The requirement should mesh with all of the other requirements in the project. You may find inconsistent requirements when a key stakeholder is forcing a particular requirement into the project as a mandate. This is when politics enter the business analysis and project management.

- **Correct**   Correct requirements describe the functionally that is to be created by the project. The author of the requirements is the individual who must fully define the correctness of the project requirement.

- **Modifiable**   Similar requirements should be grouped together so that modifications to the requirements can be made easily. When requirements are grouped by similar characteristics, it's more practical to see how a change in one requirement affects other requirements.

- **Unambiguous**   The requirements documentation should be written in such a way that all readers of the requirements documentation arrive at the same understanding of what the requirements demand. Simple, concise language is imperative for clear communication of requirements.

- **Testable**   The requirements provide evidence of completion by testing, examining, or demonstrating their existence upon completion. Each requirement must be verified upon delivery to confirm the completeness of the deliverable.

- **Feasible**   The requirements must be capable of being created considering the given timeline, budget, capabilities, and other requirements of the solution.

These characteristics are guidelines for business analysts to weigh the correctness and completeness of each requirement. You should document the existence of these attributes for each project requirement as part of your findings in requirements elicitation and requirements verification with the stakeholders. This means that if the business analyst doesn't understand the requirements the stakeholder is expressing, the business analyst should ask for clarifications, examples, and drawings to completely capture and understand the requirements.

 NOTE   Requirements should always avoid ambiguous terms. Avoid terms like "good," "valid," "fast," and "high quality." The requirements should be fully defined with exact requirements and measurements for acceptability.

A great quality control technique to use during requirements verification is a *checklist*. You can use these requirement attributes along with any additional organizational standards as a checklist to confirm the completeness of each requirement. Checklists are considered a quality control tool, as you're inspecting the documentation of each requirement to evaluate how ready the requirement is to move into project execution.

Chapter Summary

Business analysts are writers: they have to interview, elicit, and gather project requirements and then write them all down. That's really what this chapter and the CBAP exam objective is all about—you documenting the project requirements. The documentation the business analyst provides launches the real work of the project. The reliance on the business analyst to provide clear, well-written project requirements is immensely important, as these requirements steer the direction of the project execution.

The chief theme of this chapter is completeness and accuracy in documenting the project requirements. The secondary theme is that the requirements documentation must be written in clear, concise language so that all of the project stakeholders can understand each requirement and what the project aims to accomplish.

You probably noticed a subtle theme of the chapter: requirements should not be dictated by the business analyst, but rather just provide insight as to what the best solution for the end user should be. The execution of the activities to achieve the requirements is part of project planning. You'll want to steer stakeholders clear of execution demands and have them focus more on the results of execution. The approach to business solution analysis should be broad, with no attachment to only one identified solution.

The project scope will be based on the requirements as defined by the business analyst. The requirements the business analyst gathers will be collected into requirements packages. Recall that a requirements package is a single item in the project scope based on the customer requirements. The aggregation of the requirements packages will account for the project scope as a whole. The project solution should be broken down into smaller elements until the individual packages are clearly defined and can be traced to both the original requirements and the implemented solution.

Complex, technical systems are sometimes difficult to understand simply through requirements and the associated documentation. Models can help the stakeholders visualize the solution as a whole. Diagrams of the solution can show the relationship of project entities, organizational groups, and the flow of data through and out of the solution. You might also elect to use models to capture textual elements, requirements matrixes, and diagrams to completely represent the project requirements and the proposed solution.

The environment of the performing organization can also affect the requirements and the proposed solution. Politics, standards, regulations, and market conditions can all affect the prioritization of the project requirements and whether certain requirements are included in the project scope at all. The globalization of the project, legal requirements, and the potential for project audits may also affect the structure of the stakeholders' requirements. You might also have enterprise environmental factors that affect how the requirements are documented and controlled within the project. Recall that enterprise environmental factors are the rules and policies that are unique to your organization.

All requirements have expectations tied to them and how the requirements will be part of the project solution. Some requirements typically are more important than other requirements, but all requirements have an expected level of quality tied to them. The quality of service, that is, the completeness and usability of the solution, must also be recorded in the requirements documentation. Requirements quality should also include disaster and failure recovery for the project solution.

Finally, I'll leave you with good old assumptions and constraints—something you've seen a bunch of already. Assumptions are things that you believe to be true but have not been proven to be true. Assumptions can become risks for the project if they are not fully tested or prove to be false. A constraint is anything that limits the options of the project manager. Constraints can also become risks if they're too restrictive or don't mesh with other project requirements. You can bet that you'll see assumptions and constraints on your CBAP exam based on the amount of times they're mentioned in the BABOK.

Key Terms

8/80 Rule   A common rule within project management; it states that the smallest item in the scope decomposition should take no more than 80 hours and no fewer than 8 hours of labor to create. It prevents requirements packages from being too large or too small to manage.

Absolute reference   A requirement attribute where each identified requirement will have its own unique identifier that will not be assigned to any other requirement within the project. If a requirement is removed from the project, so too is the absolute reference of the requirement.

Acceptance criteria   This requirement attribute defines the conditions that prove the requirement has been delivered.

Allocation ready   The requirement can be allocated to a phase, portion, or area of the project that can be readily created. A requirement that can't be allocated usually is a sign of the requirement being too vague.

Attainable   A requirement attribute that documents the feasibility for the current project and can be created, implemented, and supported by the organization. It is possible for a requirement to be technically attainable but not feasible for the current project based on the work, time, cost, or other factors the requirement would demand.

Audit requirements   Projects may require data about the data they produce in case they're audited by an outside agency. This "data about data" is called *metadata*, and while it's a pain in the neck to create and consider, it's required for consistency and often by law depending on the industry the project is taking place in.

Author of the requirement   This requirement attribute simply defines the individual who demanded or is the author of the requirements.

Business Domain Model   A visual representation of how the business does or should work in regard to the project requirements. It defines each of the business processes affected by the project, how the process should work, and how the process interacts with other processes, functions, and project-affected users in the organization.

Business process analysis   A solution development methodology that examines and documents how the work is currently done in comparison to how the work should be done once the solution has been created. Business process analysis is also known as business process mapping, business process reengineering, business process transformation, and business process modeling.

Business Process Description   Defines the project at a high level of what the project should create. This document includes a summary of the current business model, all of the known user requirements, and any of the functional requirements that have been defined.

Business Requirements Document   This document clearly defines the behavior of a project solution for the customers and end users. It's most common for software development projects, and it's based on the business requirements defined early in the business analysis activities.

Class model   Demonstrates the attributes, operations, and relationship to entities within the solution. Classes are physical resources, solution concepts, collection of data, a function of the solution, or an action.

Complete   A requirement attribute that documents that the requirements are fully defined, which means all constraints, assumptions, potential risks, attributes, and conditions of the project are documented.

Complexity   This requirement attribute defines the scale, complexity definition, or essay on how difficult the requirement will be to implement.

Consistent   A requirement attribute where the requirement meshes with all of the other requirements in the project. You may find inconsistent requirements when a key stakeholder is forcing a particular requirement into the project as a mandate.

Correct   A requirement attribute where the requirements describe the functionality that is to be created by the project. The author of the requirement is the individual who must fully define the correctness of the project requirement.

Cost of conformance to requirements   These are the monies that an organization must spend to ascertain the expected level of quality: the correct tools, software, safety equipment, and training.

Cost of nonconformance to requirements   These are monies that an organization will pay in fines, lawsuits, loss of sales, and loss of customers should they not achieve the expected quality in the project. Consider a project that does not provide the project team with the proper safety tools or training. If someone gets injured, then there'll be repercussions. These costs also include time delays, waste of materials, loss of team morale, and poor deliverables.

CRUD Matrix   This is a table that uses the acronym CRUD to define the level of access resources have to an information system. CRUD stands for Create, Read, Update, or Delete. It's the permissions assigned to resources for system information.

Data dictionary   Describes the data used by the system. The data dictionary defines the name of the data, data aliases, values and meanings, and description of the system data.

Enterprise environmental factors   This term describes the conditions within your organization that may constrain options on the project. Consider culture, policies, rules, the chain of command, the power of the business analysts, the project manager, and the project team.

Entity relationship diagram   Visualizes the whole organization and the relationships among the organization: customers, suppliers, vendors, employees, management, and resources like data, facilities, and equipment. This is an ideal model to capture communication requirements and channels within an organization.

Feasible   A requirement attribute where the requirements are confirmed to be feasible for the project to accomplish based on the organization's resources, competencies, expected budget, and timeline for the project.

Flowchart   A structured analysis chart that shows the flow of information from one process to another.

Function   Requirements that define how something should behave. Functional decomposition identifies the high-level functions of a system, organization, or service and breaks them down into subfunctions and activities. Functional decomposition ensures that all of the active characteristics of the proposed solution are identified, documented, and can be tracked. Functional decomposition aims to capture all of the processes within the system, software, or service the project is to create.

Functional requirements   Describe how the solution will function, what it will do, and what its expected outcomes are. This is usually a more technical document than the User Requirements Document (URD), but it should mesh with the users' requirements.

Globalization and localization   Projects that span multiple countries must consider all of the laws, languages, and cultural issues of each country the project interacts with. You'll also have to consider time zone issues, languages, and monetary concerns such as the exchange rate.

Hardware interfaces   The categorization of any physical connection between technical devices. Consider servers, workstations, and other systems and the physical link between them—the network and Internet.

Key stakeholders   The stakeholders who have decision-making powers over the requirements and project.

Legal requirements   Projects and solutions must adhere to the relevant laws. It shouldn't be a surprise here, but for some industry-specific laws, the business analyst should consider or seek legal advice when there's a question of legality.

Logical view   The business requirements for the organization—documented, clearly defined, and agreed upon by the project stakeholders.

Market   Part of the organizational environment. The condition of the market is an excellent example of an environmental regulation that you have little control over. Market conditions can affect how you buy and sell, price your services and goods, and have an impact on whether the project is even launched or allowed to proceed at all.

Measurable and testable   A requirement attribute that confirms that the requirements are not described with subjective, unquantifiable terms and metrics. You'll need specific tests to measure and show a range of acceptability for satisfying the requirements.

Models   A combination of textual elements, matrixes, and diagrams that presents all or a portion of the proposed solution. Models can help stakeholders understand and relate to the requirements more easily than can a textual documentation of requirements.

Necessary   A requirement attribute that demands all personal requirements, personal agendas, and non-value-added extras be stripped from the project. Each requirement should have value and contribute to meeting defined business goals and objectives as stated in the project charter, vision document, or business case.

Object-oriented analysis   A solution development methodology that dissects a system, specifically an IT system, and shows how information, called messages, is passed from one entity in the system to another. The entities in the system are called classes, and the messages consist of data and information on how the data was created.

Ownership   This requirement attribute defines the business entity or group within the organization that will be the business owner of the requirement once it's released into production.

Physical view The map of the physical components and structure of the solution. The application developers will then create the physical view, as this information is most specific to what they'll be creating in project execution.

Political environment Every organization has politics that may influence project decisions. While you may elect not to document these politics directly, you need to consider which individuals may have power over the solution.

Prioritized A requirement attribute that allows each requirement to be assigned a level of priority based on the functional requirements, user requirements, and urgency of the deliverable.

Priority A requirement attribute that defines the order in which the requirements should be implemented. This is particularly useful when creating deliverables in stages for the project customers.

Regulations Part of the organizational environment. Your project and proposed solution may have industry regulations that you must adhere to. The regulations, even pending regulations, should always be considered, as these may hinder or constrain the project's ability to quickly and cost-effectively meet the identified requirements.

Request for Proposal (RFP) This document, often just called an RFP, is part of the procurement process in an organization. It is a request for a vendor to create a fully defined approach for the requirements of the project. It's a document that asks the vendor to provide a solution for the project—it's more than just a price request.

Request for Quote (RFQ) This document, sometimes called an RFQ, asks the vendor to create a price for the exact requirements that have already been defined. An RFQ just wants a price for the already defined requirements.

Requirements package A single item in the project scope based on the customer requirements.

Software Requirements Specification May also be called a System Requirements Specification. This requirements documentation defines the expected behavior and implementation of the software or system the developers will be creating for the project customers. This documentation starts with a definition of the problem domain and the functional requirements that will help create the solution. The document will also include the expected quality of service and will communicate any relevant assumptions or constraints the developers will need to manage as part of the solution.

Solution independent A requirement attribute where the requirements do not define the implementation of the solution but rather only the requirements. The requirements should allow for a broad selection of solution choices, not a specific implementation, resource, or approach.

Source This requirement attribute identifies the authorized entity that has the authority to approve requirements and that may need to be involved in the change control process of a project.

Stability This requirement attribute identifies how stable the requirement is based on its elaboration and supplied detail. At some point the requirement is considered stable enough for work to start.

Standards Part of the organizational environment. Standards are guidelines that are usually followed, but you won't be breaking any laws if you don't follow them. Your organization may also have standards such as forms, documentation, and processes that must be followed on most projects.

Status This requirement attribute is linked to the stability of the requirements, as it keeps track of each requirement and what its current status in the project may be: proposed, accepted, verified, or implemented.

Structured analysis This is a solution development methodology and a software development analysis tool that considers an IT system as a series of processes, and each process contributes to another process within the system. All processes stem from some user interaction. Data is also tracked in structured analysis and is seen as the result of processes and user input.

Supplemental requirements Part of the quality of service requirements that must be considered as part of a project's requirements, constraints, and quality to meet the expectations of the project customers.

Supplementary quality of service requirements The business analyst and key stakeholders must agree on what the expected level of quality of service for the project deliverable will be.

Traceable Each requirement should have the ability to be traced to its origin, owner, and author for additional information and support. Traceable also means that the requirements can be traced to their implementation in the project deliverable. Traceability is useful for audits, quality control, and end-of-project scope validation processes.

Unambiguous A requirement attribute that confirms the requirements documentation is written in such a way that all readers of the requirements documentation arrive at the same understanding of what the requirements demand.

Understandable A requirement attribute that lacks any ambiguous characteristics; the requirements must also be understandable among the project team. Terms, acronyms, and assumptions should be fully defined and explained for the requirements.

Urgency This requirement attribute defines how urgent the requirement is and when the customer needs it to be delivered as part of the solution.

User Requirements Document (URD) Defines what the user expects the solution to do. Users must agree that the business analyst understands and has captured what they want accomplished in the solution.

Verifiable   A requirement attribute that provides evidence of completion by testing, examining, or demonstrating its existence upon completion. Each requirement must be verified upon delivery to confirm the completeness of the deliverable.

Vision document   A vision document is a high-level view of the project solution. It defines a "vision" of what the project is to create for the organization. Vision documents are ideal for projects that will go through rounds of planning and where the project scope is defined through iterations.

Questions

1. You are the business analyst for your organization. You're currently documenting the requirements for a new software project. You're working with Stacey, a junior business analyst, and she wants to create a document that will define what the solution for your project will do. What type of document does Stacey want to create?

   A. User Requirements Document

   B. Vision document

   C. Project charter

   D. Project scope

2. What type of business analyst document will detail how the solution will function, what the solution will do for the organization, and the expected outcomes of the solution?

   A. User requirements

   B. Functional requirements document

   C. Vision document

   D. Request for Quote

3. You are the business analyst for your organization and are currently documenting the solution requirements for a new data redundancy system. You are ensuring that each individual requirements package includes documentation of any related constraints and assumptions. What is true about both constraints and assumptions?

   A. Constraints and assumptions don't need to be documented for every project requirement.

   B. Constraints and assumptions can become risks if they are documented within the project.

   C. Constraints and assumptions can never be fully documented, because the business analyst can never identify all of the constraints and assumptions.

   D. Constraints and assumption can become project risks.

4. Why should the business analyst verify the requirements before the project team begins execution of the project work?

   A. The verification of the requirements ensures that all of the requirements have been captured.

   B. The verification of the requirements ensures that all of the requirements risks have been addressed.

   C. The verification of the requirements ensures that the requirements have been accurately depicted and are approved by the stakeholders.

   D. The verification of the requirements means that the project scope has been approved based on the identified requirements as gathered by the business analyst.

5. Tom is the business analyst for his organization. Mary, his supervisor, asks Tom to start an analysis of a new business problem. Specifically, Tom is to examine the business problem and recommend solutions to improve the business process. Which one of the following activities does not qualify as business process analysis?

   A. Increase the revenue of the organization

   B. Reduce the costs to create a product

   C. Decrease the delivery time of product the organization creates

   D. Implement training on a new material a project will be using

6. You need to create a structured analysis chart. Which one of the following is an example of a structured analysis chart?

   A. Pareto chart

   B. Control chart

   C. Flowchart

   D. Run chart

7. You are the business analyst for your organization and are meeting with several network engineers, database administrators, and software developers. Your immediate goal is to create a diagram to capture the flow of data as it enters your IT system and to track the flow of information from application to databases, and how the data is stored. What type of chart is best suited to represent how data enters a system and what happens to the data once it enters the system?

   A. Dataflow diagrams

   B. Flowchart diagrams

   C. Pareto charts

   D. Run charts

8. What is a requirements package?

    A. It is all of the information that the customer expects the project solution to create for them.

    B. It is the decomposition of the project scope.

    C. It is a single item in the project scope based on the customer requirements.

    D. It is the documentation of all rejected and successfully completed requirements that are packaged and stored in the project archives.

9. You're working with Martha, another business analyst in your organization, to decompose the requirements of a new project. Martha is confused on how far each requirement should be decomposed, because she could continue to break down each requirement into very tiny fragments. You explain to her the 8/80 Rule of decomposition. What is the 8/80 Rule?

    A. The requirements should be decomposed to the point that it will take no fewer than 8 hours of labor, but not more than 80 hours of labor to create.

    B. The requirements should be decomposed to the point that it will take no fewer than 8 dollars of labor, but not more than 80 dollars of labor to create.

    C. The requirements should be decomposed to the point that it will take no fewer than 8 people to complete the requirements' work, but not more than 80 people to create the requirements.

    D. The requirements should be decomposed to the point that it will take no fewer than 8 days of labor, but not more than 80 days of labor to create.

10. Which one of the following could not be considered a feature of new software considering that the BABOK defines a feature as a service that the solution provides to fulfill one or more stakeholder needs?

    A. A particular font the application uses on screen

    B. The ability to print from the software

    C. The maximum cost of the software project

    D. The ability of the software to interact with SQL servers

11. What is the difference between a standard and a regulation?

    A. There is no difference; both standards and regulations are requirements.

    B. Standards are optional, while regulations may be optional.

    C. Standards are optional; regulations are requirements.

    D. Standards should always be followed; regulations should be followed if they are requirements.

12. You are the business analyst for your organization and are creating a model for a current set of requirements. What type of model view would you create if you want a model that represents all of the business requirements for the organization?

    A. Logical view

    B. Physical view

    C. Business view

    D. Structured view

13. What type of a model defines the level of access that resources have to an information system?

    A. Class model

    B. CRUD Matrix

    C. Data dictionary

    D. Entity Relationship Diagram

14. All of the following are examples of environmental requirements except for which one?

    A. Politics

    B. Regulations

    C. Market conditions

    D. Experience of the project team

15. Nancy is the business analyst for a new systems design project, and she's documenting the project requirements. She needs to create a document that communicates all of the connections among the technical components the proposed business solution will provide. What is this documentation of technical connections often called?

    A. Requirements package

    B. Technical interface documentation

    C. Interface requirements

    D. Network topology

16. An organization is considering a move from one word-processing software to a new one. Jill, the business analyst, believes that the move will increase efficiency in the long term, but the short-term results will result in a dip of efficiency because of the learning curve of the new product. Martin wants Jill to study the dip of efficiency and determine how long it'll take the staff to

reach or surpass the current level of efficiency the company enjoys. What is the study of the learning curve also known as?

A. Business analysis

B. Regression analysis

C. Parkinson's Law

D. Law of Diminishing Returns

17. Which one of the following is an example of the cost of conformance to requirements when quality is concerned?

A. Loss of customers

B. Faster equipment

C. Additional resources to help the project finish faster

D. Safety equipment for dangerous project work

18. You are the business analyst for a newly proposed business solution. Henry, the CIO of your organization, has already demanded that the project be implemented within 60 days, or it'll be considered a failure. The predetermined deadline is known as what?

A. A requirement, as Henry has created the deadline.

B. An assumption that the project can be completed in 60 days.

C. A risk, as the project cannot be completed in 60 days.

D. A business constraint created by Henry.

19. What business analysis document provides a high-level view of the project solution?

A. Project charter

B. Vision document

C. Project Work Breakdown Structure

D. Project scope

20. You are working on a document that will request a vendor to provide a solution for an identified business problem. You want the vendor to provide at least three solutions and prices for the solution you've documented. What document have you created?

A. Request for Quote

B. Invitation for Bid

C. Request for Proposal

D. Proposal

Questions and Answers

1. You are the business analyst for your organization. You're currently documenting the requirements for a new software project. You're working with Stacey, a junior business analyst, and she wants to create a document that will define what the solution for your project will do. What type of document does Stacey want to create?

   A. User Requirements Document

   B. Vision document

   C. Project charter

   D. Project scope

   A. Stacey wants to create a User Requirements Document, as this document is an easy-to-understand description of what the project solution will do. B, the vision document, provides a high-level overview of the solution. C, the project charter, is a project document that launches the project and assigns authority to the project manager. D, the project scope, is a document that defines all of the project work to complete the project.

2. What type of business analyst document will detail how the solution will function, what the solution will do for the organization, and the expected outcomes of the solution?

   A. User requirements

   B. Functional requirements document

   C. Vision document

   D. Request for Quote

   B. The functional requirements document defines the solution's abilities and place in the organization. A, user requirements, are what the functional requirements are based upon, so this choice is incorrect. C, the vision document, provides a high-level overview of the solution. D, Request for Quote, is a procurement document that asks a vendor to provide a price for a list of goods or services.

3. You are the business analyst for your organization and are currently documenting the solution requirements for a new data redundancy system. You are ensuring that each individual requirements package includes documentation of any related constraints and assumptions. What is true about both constraints and assumptions?

   A. Constraints and assumptions don't need to be documented for every project requirement.

   B. Constraints and assumptions can become risks if they are documented within the project.

    C. Constraints and assumptions can never be fully documented, because the business analyst can never identify all of the constraints and assumptions.

    D. Constraints and assumptions can become project risks.

    D. Constraints and assumption can both become project risks as constraints restrict the project options, and assumptions can prove dangerous for the project if they are not fully tested. A, B, and C are all incorrect statements about assumptions and risks, so these choices are incorrect.

4. Why should the business analyst verify the requirements before the project team begins execution of the project work?

    A. The verification of the requirements ensures that all of the requirements have been captured.

    B. The verification of the requirements ensures that all of the requirements risks have been addressed.

    C. The verification of the requirements ensures that the requirements have been accurately depicted and are approved by the stakeholders.

    D. The verification of the requirements means that the project scope has been approved based on the identified requirements as gathered by the business analyst.

    C. It's vital for the business analyst to verify the requirements with the stakeholders to prevent wasted time, monies, and effort in creating requirements that are not accurate. A is incorrect, because if all of the requirements have not been captured, then the business analyst may not know that stakeholders still need to contribute to the requirements documentation. B is incorrect, as requirements verification does not address the risks associated with the requirements. D is incorrect, because the project scope is a project document that is based on the verified requirements.

5. Tom is the business analyst for his organization. Mary, his supervisor, asks Tom to start an analysis of a new business problem. Specifically, Tom is to examine the business problem and recommend solutions to improve the business process. Which one of the following activities does not qualify as business process analysis?

    A. Increase the revenue of the organization

    B. Reduce the costs to create a product

    C. Decrease the delivery time of product the organization creates

    D. Implement training on a new material a project will be using

    D. Of all the choices, only D is not an example of a business process analysis Choices A, B, and C are all business process analysis activities, so these choices are considered incorrect for this question. Note that this question asks for which one is not an example of a business process analysis.

6. You need to create a structured analysis chart. Which one of the following is an example of a structured analysis chart?

   A. Pareto chart

   B. Control chart

   C. Flowchart

   D. Run chart

   C. Flowcharts are the most common example of a structured analysis chart. A, Pareto charts, show the distribution of results across categories. B, control charts, track trends against a defined mean. D, run charts, similar to control charts, track trends against a defined mean and against a time period.

7. You are the business analyst for your organization and are meeting with several network engineers, database administrators, and software developers. Your immediate goal is to create a diagram to capture the flow of data as it enters your IT system and to track the flow of information from application to databases, and how the data is stored. What type of chart is best suited to represent how data enters a system and what happens to the data once it enters the system?

   A. Dataflow diagrams

   B. Flowchart diagrams

   C. Pareto charts

   D. Run charts

   A. Dataflow diagrams illustrate the flow of data through a system. B, flowcharts, could be considered correct, but it doesn't answer the question as specifically as choice A. C, Pareto charts, show the distribution of results across categories. D, control charts, track trends against a defined mean.

8. What is a requirements package?

   A. It is all of the information that the customer expects the project solution to create for them.

   B. It is the decomposition of the project scope.

   C. It is a single item in the project scope based on the customer requirements.

   D. It is the documentation of all rejected and successfully completed requirements that are packaged and stored in the project archives.

   C. A requirements package is just one item in the project scope. Choice A is incorrect, as this describes the project scope. B is incorrect; this answer is the definition for the project Work Breakdown Structure. D is incorrect, as this is not a valid definition for the requirements package.

9. You're working with Martha, another business analyst in your organization, to decompose the requirements of a new project. Martha is confused on how

far each requirement should be decomposed, because she could continue to break down each requirement into very tiny fragments. You explain to her the 8/80 Rule of decomposition. What is the 8/80 Rule?

A. The requirements should be decomposed to the point that it will take no fewer than 8 hours of labor, but not more than 80 hours of labor to create.

B. The requirements should be decomposed to the point that it will take no fewer than 8 dollars of labor, but not more than 80 dollars of labor to create.

C. The requirements should be decomposed to the point that it will take no fewer than 8 people to complete the requirements' work, but not more than 80 people to create the requirements.

D. The requirements should be decomposed to the point that it will take no fewer than 8 days of labor, but not more than 80 days of labor to create.

A. The 8/80 Rule is a heuristic that says work should be decomposed down to somewhere between 8 and 80 hours of labor to complete a given requirement. This is only a suggestion, and each solution should be mapped to what's best for the project conditions. Choices B, C, and D are all incorrect statements about the 8/80 Rule.

10. Which one of the following could not be considered a feature of new software, considering that the BABOK defines a feature as a service that the solution provides to fulfill one or more stakeholder needs?

A. A particular font the application uses on screen

B. The ability to print from the software

C. The maximum cost of the software project

D. The ability of the software to interact with SQL servers

C. The maximum cost of the software project is actually a project constraint, not a feature. Choices A, B, and D are all examples of software features, so these choices are incorrect for this answer.

11. What is the difference between a standard and a regulation?

A. There is no difference; both standards and regulations are requirements.

B. Standards are optional, while regulations may be optional.

C. Standards are optional; regulations are requirements.

D. Standards should always be followed; regulations should be followed if they are requirements.

C. Standards are guidelines and are often seen as optional or best practices. Regulations, however, are actually requirements that are never optional for the project. Choices A, B, and D are all false statements about standards and regulations, so these choices are incorrect.

12. You are the business analyst for your organization and are creating a model for a current set of requirements. What type of model view would you create if you want a model that represents all of the business requirements for the organization?

   A. Logical view

   B. Physical view

   C. Business view

   D. Structured view

   A. You would create a logical view, as it provides information on all of the business requirements for the solution. B is incorrect, because the application developers will then create the physical view, as this information is most specific to what they'll be creating. Choices C and D are not valid views, and these choices are incorrect.

13. What type of a model defines the level of access that resources have to an information system?

   A. Class model

   B. CRUD Matrix

   C. Data dictionary

   D. Entity Relationship Diagram

   B. The CRUD Matrix defines the level of access that resources may have to an information system. CRUD means Create, Read, Update, or Delete. Choice A, the class model, demonstrates the attributes, operations, and relationship to entities within the solution. Classes are physical resources, solution concepts, a collection of data, a function of the solution, or an action. C, the data dictionary, describes the data used by the system. The data dictionary defines the name of the data, data aliases, values and meanings, and description of the system data. D, Entity Relationship Diagram, is a visual mapping of the system's data, its input and output, and relationship to the enterprise.

14. All of the following are examples of environmental requirements except for which one?

   A. Politics

   B. Regulations

   C. Market conditions

   D. Experience of the project team

D. The experience of the project team is not an environmental requirement. Choices A, B, and C are all examples of environmental requirements, so these choices are incorrect.

15. Nancy is the business analyst for a new systems design project, and she's documenting the project requirements. She needs to create a document that communicates all of the connections among the technical components the proposed business solution will provide. What is this documentation of technical connections often called?

A. Requirements package

B. Technical interface documentation

C. Interface requirements

D. Network topology

C. Interface requirements define how the technical components of a system interface, or communicate, with one another. Choices A, B, and D are all incorrect definitions of the interface requirements.

16. An organization is considering a move from one word-processing software to a new one. Jill, the business analyst, believes that the move will increase efficiency in the long term, but the short-term results will result in a dip of efficiency because of the learning curve of the new product. Martin wants Jill to study the dip of efficiency and determine how long it'll take the staff to reach or surpass the current level of efficiency the company enjoys. What is the study of the learning curve also known as?

A. Business analysis

B. Regression analysis

C. Parkinson's Law

D. Law of Diminishing Returns

B. Regression analysis is the study of how far backwards the organization will go in efficiency before it begins to surpass the current level of efficiency with the new software solution. Choice A, business analysis, is the overarching definition of requirements gathering, documentation, and verification. C, Parkinson's Law, states that work will expand to fill the amount of time allotted to it. D, the Law of Diminishing Returns, is a law of economics that states the duration of the work cannot be exponentially reduced by additional labor. The cost and efficiency of the added labor affect the yield, or value, of the work.

17. Which one of the following is an example of the cost of conformance to requirements when quality is concerned?

   A. Loss of customers

   B. Faster equipment

   C. Additional resources to help the project finish faster

   D. Safety equipment for dangerous project work

   D. Safety equipment is an example of the cost of conformance to requirements. Recall that the cost of conformance to requirements describes the monies the organization will have to pay to reach the expected level of quality within the project. Choice A, loss of customers, is actually an example of the cost of nonconformance to requirements. B is incorrect, as faster equipment is not an example of the cost of conformance to requirements. C is incorrect, as additional resources is not an attribute of the cost of conformance to requirements.

18. You are the business analyst for a newly proposed business solution. Henry, the CIO of your organization, has already demanded that the project be implemented within 60 days, or it'll be considered a failure. The predetermined deadline is known as what?

   A. A requirement, as Henry has created the deadline.

   B. An assumption that the project can be completed in 60 days.

   C. A risk, as the project cannot be completed in 60 days.

   D. A business constraint created by Henry.

   D. This is an example of a business constraint. Business constraints are management- or customer-set requirements such as deadlines, predefined budgets, or assigned resources to the project. Choices A, B, and C do not answer the question.

19. What business analysis document provides a high-level view of the project solution?

   A. Project charter

   B. Vision document

   C. Project Work Breakdown Structure

   D. Project scope

   B. The vision document is a high-level document that provides an overview of the proposed solution. Choice A is incorrect, as the project charter is a project document that authorizes the project manager and launches the project. C is incorrect, as the project Work Breakdown Structure is a visual decomposition of the project scope. D, the project scope, is also incorrect, because it defines all of the project work to satisfy the project objectives.

20. You are working on a document that will request a vendor to provide a solution for an identified business problem. You want the vendor to provide at least three solutions and prices for the solution you've documented. What document have you created?

    A. Request for Quote

    B. Invitation for Bid

    C. Request for Proposal

    D. Proposal

    C. You are asking for a Request for Proposal. Choice A, a Request for Quote, is only interested in the price of the solution, not proposed solutions as the question states. B, an Invitation for Bid, is identical to a Request for Quote. D is wrong, because the vendor creates the proposal as a response to your Request for Proposal.

Assessing and Validating Project Solutions

In this chapter you will
- Assess the proposed solution
- Evaluate technology options
- Ensure that the solution is viable
- Support quality assurance
- Communicate how the solution will affect stakeholders
- Complete a post-implementation review and assessment

I've got some good news and some great news for you. First, this chapter isn't that long, because this exam topic accounts for only a few questions on your CBAP exam. The great news is that it's the last exam objective you have to worry about. But let me caution you: don't let your guard down. Just because this is the end of the exam objectives doesn't mean you should dismiss this topic. A few questions may make all the difference for a passing score. You'll be tested on six business analysis processes:

- Assessing the proposed solution
- Allocating requirements
- Assessing the organization's readiness
- Defining the transition requirements
- Validating the solution
- Evaluating the solution's performance

Solution assessment and validation, the final step in business analysis, is when the business analyst plays more of a support role to ensure that the project is finished as planned. For example, the business analyst will work with the technology team, with the organization's quality assurance team, and with the end users of the product to help create and implement the project deliverables as planned.

When changes enter the project, the business analyst may be called upon to help evaluate the changes and to make decisions on their implementation. Changes can affect all areas of the project, but the business analyst's concern is ensuring the changes are implemented correctly. This can mean training, additional documentation, and confirmation of the implemented change.

Once the solution has been created, then the business analyst will assess and validate the solution. Assuming the solution meets the objectives, the business analyst will work with the project team and the end users to help the implementation go as smoothly as possible. This can mean hands-on implementation, serving as a point of reference for questions, and training of the end users. Once the solution has been implemented, the business analyst may continue to be available for related problem resolutions, training on the new procedures the solution may create, and managing change requests related to new requirements, next project phase deliverables, issues that pop up, and general support for the recipients of the solution.

Assess the Proposed Solution

Before a solution is actually implemented, the business analyst needs to review the proposed solution to determine how closely it matches what the stakeholders actually asked for. It'd be foolish to spend months of time and wads of cash collecting and prioritizing requirements only to implement a solution that didn't really meet the stakeholders' requirements. Solution assessment is a crucial piece of the business analyst's duties.

This process is all about quantified value. When you consider the myriad requirements within a proposed solution and all the different stakeholders who are contributing to those requirements, it's easy to see how complex it becomes to satisfy all of the requirements and all of the stakeholders. In assessing the proposed solution, you review the requirements and how they've been prioritized to confirm that the most valuable requirements are met for the good of the organization and the stakeholders.

Solution assessment also entertains multiple proposed solutions. When you have to deal with more than one solution, it becomes even more difficult to assess the requirements within each solution and how the solutions compare with one another in terms of value for the stakeholders. Cost benefit analysis, ranking of options, and trade-offs all come into play. The business analyst must always first satisfy the core requirements, and then examine the ancillary benefits each solution may bring the organization.

Evaluating Solution Options

Part of the role of the business analyst is to evaluate the options that the proposed solution includes—and could include. While the business analyst may not be the only person involved with this process, they should coordinate the efforts of identifying other solution options. It's dangerous for a client, business analyst, project manager, or any other stakeholder to consider only one option as the best option for the project. When you decide on a single solution without exploring other options, you may miss out on better solutions.

You'll need to have the documentation of the prioritized, approved business requirements, because these drive the project solution. You'll need to have a resource who understands the project requirements and who can link the requirements to the technical ability and constraints. It's not logical to promise the abilities of technology without understanding what the technology is capable of doing. Finally, to evaluate the options, you'll need a high-level understanding of the potential of the technology. You'll serve as the liaison between your technical resource and the project stakeholders.

Evaluating the solution options takes time, resources, and often a budget. You'll need access to resources, facilities, a schedule, and monies to test the available options for how they'll satisfy the project requirements. Depending on what the project is, you may be able to access a sample or limited version of the technology to test. You can also use simulations, interview vendors, and read white papers, historical data, and online reviews.

Evaluating the technology results may result in all or any combination of the following:

- A recommended solution that satisfies the project requirements for deliverables as identified and prioritized by the business analyst. Often the evaluation of the technical options will lead to an exact fit for the stakeholder's needs. The complexity of the project requirements, demands, and scope of the problem will affect how likely this scenario is.

- Feedback on problems, issues, or concerns for the stakeholders. The complexity of the project can affect the selected solution, and it may raise concerns about the solution. For example, the longevity, cost-effectiveness, or compatibility of the technology with the customer's operation should all be considered, documented, and communicated.

- Compliance with organizational standards. Technology comes in so many different styles, options, and abilities that the business analyst must take special care to ensure that the selected solution meets the standards defined by the organization. The size of the scope and goals of the project may help dictate what solutions would be acceptable based on existing corporate standards. These guidelines, part of enterprise environmental factors, should be identified early in the solution assessment processes.

This business analysis process helps create the final assessment of the proposed solution. The focus of the analysis is to determine the true value of the solution for the stakeholders. You'll also determine all of the possible approaches to the project solution and present these approaches to the business analysis team, the project manager, the project team, the business owner, and other key stakeholders. If there's not enough value in the solution to justify the cost, then it's reasonable to scrap the solution and try, try again.

Facilitate the Solution Selection

Value is paramount when it comes to creating a solution for the stakeholders. The deliverable of the solution must provide more benefits than the costs to create the solution. Oftentimes it just makes more sense to buy something off the shelf than to create it from scratch. The business analyst is a resource for an organization, as she can help determine the best solution based on the requirements of the business, the solutions the vendor offers, and the priority of the project and the requirements within the project. Consider the factors in purchasing a technical solution versus creating a technical solution:

- Cost of the solution
- Using in-house skills or procuring them if necessary
- Scope of the work to be complete
- Control of intellectual property
- Efficiency issues
- In-house solution may give project team opportunity to learn new skills
- Purchasing from a vendor could transfer risks
- Utilizing the project team's time

If the business analyst is to make a decision based on price alone, then there's a simple formula for determining the break-even point on a purchase versus a creation. In this scenario, let's say that Jenny has a need for a defined piece of software. The expert developers within her company report that they can create the software in-house. Jenny calculates that the in-house solution will cost $57,500 to create. In addition, the solution will cost $4,500 to maintain each month.

Jenny then checks with a favorite vendor. The vendor reports that they too can create the solution for just $39,000. As part of the pricing, however, they'll need to maintain the solution, and that'll cost $7,500 per month as part of the agreement. Jenny says that she'll think things over and make a decision. Figure 7-1 depicts what Jenny should do.

1. Find the difference of the build solution and the buy solution. In this example, the formula of the out-of-pocket fees of $57,500 minus $39,000 results in a difference of $18,500.

Figure 7-1
Make-or-buy decision can use a formula to find the break-even point.

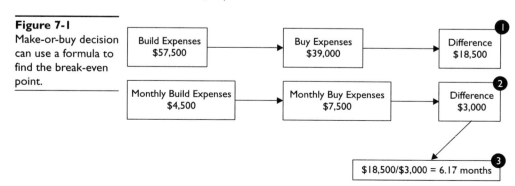

2. Find the difference between the monthly fees of the two solutions. In this example, it's $7,500 minus $4,500 for a difference of $3,000.

3. Divide the out-of-pocket difference by the monthly difference. In this example, it's $18,500 divided by $3,000 for 6.17.

Determine how long the solution will be in use and, based on that length, you'll know how long it'll take to pay for the in-house solution. In this example, Jenny can "break even" on the initial out-of-pocket expense of $57,500 in just a little over 6 months. If the solution is going to be used less than 6 months, then she'd be wiser to hire the vendor and their solution.

When making a decision to procure, the business analyst should follow the standards of his organization. Most organizations have rules about the process of procurement for solutions. The purchasing process, the initiation with bidders, the contract type, and the management of the contract may be beyond the duties of the business analyst. Here are the basic steps followed in a procurement relationship as seen in Figure 7-2:

1. The buyer creates a Statement of Work (SOW). This document defines what it is the buyer wants the vendor to provide.

2. The buyer distributes the SOW with the appropriate procurement document. There are three documents that the buyer can attach to the SOW:

   a. Invitation for Bid (IFB)—the seller is to provide just a price for the solution.

   b. Request for Quote (RFQ)—the seller is to provide just a price for the solution (bids and quotes have the same goal—just to provide a price).

   c. Request for Proposal (RFP)—the seller is to provide a detailed solution for the buyer.

3. Sellers receive the SOW and procurement form and then determine if they want to participate in a Bidders Conference. The Bidders Conference is a group meeting of all the vendors and the buyer to review the SOW and the procurement document. This is an opportunity for the bidders to ask questions about the project and for the buyer to provide clarifications when needed.

4. The buyer provides SOW updates to the bidders. If there are updates to the SOW at the Bidders Conference, then the buyer documents the changes and redistributes the SOW.

5. Sellers respond with the appropriate document; this is a bid, quote, or proposal depending on what the buyer requested.

6. The buyer then determines which of the bidders provides the best price and solution, and contract initiation begins.

While every organization has a different approach to procurement, this is the most common approach. Contract negotiations likely fall outside the domain of the business analyst, but the business analyst should insist that the vendor provides everything that the SOW calls for so that the solution can be met.

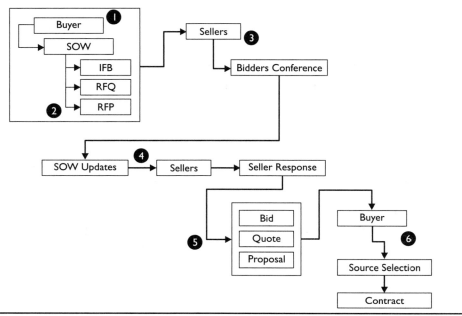

Figure 7-2 Steps to reaching a contract in the full procurement process

Buying the Best Solution

When it comes to procuring a solution, price isn't everything. Procurement really begins with first determining which requirements can best be served through procurement. This decision often focuses on a make-or-buy analysis, though price should not be the only factor in the decision. Business analysts should determine the following:

- Is it more cost-effective to make or buy the product or service?
- Is it more time-efficient to make or buy the product or service?
- Are the resources available to make the product or service?

Your organization may tick a bit differently, but most procurement decisions get started with a Statement of Work. A Statement of Work details exactly what product or service the organization is buying. The SOW will be given to potential sellers so they can prepare their offers in alignment with what is needed by the performing organization. Sure, sure, some vendors will create the SOW for you—but technically, the SOW is what you want the vendor to create.

You need some vendors to buy stuff from. Sellers can be found through a preferred vendor list, advertisements, industry directories, trade organizations, or other methods. The initial communication from the buyer to the seller is a request. Specifically, the seller issues one of the following documents:

- **Request for Proposal** These want dreamy solutions to the identified problems in the SOW. RFPs are used when multiple factors besides price determine which seller is awarded the contract. The buyer is looking for a solution to a need.

- **Request for Quotation** Used when the deciding factor is price.

- **Invitation for Bid** Used when the deciding factor is price. Yes, the IFB and the RFQ are the same type of document.

You can host a Bidders Conference to ensure that all sellers have equal opportunity to gain information about the procured work or service and that the information they do get is the same. Government contracts often are required to have a Bidders Conference and to ensure that all participants have the same information to create an accurate bid. After the Bidders Conference, the selection process is based on several things:

- Procurement documents from the sellers.

- Your company policies and procedures.

- Screening systems to sift out sellers who do not qualify.

- Weighting system to make an unbiased selection of a seller. (These can assign points to categories such as cost, experience, certifications, and so on. The seller with the most points wins!)

Once the seller has been selected, the contract is created between the buyer and seller. This formal, preferably written, agreement between the buyer and seller will define all requirements of both the buyer and seller. The seller's requirements will specify how and when the work will be completed. The buyer's requirements will specify the terms and conditions the seller is expected to maintain. The contract may also include information on resolving claims, how changes to the contract are to be made, and who are the authorities within the buyer's organization and the seller's organization.

Allocate the Solution Requirements

In life and in business analysis you can't have everything at once. Allocating the solution requirements is the process of determining which components of a solution should be implemented in what stage, release, or version of the project deliverables. It is the mapping of the solution requirements to the actual solution components and deliverables that will satisfy the scope of the project, solve the identified problem, or the business opportunity. The business analyst must find the balance of the most appropriate requirements to implement and the value of implementing those requirements in the project.

As a business analyst, you're immersed in the design strategy of a project. It's your business analysis activities, interviews with stakeholders, and the solution assessment processes that help you map and design the requirements management plan. Once you've captured the project visions and achieved stakeholder sign-off on the requirements, the technical team is responsible for actually creating the solution. This doesn't mean that your work is done—only that the foundation for the project is created.

As the technical team is creating the solution, however, they may run into roadblocks that prevent them from creating the solution exactly as you and they had agreed. Technical and environmental issues may prevent the solution from moving forward as planned. The technical team should not implement solutions on their merit, but rather you, the technical team, and the stakeholders should investigate possible solutions, trade-offs, and compromises that will allow the project to move forward.

Alternate solutions are still solutions, but they often require additional time, more funds, and loads of communication. Stakeholders may have the opinion that once they sign off on the project requirements, it's all up to you and the design team to create their deliverables. And while that's somewhat true, there needs to be an understanding among all of the stakeholders that there can always be unforeseen issues, sometimes called "unknown unknowns," that can affect the execution of the project.

 NOTE Yes, there are also known unknowns. These are things you know will likely go wrong with the project; you just aren't certain what those things may be. How will you know your key resources will leave in the middle of a project? Or how could you anticipate a new virus that wreaks havoc on the project implementation work? Unknown unknowns are an anticipation of things that will go wrong in the project—you just don't know today what those things may be. It's a way to anticipate risks, issues, and problems that you haven't clearly identified.

Reviewing User Classes

A user class is a categorization of users and how each class will use the solution. For example, a word-processing program can be used in a variety of different methods. Paralegals may create briefs with the software, while the marketing department may write press releases. User classes describe how a group of people, the users, will use the solution the project is to create for them. Understanding how the users will actually use the solution is an important part of business analysis, because it helps create a solution that can map to several different classes.

It's particularly logical to map user classes to software, as there are many different approaches to how a software solution can be used—just like the example I offered with word processing. A broader picture is to include user classes for solutions beyond software development and IT. Consider how the different employees in an organization would use a new building: the lobby, break rooms, conference rooms, offices, cubicles, shipping and receiving, and even the traffic flow of the office layout. User classes can be used to prioritize the needs of certain users, but they also can be used to show the integration of solutions across multiple classes of users.

The functions of the process and how the user classes will use each function should be documented. The business analyst and the design team should examine the solution and how each user class will operate the solution. They'll want to examine the solution in motion, step-by-step, to counteract any bottlenecks, issues, and risks the solution creates. Depending on what the solution may be, IT or otherwise, the business analyst should examine how the solution's process links classes of users together.

 NOTE User classes can help the business analyst examine alternate solutions based on how each solution would be used by the stakeholders.

Most organizations have users in multiple locations around the world. As the business analyst, you should examine the locale of the user classes to determine if there is a related impact. Language difference, customs, time zone difference, and other conditions should always be considered when designing and implementing a solution in a geographically dispersed project.

The size of each user class should be considered. The size of the user class may affect the solution, though a policy of majority rules is not always a good practice for implementing solutions. The business analyst should really examine the process, how the size of the user class will utilize the solution, and what the user class, regardless of its population, will create as a result of the process. In some instances, a small group of users can have an outstanding effect on the remainder of the organization's other employees and users. For example, consider the typically small number of people in an organization's procurement department and the large number of interactions the procurement department manages.

The business analyst and the design team should evaluate the tasks the users perform in their roles in the organization and how the solution may affect these tasks. In some instances the tasks may not be affected at all, but in other instances the tasks could be reengineered as part of the project's solution. In all instances, testing, communication, and piloting the offered solution can all be viable approaches to implementing the project solution.

As you can imagine, users are naturally going to be concerned when a change in the work flow, processes, or software takes place. Through interviews, feedback, and general communication, the business analyst should have a grasp on what the users are thinking about the solution. The users' concerns, fears, and experience with the solution could all affect a successful solution. The business analyst should document how the process is currently achieved, if at all, and what the new solution may do to each class of users. Ideally, the users have been informed of the coming change or addition of processes so they're not blindsided. No one likes to be forced into a change of action without some communication. This is not to say that communication will automatically make users thrilled with the new solution, but communication is needed, sooner rather than later, about a coming process change.

During the creation of the solution, the design phase of the project, and again during solution validation, the characteristics of each user class should be referenced. The business analyst and the design team can aim to satisfy the needs of each class of user based on the mission of the project and what the solution first aims to satisfy. Each class of user should be addressed as to the solution's impact, though it's sometimes difficult, if not impossible, to satisfy all user classes. There may be trade-offs based on priorities within the requirements, and in these instances, lucky you, it's the business analyst's role to communicate these trade-offs.

Reviewing Functions and Features

The design of a solution should address the problem the project was initiated to solve. The business analyst, design team, and subject matter experts should address the cause of the problem, not just the symptoms. A cause-and-effect chart, sometimes called the Ishikawa diagram, can help facilitate this process. The users should not be surprised at what the project creates. As they're involved in the requirements contribution, the business analyst will communicate to them what's happening with the requirements they've signed off on.

Based on the requirements, the business analyst and the design team should map out a solution that solves the identified problem or that seizes an opportunity for the organization. The users should be involved in this process, and it's often their insight, based on their regular experience with the problem or potential opportunity, that can direct the business analyst and design team to the most appropriate project solution. This does not mean, however, that the business analyst should create and adhere to only one solution. In fact, the business analyst and the design team, along with the users, should identify multiple alternate solutions.

For each alternate solution, the business analyst should identify its costs and benefits. The business analyst can consider time, cost, longevity, scalability, risk, and other relevant characteristics of each alternate solution. With each solution, there'll likely be trade-offs among the most common characteristics, such as time, cost, and the size of the solution's scope. Most solutions will have a driving factor such as urgency of the deliverable or the cost of implementation that may affect which solution is actually selected by the organization. As long as the identified solution solves the problem, the decision on the solution should not be a problem.

Managing Design Phases

Think of any solution you've ever gathered requirements for, and you'll likely be able to identify logical phases the solution followed. A *phase*, just so we're clear, is a logical grouping of activities that create a deliverable or a set of related deliverables. The design portion of your business analysis duties will also follow logical phases. It's up to the business analyst to work with the technical crew, the project team, and subject matter experts to determine how many phases the solution will entail.

Certainly some projects will follow a logical progression, and the number of phases may be established just by the nature of the work, preferences in your organization, or based on historical information. Other times, the number of phases can be based on several different factors:

- Overall project budget
- Immediacy of need for a solution
- Desire for a phased solution
- Deadline
- Cost constraints
- Business cycles
- Training schedule for end users
- How the organization will be affected by the whole solution released at once versus the solution phased into operations

Also to be considered are the technical aspect and achievability of multiple design phases, process automation, availability of resources, and the risk tied to the project. Basically, there's no definite rule for the number of design phases. The business analyst should consider what's best for the organization based on the scope of the design, the demand for the delivery, and the impact the delivery will have on the organization as a whole.

Regardless of the number of phases, the solution will require the business analyst to map each identified requirement to its corresponding design phase. Every requirement should have a unique identifier and be linked to the design phase, where the requirement will be completed. In addition, each phase should be described and summarized as to what goals the phase will accomplish. Should the number of phases change or requirements be added or removed, the business analyst must update all relevant requirements, phase mapping, and the goals of each phase.

Finalizing the Solution and Implementation

At some point the business analysis duties begin to wind down, and the solution is moved into project management for the creation of the chosen solution. These final business analysis duties ensure the smooth transfer from proposed solutions to solution implementation. A Requirements Traceability Matrix is a good business analysis tool that can track the requirements to the project's creation of the requirements.

The most compelling reason to use a Requirements Traceability Matrix, especially in these final business analysis processes, is that if it is agreed upon and followed by the design team, the project deliverables will be of quality. This is because each requirement and its subcomponents stem from the approved project requirements, and no non-value-added activities or deliverables have been introduced into the project. All deliverables, regardless of their size, originate from the requirements in the matrix.

Any scope changes that a stakeholder wants to introduce into the requirements must pass through a change control system. When considering the potential change for inclusion, the project manager and the business analyst can examine the Requirements Traceability Matrix and determine how the proposed change affects the project deliverables. Based on the project, the change could affect deliverables that were already created, so the time and cost for the proposed change would likely increase based on what's already been created—something the Requirements Traceability Matrix can quickly assess for the project manager, business analyst, and stakeholder.

Communicating and Assessing the Solution

Maybe you've noticed this phenomenon occur with a new solution. At first, people may be excited about the new software, building, or whatever deliverable the project has created. They can see the possibilities of what the solution can do for them. Then they start using the thing, and their expectations don't match what the solution delivers. It's not unlike my reaction to those x-ray vision glasses I ordered as a kid from the back of a comic book.

The business analyst needs to strip away some of the silly notions that end users, salespeople, and other stakeholders attach to project deliverables. The business analyst needs to clearly express what the deliverable will and will not do. You should be on the lookout for stakeholders with lofty expectations. I'm not saying that you should be the wet blanket and pessimist in your organization, but that you should help set appropriate expectations for the project's deliverable.

You'll also need to communicate with stakeholders about their responsibility with the new deliverable. There may be maintenance issues, initial loss of efficiency, training, and even some potential for glitches and issues in the deliverable when it first shifts into productivity. The business analyst needs to communicate how the stakeholder should report problems and to whom. Ideally the project team, support team, or some other entity is established to track the problems and communicate the problem to the appropriate people for resolution. One of the worst things for stakeholders is when a new solution is delivered and abandoned. When that happens, the stakeholders can feel angry, confused, and frustrated because there's little or no response to issues. The business analyst needs to help establish the support on the transfer of responsibilities.

Your organization's quality assurance team may work with you on assessing these impacts and post-project support. The QA team is involved, because they'll want to see evidence of the project's deliverables to confirm that it has met the quality requirements of the project. You'll need to be involved, as the business analyst, because you've helped map the project requirements from concept to the finished deliverable.

Supporting the Solution Implementation

There's a lot of excitement, usually, surrounding the release of a project's solution. Anticipation of how the solution is going fit into operations, the benefits the solution will provide the end users and the organization, and the realization of a concept into reality all contribute to some eager and anxious people. The business analyst and the project manager should work together and with the key stakeholders on transferring the solution to the organization.

Projects don't, thankfully, last forever, so the creators of the project deliverable will need a plan to transfer the solution from the temporary project into the organization. Certainly some of the people who created the solution may be the same folks who provide support to the solution post-project, but there needs to be a definite end of the project and a start of the operation. Once the project team has created the solution, they'll likely follow the *implementation plan*, sometimes called the operational transfer plan, to move the solution from the ownership of the project to operations.

The implementation plan should address how the solution will move from the project life cycle into the product life cycle. Recall that the project life cycle is the collection of phases within the project to create the deliverable. Project life cycles are unique to each project solution—an example is in Figure 7-3. Project life cycles describe all of the phases between concept and the final deliverable. Every product, from a soda to a car, has its own unique product life cycle.

The business analyst may be asked to create a product *life cycle costing*. Life cycle costing is usually created early in the solution development, but it's relevant here because it describes the actual anticipated costs of supporting the solution in operations. Life cycle costing is how much it'll cost the organization to support the deliverables the project has created per year, quarter, or whatever period the stakeholders designate.

Ensure the Solution's Usability

The solution the business analyst designs for the customer, in my view, should be as fine and user-friendly as possible. Business analysts should not overcomplicate the solution, nor should they simplify the solution: the solution should be spot on.

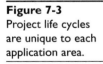

Figure 7-3
Project life cycles
are unique to each
application area.

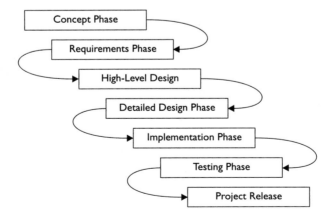

Based on the prioritized business requirements, the business analyst designs a solution that meets the objectives in the order of their priority. Truly, this is where things get sticky. Competing objectives, politics, and limitations of the technology can make this a near-impossible task at times. In addition to weighing the business requirements, the business analyst also considers the usability requirements. This means looking for or developing user case studies to determine how the solution is to be used.

 NOTE A *test plan* is mandatory in most software development projects. This plan defines how the software will be tested, adjusted, and retested before its release.

Your solution may pass through simulations, prototypes, and conceptual builds to determine its usability and acceptability. The goal here is not to necessarily gain complete approval of the proposed solution, but to determine how usable the solutions are and then to choose the most acceptable. Trade-offs and compromises aren't unusual when it comes to usability. Higher-level priorities often shift usability demands because of time, cost, and even achievability.

Whenever possible, document usability features that are de-scoped and consider in the design the possibility of adding in these solutions in later releases, additions, or renovations.

Supporting Quality Assurance Processes

Everyone talks about how important quality is when it comes to a solution—and with good reason. No one wants a shoddy deliverable that's buggy, ugly, or won't work the way the stakeholders were promised. To counteract the possible negative outcomes of a project, you have quality assurance. First, let me define quality (one more time): quality is a conformance to requirements and a fitness for use. That's a general definition from the book *A Guide to the Project Management Body of Knowledge.* Quality is, basically, satisfying the project scope.

Quality assurance, then, ensures that the designers, project team, vendors, and any other contributors to the deliverables do their job accurately and completely. Their contributions should map exactly to the project scope—nothing more and nothing less. Quality is planned into the project from the beginning. Once the requirements have been signed off by the key stakeholders, then the quality standard for acceptability has been set. It's now up to the project team to plan how to achieve the set quality standards and to meet the standards.

Before a project manager can plan for quality, he must know what the quality expectations are. The expectations are created by the business analyst along with the project stakeholders in the form of requirements. In addition, the project manager and the project will have to map to the standards of the performing organization and any relevant industry standards and regulations. As part of the planning processes, the project manager and the project team must determine how the requirements may be met, and identify the costs and time demands to meet the identified requirements.

I think you'll agree that one of the fundamentals of quality management is that quality is planned in, not inspected in. Planning for quality is more cost-effective than inspecting work results and doing the work over, or correcting problems to adhere to quality demands.

When considering the requirements, the business analyst may elect to use a *benefit/cost analysis* to help determine the acceptable level of quality. A benefit/cost analysis is a process of determining the pros and cons of any process, product, or activity. The straightforward approach is concerned with the benefits of quality management activities versus the costs of the quality management activities.

Completing quality work increases productivity, because work that's done right does not have to be corrected. If the project team wastes times, creates defective work, or doesn't map to the project requirements, then the project loses time, monies, momentum, and sometimes morale.

It's possible that the quality standard is set higher than what's actually needed for the customer's solution. Consider a low-priority project versus a high-priority project: the level of testing and planning should be great in the high-priority project and not so much so in the low-priority project. Sometimes fast and good is better than slow and perfect. Completing quality work may cost more monies than the work is worth. To deliver a level of quality beyond what is demanded costs the project additional funds. To deliver a level of quality beyond what is demanded actually misses the needed quality for acceptance. The types of quality management activities that guarantee quality may not be needed for every project.

The customer does not need or want more than what was requested. *Gold plating* is the process of adding extra features that may drive up costs and alter schedules. The project team should strive to deliver what was expected.

Chapter Summary

This short chapter was packed with all sorts of business analysis duties. While it's true that you'll probably have no more than seven or eight questions on these duties on the CBAP exam, as a business analyst you'll need to grasp these processes in your job. Every organization may have a slightly different approach to solution assessment and validation, so you'll need to know the rules in your organization. You'll also want to work with the project manager on quality assurance, quality control, and scope validation during the project planning, execution, and monitoring to ensure that the work is being done according to plan.

When the problem or opportunity is first defined, you may feel a gravitational pull toward one idea. It's wise to explore other solutions to the problem or opportunity before identifying and linking to one solution. Exploring alternate solutions ensures that the best solution based on requirements and constraints will be selected. Alternate solutions should first look at how well they meet the requirements of the project based on priority. Whatever solution is accepted, the quality assurance policies should be documented so that the project scope can meet the quality expectations of the stakeholders.

The technology that is selected should support the objectives of the project, obviously, but it should also mesh with the operations of the organization. It's easy for technology selections to solve one problem without fitting into the design, operations, and scalability of the rest of the organization. Differing software, hardware, materials, and other resources may solve an immediate problem, but may create longer and larger problems once the solution shifts into operations. The business analyst needs to examine the proposed solution and assess how she'll work with the technology already existing in the organization.

Many factors can drive the selection of a particular solution: time, resources, and regulations, though cost often seems to be the principal reason behind many decisions. The business analyst may need to examine the cost-effectiveness of buying versus building a solution. While cost is important, it's not always the most important factor in selecting a solution. There could be other considerations: risk, time, proficiency, core work, available resources, and more.

The business analyst examines each proposed solution for its usability. Usability is really linked to quality and the solution's ability to satisfy the needs of the user of the solution. In other words, a hasty decision can lead to a poor solution. A rush in judgment is really a breakdown in quality, as the selected solution may be ignored, hated, or rejected by the end users. If quality is a solution's ability to satisfy the project scope, conform to requirements, and be fit for use, then the users must actually use the deliverable.

The final project deliverable, which represents the sum of the solution, should be escorted into operations by the business analyst. Training, user guides, and ongoing support may be needed to help the recipients of the deliverable incorporate the project's product into their operations. An operational transfer plan can help with this transition. The business analyst should identify the modes of communicating problems with the solution and how these problems are to be addressed.

It's been said that quality is planned into a project. And that projects fail at the beginning, not the end. And I'm sure there a few other project management and business analysis clichés I could toss out there, but I hope you already get my point. Solution assessment and validation doesn't happen just at the end of the project. It is the responsibility of the business analyst to identify the best solution for the organization based on the identified requirements, constraints, and expectations.

Key Terms

Alternate solutions   More than one choice for a solution that may satisfy the project requirements.

Bidders Conference   A group meeting of all the vendors and the buyer to review the SOW and the procurement document. This is an opportunity for the bidders to ask questions about the project and for the buyer to provide clarifications when needed.

Buy-versus-build decision   A financially driven approach to determine which solution is the most cost-effective for the project. This approach also evaluates other factors such as employee time, efficiency, and support to make the best decision for purchasing or creating a solution.

Cause-and-effect diagram   Sometimes called a fishbone or Ishikawa diagram, it can help facilitate this root cause analysis.

Gold plating   An unscrupulous process of adding extra features that may drive up costs and alter schedules. The project team should strive to deliver what was expected.

Implementation plan   Sometimes called the operational transfer plan, it defines how to move the solution from the ownership of the project to operations. The implementation plan should address how the solution will move from the project life cycle into the product life cycle.

Invitation for Bid (IFB)   A procurement document from the buyer to seller, where the seller is to provide just a price for the solution.

Known unknowns   Things you know will likely go wrong with the project, yet you just aren't certain what those things might be. It's a way to anticipate risks, issues, and problems that you haven't clearly identified.

Life cycle costing   The estimated amount it'll cost the organization to support the deliverables the project has created per year, quarter, or whatever period the stakeholders designate.

Phase   A logical grouping of activities that create a deliverable or a set of related deliverables.

Product life cycle   The duration of the product in operations. It describes the anticipated duration of the product's usage, maintenance, and anticipated phasing out of the solution.

Quality   According to *A Guide to the Project Management Body of Knowledge,* quality is a conformance to requirements and a fitness for use. It's the deliverables, features, and functions that the customer will look at to see how well the features perform and how the solution, as a whole, operates.

Quality assurance (QA)   The assurance that the designers, project team, vendors, and any other contributors to the deliverables do their job accurately and completely. Contributions to the project scope should map exactly to the project scope—nothing more and nothing less.

Quality control (QC)   An inspection-driven process that precedes solution assessment to detect errors in the project work and to make recommendations to correct the errors before the customer sees the deliverable.

Quality of Service (QoS)   Refers to the priority level of applications and how they'll respond and act on a network. Quality of service is a way to describe the expected level of performance for an application, or in a broader sense, the expectations of reliability for a solution.

Request for Proposal (RFP)　A procurement document from the buyer to seller, where the seller is to provide a detailed solution for the buyer.

Request for Quote (RFQ)　A procurement document from the buyer to seller, where the seller is to provide just a price for the solution (bids and quotes have the same goal—just provide a price).

Requirements Traceability Matrix　Helps the business analyst trace each requirement from its origin to its final completion in the project.

Scope validation　An inspection-driven activity done with the project customer to review and ultimately accept the project deliverables.

Statement of Work (SOW)　A document that originates from the buyer to the seller that describes what the buyer is looking to purchase.

Test plan　Mandatory in most software development applications; defines how the software will be tested, adjusted, and retested before its release.

Unknown unknowns　Unforeseen issues that can affect the execution of the project.

User class　A categorization of users and how each class will use the solution.

Questions

1. You are the business analyst for the IOU Project. You're working with the technical team exploring alternate solutions to a database problem for your stakeholders. The technical team is insisting that they should use the cheapest database server, and they don't need much information to solve the problem. Why should you insist on exploring alternate solutions for the project customers?

   A. You should explore other solutions to see if a more cost-effective database server is available.

   B. You should explore other solutions to see which one fits the customer requirements the best.

   C. There's really no need to explore other solutions if the technical team has already identified the most cost-effective approach.

   D. Additional solutions are needed so that the project customers may select the solution they like the most.

2. Benjamin, the business analyst for a web application project, has identified some issues that were not identified during the project requirements-gathering processes. He has documented the issues and communicated the effects of the issues to the stakeholders. What are these issues called?

   A. Risks

   B. Uncertainties

C. Unknown unknowns

D. Constraints

3. Which one of the following statements best describes a user class?

A. It is the training of the solution for the end users.

B. It is the classification of the different stakeholders.

C. It is the classification of the ways a solution may be utilized in production.

D. It is a categorization of users and how each class will use the solution.

4. You are a business analyst for an architectural design firm. Your supervisor has asked you to create a user class to show how the lobby of a new building will be utilized. Which one of the following is not a characteristic of a user class in this architectural design project?

A. Prioritization of the purpose of the lobby.

B. Cost and schedule to create the solutions the lobby provides.

C. Utilization of the space within the lobby.

D. Documentation of how the classes of users will use the functions the lobby provides.

5. Why should the business analyst document how the stakeholders will use the solution, the processes of the solution, and the day-to-day operations the solution will affect?

A. The analysis of the solution can help counteract risks, bottlenecks, and issues.

B. The analysis of the solution can help capture exact requirements.

C. The analysis of the solution can streamline development efforts.

D. The analysis of the solution can keep time and cost estimates low.

6. You are the business analyst for a large project that will move all users to the same computer operating system, office applications, and filing structure. The IT-driven standardization for your organization aims to reduce operating costs, improve efficiency, and allow employees to access data from your company's offices, which are in several countries around the world. What characteristics of the user classes should you consider in this global effort?

A. The existing technology used in each office.

B. How the new technology will affect communications.

C. What will happen to the old technology for inventory and support purposes.

D. How the international user classes may be affected by cultural differences.

7. You are working with Angela, the technical lead for a project to create a customer relationship web site. Angela is insisting that all of the solutions identified should be scrapped, because none of the solutions satisfies the needs of all the user classes within the organization. As the business analyst, what's your best response to Angela?

   A. She does not understand the business classes.

   B. She is the technical lead and should only worry about the technical achievability, not the alternate solutions.

   C. Not all of the user classes' needs will be addressed and resolved in every project. The cost of the requirements takes precedence over the satisfaction of user needs.

   D. Not all of the user classes' needs will be addressed and resolved in every project. The prioritization of the requirements may supersede some of the user classes.

8. If a proposed solution does not meet all of the needs of the user classes, who is responsible for communicating this information to the users?

   A. Business analyst

   B. Project manager

   C. Functional management

   D. Business owner

9. You are working with the project stakeholders to help identify alternate solutions for a problem. You and your business analysis team need to explore the problem in detail, because you want to identify the root cause of the problem, not just the symptoms of the problem. What chart can help you complete root cause analysis?

   A. Ishikawa diagram

   B. Causal factor chart

   C. Pareto chart

   D. Control chart

10. What term best describes the expectation attached to the performance of a project solution?

    A. Expectation of deliverables

    B. Cost of conformance to quality

    C. Quality of service

    D. Deming Management Method

11. You are working as a business analyst for a technical solution to an identified problem. The design team has reported challenges with achieving the quality of service requirements the customer is asking for. Which one of the following is not a value that could affect the quality of service for a technical project?

    A. Limitations of the technology

    B. Competing operational needs

    C. Security issues

    D. Deadlines

12. Complete this sentence: A business analyst should never go to a stakeholder with a problem and not offer a _____.

    A. Response to the problem

    B. Solution to the problem

    C. Mitigation for the problem

    D. Documentation of the problem

13. You are the business analyst for a project in your organization. Management has asked that you create a chart that can help them and the other stakeholders visualize each of the requirements, as there are many, and see which phase each requirement should be created in. What type of chart is management asking you to create?

    A. Work Breakdown Structure

    B. Project Network Diagram

    C. Requirements Traceability Matrix

    D. Roles and Responsibilities Matrix

14. Marcy, a business analysis team member, asks, "What is the difference between quality control and scope validation?" Which one of the following provides the best definition for Marcy?

    A. Scope validation and quality control are synonymous.

    B. Quality control is the inspection of the work to keep mistakes out of the customer's hands. Scope validation is verification of the project scope before the work begins.

    C. Quality control is the inspection of the work to keep mistakes out of the customer's hands. Scope validation is an inspection of the project deliverables completed with the project customers.

    D. Quality control is the inspection of the work to ensure its completeness. Scope validation is the operational transfer of the project deliverables.

15. Holly is the project manager of the ZSW Project. Allen is the business analyst for the project. Henry is the representative of the user stakeholders for the project. Which person will serve in the role of liaison between the technical resource, Jo Anna, and the project customers?

    A. Holly

    B. Allen

    C. Jo Anna

    D. Henry

16. All of the following are results of the business analyst evaluating the technology options except for which one?

    A. User case study

    B. Recommend solution

    C. Feedback on problems, issues, or concerns

    D. Compliance with organizational standards

17. You are the business analyst for a project to create new software for your organization. You are considering outsourcing the creation of the project to a trusted vendor. Which one of the following is not a valid reason to outsource the solution to vendor?

    A. Cost of the solution

    B. Deadline for the project

    C. Risk transference

    D. Alternate identified solution

18. You have determined with the project manager that an internal solution for creating a new piece of software will cost $54,900 and will cost $12,800 each month to support the solution. A vendor has estimated that they can create a solution for you at $37,000, and the monthly support will cost your organization $15,500. What should you do considering these cost estimates?

    A. Hire the vendor, because their solution is less cost initially.

    B. Hire the vendor if the solution is going to be kept longer than 4 months.

    C. Create the solution internally if the solution is going to be kept longer than 7 months.

    D. Create the solution internally if the solution is going to be kept more than 7 months but less than 11 months.

19. You can design a solution that will cost you $67,800 initially and $13,560 monthly. A vendor can create the solution for free, but they'll support the solution for $19,000 per month. How long would it take you to break even on an internally designed solution considering the vendor's offer?

    A. You'd never break even on the offer, because the vendor's initial fee is zero.

    B. 6 months

    C. 10 months

    D. 13 months

20. What document accompanies the Request for Proposal in the procurement process?

    A. Bid

    B. Quote

    C. Statement of Work

    D. Project Scope

Questions and Answers

1. You are the business analyst for the IOU Project. You're working with the technical team exploring alternate solutions to a database problem for your stakeholders. The technical team is insisting that they should use the cheapest database server, and they don't need much information to solve the problem. Why should you insist on exploring alternate solutions for the project customers?

    A. You should explore other solutions to see if a more cost-effective database server is available.

    B. You should explore other solutions to see which one fits the customer requirements the best.

    C. There's really no need to explore other solutions if the technical team has already identified the most cost-effective approach.

    D. Additional solutions are needed so that the project customers may select the solution they like the most.

    B. The technical team should not choose the solution on their own but only recommend solutions. Choice A is incorrect, because the solution selection is not only based on cost. Choice C is incorrect, as alternate solution identification is part of the business analysis process to choose the best solution that satisfies the requirements. D is tempting, but it does not guarantee that the stakeholders will choose the best solution based on the identified requirements.

2. Benjamin, the business analyst for a web application project, has identified some issues that were not identified during the project requirements-gathering processes. He has documented the issues and communicated the effects of the issues to the stakeholders. What are these issues called?

    A. Risks

    B. Uncertainties

    C. Unknown unknowns

    D. Constraints

    C. These are sometimes called unknown unknowns; they are issues that have not been identified or even suspected of being problems during the requirements-gathering processes. Choice A is incorrect; these issues may escalate to risks, but they are not necessarily risks when they are first identified. B is not a valid choice. D, constraints, describes conditions on the project that limit the available options in the project, such as deadlines, resources, and a predetermined budget.

3. Which one of the following statements best describes a user class?

    A. It is the training of the solution for the end users.

    B. It is the classification of the different stakeholders.

    C. It is the classification of the ways a solution may be utilized in production.

    D. It is a categorization of users and how each class will use the solution.

    D. A user class is the categorization of users and how they'll use the solution. Choices A, B, and C are incorrect descriptions of a user class.

4. You are a business analyst for an architectural design firm. Your supervisor has asked you to create a user class to show how the lobby of a new building will be utilized. Which one of the following is not a characteristic of a user class in this architectural design project?

    A. Prioritization of the purpose of the lobby.

    B. Cost and schedule to create the solutions the lobby provides.

    C. Utilization of the space within the lobby.

    D. Documentation of how the classes of users will use the functions the lobby provides.

    B. Cost and schedules are examples of constraints, not user classes. Choices A, C, and D are all incorrect, because these things do describe what a user class is in this project.

5. Why should the business analyst document how the stakeholders will use the solution, the processes of the solution, and the day-to-day operations the solution will affect?

    A. The analysis of the solution can help counteract risks, bottlenecks, and issues.

    B. The analysis of the solution can help capture exact requirements.

    C. The analysis of the solution can streamline development efforts.

    D. The analysis of the solution can keep time and cost estimates low.

    A. Understanding how the solution will be used can help the technical team design the most accurate solution for the end users. B, capturing requirements, won't work, because the requirements help lead to the solution, not the other way around. C, while tempting, does not answer the question completely. Choice D is also incorrect, because understanding the problem and the solution doesn't guarantee low time-and-cost estimates. It will, however, help create accurate time and cost estimates.

6. You are the business analyst for a large project that will move all users to the same computer operating system, office applications, and filing structure. The IT-driven standardization for your organization aims to reduce operating costs, improve efficiency, and allow employees to access data from your company's offices, which are in several countries around the world. What characteristics of the user classes should you consider in this global effort?

   A. The existing technology used in each office.

   B. How the new technology will affect communications.

   C. What will happen to the old technology for inventory and support purposes.

   D. How the international user classes may be affected by cultural differences.

   D. It's essential in a project that spans multiple countries and cultures to consider the global effects of the solution for each country, language, time zones, and for cultural issues that may affect, or be affected by, the project solution. Choices A, B, and C are not categories of user classes, but map more toward operational transfer of the solution.

7. You are working with Angela, the technical lead for a project to create a customer relationship web site. Angela is insisting that all of the solutions identified should be scrapped, because none of the solutions satisfies the needs of all the user classes within the organization. As the business analyst, what's your best response to Angela?

   A. She does not understand the business classes.

   B. She is the technical lead and should only worry about the technical achievability, not the alternate solutions.

   C. Not all of the user classes' needs will be addressed and resolved in every project. The cost of the requirements takes precedence over the satisfaction of user needs.

   D. Not all of the user classes' needs will be addressed and resolved in every project. The prioritization of the requirements may supersede some of the user classes.

   D. Angela's concern is valid, but her reasoning is flawed. The prioritization of user requirements should lead to the most appropriate solution. It is common for some user classes to be dissatisfied by the solution. Choices A, B, and C would be inappropriate responses to Angela.

8. If a proposed solution does not meet all of the needs of the user classes, who is responsible for communicating this information to the users?

A. Business analyst

B. Project manager

C. Functional management

D. Business owner

A. The business analyst is the hub of communications in the project. When a solution cannot meet all of the user requirements, the business analyst is the person who must communicate the bad news. Choice B, the project manager, is incorrect, because the project manager is not the individual who has gathered the requirements; he'll manage the project execution. C, functional management, is incorrect, as this choice is too broad and not as specific as the business analyst option. D, the business owner, is not the person to share the news, as this person owns the solution and will be a recipient of the status updates.

9. You are working with the project stakeholders to help identify alternate solutions for a problem. You and your business analysis team need to explore the problem in detail, because you want to identify the root cause of the problem, not just the symptoms of the problem. What chart can help you complete root cause analysis?

A. Ishikawa diagram

B. Causal factor chart

C. Pareto chart

D. Control chart

A. An Ishikawa diagram, sometimes called a cause-and-effect diagram, can help in root cause analysis. This diagram may also be called a fishbone diagram. B, a causal factor chart, is one of the elements in the Ishikawa diagram where the effect may be stemming from. C, a Pareto chart, is incorrect, because this chart shows categories of failures. D, a control chart, tracks trends over time.

10. What term best describes the expectation attached to the performance of a project solution?

A. Expectation of deliverables

B. Cost of conformance to quality

C. Quality of service

D. Deming Management Method

C. Quality of service describes the expectation attached to the performance of a project solution. A is not a valid business analysis term. B describes the monies an organization must spend to ascertain the expected level of quality. D, the Deming Management Method, is the philosophy of quality management set forth by Edwards W. Deming.

11. You are working as a business analyst for a technical solution to an identified problem. The design team has reported challenges with achieving the quality of service requirements the customer is asking for. Which one of the following is not a value that could affect the quality of service for a technical project?

    A. Limitations of the technology

    B. Competing operational needs

    C. Security issues

    D. Deadlines

    D. While deadlines are often constraints on the project, they are not relevant to attributes possibly affecting the quality of service. Choices A, B, and C are things could affect the quality of service for a solution, so these choices are incorrect.

12. Complete this sentence: A business analyst should never go to a stakeholder with a problem and not offer a _____.

    A. Response to the problem

    B. Solution to the problem

    C. Mitigation for the problem

    D. Documentation of the problem

    B. Whenever a business analyst identifies a problem, he should document the issue and report it to the stakeholders with a possible solution. The solution may be as simple as the plan to research the problem or as in-depth as a plan to resolve the problem. Choices A, C, and D are incorrect, as responses are typically tied to risks, mitigation is a type of risk response, and simply documenting the problem is not enough for the stakeholder.

13. You are the business analyst for a project in your organization. Management has asked that you create a chart that can help them and the other stakeholders visualize each of the requirements, as there are many, and see which phase each requirement should be created in. What type of chart is management asking you to create?

    A. Work Breakdown Structure

    B. Project Network Diagram

    C. Requirements Traceability Matrix

    D. Roles and Responsibilities Matrix

    C. Management is asking you to create a Requirements Traceability Matrix; this is a simple table that identifies each requirement and links it to the phase during which the requirement will be created. The sum of all the requirements equates to the business solution. A, the Work Breakdown Structure, is a visual decomposition of the project scope. B, a project network diagram, is a visual representation of the flow of the project work. D, a Roles and Responsibilities Matrix, maps people to their assignments in the project.

14. Marcy, a business analysis team member, asks, "What is the difference between quality control and scope validation?" Which one of the following provides the best definition for Marcy?

    A. Scope validation and quality control are synonymous.

    B. Quality control is the inspection of the work to keep mistakes out of the customer's hands. Scope validation is verification of the project scope before the work begins.

    C. Quality control is the inspection of the work to keep mistakes out of the customer's hands. Scope validation is an inspection of the project deliverables completed with the project customers.

    D. Quality control is the inspection of the work to ensure it completeness. Scope validation is the operational transfer of the project deliverables.

    C. Quality control and scope validation are both inspection-driven processes. Quality control is done by the project team, the quality assurance department, or a third party without the customer's involvement. The goal is to identify mistakes and repair them before the customer inspects the work. Scope validation is a similar process, except it is done with the project stakeholders, and the focus is on scope acceptance. Choices A, B, and D are all incorrect definitions of quality control and scope validation.

15. Holly is the project manager of the ZSW Project. Allen is the business analyst for the project. Henry is the representative of the user stakeholders for the project. Which person will serve in the role of liaison between the technical resource, Jo Anna, and the project customers?

    A. Holly

    B. Allen

    C. Jo Anna

    D. Henry

    B. Allen, the business analyst, is the hub of communications. Whenever there are concerns, risks, or issues concerning the requirements, the business analyst is the communicator of the news. Choices A, C, and D are stakeholders and are not the individuals reporting the news to the other project stakeholders.

16. All of the following are results of the business analyst evaluating the technology options except for which one?

    A. User case study

    B. Recommend solution

    C. Feedback on problems, issues, or concerns

    D. Compliance with organizational standards

A. The user case study defines how the user is likely to use the solution the project creates. It will likely be an input to the project rather than an output from the evaluation of technology options. Choices B, C, and D are incorrect choices, because these are indeed outputs of evaluating the technology options.

17. You are the business analyst for a project to create new software for your organization. You are considering outsourcing the creation of the project to a trusted vendor. Which one of the following is not a valid reason to outsource the solution to a vendor?

   A. Cost of the solution

   B. Deadline for the project

   C. Risk transference

   D. Alternate identified solution

   D. It is good to identify alternate solutions, but it's not a characteristic that should be considered to outsource the work. You could argue that the vendor's solution is better, and that's an alternate solution, but your choice would be related more to the quality of the solution rather than simply an alternate solution. Choices A, B, and C are all invalid choices here, because these are reasons why the work could be outsourced.

18. You have determined with the project manager that an internal solution for creating a new piece of software will cost $54,900 and will cost $12,800 each month to support the solution. A vendor has estimated that they can create a solution for you at $37,000, and the monthly support will cost your organization $15,500. What should you do considering these cost estimates?

   A. Hire the vendor, because their solution is less cost initially.

   B. Hire the vendor if the solution is going to be kept longer than 4 months.

   C. Create the solution internally if the solution is going to be kept longer than 7 months.

   D. Create the solution internally if the solution is going to be kept more than 7 months but less than 11 months.

   C. In this buy-versus-build scenario, you'll need to identify the difference of the initial expenses, which is $54,900 minus $37,000 for $17,900. You'd then divide this value by the difference in the monthly fees of the external solution, $15,500, and the internal solution of $12,800, which is $2,700. The value is 6.63, which means that the internal solution could break even by just slightly over month 6-1/2, or in this option choice C. Choices A, B, and D do not reflect the accurate break-even point for the internal solution.

19. You can design a solution that will cost you $67,800 initially and $13,560 monthly. A vendor can create the solution for free, but they'll support the solution for $19,000 per month. How long would it take you to break even on an internally designed solution considering the vendor's offer?

    A. You'd never break even on the offer, because the vendor's initial fee is zero.

    B. 6 months

    C. 10 months

    D. 13 months

    D. In this question, you'd first find the difference of the internal and external solution, even though the external solution cost is zero. This amount is $67,800. Next, you'd find the difference of the internal solution of $13,560 and the vendor's monthly fee of $19,000, which is $5,440. By dividing $67,800 by $5,440, you get 12.46, which means your company could pay for the internal solution in 13 months. If the solution is to be used less than 13 months, the vendor has a better deal.

20. What document accompanies the Request for Proposal in the procurement process?

    A. Bid

    B. Quote

    C. Statement of Work

    D. Project Scope

    C. The Statement of Work defines what it is you'd like the vendors to create a proposal for. Choices A and B, a bid and quote, are incorrect, as these are price-driven documents from the vendor to the buyer. D, the project scope, is not valid, as the work or solution that the vendor is to provide is not always the entire project scope—it could be just a portion of the entire project solution.

CHAPTER 8

Working as a Business Analyst

In this chapter you will
- Learn the building blocks of business analysis
- Explore business and IT domains
- Apply management skills
- Host effective meetings and presentations
- Learn the fundamentals of leadership

As a business analyst, you should know some fundamental skills in your day-to-day work and for your upcoming CBAP exam. Many of the skills I'll discuss in this chapter you are likely already doing if you've found success as a business analyst. All business analysts, regardless of their years of experience, can always use a refresher on the building blocks of effective management, leadership, and analysis.

The skills in this chapter don't map to any one particular exam objective, but actually can be applied in all exam objectives. You can use these skills, techniques, and characteristics to better perform enterprise analysis, planning, requirements elicitation and analysis, communication, and even solution assessment. These are skills that will help you beyond your role as a business analyst, too. Most business analysts play more than one role in their organization, and these are practical skills that can help you in your daily assignments.

Applying Fundamental Business Analysis Skills

It's becoming clearer every day: the role of the business analyst is more valuable and important today than ever before. Business analysts are more than just requirements gatherers; they conduct gap analysis, write feasibility studies, develop case studies, serve as the hub of communications, and identify problems, solutions, and opportunities. Business analysts are the liaisons for human resources, marketing, sales, and other lines of business and the technology that's driving the business.

The cost of implementing technology correctly can be expensive and time-consuming. The cost of implementing technology incorrectly can be disastrous to an organization's bottom line. The business analyst can identify root causes, understand how the solution is to operate, document the problem the stakeholders are experiencing, and then work with experts to identify spot-on solutions.

A well-organized, intelligent, and experienced business analyst can be a valuable asset for any organization. But I don't need to tell you that. Like most successful experts, a good business analyst understands that his value is not in doing anything fancy. It's all in the fundamentals. Sure, there's the occasional magical solution or missing piece of the puzzle—but even those are founded on the basics. To be a superb business analyst, you need to be super at understanding how a business analyst is expected to operate within your organization. Understanding how to fulfill your duties and then doing them well is a sure solution for success, advancement, and leadership.

Using the Structured Systems Analysis and Design Model

There's a whole library of structured analysis techniques that a business analyst can use to elicit requirements, to document problems and solutions, and to develop methodologies to uncover opportunities. Structured analysis techniques are developed methodologies to create systems by using a model to identify the problem, to propose solutions, and to design a selected solution. There are several structured models available, and most of them provide a waterfall-approach phasing of the project.

A favored model, the Structured Systems Analysis and Design Model (SSADM) is a classic waterfall methodology, as seen in Figure 8-1, where each phase builds on the work done in the prior phase. SSADM was created in the United Kingdom as a model for developing systems and new applications. SSADM has five components from launch to completion; each component can be broken down into even more detail depending on the needs of the project:

1. **Feasibility study** A feasibility study first examines what the need is, known requirements, and if the organization can cost-effectively deliver on the identified requirements. While the focus of the feasibility study is initially on cost, you'll likely also have to investigate interoperability with current technology, processes, deadlines, and other known constraints the project would have to operate under.

Figure 8-1
The SSADM Model is a waterfall model that promotes quality.

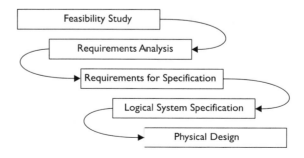

2. **Requirements analysis**   The requirements are identified in more detail, and the business analyst documents the business processes, environment, assumptions, and constraints. Technical and quality risks such as quality of service are also documented, as these attributes affect the expectations on performance for the delivered application.

3. **Requirements for specification**   The functional and nonfunctional characteristics are documented, and the stakeholders approve the requirements. These requirements map to configuration management within the project management processes, in particular, to scope management. Business analysts could begin to use a Requirements Traceability Matrix at this stage to track deliverables through the execution phase of the project.

4. **Logical system specification**   Now that the operational requirements have been detailed, the technical systems to create the deliverables are created.

5. **Physical design**   The program specifications are created based on the logical system specifications. All developers map to the same logical system for uniformity across the solution.

Each phase of the project is done completely in order, and the business analyst and the project manager maintain control over each phase. The phases may not overlap or be created in parallel, for tighter control on the process and deliverables. While this model may take longer to create a deliverable than others, its quality control, phased management, and low defects make it a viable option for high-profile development projects.

Managing Business Analysis Issues

There's a fine line between risks and issues. Depending on whom you ask, you'll get different answers for what's a risk and what's an issue. *Issues* are questions, challenges, and problems that may hinder the requirements gathering, project objectives, or identified risks that have yet to be analyzed for their cost, probability, and impact.

A *risk* is an uncertain event or condition that can have a positive or negative effect on the project. We generally think of risks as characteristics of the project that can harm the deliverables, the ability of the project to complete the work on time, or something dangerous within the project. Risks, however, also include positive characteristics; just doing the project is a risk, as the organization could lose its investment. However, investing in the project could also help the project reach its desired conclusion.

 NOTE   Recall that quantitative risk analysis examines the probability and impact of each risk in detail. Technically, a risk that has not been evaluated for time and cost impact and for the probability of happening is still an issue.

Risk management is usually handled by the project manager, not the business analyst. The business analyst does, however, need to manage issues. All issues, the things that need to be resolved within the requirements so the project team can go about creating the deliverable, need to be documented in an *issue log*. The issue log identifies the attributes of each issue, assigns an issue owner, and tracks the status of the issue. The issue owner is the individual who is closest to the issue and may be tasked with resolving the issue. Issues that are not resolved by a given date are likely to become project risks.

 For a more detailed explanation, watch the Assessing Risk Value video now.

During development of the project deliverables, new issues may appear. These new issues could be technical constraints, lagging schedules, or quality problems. Issues can come in all shapes and sizes, but they all have one common characteristic: if they are not resolved, they are likely to have an impact on the project. Issues should always be documented, discussed, and managed.

Relying on Communication Skills

Business analysts are communicators. You've got to communicate with the business owner, end users, the project team, project manager, subject matter experts, and loads of other stakeholders. You'll be talking a bunch. And don't forget that half of communicating is listening. All of these same people will want to talk to you about their needs, wants, and pet requirements they'll expect you to work into the project for them.

 NOTE It's not just what you say, it's also your body language. Fifty-five percent of communication is nonverbal.

It's not all talking, however, when it comes to business analysis. You'll also need to do plenty of writing in your role. You'll need to document conversations, e-mail threads, the outcomes of meetings, and you'll obviously need to document the requirements you captured. To be a good business analyst who's also a good communicator, you first must have a clear understanding of what the project is trying to do. You won't be able to communicate effectively if you do not understand what people are trying to tell you.

Good communicators, effective communicators, ask loads of questions. You need to understand what people are concerned about. You need to understand what they see as threats—remember, not all of your stakeholders are going to be thrilled with the project and the changes it'll bring to their lives. Use the classic 5 Ws of interviewing stakeholders:

- **Who** Who is the person and what is their role in the requirements?
- **What** What does the person want in the project requirements?
- **Where** Where is this person in the organization and where will the requirements affect them in their duties?

- **When**   When do stakeholders need to contribute to the requirements, when will you need to interact with stakeholders, and when can they expect answers to their questions?

- **Why**   Why does the stakeholder have specific concerns, requirements, and direction for the solution? This is often the most important factor to understand about any conversation. Understanding the reason behind any question can help you determine the stakeholders' motivation, needs, pains, perceived threats, and even their political agendas if they have them.

Communication also means that you'll make information available for stakeholders. You often won't have the time to broadcast information, so an internal web site, blog, or even old-fashioned e-mail lists with status updates are ideal. You want to keep stakeholders posted with concise information on what's happening in the project. While broadcasting information is a fast and wide method of communicating, it may not always be the most appropriate. The message should influence how you communicate with your stakeholders.

 NOTE   Remember that larger projects require more detail. The communications formula of $N(N - 1)/2$, where N represents the number of stakeholders, can help capture the number of communication channels. The more channels you have in a project, the more opportunities you have for communication to fail.

Learning New Skills

One of the most valuable tools for the business analyst, and really for anyone, is the ability to learn new things. Learning can be incredibly hard work, especially in a discipline you've never dealt with before. Most IT projects, for instance, are dealing with new technologies. Learning new technology can be a time-consuming activity—especially when it's a technology that may be replaced or updated in a short time.

There are many different philosophies, methodologies, and approaches to learning. Everyone learns differently. Some people can read a book and learn a new concept. Others can watch someone else do something and then emulate their actions, while others have to get in and try the activity or experience the topic in order to really understand. Chances are you're like most of us—you learn by doing, but you can also learn from reading, watching, and practicing.

New skills for business analysts often mean attending training sessions. My career started with teaching college courses. I left academia for the greener pastures of corporate education coupled with a fair amount of consulting. I can confidently tell you three things about learning:

- College students often learn in order to get a grade.

- Adult students often learn because they have to for their job requirements.

- Learners who come through my consulting experience learn because they want a new skill.

All of these learners have one thing in common: they have an objective. Whether their learning objective was conscious or not, they all entered the experience with some quantitative object, mission, or goal in mind. Occasionally, I've met students who took a class or seminar without an objective—they floundered, were visibly uncomfortable, or left the class never to return. When it comes to learning something new, my advice to you is simple: determine what you need to learn.

I often ask participants in my seminars which is more important, "for me to teach or for you to learn?" The answer should be obvious. While I give my best when I teach, it's really up to the participants to do their part in the learning process—they need to learn. When I take courses or am coached on a new skill, which I try to do often, I make myself set some learning goals for the course. I determine what specific things I'm going to learn in the class.

Learning is an active process. Learning in a classroom environment is traditionally, in my opinion, a passive process. Students sit like lumps and think about dry cleaning, what's on television, if the clock is really correct, while the teacher drones on about topic XYZ. Boring! Learning should involve the students by doing, talking, and asking questions. To learn something, get involved with the topic; embrace it.

Defining Your Business Knowledge

To be an effective business analyst, you must understand the company you're working for. When a new professional business analyst joins an organization, she has a steep learning curve to figure out how the company works, how the company makes its income, and to identify all the channels that decisions move through. Every organization has its documented means of accomplishing tasks, but politics, trade-offs, and oddballs within the organization also can sway decisions.

Beyond the internal mechanisms for accomplishing duties, there's also the knowledge of what the organization does. If you were to examine any large organization, you'd probably be amazed at all the streams of cash flow both into and out of the company. Larger companies have multiple products, joint ventures, and more to generate revenue. Then there's the stream of payments to vendors, utilities, taxes, charities, and the constant of salaries. Smaller companies also have complexities that the business analyst must learn and understand to be effective.

Large and small companies have one thing in common: they're in business to make money. Companies are not in business to provide jobs, to benefit communities, or to solve the world's problems—they exist for a profit. The primary mission and objective of any for-profit organization is to make money. I'll agree there are lofty missions, goals, and good deeds that many companies do and do well. I think of medical-related companies, and companies that share the wealth with their employees, but that goodness is still founded on making a profit.

My point in stressing the income of an organization is that the income is directly tied to the performance of the business analyst. Organizations only have so much capital to invest in projects, and projects are founded on the discoveries of the business analyst. Faulty requirements can result in lost funds, lost time, and lost opportunities. These losses can contribute to the decay of the company's primary objective—to make a profit. Even not-for-profit entities are subject to the negative effect of the business analyst's performance, as lost funds can hinder them from reaching their missions.

Business analysts must understand what a company's goal is and the means by which the company aims to reach that goal. Each business analysis activity either contributes to the goal or detracts from it.

Knowing the Products and Processes

Your company produces something. It could be a physical product, like a car, computer software, or light bulbs. Your company might be in the service industry, where you perform activities for others such as renting resources, consulting, or designing web sites. The things and services that your company produces affect the role of the business analyst.

Most organizations follow a logical pattern to create the product that generates income for the company. If you build houses, there's a logical life cycle of the construction process. If you design software, you likely subscribe to a software model. If you consult, then there's a logical approach to your consultation. While each project is unique or different, the approach of the project is probably very much the same each time.

Understanding what it is your organization creates for others can help you, the business analyst, elicit requirements, offer solutions, and control the business analysis processes to support the larger vision of the company. This is probably something you already do, because it's logical. A company that manufactures cars likely won't have requirements to start creating bicycles. The business analyst should learn as much as possible about the lines of business within an organization so that she can intelligently ask requirements-based questions, identify opportunities, and find the best solutions.

Your organization's processes were created, by design or by the logic of the inherent nature of the work, to support the creation of the products or services your company provides. Processes are actions that bring about a result. Think of the processes within your company: procurement processes, project initiation processes, quality identification, monitoring and control, and risk management to name a few. Processes are specific activities to achieve, learn, create, or confirm something.

Recognizing a Process Purpose

Just because a process exists, doesn't mean that it's a good process. When I serve as a consultant, I like to start with the flow of processes to see how a product moves from concept to creation. It doesn't matter whether the organization is creating software, designing web sites, or creating pharmaceuticals—processes move the business along. Some processes just don't provide value, don't create anything that supports the product, or can't be explained.

Not all processes contribute. Here's a story that helps prove my point. A husband and wife were cooking dinner, and the husband noticed his wife cut off the ends of the pot roast they were about to cook. "Why are you cutting off the ends of the roast?" asked the husband.

"I don't know, really. It's just what my mom used to always do," said the wife.

This puzzled the husband, so at his next chance he asked his mother-in-law why she cut the ends off the pot roast. "I don't know, really. It's just what my mom used to always do," said the mother-in-law. Now the husband was more than curious. He wondered if slicing off the ends of the roast improved the taste, helped the roast cook faster, or some other cooking secret.

The husband, wife, and mother all went to visit the grandmother, determined to learn the reason why she cut the ends off the pot roast. "Grandmother," asked the husband, "can you tell us why you always cut the ends of the pot roast off?"

The grandmother thought for a moment, and then her face lit up. "I always cut the ends off my pot roast because my cooking pan was too small."

Processes are much the same way. Just because an organization has always done the work a certain way, doesn't necessarily mean that the processes are good. A business analyst should understand how processes work and then learn why the processes are in place. Processes that can't be explained either need further exploration, documentation, and detail, or they can be attributed to grandma's pot roast.

Recognizing Market Conditions

A business analyst should be aware of the market conditions that affect the organization and its decisions on projects, requirements, and opportunities. It's usually not a secret how well the organization is performing based on the amount of work, opportunities, and growth a company is experiencing. The market conditions affect the short-term and long-term goals of an organization.

Market conditions can describe many different things. First, consider the classical supply and demand scenario of the marketplace. When demand is high and supply is low, you'll experience an increase in price and profitability. When demand is low and supply is high, prices generally fall. No mystery here, right? Supply and demand affect all businesses, and there are decisions to be made in a saturated marketplace—increase sales or reduce costs?—all of which generally involve the business analyst. Supply and demand can also prompt an organization to look for new opportunities, once again calling on the business analyst for assistance.

Beyond the classical supply and demand, all sorts of economic circumstances are attached to the health of the economy. The ability and willingness of participants in the marketplace to purchase goods and services affect decisions of the organization. The marketplace conditions are beyond the control of the organization—so it's the external constraints that affect income. The business analyst may get involved in looking for solutions, opportunities, and identifying problems of sales in less-than-desirable economic conditions.

The role of business analyst is also needed when the market is booming, times are good, and money is flowing. The business analyst often is needed in good financial markets to look for opportunities, investments for longevity, and to meet the constant need to cut costs. Removing waste, even in healthy financial times, obviously boosts profits, but also often increases productivity, quality, and ensures continued success for the organization.

Recognizing Organizational Systems

Systems are standardized process sets in an organization that has identified the flow of activities to reach a desired result. Systems are techniques unique to each organization that help its members reach results. Systems ensure that activities are done the same way, in the same order, every time. They establish a framework for common organizational activities to ensure consistency, thoroughness, and documentation.

Common organizational systems include

- Human resource management
- Procurement management
- Quality assurance and improvement
- Resource allocation management
- Facilities management and maintenance
- Project initiation and management
- Project change control
- Product configuration management

Systems are well-documented and standardized within an organization. The business analyst is to use these systems to move through the proper channels within the company to ensure that the work is done the same way every time. Circumventing a system is likely going to cause the business analyst some grief, may irritate the people that control the system, and could cause delays in the decision the system is to generate.

Systems are part of enterprise environmental factors, because they define the rules and policies for doing certain activities within the organization. The business analyst may define a system, with some caution, as a constraint on the requirements, project, or program. A constraint is anything that limits the project's options, so a stagnant, nonfunctional system may restrict the project, but not participating in the system may bring more pain than abiding by the rules. In other words, you have to follow the red tape and bureaucracy of an organization if you want to participate in the organization.

Relying on Expert Judgment

Expert judgment happens when a person relies on someone with more knowledge to help make the right decision. Consultants, subject matter experts, the technical team, and even the end users are all examples of expert judgment. All of these resources are "sources of knowledge," and it's up to the business analyst to recruit and employ these sources of knowledge to make the best decisions about the requirements.

Expert judgment, as reliable as it can be, often is tied to a fee. The business analyst should determine if the information the organization will be purchasing is from an experienced, knowledgeable resource and if the fee for that information is worth the information gained. The business analyst should determine what resources are available, the associated costs, and the benefits the costs will bring to the organization. In addition to considering the value of the immediacy of the information, the business analyst should consider the value of the time savings the information can bring to the project.

Expert judgment isn't always people, however. You can, and should, use historical information as a source of knowledge for your project. Historical information comes from previous projects, project archives, and lessons learned documentation. Every organization, regardless of its size, should have a project information archiving system to organize and store the paper documentation and provide access to project files for future reference. There's no reason to reinvent the wheel if past information is already proven.

Using past information to make current decisions is a great resource, as long as the past information is accurate. Faulty decisions, project plans that weren't updated, or deliverables that were poorly documented can haunt new projects based on this documentation. Every decision in a project should have some supporting detail not only to help the current project, but also to provide insights to future project managers and business analysts.

Mapping IT Projects

When a new business analysis effort is started in the IT arena, it's important to categorize the requirements and interoperability of the solution. It's important because it can help the business analyst identify resources, affected lines of business, and communication among the stakeholders. IT projects fall into one of four areas:

- **Applications** Includes software-driven solutions for workstations, servers, mobile devices, and the Internet
- **Hardware** Includes servers, workstations, laptops, and devices like printers, cameras, and peripherals
- **Database** Includes database servers, data management, data security, and accessibility
- **Network** Includes the connectivity and communication among computers, servers, network devices, and telecommunications

These four categories aren't isolated from one another—they're often interdependent. Consider an application like e-mail, as in Figure 8-2. While the client application

Figure 8-2
Users often interact
with several systems
without realizing it.

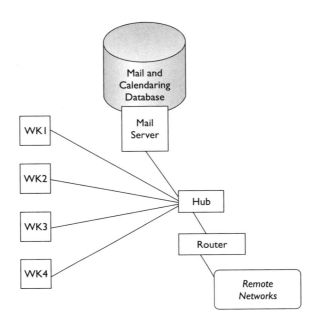

operates on a workstation, the e-mail server application is the database of messaging. The network portion includes the local area network, remote networks, and even mobile devices. The interoperability of these four systems requires analysis and consideration of the problems, constraints, and opportunities within all four areas.

NOTE It's not realistic to dive into all the bits and bytes of IT project management in this business analysis book. That's why I wrote *IT Project Management: On Track From Start to Finish*. If you are or aspire to be an IT project manager, this is a book you should read and add to your library.

Working as a Business Analyst

If you were to read a job description for a business analyst, you'd probably find requirements for the position such as the ability to identify requirements, work with different lines of business, lead technology assessments to develop business use cases, identify functional requirements, map process flow, and the usual processes you'd expect. But to work as a business analyst is more than these typical job requirements.

Business analysts need to be able to quickly learn, adapt, think logically, and make decisions that can affect the entire organization. The advanced skills of a business analyst aren't that different from the advanced skills of a team leader or project manager. You'll need to be able to facilitate meetings, create clear and concise documents, negotiate with stakeholders, and think logically and creatively about the problem, solution, and business opportunities you encounter.

You'll work with business teams, define life cycles, research problems, identify solutions, perform data analysis, and participate in creating projects that work. Business analysts work with project managers to ensure that projects are meeting the business requirements and that the solutions are cost-effective, efficient, and accurate. That's what this section of the chapter is all about: the attributes of the business analyst skills you'll need to be successful beyond passing the CBAP examination.

Hosting Effective Meetings

Meetings are actually expensive—and I'm not talking about the donuts, coffee, and soda you might provide for participants. When you invite 15 people to a typical two-hour meeting, you're really hosting a meeting that's worth 32 hours of labor. Thirty-two hours? Yep. You've 15 people in the meeting plus yourself; add four more people and you've one week of time for a two-hour meeting. Requirements meetings can last for days, so you can see why it's so important for the business analyst to host good meetings that don't waste time, have set objectives, and actually accomplish something.

This is why you should first determine who really needs to be in the meeting and what their contribution or takeaway from the meeting will be. I've sat in more than one meeting, and I'm sure you have too, where I had nothing to contribute, and the only thing I got from the meeting was a donut. As the business analyst, you should first determine who should attend the meeting and then ask some key stakeholders who else should attend and why. You don't want to waste people's time, but you also don't want to overlook stakeholders who should participate.

I'm a huge fan of agendas for any meeting. Agendas should be created and distributed a couple of days before the meeting to get feedback from the participants. Any updates to the agenda should be redistributed so everyone can anticipate what the meeting will accomplish. Whenever possible you should call the meeting attendees to remind them of the meeting and tell them what the meeting will accomplish. This can ensure that participants will attend, remind them to bring the correct information to the meeting, and collect any necessary information you'll need from the participants before the meeting. It's also a good idea to distribute the finalized agenda with a meeting notice to remind attendees when the meeting is to happen and what is to be discussed.

There's often some question about what the meeting agenda should be. It's simply an organized listing of what the goals of the meeting are. It creates order, boundaries, and a logical approach to the events of the meeting. When you start the meeting, distribute the agenda to the participants who failed to bring the copy you distributed premeeting. I like to quickly introduce the meeting's objective to match the description I've informed people about already. This keeps the objective for the meeting in mind. While an agenda can provide structure, you should allow some flexibility if the participants are accomplishing an objective.

When you start the meeting, on time of course, thank everyone for coming to the meeting to discuss the topic at hand. Review the agenda as you've designed it, and get to work quickly. People are busy—jokes, chitchat, and banter are okay for informal sessions, but wasted time can result in a wasted opportunity. I always have written on a poster or white board four simple rules for any meeting. Use 'em if you like:

- **Focus**   Turn off cell phones, e-mails, and train your brain on our immediate goals.
- **Participate**   We need your input, questions, ideas, and comments. Get involved.
- **Move**   Let's make decisions and keep the meeting momentum.
- **Close**   We have goals in this meeting. Let's accomplish and be done.

Part of meeting management is also time management. You need to facilitate the meeting, which means keeping the attendees on track to the agenda. If you have trouble keeping attendees on track or from lingering over conversations, interject, interrupt, and smile. Don't be condescending, but sometimes attendees don't realize they're rambling. One of the ground rules above is to keep the meeting's momentum; don't let the meeting stall with war stories and talk over decisions that have already been made.

You should also periodically ask attendees how they're doing. Ask if they think the meeting is accomplishing its goals and if anyone has any suggestions for the meeting. A postmeeting complaint or suggestion is valuable for the next meeting, but it doesn't do anything for the current meeting. Be accepting of input from participants, and put suggestions into action if they are good. I recommend you do this quick check of the meeting status every couple of hours and adapt accordingly.

At the end of the meeting you should also ask participants how they felt the meeting went. Verbal reviews of the meeting will usually result in generic approval, so for longer meetings distribute a quick evaluation sheet. This doesn't have to be fancy, just a five- to ten-question survey on the meeting, with space for comments or suggestions. This can help you improve your meeting management skills and help for future meetings.

When you're ready to close the meeting quickly, review assignments for participants based on the outcome of the meeting. If you're hosting a follow-up meeting, remind people of the next meeting and gain their agreement to attend. You should also follow up with participants with a thank you for participating in the meeting and remind them of their assignments as promised. End on a positive note, smile, and let people go.

NOTE   It's important to thank people for participating in the meeting. Don't thank people for attending; meetings are work.

Thinking Like a Business Analyst

As a business analyst, you need to think beyond the symptoms and look for causes. You already know through use case studies that you can experience the symptoms. You can also facilitate cause-and-effect meetings and create Ishikawa diagrams like Figure 8-3 to help you identify causal factors. You also need to ask effective questions. Strategic questioning looks for results instead of narratives. You want to ask questions that make people think about the requirements.

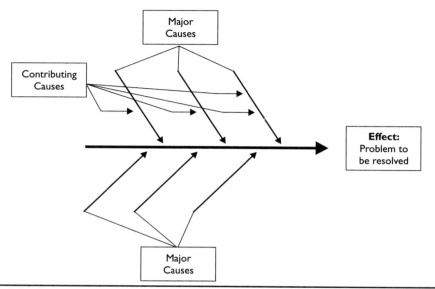

Figure 8-3 Cause-and-effect diagrams are also called fishbone diagrams.

Style your questions to create a partnership with your audience instead of challenging them. For example, here are some good questions to help your stakeholders dig deeper:

- How important is this requirement?
- Have you experienced this problem or something similar before?
- What do you think the problem is?
- What do you hope this project will accomplish?
- How soon would you like this requirement?
- If you could change one thing about your current situation, what would it be?
- What would you change next?
- Is there anything that you'd like me to ask?

These types of questions are open-ended and help the dialogue along. Based on what the stakeholders say, you can branch into more open-ended questions. Of course you're documenting their answers, so you can follow up on their input. When interviewing stakeholders, it's a good idea to check back with them later to see if they've thought of anything else you should know. It's funny how our minds will think of ideas after the meeting, so give stakeholders a second chance to add information.

One approach you may want to consider using is *system thinking*. This is a philosophy that really contrasts with the traditional decomposition of a symptom, problem, or scope. Usually when business analysts examine a problem, they'll break down and isolate the problem—which is a fine mode of attack. Systems thinking, however, examines the whole system with the belief that the symptom is a product of the system as a whole. Actions in one component of a system have effects, even subtle effects, on neighboring components. The relationships between system components are studied for effectiveness as much as the processes within the components of the system.

Systems thinking allows for the possibility that an improvement in one area of a system, such as an organization, can have negative effects on other areas of the system. A simple example is a change in the policies for accessing web sites. Blocking access based on key words can actually stop users from accessing legitimate web sites. While the inappropriate content may be blocked, time, effort, and efficiency are hindered on other levels. A broader example is seen in nature with the introduction of the Kudzu plant from Japan as an ornamental plant. The plant is a pretty, lush vine, but it has ravaged parts of the southern United States.

Business analysts also need to think about the culture that their solution may affect. With international projects, the business analyst should understand more than just the language differences, time zones, and holidays. Cultural issues can affect how well the project manager can operate in an international environment. The Sapir-Whorf hypothesis, for example, posits that the language a person speaks affects how the person thinks. It's an interesting theory created by Edward Sapir and Benjamin Whorf.

The Sapir-Whorf hypothesis is relevant to international business analysis because, if you subscribe to the theory, different language patterns affect understanding and thinking. In this theory, how you think is based on the language you speak; your thoughts may be different and in contrast to how people who speak other languages think. You need to communicate in more detail and strive to confirm a real understanding of what's being communicated between you and your international stakeholders.

Another international element that can affect your projects is ethnocentrism. Ethnocentrism is when individuals judge the world based on their own culture, usually with the belief that their culture is superior to everyone else's culture, belief, religion, and ethnicity. Being aware that other people have different values and priorities is a good method to combat ethnocentrism. You do, to a certain extent, have to be an anthropologist to overcome the self-serving beliefs ethnocentrism promotes.

Serving as a Leader

There's been an awful lot written about leadership. Cruise into your favorite bookstore, and you'll find rows of books just about leadership. Do an Internet search on leadership, and you'll be overwhelmed with results. Leadership is something we all crave, many aspire to, and all of us need. Leadership is the alignment, motivation, direction, and inspiration a person can give to others to call them to action. Leadership is inspiring people to take action because they want to, not because they are required to.

Regardless of the CBAP examination, leadership skills can help you in your career, your life, and may be the catalyst for helping people in your organization achieve great things. Organizations have people that you can identify as leaders and people who are definitely followers; leaders need followers, but more importantly, followers need someone to lead them.

People want to be led, but they want to be led by someone they can believe in. To prove themselves, leaders must be willing to do what other people are not. Leaders must be willing to act, to work, to get involved. The best leadership is leading by doing. Nothing commands respect among others more than a leader who's involved in the work, involved in the accomplishing, and puts forth as much or more effort as everyone else in the project.

Coaching and Motivating Stakeholders

Coaching is when you help another think about the actions they're required to do in order to achieve the things they want in their life. Coaching is not you doing for someone else, but rather you using activities, conversations, interviews, and exercises to help people realize what it is they want to do in their personal and professional lives and then inspiring those people to take action to accomplish goals.

In a professional organization, coaching is often limited to roles, responsibilities, and skills. A professional coach, sometimes called a life coach, is a person who uses coaching activities to help people think about and take action on changes in their lives. Both professional coaches and organizational coaches need an internal desire to help others reach their full potential.

Much of coaching, in any capacity, uses the same skills you've learned to be a business analyst. Coaches ask questions, explore solutions, listen to clients, and elicit requirements about the clients' ambitions in life. The role of a coach is to help others make decisions and determinations, create plans to achieve, and then act on those plans. Coaching as a business analyst isn't necessarily needed in every project, but business analysts have opportunities to manage others, work with others, and can serve as a coach when appropriate.

Part of coaching clients is to help them realize their long-term goals. Ambitions, dreams, and "somedays" just don't work when it comes to creating goals. Goals have specific requirements, achievable results, and deadlines to achieve them. Long-term goals such as an advanced degree, certification, or completing an event can be broken down into smaller, achievable, and traceable goals for each month, quarter, or even year.

NOTE If you're interested in goal setting, you should visit my goal-setting web site, www.lifelongproject.com. I use the principles of project management to achieve goals. It's a site chockablock with free resources, and I'd love to hear about your goals and ambitions.

Coaching and motivation go together, but motivation, real motivation, has to come from within each person. For example, if I tell you to leave a building even though it's cold, dark, and rainy outside, you might not want to. Even if I tell you to leave the building in a kind way, and smile, and hold the door open for you, you still may not want to. But if I show you that the building is on fire, now you're motivated, and you want to take action. Motivation is an internal desire that makes you want to take action.

As a business analyst, you may find sustaining motivation for the business analysis team, the project team, and the involvement of stakeholders is a hard job. You need to first identify what motivates people and use that thing to keep them moving forward. Motivating factors are different for everyone, but common motivational factors include

- **Fear**   Not acting may bring about unwanted results, attention, or punishments.

- **Ambition**   Personal achievement can motivate people to excel if they believe their current actions will help them reach future goals.

- **Recognition**   Sometimes a public recognition, commendation, or mention of their hard work is enough to motivate people. A business analyst should always thank team members, by name, for their contributions.

- **Rewards**   Financial gain, vacation days, or other rewards can motivate people to action.

- **Avoidance of consequences of inaction**   Sometimes inaction may bring about results that the person wants to avoid. Think of health issues, documentation of performance, or financial penalties.

- **Peer pressure**   When a project team, business analysis team, or any other team are all working together, it's more difficult for individuals not to contribute to their project.

- **Expectations**   When a person is assigned activities to complete from someone they admire and respect, they'll generally work harder to meet the expectations that have been placed upon them.

Coaching, long-term goal setting, and motivating are all linked together. The most important element of the three, in my opinion, is goal setting. If people are being coached but they can't see a mental image of their achievements, then coaching is just a nice conversation. Without goals there's really nothing to be motivated by. Goals are things, accomplishments, and results of hard work, but you need to be able to see exactly what you're trying to accomplish. Once you know what you want, then your motivation can help you reach that goal. Coaches can help fuel the fire and hold you accountable to taking actions to reach results.

Performing Appraisals

If you're the business analyst for a large project, you might have a group of business analysts who report to you. If that's the case, you're probably going to have to appraise their work and contribution to the project and account for their work on the business analysis duties. Appraisal skills are often handled by functional managers, but an organization can elect to have a business analyst, project manager, and even a team leader review a person's performance.

If you're assigned to complete an appraisal of someone's work, you have responsibility attached to the review. In some organizations appraisals are a joke because they're rushed, don't matter to the overall performance review, and people don't often tell the truth on the appraisal. I've seen reviews of team members where every single team member was reviewed identically to every other team member. You don't need a PhD to see that the reviewer didn't take the evaluation seriously.

Appraisals—effective appraisals—should be well-designed to capture exactly what each team member contributed to the project. Time and thought should go into the performance appraisal, and the review should reflect exactly what the team member did on the project. This means the business analyst will need good records, time to review what was or was not completed by the individual, and supporting details of the performance.

What many organizations miss is for team members to have an opportunity to appraise their functional manager, business analyst, or project manager as well. If appraisals exist to review performance and to promote better performance, it should be a two-way street. Appraisals should be made of management and not just of team members. Politics and fear of reprisal often stop that from ever happening. Whoever is performing the appraisal should follow six general rules:

- **Prepare**   As I've mentioned, it takes time to collect evidence of performance, fact, and supporting detail. Doing an appraisal of someone's performance without knowing how they actually performed is disrespectful.

- **Review performance**   The appraisal is to review what the person has done, not what was intended to be done. If the person did reach goals and expectations, that's great; if not, then an explanation is needed. There may be valid reasons why goals weren't met, and the individual should have the opportunity to explain his position and what he's contributed.

- **Listen**   As a business analyst this should not be hard for you—you listen a lot. Avoid the temptation to ramble; ask a question and allow the person to speak. Use open-ended questions rather than closed-ended questions (closed-ended questions can end with yes or no; open-ended allow people to converse).

- **Avoid politics**   Politics are a part of every organization, like it or not. The business analyst should take the high road and avoid politics, subterfuge, and reviewing personalities instead of performance.

- **Be specific**   Appraisals are a form to review performance, so you'll need to cite examples of performance. Exact details of work completeness, schedule, quality, and acceptability are needed as evidence of the person's good or bad performance.

- **Set achievable objectives**   In business analysis you want to avoid subjective definitions and characteristics such as fast, good, and happy. The same thing is true when it comes to setting objectives for the project. Good performance is too subjective to measure. When it comes to setting goals, you'll need specific, measurable results for accountability.

Appraisals aren't just for what the individual has done, but they're also an opportunity to offer encouragement and feedback on how they can improve their overall performance. Appraisals can be an excellent opportunity to set achievable goals for the team member and point them to milestones that can help them achieve their goals. If goal setting is attached to performance appraisals, the goals should be documented and reviewed with the team member throughout the year to make certain they're on their way to achieving goals.

Chapter Summary

Business analysts can help businesses identify and organize requirements for projects and business opportunities. Business analysts can help identify the most cost-effective approach to reach a solution or seize an opportunity. Business analysts work with other business analysts, the project team, the project manager, business owners, and other stakeholders to identify requirements, control requirements, and ensure that the project deliverables are created according to the demands of the requirements.

One approach to help organize requirements management and creation is the Structured Systems Analysis and Design Model (SSADM). It uses a waterfall approach that tightly controls the work and objectives of each phase before allowing the project to move on to the next phase. All projects in the SSADM model start with a feasibility study to ensure that the project goals are achievable before moving into the requirements analysis phases. The final phase of SSADM is the creation of the physical design.

Business analysts may need to do issue management for their requirements. Remember that issues and risks, while similar, are not the same thing. Issues are questions, challenges, and problems that may challenge the requirements gathering, project objectives, or identified risks that have not yet been analyzed for their cost, probability, and impact. Risks are anything that may affect the project for better or worse, though typically worse, and hinder the project from reaching its objectives. All issues, their condition, ownership, and status should be documented in an issue log.

Communication is another key business analysis skill, as business analysts need to serve as the hub of communication in the project. Effective communication means listening, asking questions, and striving to clearly understand what's being communicated to you. By understanding the requirements, you can formulate helpful questions and form conversations about what the stakeholder expects from you, the business analyst.

Another skill discussed in this chapter was understanding your organization's products and processes. By understanding what your company creates and provides for others, you're able to see project and portfolio management in light of what's most important for an organization. The systems within your organization control the flow of data, decisions, and projects that may get selected.

The market conditions that your organization must operate in have a direct correlation to the types of projects, problems, and solutions that you may be called upon to analyze. Understanding your organization and the market that's affecting its outcomes can help you perform better as a business analyst. Market conditions are more than supply and demand, though it's often as simple as that. The economy, saturation of competition, and the relevancy of what your company provides can all affect corporate income.

Key Terms

Application areas   Includes software-driven solutions for workstations, servers, mobile devices, and the Internet.

Appraisal   Review of a team member's work performance and contribution to the business analysis duties.

Coaching   Helping another person think about the actions they're required to do in order to achieve the things they want in their life. Through activities, conversations, interviews, and exercises, coaches help people realize what it is they want to do in their personal and professional lives and then inspire those people to take action to accomplish their goals.

Database areas   Includes database servers, data management, data security, and accessibility.

Hardware areas   Includes servers, workstations, laptops, and devices like printers, cameras, and peripherals.

Issue log   A document that identifies the attributes of each issue, assigns an issue owner, and tracks the status of the issue.

Issue owner   The individual who is closest to the issue and may be tasked with resolving the issue.

Issues   Questions, challenges, and problems that may hinder the requirements gathering, project objectives, or identified risks that have yet to be analyzed for their cost, probability, and impact.

Leadership   The alignment, motivation, and inspiration of people to achieve.

Meeting rules   The rules of a meeting should be posted, reviewed, and agreed upon before starting. Four simple rules for any meeting are focus, participate, move, and close.

Network areas   Includes the connectivity and communication among computers, servers, network devices, and telecommunications.

Risk   An uncertain event or condition that can have a positive or negative effect on the project.

Sapir-Whorf hypothesis   Posits that the language a person speaks affects how the person thinks. In this theory, how you think is based on the language you speak. This theory was created by Edward Sapir and Benjamin Whorf.

Structured analysis techniques Methodologies to create systems by using a model to identify the problem, propose solutions, and design a selected solution.

Structured Systems Analysis and Design Model (SSADM) Classic waterfall methodology, where each phase builds on the work done in the phase before. SSADM was created in the United Kingdom as a model for developing systems and new applications.

Supply-and-demand A classical interpretation of business, where the amount of supply (high or low) and the demand (high or low) can affect the pricing of the product or service.

Systems Standardized process sets within an organization that have identified the flow of activities to reach a desired result. Systems ensure that activities are done the same way, in the same order, every time; they establish a framework for common organizational activities to ensure consistency, thoroughness, and documentation.

Systems thinking An examination of the whole system with the belief that a known symptom is a product of the system as a whole. Actions in one component of a system have effects, even subtle effects, on neighboring components.

Questions

1. You are the business analyst of a project to create new software for your organization. This new application is considered to be mission-critical, and management stresses that there is no room for error in its development. You and the project manager are discussing approaches for creating the deliverable and its demand for quality. Which approach would be most suited to ascertaining the expected level of quality in the project?

   A. Quality assurance models

   B. Quality control models

   C. Cause-and-effect models

   D. Structured Systems Analysis and Design Model

2. What document can the business analyst create to help determine if the project can achieve the expected time, cost, and scope?

   A. Project charter

   B. Feasibility study

   C. Project scope statement

   D. Preliminary scope statement

3. You are the business analyst for the NHG Project. Fran, a member of the business analysis team, comes to you with information regarding purchasing from a particular vendor. The item that you've recommended the organization purchase is now on backorder for 2 months, and this may affect the ability of the project to finish on time. This is an example of what?

   A. Issue

   B. Risk

   C. Project procurement management

   D. Scheduling constraint

4. Which one of the following best describes a project risk?

   A. A risk is an uncertain event that can adversely affect the project.

   B. A risk is a condition that limits the options within a project.

   C. A risk is an uncertain event that will adversely affect the project.

   D. A risk is an uncertain condition that may positively or negatively affect the project.

5. You are the business analyst for a software design project. The project is a high-profile project and is considered to be one of the most important and expensive undertakings your organization has ever attempted. You have identified a new issue in the requirements. What should you do first with the issue?

   A. Add it the issue log.

   B. Discuss the issue with the project manager.

   C. Assign an issue owner.

   D. Share the issue with the project stakeholders.

6. What type of risk analysis considers the probability and impact of the risk event and assigns a cost element to each identified risk?

   A. Subjective

   B. Quantitative

   C. Qualitative

   D. Feasibility study

7. The business analyst for the NIU Project works with 74 stakeholders to elicit and manage requirements. The business analyst will be serving as the hub of communications for the project and has to speak often with stakeholders. What has the most impact on the message?

   A. Written messages

   B. Nonverbal communication

  C. Ad hoc meeting

  D. Formal presentations

8. As a business analyst, you'll be asking questions to elicit requirements, understand wants and needs, and help stakeholders prioritize demands within the requirements. What is a technique of interviewing that can help you ask better questions during stakeholder interviews?

  A. Ask who, what, where, when, and why questions.

  B. Ask how the work should be done.

  C. Ask closed-ended questions.

  D. Ask stakeholders to document all of their requirements.

9. You are the business analyst for a large project that has over 100 stakeholders. You'd like to create an internal web site to share information about the requirements. You realize that not all information can or should be posted on the web site. What component of communication influences the modality of the communication the most?

  A. Communications management plan

  B. Stakeholder status in the organization

  C. Content of the message to be communicated

  D. Stakeholder preferences

10. You are the business analyst of a new opportunity. You have identified 56 key stakeholders within the project. Because of a new vendor agreement, you'll be adding seven stakeholders next week. How many more communication channels will you have next week than now?

  A. 21

  B. 413

  C. 1,540

  D. 1,953

11. Which is considered to be the most valuable tool for a business analyst?

  A. Leadership skills

  B. Appraisal skills

  C. Learning skills

  D. Questioning skills

12. You have recently been hired by the JHY Organization. Your manager, Ellen, would like you to first spend some time learning about the JHY Organization, its history, its clients, and the services they provide. Why do you think Ellen would like you to first learn about your new employer?

   A. It gives you, the new business analyst, time to meet other people in the organization.

   B. It gives Ellen, your supervisor, time to find assignments for you to complete.

   C. It can help you elicit requirements, offer solutions, and control the business analysis processes to support the larger vision of the company if you first understand the larger vision.

   D. It can help you contribute to the organization's sales processes if you first understand the larger vision.

13. You are working with the project manager in your organization to determine how the project work will meet the expected levels of quality your client expects. The project manager has asked that you follow all of the systems within the organization to make changes or procurement requests. All of the following are considered systems except for which one?

   A. Quality change control system

   B. Scope change control system

   C. Cost change control system

   D. Contract change control system

14. You are the business analyst for a software development project. The project is somewhat similar to a project your organization completed last year, so you are using the historical information from the past project to help you make decisions on the current project. This is an example of what approach to business analysis?

   A. Expert judgment

   B. Enterprise environmental factors

   C. Analogous planning

   D. Project archiving

15. Mary Anne would like to access the organization's project archive to review information on a past project. She learns that the previous project manager did not archive the project information, but he has the information in a storage closet. Mary Anne finds the information to be sloppy, unorganized, and missing some information she expected to find. What is the danger of using historical information to plan current projects?

   A. Historical information is never reliable, as it is old information.

   B. Historical information is only as reliable as the current project allows it to be.

    C. Historical information, even sloppy, unorganized information, is still good to predict what will happen in the current project.

    D. Historical information may not be as accurate if the past owner didn't keep the information updated.

16. You are a business analyst for a new IT project. You are working with Thomas, a new project manager for your organization. You and Thomas are discussing the four categories of IT projects. All of the following are valid categories of technology projects except for which one?

    A. Application

    B. Hardware

    C. Networking

    D. Add/Move/Change Projects

17. Roberta is a new business analyst in your organization. She asks you to help her organize a requirements-gathering meeting. You agree to help, as Roberta will work with you on future projects, and you want to get things started off well and to welcome Roberta to your organization. What's the first thing that you and Roberta should create for her upcoming meeting?

    A. Meeting agenda

    B. Meeting request

    C. Meeting scope statement

    D. Meeting ground rules

18. You would like to schedule a meeting with several of the project stakeholders. You've identified seven stakeholders who should attend and are fearful you've forgotten others. Who could you most likely ask to determine what other stakeholders should attend your meeting?

    A. The project manager

    B. The stakeholders you've invited already

    C. The business owner

    D. The project sponsor

19. Management says that meetings are expensive. Why?

    A. The refreshments for meetings often cost more than what the meeting is worth.

    B. The time lost in a meeting could be time spent elsewhere.

    C. The time invested in a meeting should be equal to or less than the value of the meeting.

    D. The time preparing for a meeting may be longer than the actual meeting itself.

20. You are the business analyst for a project that will span several countries. The residents of each country speak a different language, and you're concerned that this may affect communications and how each participant thinks about your project. What theory supports your concern?

    A. Ethnocentrism

    B. Culture shock

    C. Sapir-Whorf hypothesis

    D. Cultural achievability

Questions and Answers

1. You are the business analyst of a project to create new software for your organization. This new application is considered to be mission-critical, and management stresses that there is no room for error in its development. You and the project manager are discussing approaches for creating the deliverable and its demand for quality. Which approach would be most suited to ascertaining the expected level of quality in the project?

    A. Quality assurance models

    B. Quality control models

    C. Cause-and-effect models

    D. Structured Systems Analysis and Design Model

    D. The Structured Systems Analysis and Design Model requires that each phase must be done completely, entirely, and accurately before the project is allowed to continue. While this approach is not the fastest, it does provide a high level of accuracy. Choice A, quality assurance models, is a general management approach that ensures the work is done correctly the first time. B, quality control models, is an inspection-driven process that inspects the work, looking for defects. C, cause-and-effect models, are really an analysis of a problem or goal to be achieved. They examine causes to determine what's contributing to the effects.

2. What document can the business analyst create to help determine if the project can achieve the expected time, cost, and scope?

    A. Project charter

    B. Feasibility study

    C. Project scope statement

    D. Preliminary scope statement

B. The feasibility study, often one of the first documents created during business analysis, helps determine if a project, resource, and/or technology can feasibly achieve the scope, time, and cost objectives of the project requirements. Choice A, the project charter, is a document that sets the high-level purpose of the project and assigns authority to the project manager. C, the project scope statement, defines all of the project work that must be accomplished. D, the preliminary scope statement, is a document that may precede the scope statement to establish the high-level objectives for the project.

3. You are the business analyst for the NHG Project. Fran, a member of the business analysis team, comes to you with information regarding purchasing from a particular vendor. The item that you've recommended the organization purchase is now on backorder for 2 months, and this may affect the ability of the project to finish on time. This is an example of what?

   A. Issue

   B. Risk

   C. Project procurement management

   D. Scheduling constraint

   A. This is an issue that must be resolved. It is not considered a risk, because based on the information provided, we do not know the impact of the decision or if even a probability and impact analysis has been completed, so B is incorrect. C, project procurement management, is considered wrong because project procurement management deals with purchasing and contract management and is too broad an answer. D, scheduling constraint, is also incorrect because not enough information is provided to determine what impact the change may have on the project schedule.

4. Which one of the following best describes a project risk?

   A. A risk is an uncertain event that can adversely affect the project.

   B. A risk is a condition that limits the options within a project.

   C. A risk is an uncertain event that will adversely affect the project.

   D. A risk is an uncertain condition that may positively or negatively affect the project.

   D. According to the PMBOK, a risk is an uncertain event or condition that can have a positive or negative effect on the project. Choices A and C are both incorrect, because these answers only acknowledge the negative impacts of the risk events. B is incorrect, as this defines a constraint and not necessarily a risk.

5. You are the business analyst for a software design project. The project is a high-profile project and is considered to be one of the most important and expensive undertakings your organization has ever attempted. You have identified a new issue in the requirements. What should you do first with the issue?

A. Add it the issue log.

B. Discuss the issue with the project manager.

C. Assign an issue owner.

D. Share the issue with the project stakeholders.

A. You should first add the issue to the issue log so it is documented and its characteristics are accounted for. B, C, and D are applicable activities to do once the issue has been recorded in the issue log.

6. What type of risk analysis considers the probability and impact of the risk event and assigns a cost element to each identified risk?

A. Subjective

B. Quantitative

C. Qualitative

D. Feasibility study

B. Quantitative risk analysis determines the probability, financial impact, and calculates a risk event value for risk in the project. Choice A, subjective, is not a valid risk management term. C, qualitative, also reviews the probability and impact of each risk event, but does not assign a financial value that quantitative analysis does. Generally, quantitative analysis quantifies the risk through a study, while qualitative analysis qualifies the risk event for more analysis. Feasibility studies, choice D, are usually done early in the business analysis to determine the project's ability to achieve expectations.

7. The business analyst for the NIU Project works with 74 stakeholders to elicit and manage requirements. The business analyst will be serving as the hub of communications for the project and has to speak often with stakeholders. What has the most impact on the message?

A. Written messages

B. Nonverbal communication

C. Ad hoc meeting

D. Formal presentations

B. Nonverbal communication accounts for nearly 55 percent of all communication. This is why phone calls and e-mails can be some of the worst methods to communicate. Written messages, ad hoc meetings, and formal presentations are all examples of how to communicate using the communications model, but these don't affect the communication to the degree that nonverbal communication does.

8. As a business analyst, you'll be asking questions to elicit requirements, understand wants and needs, and help stakeholders prioritize demands

within the requirements. What is a technique of interviewing that can help you ask better questions during stakeholder interviews?

A. Ask who, what, where, when, and why questions.

B. Ask how the work should be done.

C. Ask closed-ended questions.

D. Ask stakeholders to document all of their requirements.

A. The 5 Ws of questions—the who, what, where, when, and why questions— can help elicit information from stakeholders. B, asking the stakeholder how the work should be done, isn't always a good choice, as the stakeholder may have no direct knowledge of the work approach. C, closed-ended questions, should be avoided when detailed information is needed in an interview. D, the stakeholder may document some of the requirements, but this is often the responsibility of the business analyst, not the stakeholders.

9. You are the business analyst for a large project that has over 100 stakeholders. You'd like to create an internal web site to share information about the requirements. You realize that not all information can or should be posted on the web site. What component of communication influences the modality of the communication the most?

A. Communications management plan

B. Stakeholder status in the organization

C. Content of the message to be communicated

D. Stakeholder preferences

C. The content of the message should affect how the message should be communicated. The communications management plan, choice A, will determine who needs what information, when the information is needed, and in what modality the information is needed, but it's not as concise as choice C. Choices B and D, the status and preferences of the stakeholders, seem logical, but the content of the message should always determine how the communication is to happen.

10. You are the business analyst of a new opportunity. You have identified 56 key stakeholders within the project. Because of a new vendor agreement, you'll be adding seven stakeholders next week. How many more communication channels will you have next week than now?

A. 21

B. 413

C. 1,540

D. 1,953

B. 413 is the correct answer using the formula of $N(N - 1)/2$, where N represents the number of stakeholders. In this example, you first need to find the current number of communication channels, which is choice C, 1,540. Then you'll need to find the number of channels for next week based on 63 stakeholders; which is choice D, 1,953. The difference between these two numbers is the number of new communication channels you can expect. Choice A, 21, represents the number of channels if your project only had seven stakeholders total.

11. Which is considered to be the most valuable tool for a business analyst?

A. Leadership skills

B. Appraisal skills

C. Learning skills

D. Questioning skills

C. All of the skills listed are important business analysis attributes and abilities, but choice C is the most important skill from this set. Learning skills can allow you to learn how to lead, how to appraise, and how to formulate questions, so choices A, B, and D are incorrect.

12. You have recently been hired by the JHY Organization. Your manager, Ellen, would like you to first spend some time learning about the JHY Organization, its history, its clients, and the services they provide. Why do you think Ellen would like you to first learn about your new employer?

A. It gives you, the new business analyst, time to meet other people in the organization.

B. It gives Ellen, your supervisor, time to find assignments for you to complete.

C. It can help you elicit requirements, offer solutions, and control the business analysis processes to support the larger vision of the company if you first understand the larger vision.

D. It can help you contribute to the organization's sales processes if you first understand the larger vision.

C. It's important for the business analyst to understand the processes and procedures of an organization to better serve as a business analyst in the organization. Ellen is having you learn about the organization so you can operate better as a business analyst. Choice A is likely not a valid choice, though it's good to meet other people in the organization. B is not a valid choice, as it's not as important as choice C. D is not valid either, as sales were not mentioned in the question.

13. You are working with the project manager in your organization to determine how the project work will meet the expected levels of quality your client expects. The project manager has asked that you follow all of the systems within the organization to make changes or procurement requests. All of the following are considered systems except for which one?

A. Quality change control system

B. Scope change control system

C. Cost change control system

D. Contract change control system

A. There is no quality change control system. Systems are defined processes that achieve an objective. Choices B, C, and D are incorrect, because there is a scope change control system, a cost change control system, and a contract change control system. Note that the question was asking for which one is not a system.

14. You are the business analyst for a software development project. The project is somewhat similar to a project your organization completed last year, so you are using the historical information from the past project to help you make decisions on the current project. This is an example of what approach to business analysis?

A. Expert judgment

B. Enterprise environmental factors

C. Analogous planning

D. Project archiving

A. Expert judgment is relying on others to help you make the best decision. Historical information is using the information generated by the previous business analyst, project manager, and project team to make decisions on the current project. B, enterprise environmental factors, are the rules and policies the business analyst must follow in the organization. C, analogous planning, is not a valid term. D, project archiving, is the act of archiving closed project information.

15. Mary Anne would like to access the organization's project archive to review information on a past project. She learns that the previous project manager did not archive the project information, but he has the information in a storage closet. Mary Anne finds the information to be sloppy, unorganized, and missing some information she expected to find. What is the danger of using historical information to plan current projects?

A. Historical information is never reliable, as it is old information.

B. Historical information is only as reliable as the current project allows it to be.

C. Historical information, even sloppy, unorganized information, is still good to predict what will happen in the current project.

D. Historical information may not be as accurate if the past owner didn't keep the information updated.

D. The danger in historical information is that it may not be very accurate. A is incorrect, as historical information is often very reliable. B is not a valid statement, as the current project has no bearing on the accuracy of older information. C may be true in some scenarios, but not often; also if this statement is true, it's not really a danger for the current project.

16. You are a business analyst for a new IT project. You are working with Thomas, a new project manager for your organization. You and Thomas are discussing the four categories of IT projects. All of the following are valid categories of technology projects except for which one?

    A. Application

    B. Hardware

    C. Networking

    D. Add/Move/Change Projects

    D. Add/Move/Change Projects is actually a category of projects that describe one of the three activities, so this choice is incorrect. Choices A, B, and C, application, hardware, and networking, are valid categories of technology projects, so these choices are incorrect. The fourth category, which isn't an answer option, is database.

17. Roberta is a new business analyst in your organization. She asks you to help her organize a requirements-gathering meeting. You agree to help, as Roberta will work with you on future projects, and you want to get things started off well and to welcome Roberta to your organization. What's the first thing that you and Roberta should create for her upcoming meeting?

    A. Meeting agenda

    B. Meeting request

    C. Meeting scope statement

    D. Meeting ground rules

    A. Always create the meeting agenda first to determine what should be included in the meeting's discussion. B is incorrect, as the agenda should be distributed with the meeting request so attendees can offer input on what's to be discussed. C is not a valid meeting management term. D, meeting ground rules, should be established and reviewed before the meeting, but not before the agenda is created.

18. You would like to schedule a meeting with several of the project stakeholders. You've identified seven stakeholders who should attend and are fearful you've forgotten others. Who could you most likely ask to determine what other stakeholders should attend your meeting?

    A. The project manager

    B. The stakeholders you've invited already

    C. The business owner

    D. The project sponsor

    B. Asking the stakeholder you've invited to the meeting is an excellent resource for determining if additional stakeholders should also attend. A and D, the project manager and the project sponsor, aren't valid choices, as these roles may not even exist yet if the project is still in the early stages of requirements gathering. The business owner, choice C, is not likely to know who else should attend the meeting.

19. Management says that meetings are expensive. Why?

    A. The refreshments for meetings often cost more than what the meeting is worth.

    B. The time lost in a meeting could be time spent elsewhere.

    C. The time invested in a meeting should be equal to or less than the value of the meeting.

    D. The time preparing for a meeting may be longer than the actual meeting itself.

    C. Meetings are expensive because of the number of hours of labor invested in a meeting. The outcome of the meeting should be of value. The value of the meeting should equate to the time spent in the meeting. Choice A is incorrect, as refreshments may cost, but it's unlikely they'll cost more than the labor being paid to attend the meeting. B, time, should not be lost in a meeting but invested into a meeting. D, meeting preparation, may take time, but this is not the reason why meetings are considered expensive.

20. You are the business analyst for a project that will span several countries. The residents of each country speak a different language, and you're concerned that this may affect communications and how each participant thinks about your project. What theory supports your concern?

    A. Ethnocentrism

    B. Culture shock

    C. Sapir-Whorf hypothesis

    D. Cultural achievability

    C. The Sapir-Whorf hypothesis states that the language a person uses may affect their thought process. Choice A, ethnocentrism, is when a person judges other cultures by their own and assumes that other cultures are of less value. B, culture shock, is the initial disorientation you experience when you enter a foreign environment. D, cultural achievability, is a term to describe the ability of a project or idea to achieve its goals based on the reaction of the culture the project operates within.

Managing Projects

In this chapter you will
- Define business analyst, projects, and programs
- Learn how projects get initiated
- Plan for project success
- Execute the project management plan
- Monitor and control the project work
- Close the project

Business analysts and project managers should work together to help the customers get the things they require. You'll work as the business analyst to help determine the project requirements, and the project manager works with the project team to plan on how best to achieve the requirements and then to execute the project management plans. Throughout the project you will need to interact with the project manager, the project team, and other stakeholders to plow through issues, risks, and constraints in the project.

A good working relationship between the project manager and the business analyst can help both people perform better. In my experience as a consultant, I've seen business analysts and project managers that despise one another, because each thinks the other is infringing on their job duties. These people wasted energy on politics, and their projects were consistently late, riddled with rumors, and full of petty attempts to make the other person look bad. I've also seen plenty of business analysts and project managers work together to create incredible software, synergy among the team, and excitement from the customers. Business analysts and project managers must work together, but it's up to them to determine how they'll work together.

Project management is a tricky business. Project managers have loads of processes to launch; project team members to direct; management, customers, and stakeholders to communicate with; and a barrage of change requests, forms, and phone calls. Project management is somewhat unique to every organization. Some companies have a rigid, prepackaged approach to project management, and others let the project manager take the reins. In this chapter, I'm following a standardized approach that you can find in *A Guide to the Project Management Body of Knowledge* by the Project Management Institute (PMI).

Initiating the Project

Projects are initiated once they're deemed worthy by the organization. Business analysts and stakeholders are often the determining factors as to whether a project should exist based on the identified problem or opportunity. When a business analyst is brought into a scenario, either to solve a problem or to help an organization seize an opportunity, there's a pretty good chance that a project is going to be initiated. Sometimes, however, the business analyst finds that the investment is not worth the reward, and the project is scrapped before much is invested.

When a project is initiated, a project steering committee, project portfolio management board, or some other entity within the organization makes a determination that what the business analyst has learned and shared is worth investing in. Project portfolio management is the governance of the amount of funds an organization has available to invest in a project. Not every project can be initiated, as an organization only has so much capital, so many resources, and so much time to invest in opportunities.

Projects that are initiated, however, follow enterprise environmental factors in the formality of initiating and officially launching a project. For some organizations this means that there's a project kickoff meeting and formal introduction of the project manager. In other organizations the project launch is less formal, and the project manager hits the ground running to build a list of objectives for the customer. While the more formal approach is controlled, the looser approach gives more freedom to the project manager.

For a more detailed explanation watch The Project Management Life Cycle video now.

Examining the Project Charter

The project charter is a document that authorizes the project to exist within the organization. It grants the project manager authority over the resources the project needs to be successful. The person who signs the project charter needs to be high enough in the organization to ensure that the project manager has access to all of the resources needed to be successful. You need someone with organizational authority to grant the project manager the power to get the job done.

The project charter is based on the work the business analyst has done. It defines the requirements for satisfaction and the high-level purpose of the project. This can map to your initial project requirements and why the project is needed, and to what business needs the project will satisfy (seizing an opportunity or solving a problem). Your initial project requirements will define what the requirements for satisfaction are so that you, the key stakeholders, the project manager, and the project sponsor all know what the customer is expecting as a result of the project.

The project charter should also include or reference a milestone schedule. A project *milestone* is a timeless event that shows progress. You typically can identify milestones at the end of phases by the thing the phase produces. Milestones are sometimes tied to scope review, and in project management terminology these reviews are known as scope validation. It's an opportunity for the key stakeholders to examine the work that has been completed by the project manager and her team to see how valid the work results are.

In a larger project probably many stakeholders have some influence over the project work. Stakeholder influences should be documented and often include

- Internal and external stakeholders
- Stakeholder organizational power
- Stakeholder threats or perceived threats about the project
- Government agencies, laws, or customers that influence the project decisions
- Positive and negative stakeholders
- Resources to be used within the project and their managers
- Organizational structures

In addition to identifying and documenting the stakeholder influences, all of the constraints and assumptions should be documented or referenced in the project charter. Constraints in the charter could be laws, regulations, specific resources, deadlines, or budget amounts assigned to the project. Assumptions in the project charter could reference interoperability of the technology, weather, longevity of the project team, and beliefs about the technology the project centers on.

Developing the Preliminary Project Scope Statement

In some projects it may be appropriate to develop the preliminary project scope statement document as part of project initiation. This document technically spans project initiation and the project planning processes, but it is a valid document to define, in broad terms, what the project is to accomplish. It is based largely on the work of the business analyst and defines what the project objectives are for the criteria for project acceptance. The preliminary project scope statement can also define budget and schedule constraints, and customer expectations for communications, benefit management, and project deliverables.

The project scope statement, which is finalized in the project planning processes, defines all of the deliverables of the project in great detail. This initial document defines these same deliverables but at broader, functional levels. User case studies, the feasibility studies, and the project requirements documentation can all be referenced in this project document. The initial project scope statement may also define the project boundaries. *Project boundaries* are the things the project will not deliver—such as distributing software for the customer, creating user guides, or providing training of the project deliverables. It's important to define project boundaries so the project customer doesn't expect more than they're receiving.

This preliminary project scope statement should also acknowledge several other components of the project from a high level:

- **Initial project risks**   Any initial risks that have been identified should be referenced and/or recorded here.

- **Milestones**   Just as the project charter referenced the project milestones, the preliminary project scope statement should as well.

- **Initial Work Breakdown Structure**   The Work Breakdown Structure (WBS) is a key deliverable in project management, and the initial WBS can help the project manager and project team do more detailed planning, estimating, and risk assessment.

- **Rough order of magnitude (ROM) cost estimate**   The ROM estimate is a very high-level, unreliable cost estimate that "ballparks" the idea of what the project should cost. The ROM usually includes a range of variance along with the estimate costs, such as $750,000 –50 percent to +100 percent, depending on how much information, historical data, and confidence in the project estimate is available. The ROM is basically a project manager's guess of what the project will cost.

- **Configuration management requirements**   Configuration management is the documentation, control, and management of the features and functions of the project deliverable. Configuration management defines the product scope and what the customer can expect as a result of the project work. Changes to the project scope are also reflected in the configuration management of the product the project is creating.

- **Approval requirements**   Someone will need to sign off on the project scope, project documents, costs, and schedules of the deliverables. The project will also need someone to sign off on the project deliverables to verify the work has been done according to the business analyst's requirements and the project scope.

Not every project will need a preliminary project scope statement, but every project will need a project scope statement. The project scope statement is officially part of the project planning processes, but it follows much of what the preliminary project scope does. As a business analyst you'll often contribute to the project scope through your project requirements documentation, and you'll need to work with the project manager and the stakeholders to ensure that both parties are in sync with what the project promises.

Planning the Project

Projects fail at the beginning, not the end. That's a nice way of saying that if a project manager doesn't plan the project properly, the project is doomed. And it'll be time for that project manager to dust off their resume. Project planning is an essential part of the project management life cycle, as it defines all of the work for the remainder of the project. Much of the project planning, if it's to be a successful project, is based on the requirements documentation the business analyst has prepared.

Project planning doesn't happen in one fell swoop. Project planning is actually done in iterations through the project. As new issues, risks, details, and requirements are discovered, the business analyst and project manager return to the project planning phase of the project management life cycle. The project manager and the business analyst should work together on the project plan throughout the project to ensure that the deliverables for the project are in sync with what the customer has intended.

The project management plan is comprised of several project management documents and subsidiary plans that direct the project execution. The most common subsidiary project plans are:

- **Scope management plan**   Defines how the project scope should be created, decomposed into the WBS, executed, monitored and controlled, and validated.

- **Cost management plan**   Defines how the project will be estimated, budgeted, and how changes to cost will be managed.

- **Schedule management plan**   Defines how the activity duration estimates will be created, what the project schedule is, and how changes to the schedule will be managed.

- **Quality management plan**   If your organization has a quality assurance program, then the requirements of that program will be defined here; if not, a quality policy will be established for the project, and the quality control and quality assurance expectations will be defined.

- **Process improvement plan**   Defines how the project processes will be monitored and documented for accuracy, efficiency, and improvement.

- **Human Resources management plan**   Defines when the project team members will be brought onto the project, how and when they'll be utilized on the project, and when they'll be released from the project.

- **Communications management plan**   This plan defines who needs what information, when it is needed, and in what modality the stakeholders are expecting the communication. This plan can set requirements and conditions, such as cost and schedule variances, within the project that will prompt communication.

- **Risk management plan**   Risks need to be identified, documented, and recorded in the risk register. This plan defines the risk management activities, including how risks will be qualitatively and quantitatively analyzed.

- **Risk response plan**   A project manager can choose from seven risk responses, and this plan identifies each risk and the appropriate risk response based on the conditions of the project and the attributes of the risk event.

- **Procurement management plan**   When a project needs to purchase materials, services, or other resources, this plan defines the process and procedures a project manager is to follow within the organization.

Every organization has different procedures and expectations of the project manager. These somewhat generic plans are likely to be standardized for the organizational approach the project manager must follow. That standardization is part of enterprise environmental factors and constrains how the project manager is allowed to proceed in each part of the project.

Using Project Integration Management

Project integration management is a special project management knowledge area that coordinates all of the parts of a project. Project management has nine knowledge areas, and project integration management is, in a way, the parent of the other eight knowledge areas. The nine knowledge areas are

- **Project integration management** This special knowledge area coordinates the other eight knowledge areas.

- **Project scope management** This area defines, plans, and controls the project scope based on the business analyst's requirements.

- **Project time management** Time management is needed for both the project activities and the project management activities

- **Project cost management** Cost management requires the project funds be managed, controlled, and tracked, and fluctuations in project costs must be communicated.

- **Project quality management** Quality management is the assurance that the work is properly planned for project execution and then controlled to ensure the work is completed as planned.

- **Project human resources management** The management of the project human resources will vary by organization, but it takes people to complete the project work.

- **Project communications management** Project managers, like business analysts, are communicators; projects demand constant communication.

- **Project risk management** The knowledge area identifies, documents, and analyzes the project risks in order to create risks responses.

- **Project procurement management** Projects may need to purchase items, hire additional staff, and/or perform work for other organizations through a contractual relationship.

Project integration management ensures that all of the knowledge areas are considered throughout the project management life cycle. Poor performance in any of the knowledge areas could have adverse effects in all of the other knowledge areas. For example, a project manager who does a poor job of communicating will have problems in time, cost, quality, risk, and so on—just as a project manager who breezes over time management will be haunted by delays, risks, cost overruns, and more troubles.

This special knowledge area is also used in change management. Whenever a change enters the project, you'll use project integrated change control to examine the impacts of the change on the project as a whole. Project integration management requires the project manager to do a good job in every knowledge area within the project.

Planning for Scope Management

While all parts of project management planning are important, some parts are more important than others. Since the project scope is the heart of project management and is a big chunk of what the business analyst does, I consider project scope management the essential part of project management. Once the project scope has been defined, the rest of the project is really based on fulfilling the project scope. The business analyst and the project manager work together to define the project. Once the project scope has been defined, the key stakeholders, project sponsor, business analyst, and the project management should sign off on the project scope.

The project scope is then decomposed into the Work Breakdown Structure. In your organization, the WBS and the project may be the same document or an extension of the project requirements documents. That's fine. The concepts are the same, but the terminology is slightly different. Basically the project scope statement defines all of the required work to satisfy the project objectives, and then the project scope is broken down into the WBS. Along with the WBS, the project manager and project team will create a WBS dictionary. The WBS dictionary defines all of the components of the WBS and the required resources, and references any information that can explain the deliverable in more detail.

The smallest item in the WBS is the work package. The *work package* is the smallest thing that the project team will create. The accumulation of all the work packages in the WBS will equate to the project scope as seen in Figure 9-1. This is sometimes called scope aggregation, and time and cost estimates may be tied to these work packages as well. When the project manager and the project team are decomposing the project scope into work packages, it's important to not break down the project scope too small or to leave components of the scope too larger either. A heuristic is to break down the project scope components to the 8/80 Rule. The *8/80 Rule* states that the smallest item in the WBS should take no fewer than eight hours and no more than 80 hours of labor to create.

Once the scope has been defined, the project activities list can be created. The activities list is based on the work packages and reflects all of the required actions the project team will need to complete to create the work packages in the WBS. The activities list at this point isn't concerned with cost estimates or other influences on the project—the project team just wants to identify the actions they'll need to complete in order to get the work done. Once the actions have been identified, then they'll do time and cost estimates.

It's also in the planning phase of the project that the project manager, the project team, and any relevant stakeholders will complete activity sequencing. Sequencing creates a project network diagram, as in Figure 9-2, to show the relationships between activities. Each node in the network diagram represents an activity, and the lines show the predecessors and successors of each activity. The path in the network diagram that takes the longest amount of time to complete is called the *critical path*; it can't be delayed at all, or the project will be late.

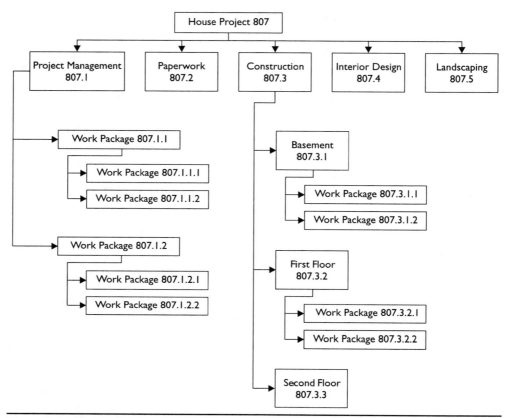

Figure 9-1   The smallest item in the WBS is the work package.

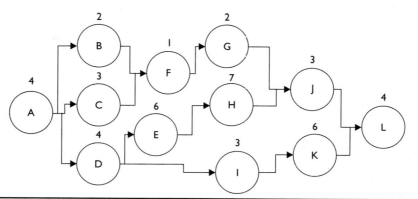

Figure 9-2   Project network diagrams show the flow of activities in the project.

NOTE   I'm giving a very high-level view of activity sequencing in this discussion. Activity sequencing can be a real science and an art. Geniuses who are called scheduling engineers examine all of the possible combinations of activities to determine the lowest risk in relation to the highest reward of scheduling. If you're really interested in network scheduling in project management, I'll once again encourage you to read Chapter 6 of my *PMP Study Guide* from McGraw-Hill Professional. If you're not so curious, that's fine too—I won't hold it against you.

You can choose from a couple of different approaches to activity sequencing, though the most common method is to use hard logic. *Hard logic* is the identification of activities that must be done in a particular order, such as installing the operating system before you can install an application. In some instances the activities can use *soft logic*, where the order of the activities such as installing the server hardware or the printer hardware doesn't really matter.

Planning for Time and Cost Estimates

The business analyst will likely be involved with the time and cost estimating activities of the project. The sum of all the costs and the total duration of all the activities should equate to how much the project will cost and how long the project will take to complete. The only trouble is that you don't really know how much a project will cost or how long a project will take until you're actually completely done with the project work. Until then you're really just making educated guesses.

Stakeholders always seem to want to know how much the project will cost before they're interested in how long it'll take to complete. Sometimes you can spend less money but take longer to complete the work the scope demands. In other instances you can spend more money and complete the work faster. And finally, there are times when the work's just going to cost what it'll cost. The biggest expense for most projects is the labor expense. When a stakeholder is in a rush, the project manager can sometimes *crash* the project by adding more resources to the project to get done faster. Yes, it's really called crashing, and it drives up cost because you're adding more labor. Crashing a project succumbs eventually to the Law of Diminishing Returns, because you can't exponentially add labor to reduce the amount of time to complete a project.

NOTE   You might be able to crash a project by adding faster equipment instead of labor, such as in construction projects and manufacturing.

Adding more labor, however, assumes that the activities within the project are effort-driven. *Effort-driven* means that the more effort you apply, the faster the job will get done. Some activities are of *fixed duration*, where it doesn't matter how much effort you add to the project, it'll still take a fixed amount of time to complete. In software development a common activity of fixed duration is testing. You have to use the software to really confirm that it works, and that takes time.

One of the best methods to estimate time and costs is based on historical information. Throughout this book I've mentioned templates, organizational process assets, and project archives—that's historical information. It's considered a form of expert judgment, because your time and cost estimates are based on proven information. You might hear some project management aficionados call these estimates *top-down estimates* or analogous estimates. Don't sweat it—they're the same thing: an estimate based on a similar project that's been completed in the past.

Depending on the work to be done in the project, you may have several activities that need to be completed over and over, such as installing 16,798 laptops. For these repetitive activities project managers can use a *parametric estimate*. This approach estimates the amount of time for one laptop installation, for example, 2 hours, and then multiplies that parameter across the number of laptops to be installed, for 33,596 hours of labor. A parametric estimate can also be used for costs: 1,235 training manuals at $20 per manual, for a grand total of $24,700. It's math-magic.

Cost estimates can also evolve over time based on the amount of information available to the project manager, and the business analyst creates a cost estimate. The broadest estimate is called the *rough order of magnitude* and has a usual range of variance of –25 percent to +75 percent, though the project manager can attach whatever range is appropriate based on the confidence in the related information. When the project scope is created, the project manager can create the *budget estimate*. This estimate type is based on the details of the project scope, but it is still pretty loose and unreliable; it has a range of variance of –10 percent to +25 percent on average. Finally, the most reliable cost estimate is based on the WBS. The *definitive estimate* is the most accurate cost estimate, but it requires the WBS to create; it has a typical range of variance from –5 percent to +10 percent.

Revisiting Project Planning

Planning is an iterative process throughout the project management life cycle as in Figure 9-3. The project can't stay in planning forever, and it's unfeasible for the project team to solve all of the project challenges in one planning attempt. As problems, issues, risks, and challenges pop into the project, the project manager shifts the project back into planning. Once the problem has been resolved, the project moves back into project execution to put the plan into action.

Some projects use rolling wave planning to allow more flexibility and quicker execution of project plans. *Rolling wave planning* uses short bursts of planning and then short sprints of project execution. These intermittent planning and executing phases allow the project team to focus on the immediate work and the project manager to focus on the long-term vision of the project execution and project scope fulfillment.

When errors are discovered in the project deliverables, the project team and the project manager shift back into planning to address the errors. The usual result of errors is to enforce corrective action to repair the defect, though not always. In some instances

Figure 9-3
Planning is iterative
in the project
management
life cycle.

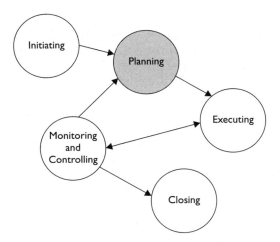

the error is more cost-effective to leave in the product than to repair. For example, a conference room was to be painted sunshine-yellow, and the project team painted it ribbon-yellow instead, a slight difference in the shade of yellow the customer asked for. For the sake of the schedule the customer agrees to keep the ribbon-yellow and receives a discount on the project cost.

Other times the error must be corrected regardless of the fee. For example, the customer could demand the room be repainted with the correct color, as sunshine-yellow could be their corporate color. This defect will cost the project time and funds, and the project manager needs to ensure that the work is done properly without additional waste or rushing through the rework. *Defect repair validation* is the inspection of the repair work to ensure that it is of the quality expected by the project manager and the customer.

The planning phase of a project aims to create preventive actions to avoid mistakes ever entering the project. Communication, documentation, and clarity of assignments are all examples of preventive actions. In the sunshine-yellow paint dilemma the project manager could have attached a paint chip, for example, to the WBS or project documentation to ensure that the right color of paint was communicated to the painters. The small amount of extra time communicating the details of a project can save the project an immense amount of time and dollars in rework.

Executing the Project Plan

It's in the project execution phase that the majority of the project schedule is focused and where the majority of the project budget is consumed. This is because in planning you're creating the schedule to complete the project work and to purchase the labor, materials, and other resources for the project to reach its conclusion. Project execution is only as good as the project planning that directs the project team on what needs to be completed.

There is a difference, I should note, in the project management life cycle and the project life cycle. The *project management* life cycle is what this chapter really focuses on; it's the initiating, planning, executing, monitoring and controlling, and closing process groups that all projects move through. The project management life cycle is universal to all projects regardless of the discipline or application area the project centers on.

The *project* life cycle, however, is unique to each project. The project life cycle is unique to the application area, such as construction, IT, and manufacturing, and it describes the life of the individual project. Projects usually follow phases, such as the construction phase in Figure 9-4. Each phase results in a milestone and allows the project to move on to the next phase in the project.

This conversation is important here in the execution of the project, because the actual execution of the project plan is unique to the project life cycle. In other words, the headlines, concepts, and ideas of project execution are universal to all projects. The actual execution of the project plan is unique to each project life cycle, because of the discipline of each project. You would not expect, I hope, the same phases and execution of a software development project as you would in the construction of a new warehouse.

Executing the Project Plan

The project team members are the people who are doing the project work as defined in the project plan. This is where the project manager really needs to just get out of the way and let the project team get the work done. This does not mean the project manager disappears; it just means that the project manager should take a support role to the project team members doing the project work. The project can't be completed when the project manager is constantly stopping progress.

The idea of a support role sometimes bothers project managers—I hope it doesn't bother you. The project manager is like the coach of a football team. The coach can't be

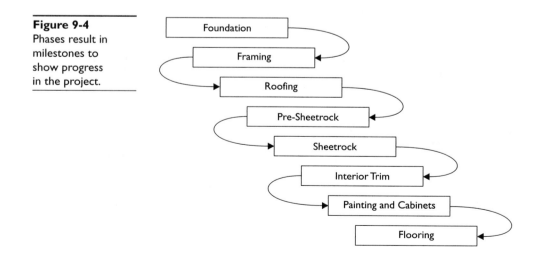

Figure 9-4
Phases result in milestones to show progress in the project.

Foundation

Framing

Roofing

Pre-Sheetrock

Sheetrock

Interior Trim

Painting and Cabinets

Flooring

on the field during the game. The coach isn't a player on the team. The coach can't even be a referee in the game. The coach directs, manages, and motivates the team and makes the decisions that should help the team reach their objectives. In project management the project manager is a person who, like the football coach, helps and supports the project team but really isn't part of the project team.

This is not to say, however, that a project manager can't help with project execution. If Shelly has years of experience as an IT consultant and she's the project manager of an IT project, there's little reason why Shelly can't help her project team when they need the help. Shelly can, if the project team needs it, help the project team executing the project plan, but she shouldn't be in the middle of every part of the project execution—she has a project to manage and lead.

Developing the Project Team

Project managers rely on the project team to complete the work the project requires. The project manager needs a cohesive team that can rely on one another to complete their assignments, communicate issues, and help one another get their work done. This does not happen easily. Project team members' abilities, personalities, interests, and other demands within the project can all affect their ability to perform as a team rather than a group of individuals.

Project team members move through a natural progression on their way to becoming a cohesive team:

- **Forming**   This is when the project team first comes together and team members are getting to know about each other. The group is simply forming based on the needs and competencies the project demands and the availability of the people in the organization to satisfy those needs. Sometimes the project has needs that can't be fulfilled internally, so procurement processes are enacted to bring on contract-based employees.

- **Storming**   As the project team members struggle for power in the project, there may be some conflicts over who'll lead the project team, who'll follow the lead, and who's indifferent as long the project work gets done. Storming can be subtle comments, alignment with key stakeholders, or combative conversations, heated arguments, and visible disgust among the project team members. The project manager needs to keep things civil, but storming will happen to some degree in all projects.

- **Norming**   Once things settle down and leaders, alliances, and acceptance have happened in the project, the team can go about getting their work done. Norming can shift back to storming when there are shifts in the project team, additions to the project scope, or new phases of the project begin.

- **Performing**   This is the ideal state for the project, when all the project team members settle into their roles and go about getting the work done. Petty differences are set aside, and the project team is hard at work accomplishing goals and moving the project toward completion. Performing is the ideal state for the project manager.

Team building activities that allow project team members to get to know and rely on each other are great exercises to facilitate team development. There are hundreds of companies offering guided team building activities such as ropes courses, whitewater rafting, and workshops with great exercises. For longer projects these can be great investments for the project team to come together faster and with better results.

Using Project Management Powers

The project manager has some special powers—really, even the business analyst has these same powers. These aren't superpowers, unfortunately, but it's how the project team members and the stakeholders perceive the project manager and his decision-making abilities. The perception of the project manager by the project team and stakeholders can help push through decisions, establish authority, and even provide leadership to the project team.

You should be familiar with five management powers:

- **Expert power**   This power exists when the project team and stakeholders recognize the project manager as an expert in the discipline the project centers on. For example, if Bob has 15 years of experience in construction, has all sorts of certifications, and has led many successful construction projects in the past, the project team should recognize Bob as an expert project manager in the field of construction.

- **Formal power**   This power, sometimes called positional power, is when a project manager is formally assigned the position of project manager. The project team may recognize the project manager as someone in charge of the project, but not necessarily someone who has any real power on the project. As the team gets to know more about the project manager, this opinion can change.

- **Reward power**   When the project team believes that the project manager can reward them for the work they complete on the project, they'll work accordingly. Reward power is tied to the announcement and ground rules for the project reward and recognition system. Knowing what motivates the project team and rewarding them accordingly is considered a win-win for the project team and the project manager.

- **Coercive power**   This is just the opposite of reward power. When the project team believes the project manager can punish them for poor performance in the project, they may feel coerced into doing their assignments in the project. Coercive power is not necessarily a bad approach for a project manager to take, but it can cause resentment when it's not coupled with reward power.

- **Referent power**   This power has a couple of different meanings. First, referent power is when the project manager refers to someone else's power to push through their project decisions. For example, "we are going to do the project this way, because Lisa the CEO put me in charge as the project manager."

The second meaning is when the project team members are familiar with the project manager from past work, so there's already a relationship established between the project team members and the project manager.

These powers can be used in combination to push through decisions and management of the project team. The structure, rules, and policies of the organization all also have an influence on how much power the project manager actually has over the project team. The project manager should have a clear understanding of how discipline, escalation processes, and rewards and recognitions can be managed within the project well before the project moves too deeply into execution.

Utilizing Human Resource Theories

Project managers should be aware of some business and psychological theories to help the project reach the big goal of its closing processes. These theories all deal with managing the project team, but they overlap some into organizational business analysis and managing the business analysis team. I doubt that you'll see these on the CBAP exam, but they'll help you be a better business analyst all the same.

First is *Maslow's Hierarchy of Needs*. Abraham Maslow created a hierarchy of needs to identify what people need in their lives and what they work for. There are five different layers, and in his theory you need to satisfy the bottom layer before you can move up and worry about satisfying the next layer. Here are the five needs we all have from the bottom working our way up:

- **Physiological**   These are the necessities to live: air, water, food, clothing, and shelter.

- **Safety**   All people need safety and security; this can include stability in life, work, and culture.

- **Social**   People are social creatures and need love, approval, and friends.

- **Esteem**   We strive for the respect, appreciation, and approval of others.

- **Self-actualization**   At the pinnacle of needs, people seek personal growth, knowledge, and fulfillment.

But not everything humans do is based on needs; there are also wants, and it's our wants that help us to achieve more. According to Frederick Herzberg, a psychologist and authority on the motivation of work, two factors affect performance of workers:

- **Hygiene agents**   These elements are the expectations all workers have: job security, a paycheck, clean and safe working conditions, sense of belonging, civil working relationships, and other basics associated with employment.

- **Motivating agents**   These are the elements that motivate people to excel. They include responsibility, appreciation of work, recognition, the chance to excel, education, and other opportunities associated with work other than just financial rewards.

Herzberg's Theory of Motivation is seen in Figure 9-5. His theory suggests that some things motivate and some things are expected in a working relationship. This theory says the presence of hygiene factors will not motivate people to perform, as these are expected attributes. However, the absence of these elements will de-motivate performance. For people to excel, the presence of motivating factors must exist.

A more reactive theory is *McGregor's Theory of X and Y*. Douglas McGregor's theory states that management believes there are two broad perspectives of workers, good and bad. X is bad; these people need to be watched all the time, micromanaged, and distrusted. X people avoid work, responsibility, and have no ability to achieve. You might guess then that Y is considered good. Y people are self-led, motivated, and can accomplish new tasks proactively. The reality is that management sometimes needs to treat people as X and other times as Y depending on the scenario and the individual.

William Ouchi's Theory Z, sometimes called the Japanese management style, is based on the participative management style of the Japanese. This theory states that workers are motivated by a sense of commitment, opportunity, and advancement. Workers in an organization subscribing to Theory Z learn the business by moving up through the ranks of the company. Ouchi's Theory Z also credits the idea of lifelong employment. Workers will stay with one company until they retire, because they are dedicated to the company that is in turn dedicated to them.

Workers expect things based on how they work. This is evident in the Expectancy Theory, which states that people will behave based on what they expect as a result of their behavior. In other words, people will work in relation to the expected reward of the work. If the attractiveness of the reward is desirable to the worker, they will work to receive the reward. In other words, people expect to be rewarded for their effort.

Monitoring and Controlling the Project

In an ideal world the project manager and the project team would develop a plan, and everything in the project would work out just dandy. In the real world, however, dandy doesn't happen often enough. Projects have constant demands, slips, cost overruns,

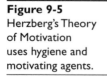

Figure 9-5
Herzberg's Theory
of Motivation
uses hygiene and
motivating agents.

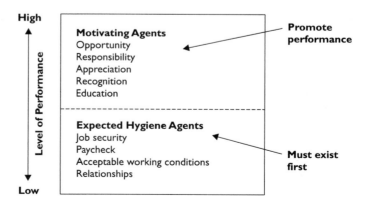

missed deadlines, and communication breakdowns. The project manager must constantly be nursing the project along, working with stakeholders, and ensuring that the project team members are completing their assignments.

Monitoring and controlling the project is a group of processes that happen in tandem with the executing processes of the project. As the project team executes the project work, control mechanisms such as quality control ensure that the work has been completed as it was planned. When the work has not been done properly, corrective actions and rework take place, and then the project can shift back to the planning activities.

Controlling Project Changes

Perhaps one of the most important activities a project manager can do is to control changes to the project scope, time, and cost. Sometimes a project manager can do little to control cost or time delays, but generally the project manager wants to communicate and demand a systemized approach to controlling changes within the project.

Early in the project, during the business analysis duties, it's pretty easy for a stakeholder to request and get a project change. Usually that's because early in the project not much time or monies have been spent on project execution. Early in the project the entire project is still in development, and not much labor has gone into the creation of the project scope. At some point, as shown in Figure 9-6, the project shifts from being open to scope changes to being a deterrent to scope changes.

All proposed changes to the project scope should be documented in a scope change request form. The change request should be part of the project management information system so the request is electronic and traceable, and it's easy to make comments about status changes and to communicate the change status. Through the change

Figure 9-6
Scope changes become more difficult as the project executes plans.

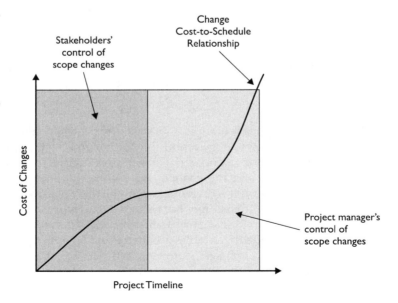

control process the project manager, business analyst, and project team will need to determine and record all of the following:

- Change request
- Date
- Why the change is needed
- Requestor of the change
- Ramifications of implementing (and not implementing) the change to the project scope
- Costs affected by the change
- Schedule affected by the change
- Human resources affected by the change
- Risks introduced or alleviated by the change
- Quality expectations
- Communication needs affected by the change
- Contracts affected by the change

Every scope change has to be considered for its total impact on the project. The examination of the proposed scope change is part of integrated change control. The examination of a scope change request may be accomplished by the project team, the business analyst, or through a change control board. The change control board is a group of project decision makers that considers the costs and benefits of a proposed change request and makes a determination about approving or declining the change request. The outcome of the decision is always documented and communicated to the relevant project stakeholders.

 NOTE If this seems awfully familiar, it's because I discussed a similar concept back in Chapter 2. You're ahead of the curve.

When a scope change request is approved, the project configuration management system is enacted. This system is responsible for documenting and controlling changes to the product scope. For example, if a stakeholder has asked for a new feature to be added to the software and the change was approved, you'd need to document the change as part of the project requirements and the project scope. This is so there's consistency between what the customer has requested and what the final deliverable of the project will be. Configuration management ensures that the features and functions of the requirements and the deliverables are the same.

When configuration management is enacted because of a project change, the following items are updated to reflect the change:

- **Product scope statement**   This document defines the deliverable the customer is expecting.

- **Project scope statement**   This document defines all the work the project manager and project team are completing to create the project product.

- **Work Breakdown Structure**   The WBS is a visual decomposition of the project scope, so changes to the project scope must be updated here as well.

- **WBS dictionary**   The WBS dictionary is a companion document to the WBS and reflects all of the work packages in the WBS. Should the WBS be updated, so too must the WBS dictionary to reflect the changes.

- **Activity list**   When additions are made to the WBS, there will likely be new activities to be included in the project activity list.

- **Project network diagram**   If the activity list has new activities, these need to be reflected in the project network diagram to be certain the project team completes all of the necessary actions to create everything the project scope requires.

A simple change request can actually cause hours of work for the project manager and the business analyst to determine if the change should be approved and to update the entire project plan to reflect the change. Project costs, schedules, resource administration, and risk management may also be changed. There will be communications to the project team, stakeholders, and other stakeholders due to an approved change request. Finally, there may be renegotiations or new contracts with vendors to accommodate the approved change request.

Just as there is a predetermined, documented process for tracking and potentially a pproving scope changes, there is also a course of action for changes to cost and to schedule. Cost changes can happen without affecting the project scope, such as a change in the cost of materials. For example, the cost of oak floors for a construction project could increase significantly, so the change in cost has to be managed. The project customer could demand oak floors regardless, so they'll pay the additional fees to maintain the project scope as it's been planned. Or the customer could opt for a different flooring material such as carpet. If the customer changes the flooring from oak to carpet, you now have a scope change, and all of the actions of the scope change request are enacted.

Changes in the project schedule should also follow a schedule change control system. The change in the schedule should be documented as to its cause, such as a new deadline or a delay in project execution. When there's a change in the project schedule, the project manager will still need to examine all areas of the project to determine the total effects the schedule change will cause in the project.

Performing Quality Control

Quality control is an inspection-driven process to make certain that the project team members are completing the project work according to the project plan. The project manager, the business analyst, project team members, and even subject matter experts inspect the project work to make certain it's being done properly. The goal is to find mistakes before the customers do, so that the project team can fix the errors. The goal of quality control is to keep mistakes out of the customer's eyesight.

Quality control activities can happen at random moments (Surprise!) and at key events throughout the project. You'll usually find quality control activities at the end of project phases in the form of walkthroughs, inspections, and audits. These inspection activities dig into the deliverables that the project team has created and document their completeness or inaccuracy.

The project manager can create some charts to track trends over time to find any instances where the project has failed, is falling into a rut, or if expectations on quality, schedules, and costs are appropriate. One of the most common charts for projects with repetitive activities is a control chart as seen in Figure 9-7. *Control charts* set the project requirements for quality for the highest expected result and the lowest acceptable result. Within the requirements are upper- and lower-control limits that are goals of where the project results should hover.

Sometimes people will ask why the project shouldn't aim for 100 percent accuracy, the highest requirement. In some projects, such as healthcare, that may be appropriate, but in manufacturing, for example, that's not always cost-effective. Consider a printing press that can print 985,800 perfect images out of a million in less than an hour. In this fictional example, the press operator could create a million out of a million perfect images, but would have to slow the machine down to print just 10 images per hour. At that hypothetical rate it wouldn't make sense, as it's more cost-effective to absorb the wasted materials than the wasted time.

In the control chart a mean is established, and the results of the measurement are plotted against the mean. Each point in the jagged line represents the sum of a predetermined amount of units; in my printing example each point in the line could represent a million copies. Each time the line goes above or below the control limit, the project is considered out of control. Yep, even when the project goes above the control limit, as the goal is to hover around the mean.

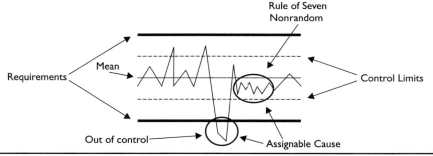

Figure 9-7   Control charts track trends over time for repetitive activities.

Every time the project is out of control it is considered an assignable cause, and there may be an investigation into the events surrounding the out of control measurement. Another assignable cause in this diagram is the Rule of Seven. The Rule of Seven applies whenever seven measurements in a row are on one side of the mean. This assignable cause, if it's lower than the mean, is a sign that there's a consistent problem or change in the project approach. When the Rule of Seven is on the positive side of the mean, it could be a signal that the mean is set too low or the project is performing better, so the mean could be raised to a new, higher level.

Another chart the project manager can create to help improve quality is a *Pareto chart*. This chart shows the distribution of defects within the project from a largest to smallest ranking. You've probably heard of the Italian macroeconomist Vilfredo Pareto in his Pareto's Law, sometimes called the 80/20 Rule. This rule states, for example, that 80 percent of your business comes from 20 percent of your customers.

Quality philosopher Joseph Juran popularized the Pareto chart, seen in Figure 9-8, as one of the key quality control charts. Each bar in the histogram is factor-ranked from most frequent to least frequent experiences. In theory, if the project manager and team attack the largest problem first, then the smaller problems should also diminish. This is because of Pareto's Law, where 80 percent of the problems, the symptoms of poor quality, are caused by 20 percent of the causes. By solving the most evident problems, the smaller problems are likely to be linked and should diminish as well.

Controlling Project Communications

Just as the business analyst's duties revolve around communications, so too do the project manager's responsibilities. Every project should have a communications management plan—not that different from what you'll create as a business analyst. This

Figure 9-8
Pareto charts show categories of defects from quality control inspections.

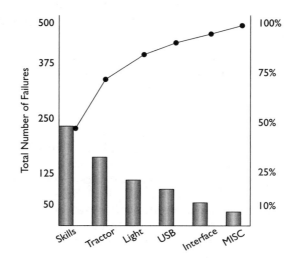

plan defines the information the stakeholders will expect and what the scenarios will be in the project to prompt communication. Good news, bad news, it doesn't matter; the project manager must communicate to the project stakeholders on a regular basis.

On larger projects the project manager can expect to communicate more information, to more people, and in more detail than in smaller, low priority projects. The more funds and time that an organization invests in a project, the more expectations management and customers will have on the project to report on how their investments are performing. Stakeholders do not like to be ignored—it's essential that the project manager create a system to quickly and accurately report project status.

Generally the project manager creates three reports on a regular basis for project stakeholders:

- **Status report** This report communicates how the project is performing overall, what objectives have been accomplished, and what activities are coming up in the project schedule. There will be updates on how vendors and project team members are performing and what deliverables and benefits have been created since the last status report.

- **Cost variance report** Whenever there is a variance in the project cost, the project manager should create a cost variance report. This report explains what the cost variance is, why the variance has occurred, and what the project manager is doing to prevent the problem from occurring again. The project manager may also recommend corrective actions for the project to recoup the costs, though this isn't always feasible.

- **Schedule variance report** Just as there are cost variance reports, so too are there schedule variance reports. These reports are generated whenever the project is slipping on the project schedule and include an explanation of the problem. Management and stakeholders are not looking for excuses, but reasons why a project is falling behind on scheduled activities and what the ramifications for the project may be.

 NOTE Variance reports are sometimes called exception reports, as there is an exception to the project plan.

Communication should be a regularly scheduled event for the project manager to perform and is part of the project schedule of events. Regular meetings such as project team meetings, conditional meetings such as at the end of project phases, and assessment meetings such as risk and performance reviews should all be scheduled in the project plan. The guidelines I discussed in Chapter 8 for meeting management are applicable to project managers, too.

All documented communication from the project manager to any stakeholder should become part of the project information management system. This knowledge retrieval process can help the project manager and team organize their promises, requirements, and requests to and from project stakeholders. This is helpful during quality control, scope validation, and during the project closeout for reference. All of this communiqué will become part of the project archives for future reference.

Closing the Project

Closing out the project is more than just putting the finishing touches on the project deliverables. In fact, those finishing touches to the things the project creates don't even happen in the official project closing processes—they happen back in project execution. Closing the project is a formality to closing out the project records, passing the project deliverables off to operations, and closing out the project contracts.

An organization can, technically, close out the entire project, or they can close out phases of the project, whichever is most appropriate. When an organization closes out phases of a project, they're usually in a large, long-term project where it's more practical to close out a phase of a project before starting a new one. You'll experience this when there are stages of deliverables the organization can put to use in the project. Staged deliverables are sometimes called benefits management, and it helps the organization to begin receiving a return for the investment in the project.

Some organizations also close out phases of a project to review the project performance to date. This is normal when it's a vendor completing a project for another organization, and each project phase is linked to a payment for the work delivered to date and a cash infusion to carry the project forward into the next phases of the project life cycle.

At some point, thankfully, all projects are officially and finally closed. This can be as informal or formal as the organization demands. For most projects it's best to have a formal closure, as it signals that the project is done and won't continue to go on and on supporting the deliverables the project created. Officially closing the project ends the project manager's responsibilities and shifts the deliverables into operations.

Closing a Project Contract

Throughout the project the project manager may rely on vendors to provide goods and services so the project can complete its objectives. Every vendor agreement is backed by a contract that specifies the terms for the project delivery, payment, and post-project support, such as a warranty when appropriate. The contract will also detail the closing processes, penalties for lateness, claim management, and sometimes a bonus structure for completing the project work early, a percentage of cost savings, or quality improvements.

When an organization is completing a project for another company, such as an IT integrator that develops software for others, the contract dictates how the project is considered final. The terms of the contract may include the acceptance of the project, allowances for change, post-implementation support, and payment details. The vendor should communicate regularly with the project customer on the status of the project and report anticipated project closure dates. Whenever a contract is involved, the terms of the contract override all other promises.

The closure of a contract is no time for negotiations—that should have happened at the start of the contractual relationship. Both the vendor and the client must live by the terms of the contract; payments, deliveries, and fulfillment of obligations by both parties is mandatory. When one or both parties believe that the other party has not lived up to their agreements in the contractual relationship, the situation could escalate to lawsuits between the two parties. The contract should, and most do, even have the terms for where the lawsuit may be filed. That's no fun for anyone.

Officially Closing a Project

When it comes to officially closing a project, every organization is different. Different forms, reviews, and procedures dictate how the project manager can consider the project closed. The rules that govern how a project manager closes the project are called the enterprise environmental factors. These rules set the expectations of communication, reviews, and documentation the project manager and sometimes the project team are expected to perform.

The project manager may also be responsible for reviewing the project team members' performance on the project. In these instances management, human resources, and, if appropriate, the project management office may have forms and procedures the project manager is to use to review each project team member's contributions to the project. A popular approach for project management performance reviews is the 360° appraisal, in which every person on the project team reviews all of the other participants in the project—including the project manager. This approach helps management find trends, make accurate assessments, and takes some of the review pressure off of the project manager.

The success of the project is based on more than declaring the project closed. Work performance information is the true reflection of the project success. Factors such as time, cost, quality, and issues that were resolved within the project are all measured to determine how successfully the project truly performed. These factors, however, should be established early in the project so the project manager and the project team know what they're graded on. It's not fair for one of the factors to be how many reports the project manager generated on Tuesdays if she didn't know that was a factor for success.

Projects do create goods and services for the project customer, but they also create other deliverables: documentations, plans, and lessons learned. These things should be catalogued, referenced in a knowledge management system, organized, and archived as part of historical information for future project managers. Historical information is considered a project deliverable and can help project managers estimate better, learn from past mistakes, and save time on future projects.

 NOTE I'm constantly amazed at how many companies do not archive their data for future usage. This is information the company has paid to have created, and it's shifted off to a random hallway closet like an old coat never to be used again.

Administrative closure is the final act of organizing all of the project data for archiving, but it's also the generation of the project final report. This report identifies all that the project created, the successes and failures within the project, and, when appropriate, recommendations for project deliverable updates, such as a bug list. The final report should also include a project certificate of completion that the project sponsor, key project stakeholders, and the project manager should all sign. And that's the end of the project.

Chapter Summary

Projects, you now know, are temporary undertakings. They create deliverables for your project stakeholders. They are not part of operations, though management, stakeholders, and customers often depend on the deliverables the project promises to create. Projects, for the most part, are based on the work of the business analyst, the requirements documentation, and the desires of the project stakeholders. Project management is a tricky, but rewarding, profession.

Projects are initiated by the project sponsor, and the project charter starts the official project. The project charter is the document that authorizes the project to exist within the organization, and the project sponsor is the person with the power to assign the project manager the resources the project needs to reach its conclusion. The project charter sets the high-level vision for the project. A more detailed document, the preliminary project scope statement, may be created during project initiation. This document is based largely on the requirements documentation and defines initial project risks, constraints, and assumptions that the project manager will need to manage.

Once the project shifts into planning, the official project scope statement is defined. This document clearly states the objectives of the project, the requirements for customer acceptance, the boundaries of the project, and the risks, constraints, and assumptions that have been identified to date. The project manager, the project team, the business analyst, and some key stakeholders develop the project management plan for all the project management knowledge areas. This group can also participate in the creation of the project Work Breakdown Structure.

Planning is an iterative process, and it is done throughout the project. Once enough of the project has been planned, the project team can go about executing the project work. Project execution is where the bulk of the project costs and time are spent. The project team is doing the work according to the project plans. Execution allows the project to move toward the project milestones, which show progress for the project.

The monitoring and controlling process group works in conjunction with the project execution. These processes ensure that the project is done according to plan. Scope, time, and costs are controlled, monitored, and responded to when situations warrant. This group also houses the ongoing quality control mechanisms to ensure that the project deliverables are of quality, and if they're not, when corrective actions are needed to fix the problems.

The project can shift from execution, to monitoring and controlling, and back to planning when needed. This transitional approach to project management allows the project manager plenty of flexibility in planning, executing changes, and responding to risks and issues within the project.

At the end of each phase of the project, the project manager can close out the project phase. This closure process is common for larger, tiered projects where the team will generate phased deliverables for the organization. Once all of the project requirements have been met, the project moves into the final closing processes. This is where the final report is generated, performance reviews are done, and the project is issued a certificate of completion. All of the project information, details, communication, and documentation should be organized and archived as part of the organization's historical information.

Key Terms

8/80 Rule   The 8/80 rule states that the smallest item in the WBS should take between 8 and 80 hours of labor to create.

Approval requirements   Someone will need to sign off on the project scope, project documents, costs, and schedules of the deliverables.

Budget estimate   Based on the details of the project scope, but it is somewhat unreliable; it has a range of variance of −10 percent to +25 percent on average.

Coercive power   When the project team believes the project manager can punish them for poor performance in the project, they may feel coerced into doing their assignments in the project.

Communications management plan   This plan defines who needs what information, when it is needed, and in what modality the stakeholders are expecting the communication. This plan can set requirements and conditions, such as cost and schedule variances, within the project that will prompt communication.

Configuration management requirements   Configuration management is the documentation, control, and management of the features and functions of the project deliverable. Configuration management defines the product scope and what the customer can expect as a result of the project work.

Control chart   A quality control chart to track trends in project execution.

Cost management plan   Defines how the project will be estimated, budgeted, and how changes to cost will be managed.

Cost variance reports   Whenever there is a variance in the project cost, the project manager should create a cost variance report. This report explains what the cost variance is, why the variance has occurred, and what the project manager is doing to prevent the problem from occurring again.

Crashing   Adding labor to a project to reduce the project duration; crashing adds costs because of the expense of added labor.

Critical path   The path in the network diagram that takes the longest amount of time to complete; the critical path cannot be delayed, or the project will be late.

Defect repair validation   The inspection of the work that has been repaired to ensure that it meets the quality expectations the project manager and the customer will have of the deliverable.

Definitive estimate   Based on the WBS. The definitive estimate is the most accurate cost estimate, but it requires the WBS to create; it has a typical range of variance from −5 percent to +10 percent.

Effort-driven activities   The more effort you apply, the faster the job will get done.

Expert power   This power exists when the project team and stakeholders recognize the project manager as an expert in the discipline the project centers on.

Fixed duration   Activities where it doesn't matter how much effort you add to the project, they'll still take a fixed amount of time to complete.

Formal power   This power, sometimes called positional power, is when a project manager is formally assigned the position of project manager. The project team may recognize the project manager as someone in charge of the project, but not necessarily someone who has any real power on the project.

Forming   This is when the project team first comes together, and team members are getting to know about each other. The group is simply forming based on the needs and competencies the project demands and the availability of the people in the organization to satisfy those needs.

Hard logic   The identification of activities that must be completed in a particular order.

Hygiene agents   From Herzberg's Theory of Motivation, these elements are the expectations all workers have: job security, a paycheck, clean and safe working conditions, sense of belonging, civil working relationships, and other basics associated with employment.

Initial project risks   Any initial risks that have been identified should be referenced and/or recorded here.

Initial Work Breakdown Structure   The Work Breakdown Structure (WBS) is a key deliverable in project management, and the initial WBS can help the project manager and project team do more detailed planning, estimating, and risk assessment.

Maslow's Hierarchy of Needs   A hierarchy of needs to identify what people need in their lives and what they work for. The hierarchy has five different layers: physiological, safety, social, esteem, and self-actualization.

McGregor's Theory of X and Y   States that management believes there are two broad perspectives of workers, good and bad. X is bad; these people need to be watched all the time, micromanaged, and distrusted. Y is considered good. Y people are self-led, motivated, and can accomplish new tasks proactively.

Milestone   A timeless event that shows project progress; milestones are typically created by completing a project phase.

Motivating agents   From Herzberg's Theory of Motivation, these are the elements that motivate people to excel. They include responsibility, appreciation of work, recognition, the chance to excel, education, and other opportunities associated with work besides financial rewards.

Norming   Once leaders, alliances, and acceptance have been settled in the project, the team can go about getting their work done.

Parametric estimate   A parameter that is used, such as cost per license or time per installation, to estimate the cost and/or duration of the current project.

Pareto chart   A histogram to show the distribution of failures within the project.

Performing   This is the ideal state for the project, when all the project team members settle into their roles and go about getting the work done. Petty differences are set aside, and the project team is hard at work accomplishing goals and moving the project toward completion.

Preliminary project scope statement   A project initiating document that defines, in broad terms, what the project is to accomplish.

Process improvement plan   This plan defines how the project processes will be monitored and documented for accuracy, efficiency, and improvement.

Procurement management plan   When a project needs to purchase materials, services, or other resources, this plan defines the process and procedures a project manager is to follow within the organization.

Product scope statement   This document defines the deliverable the customer is expecting.

Project boundaries   The things the project will not deliver.

Project charter   A document that authorizes the project to exist within the organization. It should be written by someone with the authority to grant the project manager authority over the resources the project needs to be successful.

Project communications management   Project managers, like business analysts, are communicators; projects demand constant communication.

Project cost management   Cost management requires the project funds be managed, controlled, and tracked, and fluctuations in project costs must be communicated.

Project human resources management   The management of the project human resources will vary by organization, but it takes people to complete the project work.

Project integration management   This special knowledge area coordinates the other eight knowledge areas.

Project network diagram   A diagram that shows the relationships between activities. Each node in the network diagram represents an activity, and the lines show the predecessors and successors of each activity.

Project procurement management   Projects may need to purchase items, hire additional staff, and/or perform work for other organizations through a contractual relationship.

Project quality management   Quality management is the assurance that the work is properly planned for project execution and then controlled to ensure the work is completed as it was planned.

Project risk management   This knowledge area identifies, documents, and analyzes the project risks in order to create risks responses.

Project scope management   This area defines, plans, and controls the project scope based on the business analyst's requirements.

Project time management   Time management is needed for both the project activities and the project management activities

Quality control   An inspection-driven process to make certain that the project team members are completing the project work according to the project plan.

Quality management plan   If your organization has a quality assurance program, then the requirements of that program will be defined herein; if not, a quality policy will be established for the project, and the quality control and quality assurance expectations will be defined.

Referent power   This power has a couple of different meanings. First, referent power is when the project manager refers to someone else's power to push through their project decisions. The second meaning is when the project team members are familiar with the project manager from past work, so there's already a relationship established between the project team member and the project manager.

Reward power   When the project team believes that the project manager can reward them for the work they complete on the project, they'll work accordingly. Reward power is tied to the announcement and ground rules for the project reward and recognition system.

Risk management plan   Risks need to be identified, documented, and recorded in the risk register. This plan defines the risk management activities including how risks will be qualitatively and quantitatively analyzed.

Risk response plan   A project manager can choose from seven risk responses, and this plan identifies each risk and the appropriate risk response based on the conditions of the project and the attributes of the risk event.

Rolling wave planning   Uses short bursts of planning and then short sprints of project execution.

Rough order of magnitude (ROM) cost estimate   The ROM estimate is a very high-level, unreliable cost estimate that "ballparks" the idea of what the project should cost.

Rough order of magnitude estimate   A broad, unreliable estimate.

Schedule management plan   This plan defines how the activity duration estimates will be created, what the project schedule is, and how changes to the schedule will be managed.

Schedule variance reports   These reports are generated whenever the project is slipping on the project schedule and includes an explanation of the problem.

Scope management plan   Defines how the project scope should be created, decomposed into the WBS, executed, monitored and controlled, and then validated.

Soft logic   The activities order of completion doesn't really matter.

Staffing management plan   Defines when the project team members will be brought onto the project, how and when they'll be utilized on the project, and when they'll be released from the project.

Status reports   This report communicates how the project is performing overall, what objectives have been accomplished, and what activities are coming up in the project schedule.

Storming   As the project team members struggle for power in the project, there may be some conflicts over who'll lead the project team, who'll follow the lead, and who's indifferent as long the project work gets done.

Top-down estimate   An estimate based on past projects to predict the current cost and/or duration of the current project.

WBS dictionary   The WBS dictionary is a companion document to the WBS and reflects all of the work packages in the WBS. The WBS dictionary defines all of the components of the WBS, the required resources, and references any information that can explain the deliverable in more detail.

William Ouchi's Theory Z   Sometimes called the Japanese management style, this is based on the participative management style of the Japanese. This theory states that workers are motivated by a sense of commitment, opportunity, and advancement.

Work package   The smallest item in the WBS; it is the smallest thing that the project team will put effort forth to create.

Questions

1. An organization would like to launch a new project to develop new software. They have worked with you, the business analyst, to develop project requirements. What's the first document they'll need to create to authorize this project?

   A. Contract

   B. Project scope statement

   C. Project charter

   D. Project statement of work

2. You have created the requirements for a new business opportunity. Your organization agrees with your findings and would like to create a new project. The project manager has been identified, and the newly formed project team is working with you, the business analyst, to understand all of the project requirements. What document should the project team and the project manager create that will define the high-level goals of the project, the initial project risks, project milestones, and even an initial WBS?

   A. Project charter

   B. Project requirements document

   C. Risk impact statement

   D. Preliminary project scope statement

3. Which project management plan addresses how changes to the project management team can occur? This includes adding people to the project team and removing people from the project team.

   A. Staffing management plan

   B. Human resource management plan

   C. Scope management plan

   D. Communications management plan

4. You are working with the project manager for a high-profile project for your organization. A stakeholder has introduced a new value-added change request for the project, although the project is already in project execution. The change is deemed to be valuable, and you think it should be approved. What project process can help determine if the change is worthy and the project scope should be updated?

   A. Scope management planning processes.

   B. Integrated change control.

   C. Configuration management system.

   D. A new change cannot be introduced to this project at this time, because the project is already in project execution.

5. A project manager is working with the project manager, the business analyst, and the key stakeholders to decompose the project into deliverables. The goal is to break down the project scope into smaller items that are easier to plan for. What is this process of breaking down the project scope called?

   A. WBS dictionary

   B. Work packages

   C. Scope control and management

   D. Decomposition

6. A project manager has been working with you and the project team to break down the project scope. She wants to be certain not to break down the scope into deliverables that are too small, nor does she want to leave elements too large. What heuristic can this project manager use to guide the scope breakdown?

   A. Pareto's Law

   B. 80/20 Rule

   C. 8/80 Rule

   D. Scope decomposition

7. A project manager is breaking down the project scope into smaller, more manageable components. What is the smallest element in the WBS called?

   A. Deliverable

   B. Work package

   C. Activity

   D. Project requirement

8. A project manager is estimating the costs for the project. This project is to install 17,544 new office doors in several skyscraper buildings. Each door is to be installed a particular way and will cost the organization $566 per door. If the project manager is using a parametric estimate, how much will the installation of the doors cost?

   A. There is not enough information to know.

   B. $566 per door.

   C. It depends on how many stories are in the skyscraper.

   D. $9,929,904.

9. There are several stages to team development that the project manager can attempt to facilitate. In what stage of team development does the project team go about the business of getting the project work done?

   A. Forming

   B. Norming

    C. Storming

    D. Performing

10. You are working with a project manager who has years of experience in software development. The project team respects the opinion and advice of the project manager, and they are eager to learn from the project manager based on his experience. What type of power would you deem that this project manager has?

    A. Expert power

    B. Reward power

    C. Referent power

    D. Coercive power

11. If you subscribe to Maslow's Hierarchy of Needs, you know that workers all work in order to fulfill certain needs. In Maslow's Hierarchy, all of the following are needs except for which one?

    A. Esteem

    B. Social

    C. Affiliation

    D. Safety

12. You are working with a project manager who wants to identify the things that will motivate the project team members to complete their assignments on the project. What organizational theory subscribes to the theory of hygiene agents and motivating agents?

    A. Herzberg's Theory of Motivation

    B. Maslow's Hierarchy of Needs

    C. McGregor's Theory of X and Y

    D. William Ouchi's Theory Z

13. You are the business analyst of the NHG Project. Your project stakeholders have identified a new requirement that is needed in the project, although the project is in project execution. You submit the change request to the project manager, and after a review, the change is agreed to as long as the stakeholders will pay for the additional costs and allow time to incorporate the change request. The stakeholders willingly agree, so the project manager updates the project scope, the WBS, and the activity list to reflect the change. The project manager must also update all of the following as part of this change request except for which one?

    A. Project cost baseline

    B. Project WBS

    C. Project network diagram

    D. Project charter

14. A project manager has created the project WBS, and it has been approved by the stakeholders. Management has now asked the project manager to create a visual representation of the flow of project activities to create the deliverables the WBS promises. What document will the project manager create in response to management's request?

A. WBS dictionary

B. Project network diagram

C. Activity relationship diagram

D. Activity list

15. You are working with a project manager to track the results of inspection for a manufacturing project. The project manager presents you with a chart as seen in the following illustration. What does the highlighted area in the illustration represent?

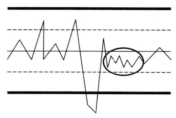

A. Defect

B. Risk

C. Quality issue testing

D. Rule of Seven

16. A project manager and a vendor are in a disagreement about the installation of new hardware for the project. The vendor believes that the project manager's team is to install the operating system and configure the device, while the project manager believes the responsibility of configuration is with the vendor. This is an example of which one of the following?

A. Risk

B. Issue

C. Litigation

D. Claim

17. You are working with a project manager on the JJJ Project. The project has delivered all of the project deliverables, the stakeholders are thrilled with the project, and they have signed the certificate of completion. What should the project manager do next?

   A. Ask for payment.

   B. Complete the final project report on why the project failed.

   C. Archive the project records.

   D. Determine the project final cost.

18. You are working with a project manager who threatens the project team if they don't complete their project assignments. The project manager insists that this method is effective and keeps the project team on schedule. While his method does work, you can tell the project team feels threatened around the project manager. What type of power is this project manager using?

   A. Reward power

   B. Expert power

   C. Coercive power

   D. Mitigating power

19. You are the business analyst for the KQL Project. This project is going along fine as the milestones are reached as planned, the deliverables are meeting quality expectations, and there are little variances on project costs or schedule. The stakeholders, however, have decided they'd like the project a month earlier than the schedule allows. What approach can the project manager take to attempt to complete the project faster than planned?

   A. Crash the project.

   B. Reduce the project costs.

   C. Use earned value management.

   D. Stop quality inspections to save time.

20. Sarah is the project manager of the JQH Project. She has created a project network diagram and is showing you, the business analyst for the project, the critical path in the project. What is the critical path?

   A. It is a path in the project network diagram that hosts the most important project activities.

   B. It is the longest path of duration in the project network diagram.

   C. It is the path in the project network diagram that has the most risks.

   D. It is the path in the project network diagram that uses the most costs.

Questions and Answers

1. An organization would like to launch a new project to develop new software. They have worked with you, the business analyst, to develop project requirements. What's the first document they'll need to create to authorize this project?

   A. Contract

   B. Project scope statement

   C. Project charter

   D. Project statement of work

   C. The project charter is the document the project manager needs to officially authorize the project in an organization. A is incorrect, as not all projects will require a contract—even those that do still need a project charter. B is wrong, as the project scope statement comes after the project charter has been created. D is incorrect, as the project statement of work is not needed on every project. When it is created, it is an input to the project charter creation.

2. You have created the requirements for a new business opportunity. Your organization agrees with your findings and would like to create a new project. The project manager has been identified, and the newly formed project team is working with you, the business analyst, to understand all of the project requirements. What document should the project team and the project manager create that will define the high-level goals of the project, the initial project risks, project milestones, and even an initial WBS?

   A. Project charter

   B. Project requirements document

   C. Risk impact statement

   D. Preliminary project scope statement

   D. The preliminary project scope statement is created during project initiation and defines the high-level objectives of the project. A is incorrect, as a project charter does not include the initial WBS. B is incorrect, as the project requirements document precedes the project. C is incorrect, as risk impact statements are project management deliverables created during project planning—after the scope statement has been approved.

3. Which project management plan addresses how changes to the project management team can occur? This includes adding people to the project team and removing people from the project team.

   A. Staffing management plan

   B. Human resource management plan

   C. Scope management plan

   D. Communications management plan

    A. The staffing management plan defines how staff members will be brought onto and released from the project team. B is incorrect, as the human resource management plan is not a valid project management plan. C is incorrect, as the project scope management plan defines how the project scope will be defined, managed, and controlled. D is incorrect, as the project communications management plan defines who needs what information, when the information is needed, and the expected modality of the information.

4. You are working with the project manager for a high-profile project for your organization. A stakeholder has introduced a new value-added change request for the project, although the project is already in project execution. The change is deemed to be valuable, and you think it should be approved. What project process can help determine if the change is worthy and the project scope should be updated?

    A. Scope management planning processes.

    B. Integrated change control.

    C. Configuration management system.

    D. A new change cannot be introduced to this project at this time, because the project is already in project execution.

    B. The integrated change control system examines all of the project knowledge areas to determine the full impact of the change on the project. A is incorrect, as the scope management planning processes do include how changes to the scope may happen and more—but the question is asking for a specific process. C is incorrect; the configuration management system controls and documents changes to the project scope. D is also incorrect, as changes can, and often do, enter the project during execution.

5. A project manager is working with the project manager, the business analyst, and the key stakeholders to decompose the project into deliverables. The goal is to break down the project scope into smaller items that are easier to plan for. What is this process of breaking down the project scope called?

    A. WBS dictionary

    B. Work packages

    C. Scope control and management

    D. Decomposition

    D. Decomposition is the correct term to describe breaking down the project scope into smaller, manageable components. A is incorrect, as the WBS dictionary is a companion document to the WBS that defines the characteristics of each work package—which is the same thing as choice B. Choice C, scope control and management, is incorrect, as scope control and management is a project management knowledge area.

6. A project manager has been working with you and the project team to break down the project scope. She wants to be certain to not break down the scope into deliverables that are too small, nor does she want to leave elements too large. What heuristic can this project manager use to guide the scope breakdown?

A. Pareto's Law

B. 80/20 Rule

C. 8/80 Rule

D. Scope decomposition

C. The 8/80 Rule is a heuristic that can guide the project team to create work packages that will not take more than 80 hours or fewer than 8 hours of labor to create. A is incorrect, as Pareto's Law is the 80/20 Law of economics—which is the same thing as choice B. D is incorrect, as scope decomposition is the process of creating the WBS.

7. A project manager is breaking down the project scope into smaller, more manageable components. What is the smallest element in the WBS called?

A. Deliverable

B. Work package

C. Activity

D. Project requirement

B. The smallest element in the WBS is called the work package. A is incorrect; while the work package may relate to a project deliverable, the smallest item is technically called the work package. C is incorrect; the WBS helps the project team create the activity list where you'll find project activities. D is incorrect; project requirements help build the project scope.

8. A project manager is estimating the costs for the project. This project is to install 17,544 new office doors in several skyscraper buildings. Each door is to be installed a particular way and will cost the organization $566 per door. If the project manager is using a parametric estimate, how much will the installation of the doors cost?

A. There is not enough information to know.

B. $566 per door.

C. It depends on how many stories are in the skyscraper.

D. $9,929,904.

D. If the project manager is using a parametric estimate, he can multiply the number of doors, 17,544, by the cost of each door, $566, for a total of $9,929,904—those are some expensive doors. A, B, and C are all incorrect, as the parametric estimate always uses a parameter to predict cost. It can also be used to predict time, such as 4 hours per door to install.

9. There are several stages to team development that the project manager can attempt to facilitate. In what stage of team development does the project team go about the business of getting the project work done?

   A. Forming

   B. Norming

   C. Storming

   D. Performing

   D. Performing is when the team settles into their roles and gets the project work done. Forming, A, is when the team first comes together. B, norming, is when things settle down and the project team accepts their role and position in the project. C, storming, is when there's competition, debate, and determination of who'll lead and who'll follow.

10. You are working with a project manager who has years of experience in software development. The project team respects the opinion and advice of the project manager, and they are eager to learn from the project manager based on his experience. What type of power would you deem that this project manager has?

    A. Expert power

    B. Reward power

    C. Referent power

    D. Coercive power

    A. When a project manager is an expert in a discipline that the project uses, that project manager is using expert power. B, reward power, is when the project team believes the project manager can reward them for their work. C, referent power, is when the project manager uses someone else's power to move project decisions forward. It's also a reference to how project team members may already know the project manager, but in this instance the project manager is clearly an expert. D, coercive power, is when the project team feels threatened by the project manager.

11. If you subscribe to Maslow's Hierarchy of Needs, you know that workers all work in order to fulfill certain needs. In Maslow's Hierarchy all of the following are needs except for which one?

    A. Esteem

    B. Social

    C. Affiliation

    D. Safety

    C. Affiliation, as nice as it may be, is not one of Maslow's identified needs. Choices A, B, and D are incorrect, as these are three of the five needs. The other two needs in Maslow's Hierarchy are physiological and self-actualization.

12. You are working with a project manager who wants to identify the things that will motivate the project team to complete their assignments on the project. What organizational theory subscribes to the theory of hygiene agents and motivating agents?

    A. Herzberg's Theory of Motivation

    B. Maslow's Hierarchy of Needs

    C. McGregor's Theory of X and Y

    D. William Ouchi's Theory Z

    A. The Herzberg Theory of Motivation uses hygiene agents, things that are expected as part of the work agreement, and motivating agents, which promote performance. Maslow's Hierarchy of Needs identifies five needs that we all have, so choice B is incorrect. C, McGregor's Theory of X and Y, is a management perspective of workers. D, William Ouchi's Theory Z, is also known as the Japanese management style and promotes a familial, participative approach.

13. You are the business analyst of the NHG Project. Your project stakeholders have identified a new requirement that is needed in the project, although the project is in project execution. You submit the change request to the project manager, and after a review, the change is agreed to as long as the stakeholders will pay for the additional costs and allow time to incorporate the change request. The stakeholders willingly agree, so the project manager updates the project scope, the WBS, and the activity list to reflect the change. The project manager must also update all of the following as part of this change request except for which one?

    A. Project cost baseline

    B. Project WBS

    C. Project network diagram

    D. Project charter

    D. The project charter is not updated once it's created. Choices A, B, and C are all incorrect, as these are components that should be updated as a result of the scope change.

14. A project manager has created the project WBS, and it has been approved by the stakeholders. Management has now asked the project manager to create a visual representation of the flow of project activities to create the deliverables the WBS promises. What document will the project manager create in response to management's request?

    A. WBS dictionary

    B. Project network diagram

    C. Activity relationship diagram

    D. Activity list

B. Management is asking the project manager to create a project network diagram to reflect the flow of activities in the project. A, the WBS dictionary, is a companion document to the WBS that details the project work packages. C is not a valid project management term. D is also incorrect, as the activity list does not show the relationship of project activities, just a list of work to be done.

15. You are working with a project manager to track the results of inspection for a manufacturing project. The project manager presents you with a chart as seen in the following illustration. What does the highlighted area in the illustration represent?

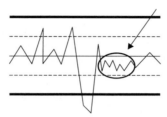

   A. Defect

   B. Risk

   C. Quality issue testing

   D. Rule of Seven

   D. The highlighted area represents the Rule of Seven. The Rule of Seven means that you have seven measurements in a row all on one side of the mean in a control chart. A is incorrect, as the measurements do not necessarily indicate there is a defect. B is incorrect; this is not a risk. C is incorrect; the control chart is part of quality control, but it's acting properly so this is not a testing issue.

16. A project manager and a vendor are in a disagreement about the installation of new hardware for the project. The vendor believes that the project manager's team is to install the operating system and configure the device, while the project manager believes the responsibility of configuration is with the vendor. This is an example of which one of the following?

   A. Risk

   B. Issue

   C. Litigation

   D. Claim

   D. When the buyer and seller are in disagreement about the terms of the contract or its deliverables, it is considered a claim. A is incorrect, as risk does not fully define the situation the project manager and vendor are experiencing. B is incorrect; issues are events, possibly risks, that have not been fully analyzed. C, litigation, may transpire if these two go to court over the claim.

17. You are working with a project manager on the JJJ Project. The project has delivered all of the project deliverables, the stakeholders are thrilled with the project, and they have signed the certificate of completion. What should the project manager do next?

A. Ask for payment.

B. Complete the final project report on why the project failed.

C. Archive the project records.

D. Determine the project final cost.

C. When the project is completely done, the project manager should archive all of the project records for future historical information. A is incorrect; payment requests are dictated by the contract terms, and this question does not stipulate that there is a contractual relationship. B is incorrect; the project has not failed. D is incorrect, as this information is part of the project final report.

18. You are working with a project manager who threatens the project team if they don't complete their project assignments. The project manager insists that this method is effective and keeps the project team on schedule. While his method does work, you can tell the project team feels threatened around the project manager. What type of power is this project manager using?

A. Reward power

B. Expert power

C. Coercive power

D. Mitigating power

C. Whenever the project team is afraid or threatened by the project manager, it is considered coercive power. A is incorrect; reward power is when the project team believes the project manager can reward the team for their work. B is incorrect; expert power is when the project team sees the project manager as an expert. D, mitigating power, is not a valid project management power.

19. You are the business analyst for the KQL Project. This project is going along fine as the milestones are reached as planned, the deliverables are meeting quality expectations, and there are little variances on project costs or schedule. The stakeholders, however, have decided they'd like the project a month earlier than the schedule allows. What approach can the project manager take to attempt to complete the project faster than planned?

A. Crash the project.

B. Reduce the project costs.

C. Use earned value management.

D. Stop quality inspections to save time.

A. Crashing the project adds project resources to the project to shorten the project duration. B, reduce the project costs, seems like a good idea, but costs are not an issue in this instance. In addition, cost reduction usually does not contribute to a shorter project duration. C is incorrect; earned value management is a suite of formulas to show project performance, not to reduce duration. D is not valid, as stopping quality inspections will reduce the overall quality of the project deliverables.

20. Sarah is the project manager of the JQH Project. She has created a project network diagram and is showing you, the business analyst for the project, the critical path in the project. What is the critical path?

    A. It is a path in the project network diagram that hosts the most important project activities.

    B. It is the longest path of duration in the project network diagram.

    C. It is the path in the project network diagram that has the most risks.

    D. It is the path in the project network diagram that uses the most costs.

    B. The critical path is the longest path in the project network diagram. This path cannot be delayed, or the project will miss its scheduled end date. A, C, and D are all wrong, as these answers do not reflect the project critical path.

CHAPTER 10

Passing the CBAP Examination

In this chapter you will
- Prepare to pass the CBAP exam
- Create CBAP study sheets
- Learn test-passing secrets
- Review the CBAP exam objectives
- Summarize the CBAP key facts

I bet you're ready to get the CBAP examination over with—after all, you've a life beyond business analysis. Just like requirements gathering, preparing for the CBAP takes time, attention to detail, and a logical approach to the objectives. Many CBAP candidates that I meet feel added pressure from their clients, bosses, friends, but most of all from themselves. You and I probably have a similar goal when it comes to your CBAP exam: pass the thing on the first attempt, and get on with your life.

This chapter is the grand finale for all you've learned in this book. It captures all of the critical exam facts in one juicy spot. This chapter includes everything that you absolutely must know to pass the CBAP. I'm not saying that knowing only this chapter will guarantee a pass on the exam. I am saying, however, that not knowing this material will likely guarantee a fail on the exam. And you and I don't want that. This chapter will give you some strategies, tips, and secrets beyond just business analysis content for passing the exam.

Preparing to Pass the CBAP Exam

If you just want to take the CBAP exam, assuming that you qualify, you don't really have to study at all. Just complete the application, get approved, and drop some cash. And then show up and take it. Preparing to pass, however, is totally different. Anyone can take an exam, but not everyone can pass an exam. The key is to enter the test-taking arena with a positive and powerful mind-set that you mean business—and the business is to pass the exam on the first attempt.

What to Do First

You cannot study, cram, and prepare for this exam forever. So the first thing you need to do is schedule your exam. Pick a date in the not-so-distant future as a deadline to pass your exam. If you haven't scheduled your exam yet, get to work on the application. The International Institute of Business Analysis requires you to complete an application in order to determine if you qualify for the exam. This application process can take up to six weeks for the IIBA approval, so complete the application, and while the IIBA does their processing, you can finalize your exam prep. If you prepare for the exam and then submit the application, you're only delaying your certification and prolonging your misery.

Once your application is approved by IIBA, then you'll need to schedule the exam through Castle Worldwide (as of this writing). Even if you don't believe you're quite ready, choose a date and schedule the exam pass date. Not a date to take the exam, this is a date to pass the exam. This is your goal, your deadline, the pinnacle of your CBAP efforts. Do not take too long to pass your exam. All these facts, figures, and formulas have a funny way of oozing out of your head the longer you wait.

You're probably wondering how long you should study before you schedule the exam. If you've not submitted your application as of right now, you've at least 60 days before you can even squeeze into the testing center—and that figure is from the IIBA. This assumes you have all of your information ready to go and there's no snag between now and test day. Here's the deal—you probably have about 75 days before you can get into a test center from right now. You're smart—plan accordingly.

I don't want you to do anything foolish and schedule an immediate exam if you're not ready for it. By taking the end-of-chapter exams in this book and the two exams available on the CD-ROM, you should have a pretty good idea of where you stand as an exam candidate. When I teach my exam prep courses based on the exams in this book or in my *PMP Study Guide,* I set your goal as an 80 percent success rate on practice questions. It's much higher than the IIBA requirements, but I feel that if someone can score an 80 on my goofy questions, they should be in alignment to pass the IIBA's goofy exam.

Take some time and look over your end-of-chapter exam scores from this book. You should have a quick SWOT analysis of your exams. And you know that SWOT is your strengths, weaknesses, opportunities, and threats. Most people, I've learned, do very well on questions that are bunched together by topic—like the chapter exams you've completed. However, it's tougher to recall the information when the question topics are all scrambled as they are on the CD—and on the CBAP examination.

What to Do Second

Now that you're excited about passing your exam, let's get on to the meaty stuffy. As soon as you've submitted your exam application, you're on your way to the test date. I recommend that you first look at your energy level. In my opinion (and based on my experience), if you're eating junk food, drinking barrels of scotch, and smoking stinky cigars, you're probably not going to feel all that great for studying. I'm no doctor, but you and I know what'll make you feel well, rested, and sharper for your exam efforts:

- *Exercise your body and your brain.* Study is hard work, and it can exhaust your brain. Get some balance and exhaust your body, too. Find time to go for a jog, lift weights, take a swim, or do whatever workout routine works best for you. Your brain works better when your body works well.

- *Put down the fries, pizza, and beer.* If you eat healthy food, you'll feel good—and feel better about yourself. Be certain to drink plenty of water, and don't overdo the caffeine. (I'm such a nag, I know.)

- *You don't need late nights, you need sleep.* You'll feel tired anyway from all of your exercise and studying. I find that when I have a well-rested brain, I have a sharp brain (and yes, I'm talking about my brain, not Abby Normal's brain, for you *Young Frankenstein* fanatics). You don't want to sit for your exam feeling tired, sluggish, and worn out.

- *Put this book down and turn on the television.* Balance really is the key to so much in life. You should not overdo your study sessions—marathon cram sessions aren't that effective. In addition, try to study every day at the same time as your exam is scheduled.

You could, for example, pick a date ten weeks from now for your exam day. That gives you plenty of time to prepare the exam application, submit the application, and for our pals at the IIBA to approve your application. Over the next ten weeks you could carve out an hour a day and study for this exam. You could read this book; complete all the exams once, twice, or eight times; create flashcards; and work out like Rocky Balboa all in the next ten weeks. Create a schedule of what you need to do and then do it.

Create a CBAP Cheat Sheet

Test anxiety haunts many adults. After all, when was the last time you took an intense exam? Most professionals that I meet haven't taken an exam in years and years. This only magnifies the test anxiety and makes it tougher to remember all the CBAP facts and formulas. Here's your secret weapon: a page of notes. If you could take one page of notes into the exam, what information would you like on this one-page document? Of course you absolutely cannot take any notes or reference materials into the exam area. However, if you can create and memorize one sheet of notes, you absolutely may re-create this once you're seated in the exam area.

 For a more detailed explanation, watch the Passing the CBAP Exam video now.

With this book, your copy of the BABOK, and any notes you've already created, you need to create a cheat sheet that you can create from memory in the testing center. Practice creating a reference sheet so that you can immediately, and legally, re-create this document once your exam has begun. In the testing facility, you'll be supplied with several sheets of blank paper and a couple of pencils. Once your exam begins, re-create your reference sheet. You know which concepts, formulas, and facts are the toughest for you—put those on your cheat sheet.

Work Smart—Not Hard

Six knowledge areas are on the CBAP exam, and some info is worth more than others. You want to study smart and adjust your study efforts for the categories of the exam where you'll find the most questions. Table 10-1 reflects each knowledge area, the exam percentage, the approximate number of questions you'll face, and which chapter in this book correlates to which knowledge area from largest number of questions to smallest.

Focus your study efforts on the chapters that'll have the most questions; Chapter 2 and Chapter 5 are almost half of the exam content. There's a hint—know these chapters, and you're well on your way. But that doesn't mean you should breeze over the other chapters. I bet you're already pretty good at communicating based on what you do as a business analyst, so there's some relative knowledge that you could brush up on and have 16 more questions in your favor.

 NOTE I strongly encourage you to check with IIBA's web site (www.theiiba. org) for the most recent exam details. While Table 10-1 is correct as of this writing, the information could change by the time you read this. If the objectives and exam distribution of questions have changed, adjust your study plans accordingly. Study the objectives the most that are the most valuable to your passing score.

Knowledge Area	Percent of Exam Questions	Number of Questions	Chapter Reference
Business Analysis Planning and Monitoring	22.7%	35	Chapter 2
Elicitation	18.7%	28	Chapter 3
Requirements Management and Communication	10.7%	16	Chapter 4
Enterprise Analysis	22%	33	Chapter 5
Requirements Analysis	20.7%	31	Chapter 6
Solution Assessment and Validation	5.3%	8	Chapter 7

Table 10-1 Exam Requirements, Questions, and Chapter Reference

My message is to take what you already know and to exploit that to help you pass the exam. For example, if you're most confident in solution assessment and validation, which only equates to eight exam questions, you'll need to relate the information to the other domains. Perhaps you can mentally match the validation of the solution with the process associated with the original creation of the requirements, so now the "Requirements Analysis and Documentation" exam details become clearer. Take what you know and grow from there.

Answering the CBAP Questions

You can expect some trick questions on your CBAP exam. Sorry. I think you'll find that the questions on your upcoming exam can be verbose and may offer a few red herrings. I tried to create some tricky test questions in the book to help prepare you for those on the exam. I really want you to take your time and think about what the question is asking. For example, you may face questions that ask, "All of the following are correct options expect for which one?" The question wants you to find the incorrect option, or the option that would be inappropriate for the scenario described.

Some questions may give you a long plot that has little to do with what the question is asking. You only have to answer the question, not what's implied in the novella behind the question, so be sure to understand what the question is asking for. It's easy to focus on the scenario presented in a question and then see a suitable option for that scenario in the answer. The trouble is, if the question is asking you to identify an option that is unsuitable, then you just missed the question. Take your time and really read and ponder each question, not the scenario. You do not get extra points for getting done early.

 NOTE I tell people in my seminars to slow down and then slow down a little more. That's my best exam advice. You have 3 hours to complete the exam, so use it all. Haste makes waste. I sometimes say it's like when I go play golf. I really get my money's worth, take lots of swings, and use the whole course.

Here's a tip that can work with many of the questions: identify what the question wants for an answer, and then look for an option that doesn't belong with the other possible answers. In other words, find the answer that doesn't fit with the other three options. Find the "odd man out." Here's an example: Deliverables from the Business Architecture initiative can include all of the following except for which one?

    A. Strategic plans

    B. Business unit goals

    C. Closing phase

    D. Business product lines

Notice how options A, B, and D are things while C is a project phase? If you choose A, strategic plans, it implies that the other options are not deliverables. The odd man out then is C, the closing phase. It's considered the "odd" choice because it, by itself, is not a project deliverable; it's a type of activity in a project. Of course, this tip won't work with every question—but it's handy to keep in mind.

For some answer choices, it may seem that two of the four options are both possibly correct answers. However, because you may choose only one answer, you must discern which answer is the best choice. Within the question, there will usually be some hint describing the progress of the work, the requirements of the stakeholders, or some other clue that can help you determine which answer is the best for the question. As a general rule, always choose what's best for the stakeholders collectively, not individually.

Answer Every Question—Once

The CBAP exam has 150 questions. You don't have to answer every question correctly, just enough to pass. In other words, don't waste 2 of your 3 hours laboring over one question—difficult questions and easy questions are worth the same amount in your exam. Never leave a question blank; a question without an answer is a wrong answer. It is better to guess than to leave an answer blank. As you move through the exam and you find questions that stump you, use the "mark question" option in the exam software, choose an answer you suspect may be correct, and then move on. When you have answered all of the questions, you are given the option to review your marked questions.

NOTE When I take exams and have to guess for an answer (yep, that happens to me, too), I always choose B. I'm not saying that choice B is used more than others, I just don't shuffle guesses around. I think sometimes B will be correct and sometimes it won't. By choosing B every time I have to guess, I increase my odds that some of my guesses will eventually, in theory, be correct about 25 percent of the time.

Some questions in the exam may prompt your memory to come up with answers to other questions you have marked for review. However, resist the temptation to review those questions you've already answered with confidence and haven't marked. Stick with your gut instinct; more often than not, your first choice is the correct choice. If you want to test that theory, look over your exam scores from this book. Did you change answers more often to wrong or to correct choices?

Use the Process of Elimination

Just because you don't know the answer to a question doesn't mean you must guess the answer. You can use some deductive reasoning to increase your odds of answering the question correctly. If you were to guess A out of ABCD, you'd have a 25 percent chance of being correct. But for every answer you can safely rule out of consideration, you'll increase your odds of answering correctly.

When you're stumped on a question, use the process of elimination. You know each question has four choices. On your scratch paper, write down "ABCD." If you can safely rule out A, cross it out of the "ABCD" you've written on your paper. You have just increased your odds of guessing correctly from one in four to one in three. Now focus on which of the other answers won't work. If you determine that C won't work, cross it off your list. Now you've got a 50-50 chance of finding the correct choice. If you can rule out D, then you know that the correct choice must be choice B, even if you don't know why.

If you cannot determine which answer is best, B or D in this instance, here's the best approach:

1. Choose an answer in the exam (no blank answers, remember?).
2. Mark the question in the exam software for later review.
3. Circle the "ABCD" on your scratch paper, jot any relevant notes, and then record the question number next to the notes.
4. During the review, or from a later question, you may realize which choice is the better of the two answers. Return to mark the question and confirm that the best answer is selected.

Everything You Must Know

As promised, this section covers all of the information you must know going into the CBAP exam. This section contains snippets from all the chapters you've read in this book (assuming you've read all the chapters up to here). You can use this information as a quick recap of what to expect on your exam. You should review this material, create flashcards, and even make up your own practice questions. Here goes.

Managing and Planning Requirements

Requirements planning is at the heart of business analysis duties. You'll have 35 questions on this exam objective. These topics are the most essential from that chapter as you prepare to pass your CBAP exam.

First off, be familiar with your business analysis team roles. Typical team roles you should know for your CBAP examination are shown in Table 10-2.

Role	Role Description	Responsibility
Application architect	This role defines the technical direction for the project solution, creates the architectural approach, and serves as project expert for the project solution structure.	Responsible for choosing and designing the architectural approach, high-level application design, and requirements review.
Business analyst	Smart, good-looking individual who elicits, documents, and reviews the requirements for projects. This role is the key facilitator for requirements gathering, planning, and communicating.	Responsible for the identification, documentation, and management of requirements. The business analyst will also manage requirements modifications and the change approval process.
Database analyst	This role, sometimes called the DBA, designs, creates, and maintains databases for the project.	Responsible for the creation, management, configuration, design, and performance of any databases interacting with the project work, deliverables, or requirements.
Developer	The technical resource within the project; may serve as a designer, tester, coder, application developer, or other job titles. Developers help plan the operational transfer of the deliverable to the user.	Participates in the requirements review, sign-off, and project deliverables approval and validation processes.
End user	The recipient and user of the project deliverables.	Participates during the requirements gathering process; may participate in user acceptability testing and pilot groups.
Executive sponsor	Responsible for the project funding, go/no-go decisions, resource support. Approves schedules, budgets, and chief decisions. This role may also be known as the solution owner, project sponsor, or champion.	Approves the requirements and the management processes.

Table 10-2 Roles and Responsibilities Should Be Clearly Identified

Role	Role Description	Responsibility
Information architect	This role, sometimes called the data modeler, helps assess the data requirements of a project, identifies data assets, and helps the project team complete data modeling requirements.	Identifies data requirements; involved in the requirements' review, approval, and modification processes.
Infrastructure analyst	This role designs the hardware, software, and technical infrastructure required for the project application development, operation requirements, and ongoing solution of the project.	Responsible for designing the hardware, software, and technical structure to conform to the project requirements.
Project manager	Manages the project management life cycle to ensure that the project team is completing the project work with quality and according to the project objectives and requirements. This role works with the business analyst, executive sponsor, and key stakeholders to gain approval on project deliverables.	Responsible for management of the project management life cycle, the project team work, facilitating deliverable approval processes, and the project success or failure.
Quality assurance analyst	This role maps the quality assurance requirements of the organization and the stakeholders to the project, ensures that the project deliverables meet the quality requirements, and works with the project manager and the project team on quality standards compliance.	Participates in requirements review, validation; ensures project deliverables adhere to quality standards and scope fulfillment.
Solution owner	This role approves the project scope statement, phase gate reviews, solution validations, scope changes, and project success criteria. This role may often be the same as the executive sponsor, though sometimes the project customer may serve in this role.	Provides requirements and information; approves functional requirements.

Table 10-2   Roles and Responsibilities Should Be Clearly Identified *(continued)*

Role	Role Description	Responsibility
Stakeholders	This role is fulfilled by anyone who is affected by the outcome of the project deliverables. Stakeholders who make decisions on the project, influence the project requirements, or contribute to the project are sometimes called key stakeholders.	The responsibilities shift depending on which stakeholder is identified.
Subject matter expert	This role is sometimes called the SME and consults the business analyst, project manager, and project team on decisions, directions, and other information needed to elicit requirements and build the project deliverables. This role can be someone on the project team, someone within the organization who provides expert judgment, or a consultant hired to contribute to the project work.	Responsible for contributing information, advice, and contributing to requirements gathering activities.
Trainer	This role works with the project team to understand the deliverables and then teaches the users of the deliverables how to utilize the project product. This person may teach, coach, write, and do instructional design to educate the users of the project deliverable.	Develops training materials, facilitates knowledge transfer, and may participate in the development and approval of requirements.

Table 10-2   Roles and Responsibilities Should Be Clearly Identified *(continued)*

Here are the most common approaches to dividing the work strategy:

- **Subject matter expert**   If one member of the business analysis team is an SME in a given topic, then it's logical to assign that person to the business analysis activities that deal with the given topic. For example, if one member of the business analysis team also serves as an application developer, then it'd make sense to allow that business analyst to manage that portion of the business analysis duties.

- **Complexity**   Projects, programs, and opportunities can be very complex things. The more complex the project, the more business analysis is usually required. In this instance the business analysis team may elect to assign a senior business analyst to the core, more advanced themes of the project, and to assign junior members of the team to extraneous, optional, and straightforward issues. Note that this approach is not based on seniority, necessarily, but more on business analysis experience.

- **Previous work experience with stakeholders**   When you consider that most organizations do the same types of projects over and over, it's highly likely that a business analyst will become familiar with certain stakeholders. Past experiences with stakeholders may help the business analyst streamline the business analysis procedures because of their existing relationship, knowledge of how each other operates, and positive past experiences with one another. The opposite of this is true, too; if Bob the business analyst doesn't mesh well with Barb the stakeholder, it's probably a good idea to keep those two away from each other and to assign a different business analyst to the duties where Barb is involved.

- **Geography and culture**   You can divide the business analysis duties based on geographic locations; no need to send a business analyst from New York to Antwerp when there's already a business analyst in Antwerp who can complete the same duties. This approach is also good for cultural considerations. When you consider a worldwide project, it's good to have people work together who have the same culture, beliefs, and approach to work.

- **Interest**   Sometimes business analysis presents opportunities to broaden competencies or to linger in areas of technology that are dear to business analysts. It's a great opportunity when a business analyst can work on areas of requirements gathering and business analysis that are of high interest. This is also an opportunity for a business analyst to work in a new area and learn new skills and competencies in subjects that are new to him or her.

- **Physical limitations**   Sometimes the business analysis duties may need to be divided among the business analysts based on physical limitations such as mobility issues, work-from-home issues, and the physical requirements of the analysis duties. Travel, physical challenges, and locale are all considerations the business analysis team should consider.

- **Availability**   Many companies are matrix structured, where a business analyst may be working on many projects at once. It's a rare thing to have a business analyst dedicated to one project 100 percent of the time. When business analysts are shared across multiple projects, the assignment of duties should be considered based on each business analyst's schedule and availability.

Review of Key Terms for Requirements Management

You'll need to know, for starters, these core key terms about requirements management:

Configuration management   Defines the features and functions of the approved change request and how it will be used as part of the deliverables.

Explicit knowledge   Documentation, written instruction, charts, graphs, and openly shared information that any business analyst could use in their requirements management activities.

Incremental   An SDLC method that uses a granular approach for quicker deliverables, easier risk management, and easier change control on the smaller segments of the project work. This approach can also use a series of waterfalls for phases and deliverables rather than one large waterfall model. This model is ideal for large projects.

RACI chart   A RAM (Responsibility Assignment Matrix) that defines each role by using the RACI legend of responsible, accountable, consult, and inform for each activity.

Requirement elicitation   This task determines which stakeholders should be identified as contributors to the requirements gathering process. Based on the stakeholder, type of project, and conditions within the organization, the business analyst will decide which elicitation activities are most appropriate.

Requirements analysis and documentation   The business analysis activity defines the modeling and business analysis documentation technique the organization requires. Policies within the organization, business analyst preferences, or industry standards may influence the documentation and modeling approaches the business analyst uses.

Requirements communication   Communication is a key activity for a business analyst. This activity defines what types of communication, best practices for communication, and the organizational requirements for communication may be. Based on the size of the project, organizational procedures, and requests from stakeholders, the business analyst will document and adapt the communication to what's best for the project.

Requirements Traceability Matrix (RTM)   A table that tracks many actions to many requirements of the project. It maps the deliverables to the specific requirements and the verification that the deliverables do or don't satisfy the requirements.

Risk   An uncertain event that could have a positive or negative effect on the project.

Risk trigger   A warning sign or condition that the risk event is becoming an issue.

Spiral   An SDLC approach, sometimes called the cinnamon roll, that uses a series of planning, objective determination, alternative identification, and development for the life cycle. It's ideal for projects that are sensitive to risk avoidance. The downside of this model is that it's unique for each project and can't usually be used as a template for future similar projects.

System Development Life Cycle (SDLC)   A generic way of describing the life cycle of an information system and the phases the system goes through.

Waterfall   An SDLC methodology that divides the project into phases, with the project manager focusing on control of time, cost, and scope. Intense documentation happens throughout the creation of the software or system. The waterfall approach is not the fastest or most flexible approach, but it does work. A new project team or teams that shift in resources often subscribe to this approach.

Eliciting Requirements

You'll have 28 questions on eliciting requirements from stakeholders, so pay attention to these key facts for your exam. The business analyst will also need to be familiar with these skills to complete requirements elicitation:

- Information assessment
- Interviewing people
- Facilitating joint sessions among functional management, end users, customers, and other stakeholders
- Observing processes, work flow, and how tools, software, and other related resource are utilized within the organization
- Conflict resolution and consensus achievement among stakeholders
- Finding and leveraging patterns
- Writing
- Effective communications

You'll also use time management, planning, and resource management to effectively and quickly gather requirements. The goal of requirements elicitation is to determine what's needed by the stakeholders so a solution can be created in the least amount of time for the lowest and most accurate price possible. Charts can help organize thoughts, processes, and communication needs. Here are some common charts you should be familiar with:

- **Organization chart**   This traditional chart shows how the organization is broken down by department and disciplines. This chart is sometimes called the Organizational Breakdown Structure (OBS) and is arranged by departments, units, or teams.
- **Resource Breakdown Structure (RBS)**   This hierarchical chart can break down the business problem or opportunity by the type of resources affected by the project. For example, your project might need several database administrators and programmers in several likely deliverables throughout the project. The RBS would organize all of the usage of the resources by their discipline rather than by where the discipline is being utilized.

- **Responsibility Assignment Matrix (RAM)** A RAM chart shows the correlation between project team members and the work they've been assigned to complete. A RAM chart doesn't necessarily have to be specific to individual team members; it can also be decomposed to project groups or units. When you first begin elicitation, you likely won't have a RAM to reference, but on larger projects that have a series of elicitations this can be useful.

These five approaches are where you'll likely have a generous number of questions for the requirements elicitation knowledge area on your exam. Spend a little time learning all about these approaches:

- Leading a brainstorming session
- Hosting a focus group
- Observing stakeholders
- Facilitating a requirements workshop
- Managing a stakeholder survey

Requirements workshops are great tools to focus on the exact requirements needed for the project to be successful. The facilitator has many responsibilities before, during, and after a requirements workshop. For every workshop, the facilitator must prepare to lead the event to ensure it's productive and meaningful. Before the workshop the facilitator must:

- Document what the business problem or opportunity is
- Communicate the purpose of the requirements workshop to the key stakeholders
- Create an agenda for the workshop
- Schedule a scribe or recorder to document the minutes and conversations of the workshop for future reference
- Complete interviews with the stakeholder to help facilitate the workshop

During the workshop the facilitator will engage and interact with the participants to elicit information about the project. He'll need to work with the participants to help them reach consensus and agreement on conflicting views and competing objectives. Throughout the conversations, the facilitator will need to keep the session on track by following the agenda and the objectives of the workshop.

It's helpful to identify the different types of interactions and interfaces when you're identifying requirements. There are three categories of interfaces that the business analysts need to identify:

- **User interfaces** People who interact with one another, a system, or data moved between two users.

- **External systems**   Links between internal systems and external systems, such as vendors, regulatory agencies, and technical interfaces.

- **Hardware devices**   Identification of links between any hardware device that may be affected by the proposed project. Consider servers, workstations, kiosks, and printers.

Prototypes are like pseudo-working solutions created to test their viability. The functional scope of the prototype can be developed in two different approaches, depending on the project:

- **Horizontal method**   Quick, shallow, and wide view of the system without any real functionality behind the prototype. Easy to create, modify, and explain.

- **Vertical method**   Creates an in-depth analysis, deep prototype of just one portion of the system functionality. Can be costly and time intensive, but proves the functionality of the system key processes.

There are also two prototype approaches for system design and creation during the development life cycle:

- **Throwaway prototype**   As its name suggests, this prototype is simple and may often just be a sketch of the proposed system. It helps the customer and the developer see the system in recognizable components.

- **Evolutionary prototype**   This approach, sometimes called a working prototype, creates an operating prototype that will eventually evolve into the delivered solution. Each addition to the system evolves it another step until it reaches the complete scope of requirements and the project is closed.

Review of Key Terms for Requirements Elicitation

Some key terms on requirements elicitation:

Active stakeholder observation   The business analyst seeks to understand the reason behind every step in the business process. Sometimes the business analyst will actually get involved in the work to fully understand the process and how the person performing it completes the process.

Evolutionary prototype   Sometimes called a working prototype, creates an operating prototype that will eventually evolve into the delivered solution. Each addition to the system evolves it another step until it reaches the complete scope of requirements and the project is closed.

External systems interfaces   These are the links between internal systems and external systems, such as vendors, regulatory agencies, and technical interfaces.

Focus group This is a structured, facilitated meeting to gather ideas and determine opinions and feelings about a product, service, problem, or opportunity.

Horizontal method prototyping This is a quick, shallow, and wide view of the system without any real functionality behind the prototype. Easy to create, modify, and explain.

Interface analysis This defines and documents all of the links between two or more components in a system.

Organization chart This traditional chart shows how the organization is broken down by department and disciplines. This chart is sometimes called the Organizational Breakdown Structure (OBS) and is arranged by departments, units, or teams.

Passive stakeholder observation Sometimes called invisible observation, this is when the business analyst observes the stakeholder's activity without any interaction with the person doing the work.

Communicating Requirements

Business analysts are more than just talkers—they're communicators. Communication is talking, listening, and transferring ideas from one person to other people. There are many facts to know about communication when it comes to business analysis. Fortunately, this objective only accounts for about 16 questions on your CBAP exam. When the business analyst begins to identify communication requirements and create the Requirements Communication Plan, she should consider

- Each stakeholder's time availability to contribute to the project
- Each stakeholder's physical location and the communication challenges of time zone differences, language differences, and cultural differences such as holidays and customs
- What authority level the stakeholder has to contribute to the requirements
- The information that will be elicited during requirements gathering activities
- The best communication approach to elicit requirements
- The appropriate forms, templates, and other modalities to communicate identified requirements, conclusions, and requirements packages

There's a nifty formula to demonstrate project communication demands based on the size of the project stakeholders. The formula, $N(N-1)/2$, where N represents the number of project stakeholders, shows the number of communication channels in the project.

The BABOK tells us directly that the business analyst is the chief communicator for everything about requirements. As the chief communicator, you've loads of responsibility riding on your shoulders to be certain that all stakeholders are identified and communicated with. You can use a Communications Requirements Matrix to help you identify the communication interaction of the stakeholders.

Here are some conflict resolution approaches that a business analyst can participate in:

- **Problem solving**   This conflict resolution approach uses a spirit of cooperation among the stakeholders. Problem solving tackles the problem head-on and is the preferred method of conflict resolution. Sometimes this approach is defined as "confronting" rather than problem solving. Problem solving calls for additional research to find the best solution for the problem, and it's a win-win solution. It should be used if there is time to work through and resolve the issue. It also serves to build relationships and trust. The business analyst is the facilitator of the problem-solving technique.

- **Forcing**   You've seen forcing used when the person in the conflict with the most power forces the decision. The decision made may not be the best decision for the project, but it's fast. As expected, this autocratic approach does little for relationship building and is a win-lose solution. You know a solution is being forced when someone with seniority or power makes a decision without considering the other parties' objections or concerns.

- **Compromising**   While compromising sounds nice, it really means that both parties must give up something. The decision made is a blend of both sides of the argument. Because neither party really wins, it is considered a lose-lose solution. The business analyst can use this approach when the relationships are equal and no one can truly "win."

- **Smoothing**   This approach "smoothes" out the conflict by minimizing the perceived size of the problem. It is a temporary solution, but can calm stakeholder relations and boisterous discussions. Smoothing may be acceptable when time is of the essence or when any of the proposed solutions will not currently settle the problem. This can be considered a lose-lose situation as well, since no one really wins in the long run. The business analyst can use smoothing to emphasize areas of agreement between disagreeing stakeholders and, thus, minimize areas of conflict. It's used to maintain relationships and when the issue is not critical.

- **Withdrawal**   This conflict resolution approach has one side of the argument walking away from the problem, usually in disgust. You can recognize withdrawal when one party refuses to participate in the conflict resolution any longer and surrenders to the other stakeholders. The conflict is not really resolved, and it is considered a yield-lose solution. The approach can be used, however, as a cooling-off period or when the issue is not critical.

In all of these instances the business analyst should document the conversation, the details of the conflict resolution meeting, and update the Requirements Issue Log. Once the decision has been made about the conflict, the business analyst should obtain signatures from all parties involved in the conflict on a conflict resolution document.

Typical stakeholders and their communication expectations include

- **Executive sponsors and management**   This group will likely want high-level requirements and summaries. They're not interested, usually, in the fine details and inner workings of the requirements. Management will want to see how the investment in the solution will help the organization grow, what the return on investment will be, and in some instances how operation costs can be cut by implementing the requirements.

- **Technical designers**   These people will want the specifics of the requirements as they relate to the form, function, interface, and how the solution will be used once it's created. While business objectives are often included, for technical designers the primary focus will be on how the deliverables are to be utilized in the organization.

- **End users**   The recipients of the deliverables, often the largest audience, need clear and easy-to-understand requirements. End users may be the group that is affected the most by the solution, with the least amount of influence over the solution.

- **Project team**   The project team, if they're known at this point, will need information about the success criteria for the requirements so they may plan accordingly.

- **Quality assurance team**   The QA group will want to know the business benefits so that they can create testing for the project deliverable. They'll also want to create plans based on the requirements to ensure that the proposed solution matches the expectations of the project customer.

- **Vendors**   Depending on the type of project, the vendor will need information about the technical requirements, required materials, and other relevant requirements information.

Multiple communications of requirements take time, redundancy, and thoroughness to ensure consistency through each depiction of the project requirements. A checklist can help the business analyst determine what needs to be communicated and to whom. When you are considering multiple versions of requirements, you should consider several factors first:

- The level of detail the requirements must possess
- The information that must be communicated
- What each stakeholder audience needs to understand about the requirements
- Each stakeholder audience's preferred method of communication
- The characteristics of the requirement (technical constraint or business function)
- The extent that the requirement is traceable through phases, implementation, and project delivery

A requirements package is the collection of the business analyst's work results. It is the documentation, formulation, and organization of all the requirements the business analyst has gathered from the stakeholders packaged in a comprehensive set of project requirements. It's what the business analyst creates to fully communicate the intent, demands, and requirements for the proposed solution.

For your CBAP examination, you should pay special attention to the completeness and accuracy of the requirements package. The requirements package is the culmination of the work the business analyst has completed, and it's a reflection of the business analyst's performance in the organization. A sloppy, rushed requirements package will certainly result in either rework or defects within the project.

You need the project stakeholders before and during the project to participate in formal requirements review meetings. It's much more cost-effective to catch mistakes, errors, and omissions on paper than to fix problems that have already been implemented by the project team. Initially, formal reviews are completed with your fellow business analysts, certain key stakeholders, and subject matter experts. This gives all of you a chance to confer on the requirements before things become too formal. As time progresses, you'll move to a more formal approach in your reviews. Formal requirements review can include any and all of the following purposes:

- Review by all the stakeholders to see that all of the requirements have been captured
- Opportunity to cut unessential requirements (goodbye to pet requirements)
- Confirmation that the requirements are exact and easy to understand
- Review of the requirements for correctness
- Confirmation that the requirements will adhere to the organizational standards, policies, and quality expectations
- Review of requirements feasibility
- Opportunity for the stakeholders to prioritize the requirements

The formal requirements review usually includes all of the stakeholders or authorized representatives from large groups of stakeholders. When you've a large group of stakeholders, such as end users, there may be a selection of stakeholders that represents the interests of the larger group of stakeholders. These representatives should be authorized to comment on and approve the requirements on behalf of the stakeholders being represented. Typical roles for the formal requirements review include

- **Requirements author** This is the person who created the requirements document; typically this is the business analyst. The requirements review meeting can't happen without this person present.
- **Recorder** This lucky person gets to record all the comments, suggestions, questions, and prompts for clarification about the requirements document.
- **Moderator** This is the person who actually facilitates the meeting. It's possible that this person is the business analyst, but generally this role is

performed by a neutral person who can move the meeting along and stick to the meeting rules. The moderator has the responsibility of ensuring that all participants have reviewed the requirements documentation prior to the start of the meeting and of keeping stakeholders on track during the meeting.

- **Author peer reviewer**   This person completes peer review of the requirements documentation to ensure that it meets the expected quality of the organization and inspects the requirements documentation for completeness. The author peer reviewer is often another business analyst.

- **Appropriate stakeholders**   The business analyst and the project manager may invite other key stakeholders who are not necessarily decision makers on the requirements but who can offer input and direction to technicalities, quality, and expert judgment about the content and accuracy of the requirements and deliverables.

Review of Key Terms for Communication

There are a few key terms you should make certain that you know for requirements communications:

Author peer reviewer   This person completes peer review of the requirements documentation to ensure that it meets the expected quality of the organization and inspects the requirements documentation for completeness. The author peer reviewer is often another business analyst.

Barrier   Anything that prevents communication from occurring at optimum levels.

Decoder   The device that decodes the message as it is being received.

Deliverable   A document that clearly identifies the project deliverables the customer is expecting and that the project is to produce for the stakeholders.

Encoder   The device that encodes the message to be sent.

Feedback loop   A conversation between one or more speakers centering on one specific topic.

Media   The best modality to use when communicating is the one that is relevant to the information that's being communicated. Some communications demand a formal presentation, where others only warrant a phone call, an ad hoc meeting, or a quick e-mail. The right modality is dictated by what needs to be communicated.

Noise   Anything that interferes with or disrupts the message. Anything that distracts you or me from the message is noise.

Receiver   The person who receives the message.

Sender   The party sending the message is the sender.

Working as an Enterprise Business Analyst

This is the most important information on enterprise business analysis. You'll have approximately 33 questions for this exam objective. First off, Table 10-3 shows the expected activities, roles, and responsibilities from the project stakeholders you have to deal with as a business analyst.

Activity	Owner	Deliverables	Business Analyst Duties
Develop the strategic plan	Executive team	Strategic plan	Competitive analysis. Create benchmark studies. Plan and lead strategic planning sessions.
Develop strategic goals	Executive team	Strategic goals Organizational themes and benefit measurements	Plan and lead strategic planning sessions.
Develop business architecture	Business analyst	Business architecture	Based on executive vision, develop and maintain current and future state of the business architecture.
Perform feasibility studies	Business analyst	Feasibility study	Identify alternative solutions. Examine feasibility of options. Determine most feasible solution.
Business case development	Business analyst	Business case	Create project scope. Create time and cost estimates. Quantify benefits. Create business case document.
Project proposal	Business sponsor	Executive presentation Decision package	Create executive presentation documentation. Create decision package.
Select and prioritize opportunities	Enterprise governance group	Project selection Project priority Project charter	Facilitate portfolio management meeting. Present new project proposals.
Launch new projects	Project manager	Project plans	Assist with project initiating and planning. Collaborate with system architect on project solution.

Table 10-3 Stakeholder Roles the Business Analyst Interacts With

Activity	Owner	Deliverables	Business Analyst Duties
Manage projects for value	Business analyst	Updated business case at control gates	Work with project manager to update the business case. Help executive make decision to continue to invest in project based on project performance, discovery, risk, and findings.
Tracking project benefits	Business sponsor	Balanced Scorecard reports	Ensure metrics are present, analyzed, and reported to business sponsor. Track actual and planned performance.

Table 10-3 Stakeholder Roles the Business Analyst Interacts With *(continued)*

The idea of the Balanced Scorecard uses four predetermined metrics to measure the components of an organization:

- **Financial**   This metric states the specific financial goals of the organization, such as to reduce costs by 10 percent and increase revenue by 8 percent.

- **Customer**   This metric states the goal for customer satisfaction, such as based on a customer service survey, to earn a 98 percent approval rating. It could also include customer retention and new customer additions to be measured.

- **Internal**   Internal processes are measured between periods, and goals are set to improve process performance. Industry benchmarks such as IT and construction could also be used as internal metrics for measurement.

- **Learning and innovation**   This goal measures new product development, measurable competencies achieved, skill development, and proper application of knowledge learned to projects, operations, and issues.

According to the BABOK it's the senior business analysts, along with the executive team, who serve as the business architects. Just keep in mind that business architects are creating systems, documentation, and components so business decisions can be made as efficiently as possible. Business architects need the ability to understand and apply

- Generally accepted business practices
- Relevant knowledge of industry domains
- IT-enabled business solutions
- Emerging business concepts, strategies, and practices
- Internal lines of business and how they interact
- Organization of the enterprise knowledge

- How the organization business issues drive the organization demand for technology
- Business process engineering
- Business analysis abilities
- Business modeling, concepts, rules, policies, and terminology

Review of Key Terms for Enterprise Analysis

And you should know, at a minimum, these key terms on enterprise analysis:

Activity Based Costing   Examines the true cost of any business process the project may invoke. It examines the performance or resources, the activities resources will complete, and includes the cost-effectiveness of nonhuman resources such as equipment and facilities.

Analytic Hierarchy Process   This approach uses both qualitative (subjective) and quantitative (in-depth) analysis for each solution to compare and contrast each solution based on a series of comparisons.

Business case   A document that reports on the value that the business will gain by investing in the initiative.

Business process model   Sometimes called an activity model, this captures all of the activities within a business, the inputs and outputs of each activity, and the required resources to complete each activity.

Business process reengineering   This approach studies the current flow of business processes, looks for strengths, weaknesses, opportunities, and threats (SWOT), and considers everything from minor adjustments to entire new designs to investigate improvements.

Component business model   This is the most common business model and was formulated by IBM. It provides a direct and traditional view of an enterprise, providing nomenclature to lines of business, functional units, departments, groups, and other organizational resources.

Current state assessment   Part of the feasibility study to determine the current status of the organization. An understanding of the current organizational status can be compared with the desired future status of the company.

Data flow diagrams   The type and traffic of information within the organization is captured and displayed.

POLDAT Technique   A requirements gathering and business architecture technique that captures information about processes, organization structure, location, data, applications, and technology.

Requirements Traceability Matrix (RTM)   A table that facilitates the identification and documentation of the categories of needs, specific requirements within the categories of needs, functional or operational identification for each identified requirement, and any additional characteristics.

Technology architecture diagrams   The topology and relationship of the IT infrastructure are mapped in these diagrams.

Theme   Premise of a strategic goal; allows the large organizational goals to be broken down into smaller projects and opportunities.

Use case models   Captures the business processes by showing how customers, vendors, management, departments, and other enterprisewide stakeholders interact with the business.

Work Breakdown Structure (WBS)   The WBS is a visual decomposition of the scope; it is deliverables-based and typically does not include activities.

Zachman Framework   A matrix, created by John Zachman, that provides structure and helps stakeholders describe complex enterprises. The Zachman Framework uses predefined questions that must be answered for each component of any organization.

Performing Requirements Analysis and Documentation

For the CBAP exam, when it doubt, document whatever it is you're doing in the project. This domain accounts for approximately 31 questions on your exam. You'll complete loads of documentation as a business analyst. These iterations of requirements review are completed through many different activities, though not all of these are necessary for every project. You should be familiar with these activities and the documents they create:

- **Structure requirements**   The requirements are logically organized and documented.

- **Create a business domain model**   This is a visual representation of how the business works, or should work, in regard to the project requirements. In particular, it defines each of the processes affected by the project, how the process should work, and how the process interacts with other processes, functions, and project-affected users in the organization.

- **Analyze user requirements**   Documents what the user expects the solution to do; in a software project, this is the creation of the User Requirements Document (URD). Users must agree that the business analyst understands and has captured what they want accomplished in the solution.

- **Analyze functional requirements**   Functional requirements describe how the solution will function, what it will do, and what its expected outcomes are. This is usually a more technical document than the URD, but it should mesh with the users' requirements.

- **Analyze supplementary quality of service requirements**   The business analyst and key stakeholders must agree on what the expected level of quality of service for the project deliverable will be. This term lends itself most to IT solutions where a benchmark has been created for an acceptable level of quality, and the solution is measured above or below the defined benchmark. In other words, based on the solution and previous history, what's the expected level of quality and an acceptable level of errors in relation to the expected quality? Generally, the higher the quality, the more mission-critical the solution is and the higher the costs to achieve the solution.

- **Determine assumptions and constraints**   This is an ongoing activity to define, test, and document the assumptions and constraints of the requirements. Recall that an assumption is something that you believe to be true but haven't yet proven to be true. A constraint is anything that limits the project options, such as a deadline or predetermined budget. Assumptions and constraints can both become project risks.

- **Determine requirements attributes**   All of the identified requirements have attributes that should be documented; attributes can include status, associated risks, cost and time estimates, dependencies, resources needed, and more.

- **Verify requirements**   The verification of the known requirements is an opportunity for the business analyst to confirm with the stakeholders that all of the requirements have been captured, documented, and are accurately represented. In other words, the business analyst gets to ask the key stakeholders, "Do we have the requirements correct?"

- **Validate requirements**   Validation of the requirements is a test of the actual deliverables, a prototype of the deliverables, or a small batch run.

Flowcharts are excellent diagrams to visually demonstrate how the components of a system are interrelated. A fully developed flowchart has lots of parts. Components of a flowchart can include

- **Activities**   These are the processes, work, or functions, represented by rectangles.
- **Flow**   The flow is the direction of the data, represented by arrows.
- **Branches**   When conditions allow the flow of activities to branch into multiple streams, a diamond is used to represent the split in the flowchart.
- **Forks**   Sometimes the flow will need to choose one of two paths to continue; this is called a fork. Forks in the flowchart are represented by a double line above the two paths in the flowchart.

- **Joins** Just as the flow can split into two paths, so too can two paths merge together through a join. Joins are also represented by a double line, but joins come after multiple paths.

- **Other items** Depending on your industry, you can have other items in your flowchart like documents, databases, storage, and other media.

- **Starting point** This is the first item in the flowchart, and it's represented by a rounded rectangle.

- **End point** This is the final item in the flowchart, and it, too, is represented by a rounded rectangle.

On a larger scale is an entity relationship diagram. This diagram considers the whole picture of an organization rather than just the IT systems the business interacts with. An entity relationship diagram visualizes all of the components of an organization and the relationships among the organization: customers, suppliers, vendors, employees, management, and resources like data, facilities, and equipment. Components of an entity relationship diagram are

- **Entities** It's good for an entity relationship diagram to have entities; these are the people, resources, vendors, and data sources that contribute to the communication and processes within the organization.

- **Attributes** The characteristic of the entity identified in the chart; consider the details of a piece of equipment, contact information for a vendor, and employee information.

- **Unique identifiers** Each entity in the chart needs to be uniquely identified. Consider all of the system engineers who could be included in the chart; the unique identifiers distinguish between Marcy the system engineer and Steve the system engineer. This is used for each entity in the chart: vendors, equipment, and so on.

- **Relationships** These show how communication flows from one entity to another. The rules of the organization, established flow of communication, and demands for communication are considered.

Both user and functional requirements may overlap each other. Attention to the documentation of the requirements is needed to ensure that there is no duplication in requirements, no conflicts within the requirements documentation, and a clear understanding among the stakeholders. Requirements should be written clearly, precisely, and exactly, so there's no confusion or misinterpretation of what the requirements are. Follow these rules when writing requirements:

- State the requirements as simply as possible.

- Avoid complex conditional clauses.

- Confirm that terminology is accurately defined and used consistently throughout all the requirements documentation.

- Don't make assumptions; spell out acronyms and define new terms.
- Don't group requirements; define them one at a time.

Your goal as a business analyst is to create well-formed requirements for your stakeholders. Anyone related to the project should be able to read the requirements documentation and understand what the project is to do. The reader should be able to understand what the solution is, the conditions that will define when the solution exists, and which people are responsible for which elements of the solution.

Good writing uses the active voice and defines what the subject must do. For example, "the database administrator creates the database." Passive voice can leave things open for interpretation, is not as commanding as active, and makes me sleepy. Avoid the passive voice; here's an example: "The database was created by the database administrator." Your requirements want strong, imperative roles and responsibility definitions. Leave nothing to interpretation.

Models can also help stakeholders understand and relate to the requirements more easily than textual documentation can. Models are a mesh of textual elements, matrixes, and diagrams, and they present all or a portion of the proposed solution. You'll typically find yourself using a model in complex solutions and long-term project schedules. There are several benefits to using models:

- Core requirements are focused on; the business analyst can filter out descriptions, opinions, and other noise.
- Complex systems and solutions can be understood more easily through models.
- Perspectives on the system can shift using models.
- Models can help ensure that all of the business requirements are captured.
- Models can help the business analysis team define a solution design.

Models can be formal or informal, depending on the organization, but both should be created with clearly defined boundaries, terminology, and designs. The complexity of the model often depends on how complex the problem is, the timeline for the implementation, and the number of requirements already identified. So here's a quick definition of these models that may appear on your CBAP exam:

- **Class model** Demonstrates the attributes, operations, and relationship to entities within the solution. Classes are physical resources, solution concepts, a collection of data, a function of the solution, or an action.
- **CRUD Matrix** This is a table that uses the acronym CRUD to define the level of access resources have to an information system. CRUD stands for Create, Read, Update, or Delete. It's the permissions assigned to resources for system information.
- **Data dictionary** Describes the data used by the system. The data dictionary defines the name of the data, data aliases, values and meanings, and descriptions of the system data.

- **Entity relationship diagram** This is a visual mapping of the system data, its inputs and outputs, and relationship to the enterprise. The entity relationship diagram links the data to operations such as customers, invoices, accounts payable, and products.

Assumptions are tied to project risks. Negative risks are things that hurt the project, while positive risks actually help the project. You can have both positive and negative assumptions in every project. Here are samples of things that may be currently known and that are usually assumed won't change:

- Availability of project resources
- Availability of project budget
- Reliance on identified vendors
- Accuracy of project requirements
- Abilities of the project team
- Law, standards, and regulations

There can be countless other assumptions in a project that you have to consider. Should any of these assumptions change, the project could be affected. Sometimes a change in assumption could be seen as a boon to a project, such as an assumption in the cost of a certain material. Consider the cost of fuel, shipping, and travel; these are variable costs that can change based on market conditions. The shift up or down on costs could help or hinder the project as a whole.

Since this domain is about requirements analysis and documentation, you should be familiar with these documents for your CBAP exam:

- **Vision document** A vision document is a high-level view of the project solution. It defines a "vision" of what the project is to create for the organization. Vision documents are ideal for projects that will go through rounds of planning and where the project scope is defined through iterations.

- **Business Process Description** Like the vision document, the Business Process Description defines the project at a high level of what the project should create. Where this document differs, however, is that the Business Process Description also includes a summary of the current business model, all of the known user requirements, and any of the functional requirements that have been defined. This document may also move through iterations of planning.

- **Business Requirements Document** This document clearly defines the behavior of a project solution for the customers and end users. It's most common for software development projects, and it's based on the business requirements defined early in the business analysis activities. This document is great for confirming that the business analyst, the project manager, and the stakeholders all agree on what the project should create.

- **Software Requirements Specification**   Depending on the situation, this document may also be called a System Requirements Specification. This requirements documentation defines the expected behavior and implementation of the software or system the developers will be creating for the project customers. This documentation starts with a definition of the problem domain and the functional requirements that will help create the solution. The document will also include the expected quality of service and will communicate any relevant assumptions or constraints the developers will need to manage as part of the solution.

There are eight conditions for each requirement that you should confirm before the project execution. These eight criteria help you and the project stakeholders review the completeness and accuracy of the requirements prior to project execution. You should be familiar with these criteria for your CBAP exam:

- **Necessary**   Each requirement should have value and contribute to meeting defined business goals and objectives as stated in the project charter, vision document, and the business case.

- **Complete**   The requirements are fully defined, which means that all constraints, assumptions, potential risks, attributes, and conditions of the project are documented. The complete attribute also means there is enough accurate information that the project team may begin creating the requirements based on the documentation provided.

- **Consistent**   The requirement should mesh with all of the other requirements in the project. You may find inconsistent requirements when a key stakeholder is forcing a particular requirement into the project as a mandate. This is when politics enter the business analysis and project management.

- **Correct**   Correct requirements describe the functionally that is to be created by the project. The author of the requirements is the individual who must fully define the correctness of the project requirement.

- **Feasible**   Each requirement should be feasible to implement based on the needed resources, schedule, cost, quality, risks, and capabilities.

- **Modifiable**   Similar requirements should be grouped together so that modifications to the requirements can be made easily. When requirements are grouped by similar characteristics, it's more practical to see how a change in one requirement affects other requirements.

- **Unambiguous**   The requirements documentation should be written in such a way that all readers of the requirements documentation arrive at the same understanding of what the requirements demand. Simple, concise language is imperative for clear communication of requirements.

- **Testable**   The requirements provide evidence of completion by testing, examining, or demonstrating their existence upon completion. Each requirement must be verified upon delivery to confirm the completeness of the deliverable.

These characteristics are guidelines for business analysts to use to weight the correctness and completeness of each requirement. You should document the existence of these attributes for each project requirement as part of your findings in requirements elicitation and requirements verification with the stakeholders.

Review of Key Terms for Requirements Analysis and Documentation

Here are some key terms in addition to those I've already mentioned:

Business Domain Model   A visual representation of how the business works, or should work, with regard to the project requirements. It defines each of the business processes affected by the project, how the process should work, and how the process interacts with other processes, functions, and project-affected users in the organization.

Business process analysis   A solution development methodology that examines and documents how the work is currently done in comparison with how the work should be done once the solution has been created. Business process analysis is also known as business process mapping, business process reengineering, business process transformation, and business process modeling.

Cost of conformance to requirements   These are the monies that an organization must spend to meet the expected level of quality: the correct tools, software, safety equipment, and training.

Cost of nonconformance to requirements   These are monies that an organization will pay in fines, lawsuits, loss of sales, and loss of customers should they not achieve the expected quality in the project. Consider a project that does not provide the project team with the proper safety tools or training. If someone gets injured, then there'll be repercussions. These costs also include time delays, waste of materials, loss of team morale, and poor deliverables.

Market   Part of the organizational environment. The condition of the market is an excellent example of an environmental regulation that you have little control over. Market conditions can affect how you buy and sell, price your services and goods, and can have an impact on whether the project is even launched or allowed to proceed.

Measurable and testable   A requirements attribute that confirms the requirements are not described with subjective, unquantifiable terms and metrics. You'll need specific tests to measure and show a range of acceptability for satisfying the requirements.

Regulations   Part of the organizational environment. Your project and proposed solution may have industry regulations that you must adhere to. Regulations, even pending regulations, should always be considered, because these may hinder or constrain the ability of the project to quickly and cost-effectively meet the identified requirements.

Assessing and Validating Project Solutions

The last exam domain accounts for just eight questions on your CBAP exam.

First off is the user class. A user class is a categorization of users and how each class will use the solution. For example, a word-processing program can be used in a variety of different methods. Paralegals may create briefs with the software, while the marketing department may write press releases. User classes describe how a group of people, the users, will use the solution the project is to create for them. Understanding how the users will actually use the solution is an important part of business analysis, because it helps create a solution that can map to several different classes.

The design of a solution should address the problem the project was initiated to solve. The business analyst, design team, and subject matter experts should address the cause of the problem, not just the symptoms. A cause-and-effect chart, sometimes called the *Ishikawa chart*, can help facilitate this process. The users should not be surprised as to what the project creates, because they're involved in the requirements contribution, and the business analyst will communicate to them what's happening with the requirements they've signed off on.

Based on the requirements, the business analyst and the design team should map out a solution that solves the identified problem or that seizes an opportunity for the organization. The users should be involved in this process, and it's often their insight, based on their regular experience with the problem or potential opportunity, that can direct the business analyst and design team to the most appropriate project solution. This does not mean, however, that the business analyst should create and adhere to only one solution. In fact, the business analyst and the design team, along with the users, should identify multiple alternate solutions.

In computer networking, quality of service (QoS) refers to the priority level of applications, and how they'll respond and act on a network. For example, a company may place a higher priority on network traffic for a sales application than on an application for web browsing their Internet server. Quality of service is a way to describe the expected level of performance for an application, or in a broader sense, the expectations of reliability for a solution.

Quality of service, for an IT solution, is considered by the business analyst and the design team because the expectations may affect the actual solution, creation, and implementation of the project deliverable. Stakeholders, however, don't often define the expected quality of service, because they don't know about QoS; they just know that when they use a device or software program, they expect it to work every single time. Consider these typical constraints that can affect QoS:

- Limitations of the technology
- Competing operational needs such as reliability, disaster recovery, and the product life cycle
- Politics
- Legal requirements and constraints

- Security issues
- Physical environment constraints
- Global and local constraints
- Connectivity with internal and external interfaces

In some application areas, such as healthcare and financial, government regulations may be in place, so it's more than logical to use a Requirements Traceability Matrix. In other areas, such as IT and manufacturing, it's really up to the project team to determine the level of traceability between requirements and the actual project work. The size of the project scope and the overall priority of the project will likely affect the level of traceability a project keeps. There are many good reasons to implement traceability in a project:

- The business analyst can trace a requirement from its start, through design, testing, implementation, and into operations.
- Stakeholders can visualize all of the phases a requirement passes through as it moves from concept to implementation.
- A Requirements Traceability Matrix can help the project manager and the business analyst ensure that all of the features and functions are accounted for in the project solution.
- A Requirements Traceability Matrix can help deter unapproved scope changes, sometimes called *scope creep*, from entering the project, as each deliverable must be tracked back to the matrix.

The most compelling reason to use a Requirements Traceability Matrix is that if it is agreed upon and followed by the design team, the project deliverables will be of quality. This is because each requirement and its subcomponents stem from the approved project requirements, and no non-value-added activities or deliverables have been introduced into the project. All deliverables, regardless of their size, originate from the requirements in the matrix.

Make or buy decisions can use a formula to find the break-even point:

1. Find the difference of the build solution and the buy solution.
2. Find the difference of the monthly fees between the two solutions.
3. Divide the out-of-pocket difference by the monthly difference.

Determine how long the solution will be in use, and based on that length, you'll know how long it'll take to pay for the in-house solution. In this example, Jenny can "break even" on the initial out-of-pocket expense of $57,500 in just a little over 6 months. If the solution is going to be used less than 6 months, then she'd be wiser to hire the vendor and their solution.

When you need to buy stuff from vendors, you'll start the procurement process as the buyer. Sellers can be found through a preferred vendor list, advertisements, industry directories, trade organizations, or other methods. The initial communication from the buyer to the seller is a request. Specifically, the seller issues one of the following documents:

- **Request for Proposal (RFP)** These want dreamy solutions to the identified problems in the Statement of Work. RFPs are used when multiple factors besides price determine which seller is awarded the contract. The buyer is looking for a solution to a need.

- **Request for Quotation (RFQ)**   Used when the deciding factor is price.

- **Invitation for Bid (IFB)**   Used when the deciding factor is price. Yes, the IFB and the RFQ are the same type of document.

The business analyst needs to strip away some of the silly notions that end users, salespeople, and other stakeholders attach to project deliverables. The business analyst needs to clearly express what the deliverable will and will not do. You should be on the lookout for stakeholders with lofty expectations. I'm not saying that you should be the wet blanket and pessimist in your organization, but that you should help set appropriate expectations for the project deliverable.

You'll also need to communicate to stakeholders about their responsibility with the new deliverable. There may be maintenance issues, initial loss of efficiency, training, and even some potential for glitches and issues in the deliverable when it first shifts into productivity. The business analyst needs to communicate how the stakeholder should report problems and to whom. Ideally the project team, support team, or some other entity is established to track the problems and communicate the problem to the appropriate people for resolution.

Review of Key Terms for Assessment and Validation

There are a few key terms you should make certain you know for solution assessment and validation:

Alternate solutions   More than one choice for a solution that may satisfy the project requirements.

Bidders Conference   A group meeting of all the vendors and the buyer to review the SOW (Statement of Work) and the procurement document. This is an opportunity for the bidders to ask questions about the project and for the buyer to provide clarifications when needed.

Cause-and-effect diagram   Sometimes called a fishbone or Ishikawa chart, this can help facilitate root cause analysis.

Gold plating   An unscrupulous process of adding extra features that may drive up costs and alter schedules. The project team should strive to deliver what was expected.

Implementation plan   Sometimes called the operational transfer plan, it defines how to move the solution from the ownership of the project to operations. The implementation plan should address how the solution will move from the project life cycle into the product life cycle.

Life cycle costing   The estimate of how much it'll cost the organization to support the deliverables the project has created per year, quarter, or whatever period the stakeholders designate.

Phase   A logical grouping of activities that create a deliverable or a set of related deliverables.

Product life cycle   The duration of the product in operations. It describes the anticipated duration of the product usage, maintenance, and anticipated phasing out of the solution.

Unknown unknowns   Unforeseen issues that can affect the execution of the project.

Chapter Summary

If you follow my advice, your gut instinct, and some common sense, you'll be on your way to passing your exam. My goal for you is to pass your exam. As I teach business analysis, project management, and program management for different organizations around the globe, I'm struck by one similarity among the most excited course participants: these people want to pass their exam. Sure, business analysis is not the most exciting topic, but the individuals are excited about passing their exam. They correlate the rewards, personal and professional, to the hard work it takes to prepare.

I hope you feel the same way about passing your test. I believe that passing the CBAP exam is like most things in life: you'll only get out of it what you put into it. I challenge you to become excited, happy, and eager to pass the exam.

Here are ten final tips for passing your CBAP examination:

- Prepare to pass the exam, not just take it.
- If you haven't done so already, schedule your exam. Having a deadline makes that exam even more of a reality.
- If you haven't done so already, create a clutter-free area for studying.
- Study in regular intervals right up to the day before your examination.
- Repetition is the mother of learning. If you don't know the formula, repeat and repeat. And then repeat it again.
- Create your own flashcards from the terms and glossary in this book.

- Always answer the exam questions according to the IIBA, not how you'd do it at your organization.

- Practice making the one page of notes that you'll create at the start of your exam.

- Create a significant reward for yourself as an incentive to pass the exam.

- Make a commitment to pass.

If you're stumped on something I've written in this book, or if you'd like to share your success story, drop me a line: certified@projectseminars.com. Finally, I won't wish you good luck on your CBAP exam—luck is for the ill-prepared. If you follow the strategies I've outlined in this book and apply yourself, I am certain you'll pass the exam.

All my best,

Joseph Phillips, PMP, Project+, CBAP
www.projectseminars.com

About the CD

The CD-ROM included with this book comes complete with MasterExam and the electronic version of the book. The software is easy to install on any Windows 2000/XP/Vista computer and must be installed to access the MasterExam feature. You may, however, browse the electronic book and the CBAP video training directly from the CD without installation. To register for the bonus MasterExam, simply click the Bonus MasterExam link on the main launch page, and follow the directions to the free online registration.

System Requirements

The software requires Windows 2000 or later and Internet Explorer 6.0 or later and 20MB of hard disk space for full installation. The electronic book requires Adobe Acrobat Reader.

Installing and Running MasterExam

If your computer CD-ROM drive is configured to autorun, the CD-ROM will automatically start up when you insert the disc. From the opening screen, you can install MasterExam by clicking the MasterExam link. This will begin the installation process and create a program group named LearnKey. To run MasterExam, use Start | All Programs | LearnKey | MasterExam. If the autorun feature did not launch your CD, browse to the CD and click the LaunchTraining.exe icon.

MasterExam

MasterExam provides you with a simulation of the actual exam. The number of questions, the type of questions, and the time allowed are intended to be an accurate representation of the exam environment. You have the option to take an open-book exam, including hints, references, and answers; a closed-book exam; or the timed MasterExam simulation.

When you launch MasterExam, a digital clock display will appear in the lower-right corner of your screen. The clock will count down to zero and the exam will end unless you choose to end the exam before the time expires.

CBAP Video Training

CBAP video training clips on the CD provide detailed examples of key certification objectives in audio/video format direct from the author, Joseph Phillips. These clips walk you step-by-step through various certification objectives. You can access the clips directly from the videos table of contents by clicking the videos link on the main launch page.

The CBAP video training clips are recorded and produced using Adobe Flash. You can download the most recent Adobe Flash player free of charge from www.adobe.com.

Electronic Book

The entire contents of the Exam Guide are provided in PDF (portable document format) files, readable by Adobe Acrobat Reader, which is included on the CD.

Help

A help file is provided through the help button on the main page in the lower-left corner. An individual help feature is also available through MasterExam.

Removing Installation(s)

MasterExam is installed to your hard drive. For best results removing programs, use the Start | All Programs | LearnKey | Uninstall option to remove MasterExam.

Technical Support

For questions regarding the content of the electronic book, MasterExam, or CBAP video training, please visit www.mhprofessional.com or e-mail customer.service@mcgraw-hill.com. For customers outside the 50 United States, please e-mail international_cs@mcgraw-hill.com.

LearnKey Technical Support

For technical problems with the software (installation, operation, removing installations), please visit www.learnkey.com, e-mail techsupport@learnkey.com, or call toll free 1-800-482-8244.

Glossary of Key Terms

8/80 Rule   A common rule within project management, it states that the smallest item in the scope decomposition should take no more than 80 hours and no fewer than 8 hours of labor to create. It prevents requirements packages from being too large or too small to manage.

***A Guide to the Business Analysis Body of Knowledge* (BABOK)**   The BABOK book is published by the IIBA and supports and defines the business analysis role, processes, and generally accepted practices of the community. The CBAP examination is based largely on the BABOK.

Absolute reference   A requirements attribute where each identified requirement will have its own unique identifier that's used only once within the project. If a requirement is removed from the project, so too is the absolute reference of the requirement.

Acceptance criteria   This requirements attribute defines the conditions that prove the requirement has been delivered.

Action plan   This business analysis plan defines what the risk responses are and which members of the business analysis team will own which risks.

Active stakeholder   The business analyst seeks to understand the reason behind every step in the business process to fully understand the process. Sometimes the business analyst will actually get involved in the work as an active stakeholder to fully understand the process and how the person completes the process.

Activity Based Costing   Examines the true cost of any business process the project may invoke. It examines the performance of resources, the activities the resources will complete, and includes the cost-effectiveness of nonhuman resources, such as equipment and facilities.

Agile   An SDLC (System Development Life Cycle) methodology that uses quick execution; daily meetings; isolated, protected developers; and adaptability to changes. The model uses small increments of planning and execution of the requirements. The benefit of this model is that the team can quickly create deliverables for the project stakeholders. The downside of this model is that an early mistake can cause huge ramifications and rework throughout the project.

Allocation ready   Refers to the requirement that can be allocated to a phase, portion, or area of the project where it can be readily created. A requirement that can't be allocated usually is a sign that the requirement is too vague.

Alternate solutions   More than one choice for a solution that may satisfy the project requirements.

Alternative identification   An approach to consider all of the available and possible solutions and then to pare down the solutions to the most likely and feasible options.

Analytic Hierarchy Process   This approach uses both qualitative (subjective) and quantitative (in-depth) analysis for each solution to compare and contrast each solution based on a series of comparisons.

Application architect   This role defines the technical direction for the project solution, creates the architectural approach, and serves as project expert for the project solution structure.

Application areas   Software-driven solutions for workstations, servers, mobile devices, and the Internet.

Appraisal   Review of a team member's work performance and contribution to the business analysis duties.

Approval requirements   Identify who will need to sign off on the project scope, project documents, costs, and schedules of the deliverables.

Assume   To assume the risk is to accept the risk. This business analysis risk response is an acceptance of the risk event and is used when the identified risk event is particularly low in probability and impact.

Assumption   Anything that you believe to be true, but you've not proven to be true.

Attainable   A requirements attribute that documents the feasibility for the current project—that it can be created, implemented, and supported by the organization. It is possible for a requirement to be technically attainable but not feasible for the current project based on the work, time, cost, or other factors the requirement would demand.

Audit requirements   Projects may require data about the data they produce in case they're audited by an outside agency. This "data about data" is called metadata, and while it's a pain in the neck to create and consider, it's required for consistency and often by law, depending on the industry the project is taking place in.

Author of the requirement   This requirements attribute simply defines the individual who demanded or is the author of the requirements.

Author peer reviewer   This person completes peer review of the requirements documentation to ensure that it meets the quality expected by the organization and inspects the requirements documentation for completeness. The author peer reviewer is often another business analyst.

Avoid   Avoid the risk by changing processes and activities to circumvent the risk event.

Balanced scorecard   A management approach that tracks and grades financial performance, customer satisfaction, internal processes, and enterprisewide learning and innovation.

Barrier   Anything that prevents communication from occurring at optimum levels.

Benchmarking   Benchmarking compares two or more systems, states, services, products, or things to determine the best viable choice.

Benefit/cost ratio (BCR) models   Examine the benefit-to-cost ratio.

Bidders conference   A meeting of all the vendors and the buyer to review the SOW (Statement of Work) and the procurement document. This is an opportunity for the bidders to ask questions about the project and for the buyer to clarify as needed.

Black box reverse engineering   Examines the structure and workings of a system without physically breaking down its internal structure.

Brainstorming session   A facilitated meeting with a group of stakeholders to attack a problem or opportunity with as many ideas as possible. The term "brainstorm" was created by advertising guru Alex Osborn in 1939.

Budget estimate   Based on the details of the project scope but it is somewhat unreliable. It has a range of variance of –10 percent to +25 percent on average.

Business analyst   An individual who identifies the business needs of the organization's clients and stakeholders, helps determine solutions to business problems, and completes requirements development and requirements management. The business analyst also facilitates communications among clients, project stakeholders, and the defined solutions team.

Business architecture   The intangible structure that constitutes a business entity. It is the culture, enterprise environmental factors, business structure, and policies that guide and direct the selection, funding, and management of programs and projects.

Business case   A document that reports on the value that the business will gain by investing in the initiative.

Business Domain Model   A visual representation of how the business does or should work with regard to the project requirements. It defines each business process that is affected by the project, how the process should work, and how the process interacts with other processes, functions, and project-affected users in the organization.

Business process analysis   A solution development methodology that examines and documents how the work is currently done in comparison to how the work should be done once the solution has been created. Business process analysis is also known as business process mapping, business process reengineering, business process transformation, and business process modeling.

Business Process Description   Defines the project at a high level of what the project should create. This document includes a summary of the current business model, all of the known user requirements, and any of the functional requirements that have been defined.

Business process model   Sometimes called an activity model, this captures all of the activities within a business, the inputs and outputs of each activity, and the required resources to complete each activity.

Business process reengineering   This approach studies the current flow of business processes, looks for strength, weaknesses, opportunities, and threats (SWOT), and considers everything from minor adjustments to entire new designs to investigate improvements.

Business Requirements Document   A snapshot of the requirements documentation that will serve as the requirements scope baseline (synonymous with Specification System Requirements Document). This document clearly defines the behavior of a project solution for the customers and end users. It's most commonly used for software development projects, and it's based on the business requirements defined early in the business analysis activities.

Business scenarios   A hypothetical situation that portrays how the organization processes are to operate. Business scenarios can depict typical operations, planned processes, and responses to situations when things don't go as planned.

Business sponsor   An individual who has the positional power and decision-making ability to launch new projects and organizational initiatives, and to grant resources to business analysts and project managers.

Buy-versus-build decision   A financially driven approach to determine which solution is the most cost-effective for the project. This approach also evaluates other factors, such as employee time, efficiency, and support to make the best decision for purchasing or creating a solution.

Cause-and-effect diagram   Sometimes called a fishbone or Ishikawa diagram, it can help facilitate root cause analysis. The diagram can be massive, as each contributing factor must be reviewed to determine what things, events, and processes may be contributing to it. In most cases, a combination of contributing factors creates the problem the organization is experiencing.

CBAP Code of Ethical Conduct and Professional Standards   An IIBA document that defines the expected ethical and professional standards for all CBAPs.

Certified Business Analysis Professional (CBAP)   An individual who has the required education, professional development, and work experience, and who has proven it by passing a business analysis exam governed by the International Institute of Business Analysis.

Class model   Demonstrates the attributes, operations, and relationships to entities within the solution. Classes are physical resources, solution concepts, a collection of data, a function of the solution, or an action.

Closed-ended questions   Used in interviews and surveys, these questions can gain specific information, be multiple-choice answers, or provide yes or no answers.

Closing   The final project management process group, where the project's phase or entire scope has been completed, and the project manager performs administrative closure. This includes sign-off from the customer on the scope validation, final findings, and then the project manager archives all of the project documentation.

Coaching   Helping other people think about the actions they're required to do in order to achieve the things they want in their life. Through activities, conversations, interviews, and exercises, coaches help people realize what it is they want to do in their personal and professional lives, and then inspire those people to take action to accomplish their goals.

Coercive power   When the project team believes the project manager can punish them for poor performance in the project, they may feel coerced into doing their assignments.

Communications formula   The formula $N(N - 1)/2$, where N represents the number of project stakeholders. It shows the number of communication channels in the project.

Communications management plan   This plan defines who needs what information, when it is needed, and in what modality the stakeholders are expecting the communication. This plan can set requirements and conditions, such as cost and schedule variances, within the project that will prompt communication.

Communications Requirements Matrix   Identifies the stakeholders and their communication interactions with other stakeholders.

Competitive analysis   This is a marketplace study to determine the feasibility of a proposed solution as compared with competition.

Complete   A requirements attribute that documents that the requirements are fully defined, which means that all constraints, assumptions, potential risks, attributes, and conditions of the project are documented.

Completing the Solution Assessment and Validation   This business analysis knowledge area works with the project manager, technology team, project team, and stakeholders to analyze the detailed design documents. You'll define the logical phases of the project, the technical design, and the quality assurance activities.

Complexity   This requirements attribute defines the scale, complexity definition, or overview on how difficult the requirement will be to implement.

Component business model   This is the most common business model and was formulated by IBM. It provides a direct and traditional view of an enterprise, providing nomenclature to lines of business, functional units, departments, groups, and other organizational resources.

Compromising   Requires that all parties in the conflict must give up something. The decision made is a blend of both sides of the argument. Because neither party really wins, it is considered a lose-lose solution. The business analyst can use this approach when the relationships are equal and no one can truly "win."

Configuration management requirements   Configuration management is the documentation, control, and management of the features and functions of the project deliverable. Configuration management defines the product scope and what the customer can expect as a result of the project work.

Conflicting requirements   When two or more requirements conflict in scope, time, cost, or objective. Conflicting requirements should be documented in the Requirements Issues Log, and a conflict resolution process should begin. Updates to the resolution should be documented in the issues log as well.

Consistent   A requirements attribute where the requirement meshes with all of the other requirements in the project. You may find inconsistent requirements when a key stakeholder is forcing a particular requirement into the project as a mandate.

Constraint Anything that limits your option. Time and cost limits are examples of constraints.

Contingency plan Should a risk event become an issue, then there should be a contingency action, sometimes called a correction action, to respond to the issue. The contingency plan also defines what the risk triggers are.

Continuing Development Units (CDUs) CBAPs must earn 60 CDUs per three-year cycle to maintain their CBAP status. CDUs can be earned through education, professional activities, and professional development.

Control chart A quality control chart to track trends in project execution.

Correct A requirements attribute where the requirements describe the functionality that is to be created by the project. The author of the requirements is the individual who must fully define the correctness of the project requirement.

Cost benefit analysis Measures the early known cost and benefits to create a cost benefits ratio of each potential solution. The cost benefit ratio will be elaborated during the business case creation.

Cost management plan Defines how the project will be estimated, budgeted, and how changes to cost will be managed.

Cost of conformance to quality These are expenses that must be spent to achieve the expected level of quality by the organization. Consider training, correct materials, additional resources, and in some instances safety, inspections, and compliance issues. This is also known as the **cost of conformance to requirements**.

Cost of nonconformance to quality These are the costs of not conforming to the expected level of quality. For example, if the project team doesn't have the correct training, then the project may take longer to complete, cost more due to errors and omissions, and customers may reject the deliverables.

Cost of nonconformance to requirements Monies that an organization will pay in fines, lawsuits, loss of sales, and loss of customers should they not achieve the expected quality in the project. Consider a project that does not provide the project team with the proper safety tools or training. If someone gets injured, then there'll be repercussions. These costs also include time delays, waste of materials, loss of team morale, and poor deliverables.

Cost variance reports Whenever there is a variance in the project cost, the project manager should create a cost variance report. This report explains what the cost variance is, why the variance has occurred, and what the project manager is doing to prevent the problem from occurring again.

COTS   Examines in-house creation versus a commercial off-the-shelf (COTS) solution.

Crashing   Adding labor to a project to reduce the project's duration. Crashing adds costs because of the expense of added labor.

Critical path   The longest path in a project network diagram to project completion. No delays are allowed on the critical path, or the project will be late for delivery.

CRUD Matrix   This is a table that uses the acronym CRUD to define the level of access that resources have to an information system. CRUD stands for Create, Read, Update, or Delete. It's the permissions assigned to resources for system information.

Current state assessment   Part of the feasibility study to determine the current status of the organization. An understanding of the current organizational status can be compared with the desired future status of the company.

Data dictionary   Describes the data used by the system. The data dictionary defines the name of the data, data aliases, values and meanings, and description of the system data.

Data flow diagrams   The type and traffic of information within the organization is captured and displayed.

Database analyst   This role designs, creates, and maintains databases for the project.

Database areas   Include database servers, data management, data security, and accessibility.

Decision Analysis   This statistical reasoning approach allows the study team to measure and compare the probabilities of each identified solution outcome.

Decision tables   A matrix that illustrates the logic of decisions and leads the study team to a recommended option based on the qualifiers the table identifies and the initial feasibility study requirements for the proposed solution.

Decoder   The device that decodes the message as it is being received.

Defect repair validation   The inspection of the work that has been repaired to ensure that it reaches or exceeds the quality expectations the project manager and the customer will have of the solution.

Definitive estimate   Based on the WBS (Work Breakdown Structure). The definitive estimate is the most accurate cost estimate, but it requires the WBS to create; it has a typical range of variance from –5 percent to +10 percent.

Deliverable   A document that clearly identifies the project deliverables the customer is expecting and that the project is to produce for the stakeholders.

Dependent task   This task cannot start until other tasks are completed; this is sometimes called a successor task.

Developer   This role is the technical resource within the project and may serve as a designer, tester, coder, application developer, or other job title. Developers help plan the operational transfer of the deliverable to the user.

Document analysis   A requirements elicitation technique that examines current documentation of project, product, organization, service, or process to help determine how these things could become better or contribute to the existing business problem solution or opportunity.

Domain modeling   Domain modeling charts the area of organization that's under construction, analysis, or creation so that all stakeholders can visualize the areas that are affected.

Effort-driven activities   The more effort you apply to the activity, the faster the job will get done.

Encoder   The device that encodes the message to be sent.

End user   The recipient and user of the project's deliverables.

Endorsed Education Provider (EEP)   Educational providers, such as training centers or colleges, that have paid a fee to the IIBA to have their materials reviewed and endorsed by the IIBA as being accurate business analysis courses. EEPs may provide professional development courses and seminars that offer continuing development units.

Enhancing   This risk response seeks to modify the size of the identified opportunity. The goal is to strengthen the cause of the opportunity to ensure that the risk event does happen. Enhancing a project risk looks for solutions, triggers, or other drives to ensure that the positive risk will happen so the rewards of the risk can be realized by the performing organization.

Enterprise analysis   The business analysis activities that help define and identify business opportunities for an organization.

Enterprise environmental factors   Part of the business architecture, the definition of the policies, procedures, and rules that project managers and employees must follow. Enterprise environmental factors are unique to each organization.

Enterprise governance group   A committee of organizational leaders that ensures groups, functional departments, projects, and other members of the organization are following the established organizational rules, procedures, and business directives of the organization.

Entity relationship diagram   This is a visual mapping of the system's data, its input and outputs, and its relationship to the enterprise. The entity relationship diagram links the data to operations such as customers, invoices, accounts payable, and products. It can visualize the whole organization and the relationships among the organization: customers, suppliers, vendors, employees, management, and resources like data, facilities, and equipment. This is an ideal model to capture communication requirements and channels within an organization.

Environment impact analysis   Each option is measured for its impact on the environment in consideration of culture, compliance, regulation, and laws.

Evolutionary prototype   Sometimes called a working prototype, an operating prototype that will eventually evolve into the delivered solution. Each addition to the system evolves it another step until it reaches the complete scope of requirements and the project is closed.

Execution   The third project management process group, where the project plans are executed. The project manager ensures that the work is done with quality, that the project team are completing their assignments, and that the outcomes of the work are documented.

Executive sponsor   Responsible for the project funding, go/no-go decisions, resource support, and approves schedules, budgets, and chief decisions. This role may also be known as the solution owner, project sponsor, or champion.

Executive team   These people constitute the organization's upper management who create the vision, leadership, direction, strategy, and tactics for the organization.

Expert power   This power exists when the project team and stakeholders recognize the project manager as an expert in the discipline the project centers on.

Explicit knowledge   Documentation, written instruction, charts, graphs, and openly shared information that any business analyst could use in her requirements management activities.

Exploiting   Not all risks are bad; some risks you actually want to happen. When you want to take advantage of a positive risk, you exploit the risk. Some examples of positive risk exploitation: adding resources to finish faster than planned, increasing quality to recognize sales and customer satisfaction, and utilizing a better way of completing the project work.

External systems interfaces   Links between internal systems and external systems, such as vendors, regulatory agencies, and technical interfaces.

Feasibility study   The research of the possible solutions to determine each solution's likelihood of meshing with the business architecture, the organizational mission, and reaching financial, operational, and technical achievability.

Feasible   A requirements attribute where the requirements are confirmed to be feasible for the project to accomplish based on the organization's resources, competencies, expected budget, and timeline for the project.

Feedback loop   A conversation between two or more speakers centering on one specific topic.

First-Time First-Use Penalty   States that the first time you try something new, you can't know how long it'll take to complete and what the financial impact of the project may be, because you've never attempted the activity before.

Fixed duration   Activities where it doesn't matter how much effort you add to the project, it'll still take a fixed amount of time to complete.

Flowchart   A structured analysis chart that shows the flow of information from one process to another.

Focus group   A structured, facilitated meeting to gather ideas and to determine opinions and feelings about a product, service, problem, or opportunity.

Forcing   When the person in the conflict with the most power forces the decision. The decision made may not be the best decision for the project, but it's fast. As expected, this autocratic approach does little for relationship building and is a win-lose solution. You know a solution is being forced when someone with seniority or power makes a decision without considering the other parties' objections and concerns.

Formal power   This power, sometimes called positional power, is when a project manager is formally assigned the position of project manager. The project team may recognize the project manager as someone in charge of the project, but not necessarily someone who has any real power on the project.

Formal requirements presentation   A structured meeting to review requirements status, changes, and progress. Formal presentations are often hosted by the business analyst for all of the stakeholders to attend.

Formal requirements review   A meeting that brings together all of the stakeholders to identify any errors or omissions in the identified requirements. Should no errors exist, requirements sign-off is needed.

Forming   When the project team first comes together and team members are getting to know about each other. The group is simply forming based on the needs and competencies the project demands and the availability of the people in the organization to satisfy those needs.

Function   Requirements that define how something should behave. Functional decomposition identifies the high-level functions of a system, organization, or service and breaks them down into subfunctions and activities. Functional decomposition ensures that all of the active characteristics of the proposed solution are identified, documented, and can be tracked. Functional decomposition aims to capture all of the processes within the system, software, or service the project is to create.

Functional requirements   Define the specific operations and characteristics of a system. The definition of specific components, and expectations for how those components are to operate. These requirements describe how the solution will function, what it will do, and what its expected outcomes are. This is usually a more technical document than the URD (User Requirements Document), but it should mesh with the users' requirements.

Future value   Determine the future value of an amount of funds based on the present value of the funds. The formula for future value is $FV = PV (1 + I)^n$, where FV is future value; PV is present value; I is the interest rate; and N is the number of periods.

Geographical maps   Show the physical location of the business units that can help address logistical concerns such as shipping, travel, communication, and IT issues.

Global Balanced Scorecard for U.S. Government   A scorecard that measures government agency performance, customer perception, financial and internal responsibilities, and innovation.

Globalization and localization   Projects that span multiple countries must consider all of the laws, languages, and cultural issues of each country the project interacts with. You'll also have to consider time zone issues, languages, and monetary concerns such as the exchange rate.

Gold plating   An unscrupulous process of adding extra features that may drive up costs and alter schedules. The project team should strive to deliver what was expected.

Hard logic   The identification of activities that must be completed in a particular order.

Hardware areas   Include servers, workstations, laptops, and devices like printers, cameras, and peripherals.

Hardware devices interfaces   Identification of links between any hardware device that may be affected by the proposed project. Consider servers, workstations, kiosks, and printers.

Horizontal method prototyping   A quick, shallow, and wide view of the system without any real functionality behind the prototype. Easy to create, modify, and explain.

Hygiene agents   From Herzberg's Theory of Motivation, these elements are the expectations all workers have: job security, a paycheck, clean and safe working conditions, sense of belonging, civil working relationships, and other basics associated with employment.

Implementation plan   Sometimes called the operational transfer plan, it defines how to move the solution from the ownership of the project to operations. The implementation plan should address how the solution will move from the project life cycle into the product life cycle.

Incremental   An SDLC method that uses a granular approach for quicker deliverables, easier risk management, and easier change control on the smaller segments of the project work. This approach can also use a series of waterfalls for phases and deliverables rather than one large waterfall model. This model is ideal for large projects.

Independent task   This task is not reliant on other activities, and no other activities are reliant on this task completing.

Informal requirements presentations   Somewhat structured, but less formal and more conversational in nature.

Information architect   This role, sometimes called the data modeler, helps assess the data requirements of a project, identifies data assets, and helps the project team complete data modeling requirements.

Infrastructure analyst   This role designs the hardware, software, and technical infrastructure required for the project's application development, operation requirements, and the project's ongoing solution.

Initial project risks   Any initial risks that have been identified should be referenced and/or recorded here.

Initial Work Breakdown Structure   The Work Breakdown Structure (WBS) is a key deliverable in project management, and the initial WBS can help the project manager and project team do more detailed planning, estimating, and risk assessment.

Initiating   The first project management process group where the project is charted with a broad vision of what the project is to create. The project manager is named and given autonomy over the feasibility study project.

Integrated change control   Project management process of examining all areas of the project and how a proposed change may affect time, cost, scope, quality, human resources, communication, risk, and any procurement issues.

Interface analysis   Defines and documents all of the links between two or more components in a system.

Internal rate of return   A complex formula to calculate when the present value of the cash inflow equals the original investment.

International Institute of Business Analysis   The IIBA is a nonprofit entity headquartered in Toronto, Canada. IIBA aims to develop and propel the business analysis role and career through its mission "to develop and maintain standards for the practice of business analysis and for the certification of its practitioners." The IIBA is the governing body for the CBAP examination and certification.

Invitation for Bid (IFB)   A procurement document from the buyer to seller, where the seller is to provide just a price for the solution.

Issue   A negative risk that has come to fruition. Issues are conditions that you'll have to react to in order to offset the negative impact of the negative risk.

Issue log   A document that identifies the attributes of each issue, assigns an issue owner, and tracks the status of the issue.

Issue owner   The individual who is closest to the issue and may be tasked with resolving the issue.

Key stakeholders   The stakeholders who have decision-making powers over the requirements and the project.

Knowledge management   The collection, storage, accessibility, and accuracy of the wealth of information an organization creates.

Known unknowns   Conditions and events that will likely go wrong with the project; you just aren't certain what those things maybe. It's a way to anticipate risks, issues, and problems that you haven't clearly identified due to the nature of the project work.

Leadership   The alignment, motivation, and inspiration of people to achieve.

Legal requirements   Projects and solutions must adhere to the relevant laws. It shouldn't be a surprise here, but there may be some industry-specific laws the business analyst should consider or seek legal advice on when there's a question of legality.

Life cycle costing   The estimated amount of cost for the organization to support the deliverables the project has created per year, quarter, or whatever period the stakeholders designate.

Logical view   The business requirements for the organization, documented, clearly defined, and agreed upon by the project stakeholders.

Market   Part of the organizational environment. The condition of the market is an excellent example of an environmental regulation that you have little control over. Market conditions can affect how you buy and sell, price your services and goods, and have an impact on whether the project is even launched or allowed to proceed.

Maslow's Hierarchy of Needs   A hierarchy of needs to identify what people need in their lives and what they work for. There are five different layers: physiological, safety, social, esteem, and self-actualization.

McGregor's Theory of X and Y   States that management believes there are two broad perspectives of workers: good and bad. X is bad; these people need to be watched all the time, micromanaged, and distrusted. Y is considered good. Y people are self-led, motivated, and can accomplish new tasks proactively.

Measurable and testable   A requirements attribute that confirms the requirements are not described with subjective, unquantifiable terms and metrics. You'll need specific tests to measure and show a range of acceptability for satisfying the requirements.

Media   The best modality to use when communicating is the one that is relevant to the information that's being communicated. Some communications demand a formal presentation, where others only warrant a phone call, an ad hoc meeting, or a quick e-mail. The right media is dictated by what needs to be communicated.

Medium   This is the device or technology that transports the message.

Meeting management techniques   Meetings should have an agenda and order, and someone needs to keep the meeting minutes for the project.

Meeting rules   The rules of meeting should be posted, reviewed, and agreed upon before starting. Four simple rules for any meeting are focus, participate, move, and close.

Milestone   The significant deliverable of a project phase; it is a timeless project event that shows progress toward completing the project requirements.

Mitigate   To mitigate a risk event is to spend more, add time, or take extra steps in the processes to reduce the probability and/or impact of the risk event should it happen. Mitigation is a risk response.

Models   A mesh of textual elements, matrixes, and diagrams that present all or a portion of the proposed solution. Models can help stakeholders understand and relate to the requirements more easily than a textual documentation of requirements can.

Moderator   The person who actually facilitates the requirements review meeting. This person may be the business analyst, but generally this role is performed by a neutral person who can move the meeting along and stick to the meeting rules. The moderator has the responsibility of ensuring that all participants have reviewed the requirements documentation prior to the start of the meeting and of keeping stakeholders on track during the meeting.

Monitoring and controlling   The fourth project management process group, where processes are completed in tandem with project execution. The project work is monitored and controlled.

Motivating agents   From Herzberg's Theory of Motivation, these are the elements that motivate people to excel. They include responsibility, appreciation of work, recognition, the chance to excel, education, and other opportunities associated with work besides financial rewards.

Necessary   A requirements attribute that demands all pet requirements, personal agendas, and non-value-added extras be stripped from the project. Each requirement should have value and contribute to meeting defined business goals and objectives as stated in the project charter, vision document, or business case.

Net Present Value   Evaluates the monies returned on a project for each period that the project exists; based on the present value formula for each period.

Network areas   Include the connectivity and communication among computers, servers, network devices, and telecommunications.

Noise   Anything that interferes with or disrupts the message. Anything that distracts you or me from the message is noise.

Nonfunctional requirements   Define how a system is supposed to operate. It is the qualities, characteristics, and constraints of any given system.

Norming   Once things settle down and leaders, alliances, and acceptance have emerged in the project, the team can go about getting their work done.

Object-oriented analysis of an information system   A solution development methodology that dissects a system, specifically an IT system, and shows how information (called messages) is passed from one entity in the system to another. The entities in the system are called classes, and the messages consist of data and information on how the data was created.

Open-ended question   Used in interviews and surveys, these questions can't be answered with a "yes" or "no" and allow the participant to elaborate on the question's topic.

Organization chart   This traditional chart shows how the organization is broken down by department and disciplines. This chart is sometimes called the Organizational Breakdown Structure (OBS) and is arranged by departments, units, or teams. These will show the hierarchical structure of the company and which units of the company are affected by the feasibility study.

Organizational process assets   The collection of historical information, templates, processes, procedures, and other documents that support the business analysis duties.

Ownership   This requirements attribute defines the business entity or group within the organization that will be the business owner of the requirement once it's released into production.

Parametric estimate   A parameter, such as cost per license or time per installation, that is used to estimate the cost and/or duration of the current project.

Pareto chart   A histogram to show the distribution of failures within the project. It shows the categories of defects, range of solution costs, income potential, and other categorization of components from largest to smallest.

Parkinson's Law   States that work expands to fill the amount of time allotted to it.

Passive stakeholder observation   Sometimes called invisible observation. When the business analyst observes the stakeholder's activity without any interaction with the person doing the work.

Payback period   The amount of time it takes the project to "pay back" the costs of the project.

Performing   This is the ideal state for the project, when all the project team members settle into their roles and go about getting the work done. Petty differences are set aside, and the project team is hard at work accomplishing goals and moving the project toward completion.

Phase   A logical grouping of activities that create a deliverable or a set of related deliverables.

Physical view   The map of the physical components and structure of the solution. The application developers will then create the physical view, as this information is most specific to what they'll be creating in project execution.

Planning   The second project management process group, where the project is planned based on the determined requirements for scope, time, cost, quality, human resources, communications, risk, and procurement.

POLDAT Technique   A requirements gathering and business architecture technique that captures information about processes, organization structure, location, data, applications, and technology.

Political environment   Every organization has politics that may influence project decisions. While you may elect not to document these politics directly, consider what individuals may have power over the solution.

Portfolios   The organizational management of projects, programs, and undertakings that support the vision, strategy, and tactics of the enterprise. Portfolio management is the measurement, selection, and management of the funds, time, and effort to support the enterprise ventures beyond day-to-day operations.

Predecessor task   Other tasks cannot begin until this task is completed, as it precedes them in the order of activities.

Preliminary project scope statement   A project initiating document that defines, in broad terms, what the project is to accomplish. This is a document that establishes the boundaries, initial requirements, broad cost and time estimates, and sets the expectations for what the project should do and create for the organization.

Preliminary scope   A document that establishes the boundaries, initial requirements, broad cost and time estimates, and sets the expectations for what the project should do and create for the organization.

Present Value   A formula that determines the present value of a future amount of money. The present value formula is $PV = FV \div (1 + I)^n$, where FV is future value; PV is present value; I is the interest rate; and N is the number of periods.

Prioritized   A requirements attribute that allows each requirement to be assigned a level of priority based on the functional requirements, user requirements, and urgency of the deliverable.

Priority   A requirements attribute that defines the order in which the requirements should be implemented. This is particularly useful when creating deliverables in stages for the project customers.

Problem solving   A conflict resolution approach that uses a spirit of cooperation among the stakeholders. Problem solving tackles the problem head-on and is the preferred method of conflict resolution. Sometimes this approach is called "confronting" rather than problem solving. Problem solving calls for additional research to find the best solution for the problem, and it's a win-win solution. It should be used if there is time to work through and resolve the issue. It also serves to build relationships and trust. The business analyst is the facilitator of the problem-solving technique.

Process flow diagram   A diagram that captures the inputs and outputs of current (and in some instances, future) processes within the organization.

Process improvement plan   This plan defines how the project processes will be monitored and documented for accuracy, efficiency, and improvement.

Procurement management plan   When a project needs to purchase materials, services, or other resources, this plan defines the processes and procedures a project manager is to follow within the organization.

Product life cycle   The duration of the product in operations. It describes the anticipated duration of the product's usage, maintenance, and anticipated phasing out of the solution.

Product scope statement   This document defines the deliverable the customer is expecting.

Program   A program is a collection of projects working together with a common vision to take advantage of benefits that would not be realized if the projects worked independently of each other.

Project   A short-term endeavor that will create something unique for the organization. Projects have a definite ending.

Project boundaries   The things the project will not deliver.

Project charter   A document that authorizes the project to exist within the organization. It should be written by someone with the authority to grant the project manager authority over the resources the project needs to be successful.

Project communications management   Project managers, like business analysts, are communicators; projects demand constant communication.

Project cost management The funds that a project requires must be managed, accounted for, and fluctuations in project costs must be communicated.

Project human resources management The management of the project human resources will vary by organization, but it takes people to complete the project work.

Project integration management This special project management knowledge area coordinates the other eight project management knowledge areas.

Project life cycles A project life cycle is the unique life and phases of a project. A project life cycle is unique to each project; for example, the project life cycle of a software development project does not have the same project life cycle as a bridge construction project.

Project management process groups There are five project management process groups that are universal to all projects: initiating, planning, executing, monitoring and controlling, and closing.

Project manager Manages the project management life cycle of a project to ensure that the project team is completing the project work with quality and according to the project objectives and requirements. This role works with the business analyst, executive sponsor, and key stakeholders to gain approval on project deliverables.

Project network diagram A diagram that shows the relationships between activities. Each node in the network diagram represents an activity, and the lines show the predecessors and successors of each activity.

Project phases The incremental progression of the project through logical, work-producing sections of a project. The end of a project phase results in a project deliverable and often coincides with a milestone.

Project procurement management Projects may need to purchase items, hire additional staff, and/or perform work for other organizations through a contractual relationship.

Project quality management Quality management is the assurance that the work is properly planned for project execution and then controlled to ensure the work is completed as it was planned.

Project risk management This knowledge area identifies, documents, and analyzes the project risks in order to create risk responses.

Project scope management This area defines, plans, and controls the project scope based on the business analyst's requirements.

Project time management   Projects require time to do the project work but also to complete the project management activities.

Prototype   A basic mockup of what the final project deliverable may look like.

Prototyping   This approach creates the highest-risk component of a proposed solution to determine if the solution is feasible in light of the known risk. In other words, the team must create the solution to determine if the actual solution can be created considering the largest known risk.

Quality   According to *A Guide to the Project Management Body of Knowledge*, quality is a conformance to requirements and a fitness for use. It's the deliverables, features, and functions that the customer will look at to see how well the features perform and how the solution, as a whole, operates.

Quality assurance (QA)   The assurance that the designers, project team, vendors, and any other contributors to the deliverables do their jobs accurately and completely. Contributions to the project scope should map exactly to the project scope—nothing more and nothing less.

Quality assurance analyst   This role maps the quality assurance requirements of the organization and the stakeholders to the project, ensures that the project deliverables meet the quality requirements, and works with the project manager and the project team on quality standards compliance.

Quality control (QC)   An inspection-driven process that precedes solution assessment, sometimes called scope validation, to detect errors in the project work and make recommendations to correct the errors before the customer sees the deliverable.

Quality management plan   If your organization has a quality assurance program, then the requirements of that program will be defined herein; if not, a quality policy will be established for the project, and the quality control and quality assurance expectations will be defined here.

Quality of Service (QoS)   Refers to the priority level of applications and how they'll respond and act on a network. Quality of service is a way to describe the expected level of performance for an application, or in a broader sense, the expectations of reliability for a solution.

RACI chart   A chart that defines each role's participant with the legend of responsible, accountable, consult, and inform for each activity.

Receiver   The person who receives the message.

Recorder The person who will record all the comments, suggestions, questions, and prompts for clarification about the requirements document during the formal requirements review meeting.

Referent power This power has a couple of different meanings. First, referent power is when the project manager refers to someone else's power to push through his project decisions. The second meaning is when the project team members are familiar with the project manager from past work, so there's already a relationship established between the project team member and the project manager.

Regulations Part of the organizational environment. Your project and proposed solution may have industry regulations that you must adhere to. Consideration of the regulations, even pending regulations, should always be made, as these may hinder or constrain the project's ability to quickly and cost-effectively meet the identified requirements.

Request for Proposal (RFP) A procurement document from the buyer to seller where the seller is to provide a detailed solution for the buyer. It is often just called an RFP and is part of the procurement process in an organization. It is a request for a vendor to create a fully defined approach for the requirements of the project. It's a document that asks the vendor to provide a solution for the project—it's more than just a price request.

Request for Quote (RFQ) A procurement document from the buyer to seller where the seller is to provide just a price for the solution (bids and quotes have the same goal—just provide a price). It is sometimes called an RFQ and asks the vendor to create a price for the already defined requirements.

Requirement elicitation This task determines which stakeholders should be identified as contributors to the requirements gathering process. Based on the stakeholder, type of project, and conditions within the organization, the business analyst will decide which elicitation activities are most appropriate. This is a structured approach to systematically and accurately draw out or confirm the project or opportunity requirements from the project stakeholders and clients.

Requirements analysis and documentation The business analysis activity that defines the modeling and business analysis documentation technique the organization requires. Policies within the organization, business analyst preferences, or industry standards may influence the documentation and modeling approaches the business analyst uses.

Requirements author The person who created the requirements document; typically this is the business analyst. The requirements review meeting can't happen without this person present.

Requirements communication Communication is a key activity for the business analyst. This activity defines what types of communication, best practices for communication, and the organizational requirements for communication may be. Based on the size of the project, organizational procedures, and requests from stakeholders, the business analyst will document and adapt the communication to what's best for the project.

Requirements Communication Plan Documents communication requirements for the business analysis activities. It's a plan to ensure that all of the proper communication channels are identified, documented, and communicated throughout the pre-project activities.

Requirements format The format of and information included in the requirements document; there may be multiple versions of the requirements document, depending on the stakeholders in the project.

Requirements Issue Log Central log to document conflict issues, the attributes of the conflict, the stakeholders involved, and the ramifications of the conflict on the other requirements within the project.

Requirements package The collection of the business analyst's work results. It is the documentation, formulation, and organization of all the requirements the business analyst has gathered from the stakeholders, packaged in a comprehensive set of project requirements.

Requirements planning and management A business analysis activity that works with the project and organizational stakeholders to determine the required resources to complete the requirements gathering. A business analyst completing these tasks is determining the key roles, managing the requirements scope, and serving as a communicator.

Requirements sign-off The stakeholders signing off on the requirements; demonstrates the stakeholder approval of the identified requirements. Stakeholders can sign off on requirements in ink or electronically—either is acceptable as you're creating an audit trail of activity.

Requirements traceability A communication process that allows for each project requirement to be traced from its conception in the requirements documentation to its implementation in the project execution phase. Traceability ensures that each requirement is accounted for and its implementation is tracked to execution, costs, and timing.

Requirements Traceability Matrix (RTM) A table that tracks many actions to many requirements of the project. It maps the deliverables to the specific requirements and the verification that the deliverable does or does not satisfy the requirements.

Requirements workshop Sometimes called a Joint Application Design (JAD) workshop, it brings the key stakeholders together to define the requirements for the project. This meeting can be used to clarify the project scope, refine existing requirements, and gain stakeholder consensus on the priorities of the project.

Resource Breakdown Structure (RBS) This hierarchical chart can break down the business problem or opportunity by the type of resources affected by the project. An RBS is an excellent tool for tracking resource utilization, resource costs, and to help formulate questions.

Responsibility Specifies the amount of control a role has over the decision, direction, quality, and accountability of the facets of the project; defines what the role is accountable for.

Responsibility Assignment Matrix (RAM) A RAM chart shows the correlation between project team members and the work they've been assigned to complete. A RAM chart doesn't necessarily have to be specific to individual team members; it can also be decomposed to project groups or units. It's a table that maps roles to responsibilities.

Reward power When the project team believes that the project manager can reward them for the work they complete on the project, they'll work accordingly. Reward power is tied to the announcement and ground rules for the project's reward and recognition system.

Risk An uncertain event or condition that can have a positive or negative effect on the project.

Risk management plan Risks need to be identified, documented, and recorded in the risk register. This plan defines the risk management activities including how risks will be qualitatively and quantitatively analyzed.

Risk response plan There are seven risk responses that a project manager can choose from, and this plan identifies each risk and the appropriate risk response based on the conditions of the project and the attributes of the risk event. The seven risk responses that the risk response plan documents are acceptance, mitigation, transference, avoidance, enhance, exploit, and share.

Risk trigger A warning sign or condition that the risk event is becoming an issue.

Role Defines the function the person plays on the business analysis team or the project team.

Rolling wave planning Uses short bursts of planning and then short sprints of project execution.

Root cause analysis   This process investigates causes, contributing causes, and causal factors that are creating the effect to be solved (which may turn out to be a business problem).

Rough order of magnitude (ROM) cost estimate   The ROM estimate is a very high-level, unreliable cost estimate that "ballparks" the idea of what the project should cost.

Sapir-Whorf hypothesis   Posits that the language a person speaks affects how the person thinks. This theory was created by Edward Sapir and Benjamin Whorf.

Schedule management plan   This plan defines how the activity duration estimates will be created, what the project schedule is, and how changes to the schedule will be managed.

Schedule variance reports   These reports are generated whenever the project is slipping on the project schedule and provide an explanation of the problem.

Scope management plan   Defines how the project scope should be created, decomposed into the WBS (Work Breakdown Structure), executed, monitored, and controlled, and the scope validated.

Scope validation   An inspection-driven activity done with the project customer to review and ultimately accept the project deliverables.

Sender   The party sending the message is the sender.

Sender-receiver models   The flow and rhythm to conversation, formal or informal, composed of feedback loops.

Sharing   Sharing a mutually beneficial opportunity between two organizations or projects, or creating a risk-sharing partnership. When a project team can share the positive risk, ownership of the risk is given to the organization that can best capture the benefits from the identified risk.

Six Sigma programs   These quality improvement approaches rely on data and statistical analysis to measure accuracy, efficiency, and trend analysis.

Smoothing   "Smoothes" out the conflict by minimizing the perceived size of the problem. It is a temporary solution, but can calm relations and boisterous discussions. Smoothing may be acceptable when time is of the essence or any of the proposed solutions will not currently settle the problem. This can be considered a lose-lose situation, since no one really wins.

Soft logic   The activities can be completed in any order without affecting the deliverable.

Software Requirements Specification   May also be called a System Requirements Specification. This requirements documentation defines the expected behavior and implementation of the software or system the developers will be creating for the project customers. This documentation starts with a definition of the problem domain and the functional requirements that will help create the solution. The document will also include the expected quality of service and will communicate any relevant assumptions or constraints the developers will need to manage as part of the solution.

Solution assessment and validation   Once all parties are in agreement on the requirements, then the solution for the requirements can be presented. This activity assesses the proposed solution(s) and validates that the solution can or has met the requirements of the stakeholders.

Solution independent   A requirements attribute where the requirements do not define the implementation of the solution but rather only the requirements. The requirements should allow for a broad selection of solution choices, not a specific implementation, resource, or approach.

Solution owner   This role approves the project scope statement, phase gate reviews, solution validations, scope changes, and project success criteria. This role may often be the same as the executive sponsor, though sometimes the project customer may serve in this role.

Source   This requirements attribute identifies the authorized entity that has the authority to approve requirements and that may need to be involved in the change control process of a project.

Specification System Requirements Document   A snapshot of the requirements documentation that will serve as the requirements scope baseline (synonymous with Business Requirements Document).

Spiral   An SDLC approach, sometimes called the cinnamon roll, that uses a series of planning, objective determination, alternative identification, and development for the life cycle. It's ideal for projects that are sensitive to risk avoidance. The downside of this model is that it's unique for each project and can't usually be used as a template for future similar projects.

Stability   This requirements attribute identifies how stable the requirement is based on its elaboration and supplied detail. At some point the requirement is considered stable enough to start work.

Staffing management plan   Defines when the project team members will be brought onto the project, how and when they'll be utilized on the project, and when they'll be released from the project.

Stakeholder observation   A requirements elicitation approach where the business analyst observes the stakeholder working to determine how the work is actually completed.

Stakeholders   This role is fulfilled by anyone who is affected by the outcome of the project deliverables. Stakeholders who make decisions on the project, influence the project requirements, or contribute to the project are sometimes called key stakeholders.

Standards   Part of the organizational environment. Standards are guidelines that are usually followed, but you won't be breaking any laws if you don't follow them. Your organization may also have standards such as forms, documentation, and processes that must be followed on most projects.

Statement of Work (SOW)   A document originating from the buyer to the seller that describes what the buyer is looking to purchase.

Status   This requirements attribute is linked to the stability of the requirements, as it keeps track of each requirement and what its current status in the project may be: proposed, accepted, verified, or implemented.

Status report   This report communicates how the project is performing overall, what objectives have been accomplished, and what activities are coming up in the project schedule.

Storming   As the project team members struggle for power in the project, there may be some conflicts over who'll lead the project team, who'll follow the lead, and who's indifferent as long the project work gets done.

Structured analysis   This is a solution development methodology and a software development analysis tool that considers an IT system as a series of processes, and each process contributes to another process within the system. All processes stem from some user interaction. Data is also tracked in structured analysis and is seen as the result of processes and user input.

Structured analysis techniques   Methodologies to create systems by using a model to identify the problem, propose solutions, and design a selected solution.

Structured problem-solving techniques   Receive and retrieve information within an organization. They keep communication happening, involve stakeholders, and plot out expected responses based on a survey, form, or structured interview.

Structured Systems Analysis and Design Model (SSADM)   Classic waterfall methodology, where each phase builds on the work done in the phase prior. SSADM was created in the United Kingdom as a model for developing systems and new applications.

Subprojects   A subproject is a smaller project within a larger project. Subprojects are managed as their own project reporting to the project manager of the parent project.

Supplementary quality of service requirements   The business analyst and key stakeholders must be in agreement on what the expected level of quality of service for the project deliverable will be.

Supplemental requirements   Part of the quality of service requirements that must be considered as part of a project's requirements, constraints, and quality to meet the expectations of the project customers.

Supply-and-demand   A classical interpretation of business, where the amount of supply (high or low) and the demand (high or low) can affect the pricing of the product or service.

Surveys   A requirements elicitation technique to quickly gain insight and feedback from a large group of stakeholders. Surveys can be anonymous, or participants could be known for follow-up questions from the survey.

SWOT Analysis   The business analysis team can identify the strengths, weaknesses, opportunities, and threats (SWOT) of each requirement to determine if there are risks to be documented.

System Development Life Cycle (SDLC)   A generic way of describing the life cycle of an information system and the phases the system goes through.

Systems   Standardized process sets within an organization that have identified the flow of activities to reach a desired result. Systems ensure that activities are done the same way, in the same order, every time. They establish a framework for common organizational activities to ensure consistency, thoroughness, and documentation.

Systems thinking   An examination of the whole system with the belief that a known symptom is a product of the system as a whole. Actions in one component of a system have effects, even subtle effects, on neighboring components.

Tacit knowledge   Assumed information, application by experience, and unstated information. It's the type of information that a business analyst who's served for years in the IT industry might take for granted but a new business analyst might crave.

Technology advancement analysis   Examines the most recent technical solutions that may be applied to the business problem or opportunity.

Technology architecture diagrams   Maps of the topology and relationship of the IT infrastructure.

Test plan   Mandatory in most software development applications. Defines how the software will be tested, adjusted, and retested before its release.

Theme   Premise of a strategic goal; allows the large organizational goals to be broken down into smaller projects and opportunities.

Throwaway prototype   A simple prototype sample that may be just a sketch of the proposed system. It helps the customer and the developer see the system in recognizable components.

Top-down estimate   An estimate based on past projects to predict the current cost and/or duration of the current project.

Traceable   Each requirement should have the ability to be traced to its origin, owner, and author for additional information and support. Traceable also means that the requirements can be traced to their implementation in the project deliverable. Traceability is useful for audits, quality control, and end-of-project scope validation processes.

Trainer   This role works with the project team to understand the deliverables and then teaches the users of the deliverables how to utilize the project's product. This person may teach, coach, write, and do instructional design to educate the users of the project's deliverable.

Transference   This is the transfer of the risk (and the ownership of the risk) to a third party. The risk doesn't go away; it's just becomes someone else's problem. There's usually a fee for transference, and great examples include insurance, warranties, guarantees, and fixed-priced contracts with vendors.

Unambiguous   A requirements attribute that confirms the requirements documentation is written in such a way that all readers of the requirements documentation arrive at the same understanding of what the requirements demand.

Understandable   A requirements attribute for which, like the unambiguous characteristic, the requirements must also be understandable among the project team. Terms, acronyms, and assumptions should be fully defined and explained for the requirements.

Unknown unknowns   Unforeseen issues called unknowns that can affect the execution of the project.

Urgency   This requirements attribute defines how urgent the requirement is and when the customer needs it to be delivered as part of the solution.

Use case models   Captures the business processes by showing how customers, vendors, management, departments, and other enterprisewide stakeholders interact with the business.

User class   A categorization of users and how each class will use the solution.

User interfaces People who interact with one another, a system, or data moved between two users.

User Requirements Document Defines what the user expects the solution to do. Users must be in agreement that the business analyst understands and has captured what they want accomplished in the solution.

Utility function The willingness of a person or organization to accept risk. The higher the utility function, the more willing the person or organization are to accept risk.

Verifiable A requirements attribute that provides evidence of completion by testing, examining, or demonstrating its existence upon completion. Each requirement must be verified upon delivery to confirm the completeness of the deliverable.

Vertical method prototyping An approach that creates an in-depth analysis, deep prototype of just one portion of the system's functionality. Can be costly and time-intensive, but proves the functionality of a system's key processes.

Vision document A vision document is a high-level view of the project solution. It defines a "vision" of what the project is to create for the organization. Vision documents are ideal for projects that will go through rounds of planning and where the project scope is defined through iterations.

Waterfall An SDLC (System Development Life Cycle) methodology that divides the project into phases. The project manager focuses on control of time, cost, and scope. Intense documentation happens throughout the creation of the software or system. The waterfall approach is not the fastest or most flexible approach, but it does work. A new project team or teams that shift in resources often subscribe to this approach.

WBS dictionary The WBS dictionary is a companion document to the WBS (Work Breakdown Structure) and reflects all of the work packages in the WBS. The WBS dictionary defines all of the components of the WBS, the required resources, and references any information that can explain the deliverable in more detail.

White box reverse engineering Decompiles the software to see how it works by examining the actual coding of the software.

William Ouchi's Theory Z Sometimes called the Japanese management style, it is based on the participative management style of the Japanese. This theory states that workers are motivated by a sense of commitment, opportunity, and advancement.

Withdrawal This conflict resolution has one side of the argument walking away from the problem, usually in disgust. You can recognize withdrawal when one party refuses to participate in the conflict resolution any longer and surrenders to the other stakeholders. The conflict is not really resolved, and it is considered a yield-lose solution. The approach can be used, however, as a cooling-off period or when the issue is not critical.

Work Breakdown Structure (WBS)   The WBS is a visual decomposition of the scope; it is deliverables-based and typically does not include activities.

Work package   The smallest item in the WBS; it is the smallest thing that the project team will put effort forth to create.

Work product   A work-in-progress version of the requirements presentation.

Writing style   The tone, language, and formality of a written topic.

Zachman Framework   A matrix, created by John Zachman, that provides structure and helps stakeholders describe complex enterprises. The Zachman Framework uses predefined questions that must be answered for each component of any organization.

INDEX